Still Invisible?

Still Invisible?

Elvin J. Dowling

Elvin J. Dowling
Copyright 2020
Inspira Communications, LLC
Miramar, Florida.

All rights reserved.

Table of Contents

Dedication

"

"I denounce because though implicated and partially responsible, I have been hurt to the point of abysmal pain, hurt to the point of invisibility. And I defend because in spite of it all, I find that I love."

- Ralph Waldo Ellison

(Ralph Waldo Ellison: Groundbreaking Author & Literary Genius)

"

To the memory of the late, great Ralph Waldo Ellison. May your literary brilliance continue to be seen by all;

"

To my wife Yadira, my children Josiah, Joshua and Eden and my family members and friends. May the joy of the love we have shared together in this life meet us on the other side;

"

To the generations unborn who will one day dare to seek truth and understanding. May the hope of a better tomorrow become the reality of your today;

"

To my mother, Essie Dowling, and all of the single mothers doing their best to improve the lives of their children. Please know that your sacrifices are most appreciated and shall never be forgotten;

"

To the mentors in my life, Alcee L. Hastings, Harry E. Johnson, Sr., William F. Pickard, Lia T. Gaines, Gregory Phillips, the late Maude Ford Lee, and the late William M. Batts, III, who helped shaped me into the man I am today. I attribute many of the vast experiences I have enjoyed as a direct result of having passed your way, and I am grateful;

"

To my brothers in the struggle simply yearning to be seen. May you always leave a positive impact upon the world that can never be erased;

"

To my dearest friends Myles B. Caggins III, Ian A. Davis, C. Marc Harper, Reuben Ahmed Munday, Kent M. Stone, who have helped to pick me up when I have been down and continue to encourage me to reach my full potential. Thank you for never allowing me to take myself too seriously;

"

To my constant supporters and friends, Michael and Lori Armstrong and their children Caleb and Coleman. Thank you for always believing in and encouraging me to step into my greatness.

"

To my dear friends Richy Gray, C. Ron Allen, the Honorable Wayne Messam of the City of Miramar, Florida, and my cousin, Kay Dowling, for being early financial contributors to the completion of this project; without your support this work would not have been possible;

"

To the late Gregory Diggs, Tamir Rice, Kalief Browder and Tayvon Martin, subjects in this book , all of whom have "slipped the surly bonds of earth to kiss the face of God." May your memory live through the ages;

"

To each of you, from the depths of my soul, this book is respectfully dedicated.

Endorsements

"As a former classroom teacher, superintendent of schools, and America's first Black U.S. Secretary of Education, I have witnessed up close the impact that a quality education, or the lack thereof, can have on the lives of Black boys in this country. This book is a must read for anyone who is concerned about the state of young Black men in America and want to do their part to help strengthen and protect their future."

– The Honorable Dr. Roderick R. Paige, 7th Secretary of the *United States Department of Education*

"History has shown us that when given an equal opportunity, Black men in America can achieve almost anything. *Still Invisible?* provides America with a blueprint for truly becoming that shining city on a hill."

– The Honorable Marc H. Morial, President & CEO, *National Urban League* & 48th Mayor of the *City of New Orleans, Louisiana*

"We all deal with the stresses of being marginalized because we are not part of an "in" group in various life situations. Mr. Dowling has compellingly described the challenges of experiencing that marginalization continuously throughout the life of a Black male. This is an extremely important book to help us empathize and address the pathology of marginalization of Black males and what we need to understand far more deeply than we do today."

– Michael Critelli, CEO of *MovieFlux Corporation* and Former Chairman & CEO of *Pitney Bowes*

"Be prepared to have a tough conversation within yourself before picking up this book! *Still Invisible?* will challenge many of the pre-conceived notions you may carry about the issues of race and culture in America, regardless of what side of the color line you fall."

– Kelvin Boston, Host - *Money Wise with Kelvin Boston* on *PBS*

"Still Invisible? is a must-read for anyone interested in understanding and addressing the issues and challenges facing Black men in America."

– Lawrence C. Ross, Author - *Blackballed: The Black & White Politics of Race on America's Campuses*

"As a clinical psychologist, I understand all too well the impact that continued oppression, hopelessness and anxiety have on vulnerable populations. *Still Invisible?* sheds light on the urgent need to identify and address the social, emotional, and mental health concerns of Black males in America."

– Dr. Jari Santana, President of *Aspira Delaware* and an Expert on Acculturation Stress

Foreword

"Forward Ever... Backwards Never!"

"

The white folk tell everybody what to think – except men like me. I tell them;
that's my life, telling white folk how to think about the things I know about..."

- Ralph Ellison, "Invisible Man" (Shmoop Editorial Team)

(Pictured above are the first Black Members of Congress [circa 1868], elected after the
passage of the 15th Amendment to the U.S. Constitution guaranteeing the right to vote
to newly freed African-American citizens.)

Never Give Up the Fight!

The late, great newspaper man and founder of the *Washington Informer*, Dr. Calvin Rolark, so often said, *"No one can save us, for us, but us. If it is to be, it's up to me."* Throughout my time here on this earth, I have not only believed those words, I have lived them. In doing so, I would like to think that I have "let my life to do the singing", in service to God and all humanity. In fact, as the longest serving member and dean of the Florida Delegation to the United States House of Representatives, I know what it's like to be "buffeted to and fro" by the vicissitudes of life and winds of time, and yet come out standing. I know, because I am a survivor.

As a grade school student at *Crooms Academy* in Sanford, Florida, we were taught and expected to recite each day the words to the poem, *"It Couldn't Be Done"*, penned a century ago by journalist Edgar Albert Guest, who wrote:

❝

"Somebody said that it couldn't be done, But

he, with a chuckle replied,

That "maybe it couldn't," but he would be one

Who wouldn't say so till he tried.

So, he buckled right in with the trace of a grin

On his face. If he worried, he hid it.

He started to sing, as he tackled the thing,

That couldn't be done, and he did it!"

For more than eighty years, there have been those who have told me that the hopes and dreams I have had not only for myself, but also for oppressed people everywhere, just simply "couldn't be done". And, for more than eighty years, I have refused to believe them.

In 1936, the year I was born, my life was one that was marked for infinite possibilities, in spite of a world that was quick to remind me that the successes I have experienced, having started out a poor Black kid from a segregated town, were simply impossible to achieve. But less than one month before my birth, however, Olympian Jesse Owens obliterated the notion, once again, that African-American males were incapable of achieving greatness; shattering Adolph Hitler's "master race" theory when he won four gold medals at the Berlin Olympics. In doing so, Owens paved the way for young boys like me to believe that anything was possible when you work hard and ignore your critics--popular opinion be damned!

As an individual who has learned to not take "no" as a first answer, I have been defying the odds and shattering expectations all of my life. Born at home, in a little house in Altamonte Springs, Florida, I am the only child of the late Julius and Mildred Hastings, my wonderful parents, who instilled within me the drive to reach my full potential. As domestic workers, they labored day and night, cleaning other people's homes to provide one for me, while continuing to impress upon me the belief that the extent to which I could dream was my only limitation. To that end, as the great-grandson of enslaved Africans, I understand what it's like to be picked on and counted out.

Nominated by President Jimmy Carter in 1979, I was the first Black Floridian appointed as a *United States District Court* Judge in America. After several years on the bench, I was falsely accused of crimes in which I have steadfastly maintained my innocence, and placed on trial. And I emerged victorious! But that victory would be short lived, however, having "fought the law" and won. In fact, despite having been found not guilty on all charges and exonerated of wrongdoing by a jury of my peers, I was impeached anyway and removed from the federal bench in 1989 by the very same body that had approved my nomination just ten years previously. But that's not how my story ends...

After having endured what I thought was the fight of my life, one that would cost me not only my job, but millions of dollars in legal fees, I picked myself up and dusted myself off; determined that I would not let a system that mistreated me to do the same thing to someone else. And so, I ran for office-- and I lost. In fact, I have run and lost eight times. EIGHT TIMES! But in defeat, however, I was ever mindful of the fact that "a setback is a set-up for a comeback" and I never gave up on my dreams and a belief in the promise of a better tomorrow. (And you ought not give up on your dreams either)! For it was during those difficult days that I would hearken back to the lessons taught to me by my parents, who would remind me that it didn't matter how often I got knocked down, I still owed it to myself, and to those who came before me, to get back up again. And so, I did...

In 1992, after the results of the 1990 *U.S. Census* led to the apportionment of additional congressional seats to Florida, and offered the possibility of an African-American being elected to *Congress,* I saw another opportunity to serve my community while simultaneously fulfilling my purpose and so I ran—again—and won. And I haven't lost since! In fact, as the first Black congressman elected from Florida in 116 years, having only been preceded by the Honorable Josiah T. Walls who served in the *United States House of Representatives* from 1871-1876, I have served in Congress with the firm realization that I am merely a caretaker for a seat that belongs to the people of my great state. Yet, through it all, I have been able to do so, understanding that I stand on the shoulders of those who paid the ultimate price, while reaching back to prepare those who will take the mantle of leadership and carry the torch that I have been privileged to hold aloft, of advocacy, action and service above self.

In 1994, having just completed my first term in Congress, I received a letter from a student in my district seeking an internship opportunity in our Washington, DC Office. The young man, Elvin Dowling, the author of this most important work and a community leader in his own right, was not unknown to me, having been previously recognized by the local newspaper, *The Palm Beach Post,* for his community service efforts. As such, giving him an opportunity to serve alongside me was an easy decision; one that would result in a longstanding mentoring relationship for a quarter-century. In fact, since that time, Elvin has stood with me, and those of us in the struggle for civil rights and social justice, fighting for the voiceless and the "least of these" on the issues that matter most to those in need.

(Congressman Alcee L. Hastings and Author Elvin J. Dowling, pictured at the
Congressman's Office on Capitol Hill in Washington, DC, circa 1994.)

As one of my trusted aides, Elvin worked hard to help me understand the
complexities facing young men of color in this country; effectively articulating
their concerns in a way that facilitated my better appreciation of the impact of

public policy on younger generations. As the youngest chief of staff to one of our nation's oldest and most historic civil rights organizations, the *National Urban League*, Elvin's comprehensive understanding of the state of Black America has uniquely positioned him to articulate the challenges African-American men face today, both within this book and throughout the world. As an author and master communicator, Elvin's ability to tell a story, particularly one that deserves to be heard, will leave each of us more hopeful and generations more enlightened, with each turn of phrase. More importantly, however, as a survivor like me, having lost siblings and family members to inner city violence, Elvin Dowling's understanding of what it means to be a successful Black man in an often-hostile country, lends greater credence to his ability to articulate the crucial messages that resonate throughout this book.

Steve Goodier, author of "One Minute Can Save a Life", once said:

❝

"My scars remind me that I did, indeed, survive my deepest wounds. That, in itself, is an accomplishment. And they bring to mind something else, too. They remind me that the damage life has inflicted on me has, in many places, left me stronger and more resilient. What hurt me in the past has actually made me better equipped to face the present."

I agree and understand. Today, as I now face the twilight of a remarkable journey that, I would like to believe, has made a mark on the world that can never be erased, I do so, knowing that the future of our nation—and our people—is hopeful; should we choose to rise to the challenge and fight for America's future.

For until the day comes when minorities in this country are no longer denied the things that others take for granted, the struggle must continue. Until we live in a nation that celebrates our diversity and does not demonize it, the fight must go on. And until black men are no longer invisible in this, the most prosperous nation in history, change cannot wait. Like Jesse Owens in 1936, I am heartened to know that a new generation of leaders, like my friend Elvin Dowling, will pick up the baton and run the race for such a time as this. As such, I urge you to give this book the attention it deserves, as I am confident that you will be informed and inspired by the words and ideas of this powerful and anointed servant of all mankind.

Yours In the Struggle,

Alcee L. Hastings

Alcee L. Hastings, Member of Congress

Editor's Note: *The Honorable Alcee L. Hastings has represented the citizens of South Florida in the United States House of Representatives since 1992. Florida's longest serving Member of Congress, Hastings has served as a United States District Court Judge and attorney in private practice.*

(Alcee L. Hastings, Sr.: Congressman & Statesman)

Works Cited

1. Shmoop Editorial Team. "Invisible Man Race Quotes Page 6." *Shmoop*. Shmoop University, Inc., 11 Nov. 2008. Web. 8 Sep. 2019.

Author's Note

Why I Wrote This Book

The late, great Toni Morrison, once said, *"If there is a book you want to read and it hasn't been written yet, then you must write it."* For more than five years, I carried the conceptual framework for this book in both my heart and my head, with the idea that someone, anyone, should author a comprehensive narrative on the challenges impacting Black Males in America, particularly in the wake of a more awakened populace who, through the proliferation of cameras and social media technology, have more recently discovered what African-Americans already know: racism, discrimination and disparate treatment, based on conscious and unconscious bias does, indeed, exist and is played out repeatedly in law enforcement interactions between minorities and the police each and every day.

While this book is, in no way the answer to the greatest challenges facing our country, the challenges examined herein, and the prescriptions for progress proposed, make up what portends to be the beginnings of a meaningful national dialogue on one of the most pressing sociodemographic issues of our time: the perilous prognosis facing African-American men and boys.

Offensive Language Warning

Please be advised that this book contains discussions of race, culture and stereotypes and, when contextually relevant, uses the *"n-word"* in its historical application. The purpose of this book is to explore mischaracterizations and epithets, including the un-redacted use of the *"n-word"*, with the goal of bringing greater understanding around the use of this and other pejoratives, their origins, applications and impact upon African-Americans and other individuals of color. Historically in the United States, the term *"nigger"* (*also known as the "n-word"*) was first used as a racial epithet in the early nineteenth century. Today, however, while usage of the word within the African-American community is complex in that it is used interchangeably as a term of endearment, as a political descriptor or as an insult, it is still considered an abusive slur when used by whites.

Survey Methodology

To complete this most-important research component for this book, I partnered with an experienced third-party vendor, *Pollfish**, and utilized proprietary technology that natively integrated with partner apps, to randomize the delivery of our survey to real consumers, in targeted demographics, while they were organically engaged with the apps on their devices. This survey's audience consisted of actual and real consumers like you and I, who were selected automatically through a vast network of partner smartphone apps and websites. The survey methodology deployed is based on a revolutionary way of targeting audiences and collecting data, through the use of proprietary and third-party mobile phone applications. Additionally, our research process applied several safeguards, like weighting adjustments, which provided fast and reliable data, whilst keeping selection and/or non-response bias under control. Furthermore, to ensure our data's integrity, we utilized a set of automated techniques and algorithms to ensure that this project received only legitimate responses. Some of those processes took into account Unique Device I.D., IP, proxy, device type, location, and more. Just as importantly, as a researcher, because I understand that, without quality, the data that we have painstakingly gathered means nothing, we implemented a number of technical measures to ensure the integrity of our results, by injecting quality questions, avoiding pitfalls such as speeding through surveys and checking on the survey results to ensure accuracy, reliability and validity.

Finally, it should be noted that all of the demographic data we provide on each of our respondents is first-hand information, gathered through comprehensive questionnaires completed by each of our survey's respondents prior to their participation.

Survey Demographics

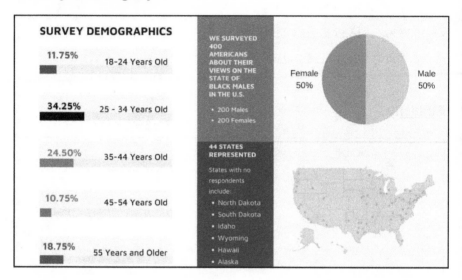

As a key component of this book, we conducted a survey of 400 Americans from various walks of life, to gauge their opinions, attitudes and perspectives on the various issues discussed in this work. We aimed to have a research sample that was reflective of the current demographic makeup of country, to as great an extent as possible, based on the statistical findings from the *2010 United States Census*. Additionally, the poll's population size was 321,646,250 individuals; hailing from all U.S. States except, Alaska, Hawaii, Idaho, North Dakota and South Dakota. Furthermore, with a confidence level of 95%, the poll's overall margin of error is (+/- 5%). An acceptable margin of error used by most survey researchers typically falls between 4% and 8%. Our calculations used a normal distribution (50%) to determine our optimum margin of error. To that end, the following data-points are critical to understanding the demographic composition of our research population, to include the following statistics:

- 50% - Male Respondents
- 50% - Female Respondents
- 11.75% - 18 to 24 Years Old
- 34.25% - 25 to 34 Years Old
- 24.50% - 35 to 44 Years Old
- 10.75% - 45 to 55 Years Old
- 18.75% - 55 Years and Older

Ethnicity

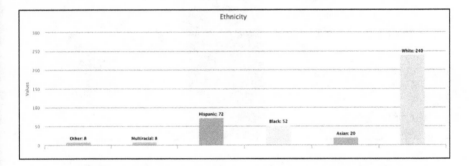

Racial Demographics of Respondents

- Other - 2.00%
- Multiracial - 2.00%
- Hispanic - 18.00%
- Black - 13.00%
- Asian - 5.00%
- White - 60.00%

Career

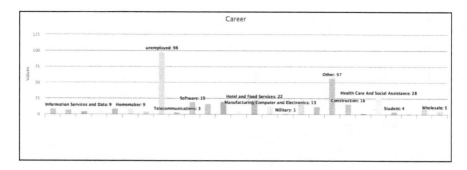

Jobs/Professional Services Represented

- Information Services and Data - 2.25%

- Retail - 1.75%

- Real Estate Rental or Leasing - 1.00%

- Legal Services - 2.00%

- Transportation and Warehousing - 2.25%

- Homemaker - 2.25%

- Science or Technical Services - 1.00%

- Unemployed - 24.50%

- Telecommunications - 0.75%

- Software - 4.75%

- Arts, Entertainment or Recreation - 4.00%

- Education - 5.00%

- Retired - 1.25%

- Hotel and Food Services - 5.50%

- Manufacturing, Computer and Electronics - 3.25%

- Military - 0.25%

- Finance and Insurance - 4.75%

- Manufacturing (Other) - 3.00%

- Other - 14.25%

- Construction - 4.00%

- Agriculture, Forestry, Fishing or Hunting - 0.50%

- Healthcare and Social Assistance - 7.00%

- Student - 1.00%

- Information (Other) - 0.25%

- Government and Public Administration - 2.25%

- Wholesale - 1.25%

Education

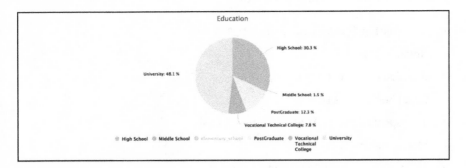

Highest Academic Level Completed

- High School - 30.25%

- Middle School - 1.50%

- Elementary School - 0.08%

- Post Graduate - 12.28%

- Vocational Technical College - 7.77%

- University - 48.12%

Income

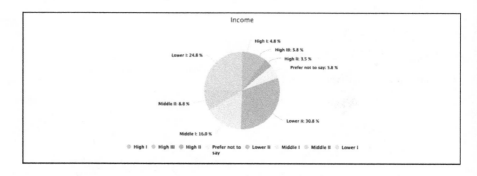

Annual Income of Respondents

- High I (Between $100,000 - $124,999) - 4.75%

- High II (Between $125,000 - $149,999) - 5.75%

- High III ($150,000 and More) - 3.50%

- Prefer Not to Say - 5.75%

- Lower Level II (Between $25,000 - $49,999) - 30.75%

- Middle I (Between $50,000 - $74,999) - 16.00%

- Middle II (Between $75,000 - $99,999) - 8.75%

- Lower Level I (Under $25,000) - 24.75%

Employment Status

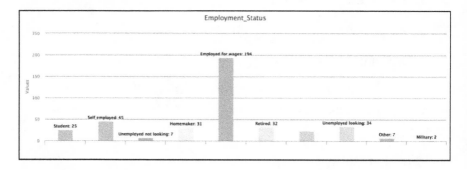

Source of Respondent's Income

- Student - 6.25%
- Self-Employed - 11.25%
- Unemployed Not Looking - 1.75%
- Homemaker - 7.75%
- Employed for Wages - 48.50%
- Retired - 8.00%
- Unable to Work - 5.75%
- Unemployed but Looking - 8.50%
- Other - 1.75%
- Military - 0.50%

Marital Status

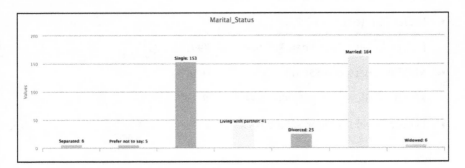

Relationship Status of Respondents

- Separated - 1.50%
- Prefer Not to Say - 1.25%
- Single - 38.25%
- Living with Partner - 10.25%
- Divorced - 6.25%
- Married - 41.00%
- Widowed - 1.50%

Parental Status

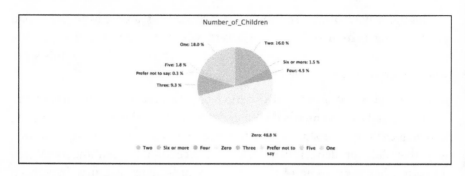

Respondent's Number of Children

- Two - 16.00%

- Six or More - 1.50%

- Four - 4.50%

- Zero - 48.75%

- Three - 9.25%

- Prefer Not to Say - 0.25%

- Five - 1.75%

- One - 18.00%

All survey results displayed above are represented by the overall percentage of survey respondents. To review raw survey results, visit: http://bit.ly/stillinvisiblesurvey.

Special Thanks & Final Thoughts

In closing, a note of appreciation to my trusted research partners, **Kendall Finlay, Tyler Brown and Joseph Garrett,** who helped to keep the vision of this project alive until it was finished. Without your contributions this work would not have been completed.

Over the course of an extended period of time, recorded interviews were conducted and then transcribed with each chapter's leading subjects. Our goal, in telling each of their stories, was to accurately reflect their expressions in a way that did not detract from the substance of their sentiments. When necessary, however, some of the subject's words or phrases may have been changed, but only to provide clarity, brevity or context. Further, _from a stylistic perspective, I have chosen to capitalize the word "Black" when referencing the African-American experience or identity._ While it may not necessarily be grammatically correct (depending upon when and how it is being used), I do so because Black people in America are often marginalized and overlooked in society. In the pages of this book, however, they are very much seen, heard and appreciated, thus the capitalization. Additionally, please note that any conclusions made in this book, to the extent that there are any, are those of the author and do not necessarily represent the views and opinions of the subjects of this work or those who may have offered endorsements of this work.

Finally, this book was created as a tool to be used to further promote understanding, while simultaneously debunking false narratives, misperceptions, and racist tropes, with verifiable facts and workable solutions aimed at helping the United States of America to achieve a "more perfect union". Please feel free to share with me, and others, your thoughts and ideas, by tweeting, texting, posting and chatting about your take on the issues discussed herein. I would love to hear your opinion and please know that I am grateful that you _"thought it not robbery"_ to read this work and add to what I pray will be a substantive conversation about how, together, we can help make America better, using the hashtag_: #StillInvisible._

In the spirit of high idealism, I remain,

Sincerely yours,

Elvin J. Dowling

Elvin J. Dowling

(Elvin J. Dowling: Author, Activist & Architect of Change)

Preface

Or again, you often doubt if you really exist. You wonder whether you aren't simply a phantom in other people's minds. Say, a figure in a nightmare which the sleeper tries with all his strength to destroy. It's when you feel like this that, out of resentment, you begin to bump people back. And, let me confess, you feel that way most of the time. You ache with the need to convince yourself that you do exist in the real world, that you're a part of all the sound and anguish, and you strike out with your fists, you curse and you swear to make them recognize you. And, alas, it's seldom successful."

- Ralph Ellison, "Invisible Man" (Shmoop Editorial Team. Prologue.2)

(This image of an "Invisible Man", rendered in scratchboard art form, is emblematic of the "invisibility" Black men in America feel and experience daily.)

Paying Homage to An American Classic

In 1952, famed author Ralph Ellison penned the fictional classic, *"Invisible Man"*, chronicling the challenges of early twentieth century life in America for her citizens of color. In its gripping and often gritty depiction of the travails of a college educated, young Black man who often felt himself unnoticed in the rest of society, this literary masterpiece helped to shed light on the harsh realities that most Black males face each and every day—from the womb to the tomb—as they are forced to swim against the tide of negative public perception, institutional disadvantage, and creative disenfranchisement; further stacking the odds of success against them. Trapped in the alternate reality of being "seen, but not seen", present but unaccounted for—and in many aspects unaccountable—Ellison's work brought light to the plight of Blacks in America. Today, however, nearly seventy years since the book's release marked a watershed moment for a slowly evolving society, many argue that very little has changed for the plight of America's Black males. And, in many instances, a "reversal of fortune" has occurred, as Black men in America continue to lose ground and get left behind in today's changing global marketplace.

Since the first African slaves were brought to the Spanish settlement in what is now St. Augustine, Florida in 1581, Black males in America have been systematically marginalized and told they were inferior in most aspects of American life. In spite of this uncontested truth, however, Black males, as a subset of the broader cultural fabric, have achieved remarkable feats that can't be overlooked. Yet and still, even with the election of America's first President of color, very little has changed for African-American men, as they continue to lag behind in all measurable indicators of success in twenty-first century America.

At this point in the journey of the Black man in America, no one can argue with the effects of generations of systematic racism and a pathology of "low expectations" that Black males sometimes embrace for themselves. This pervasive attitude, born, more often than not, from a culture of poverty, is a result of the combined effects of hundreds of years of psychological terrorism that is permanently embedded within the DNA of the survivors of one of the world's most brutal example of "man's inhumanity to man". So, what must we do? For starters, we must get real about how America arrived here in the first place, while offering real solutions to begin addressing these intractable issues. and what we must do to fix it. And that requires hard choices—and tough conversations—if we ever want to get to the root of the problem, instead of uselessly treating symptoms.

What Makes This Book Different?

It has often been said, "You're only as strong as your weakest link." *Still Invisible?* is an explosive narrative that examines many of the reasons Black men have been left behind in the shadows of a twenty-first century economy. The goal of this work is to remind America that the problems we will explore throughout this book are not just Black America's problem, its America's problem! Just as importantly, this book, not only examines the current and, if nothing is done, future prospects for countless Black males.

Narrated by "Lady Justice", the symbolic embodiment of moral justice and fair play in the judicial system, each chapter of *Still Invisible?* will not only feature the shared experiences of African American males from all walks of life, from working class men striving to make ends meet, to power professionals and recognizable figures, all of whom get that same feeling in their stomach whenever they see the police, it will also provide the reader with the tools and resources they need to accurately and factually contextualize the issues facing Black men today, while taking into account the attitudes and perspectives of those who experience them differently.

Special sections at the end of each chapter include:

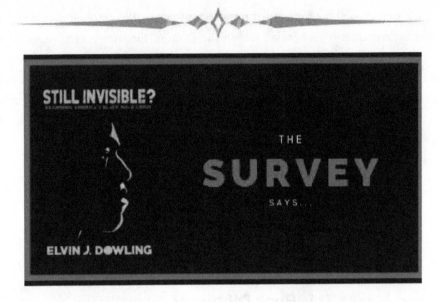

In this section, we will examine the opinions, beliefs and assumptions of many in society, as it pertains to their overall views of Black males in America. As a part of this discussion, we will explore stereotypes, taboos and preconceived notions that help to drive the negative narrative attributed to African-American men, how they came to exist, and what fuels them today.

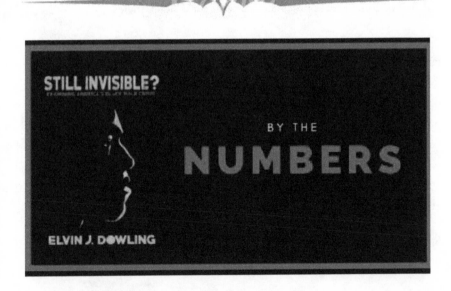

Perhaps the most useful resource in this book, this section will provide data and statistics that directly address each of the issues explored within the chapter. Challenging widely held misconceptions about Black males in America, such as the erroneous belief that there are more Black males in prison than there are in college, or the false narrative that Black males are more prone to violence than other members of American society, this section will help to arm the reader with accurate information, facts and empirical evidence that they can use to help reshape a false narrative. Those pesky things called facts are always critical when wading into the raging debate on race and culture in America.

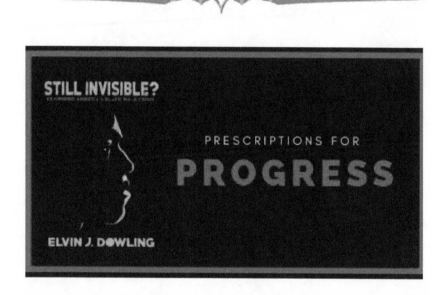

After considering the opinions and perspectives of others as it relates to their views on Black males in *"THE SURVEY SAYS"*, and providing the requisite facts and figures each reader needs to inform their own perspectives in *"BY THE NUMBERS"*, we will then offer thoughtful solutions on what to do next in *"PRESCRIPTIONS FOR PROGRESS."*

As an author committed to chronicling the truth in a way that examines all sides of the argument, while offering a compellingly transparent perspective buttressed by unassailable evidence, my aim is to present to you, the reader, a seminal narrative that will last the test of time. To that end, it is my hope that *Still Invisible?* will be for you what Invisible man was for me: the definitive narrative of what it means to be a Black man in a white country.

Works Cited

1. Shmoop Editorial Team. "Invisible Man Identity Quotes   Page 1." *Shmoop*. Shmoop University, Inc., 11 Nov.   2008. Web. 19 Aug. 2019.

Introduction

❝

I am an invisible man. No, I am not a spook like those who haunted Edgar Allan Poe; nor am I one of your Hollywood-movie ectoplasms. I am a man of substance, of flesh and bone, fiber and liquids -- and I might even be said to possess a mind. I am invisible, understand, simply because people refuse to see me."

- Ralph Ellison, "Invisible Man" (Schmoop Editorial Team. Prologue.1)

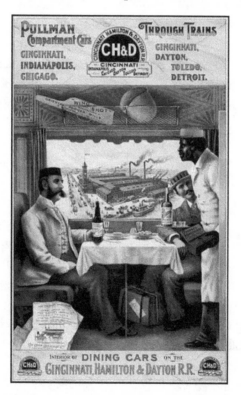

(Hired for their ability to be "seen and unseen" at the same time, African-American men working along the railways as Pullman Porters were generally stripped of their own identity and called "George" in homage to the company's founder, George Pullman).

I am the Beholder

What's in a Name?

It has often been said that justice, like beauty, is in the eye of the beholder. Well, darling, that's me ...

I am Lady Justice.

I was born into the world the brainchild of Augustus, the first emperor of Rome, who wanted to present himself as the paragon of impartiality and, in doing so, created me. I am the personification of fair play for those seeking truth and a redress of their grievances. From the moment I was crowned as the Roman goddess Justitia (Lady Justice, if you will), until this very day, the world has taken note of the power I wield in temples of jurisprudence everywhere. In fact, the very mention of my name demands immediate respect and invokes a modicum of fear from even the strongest of individuals. You may not like me, but you will respect me. Of this, I have no doubt.

Having a name is the first and most important gift that each of us are given at birth, one that will generally follow us for the rest of our lives. As babies, we immediately identify with, and respond to, the sound of our names when uttered by the ones we love and those who love us. As children, we begin to build our names, our brand if you will, and start to understand that our reputations truly proceed us. As adults, we hope to cultivate a name that is integral to the legacy we will leave long after we are gone. But having no name at all, is both wounding to the spirit and debilitating to one's own sense of self, rendering that individual worthless to those that choose to see them, and all but invisible to everyone else. Just as it was intended.

For nearly one hundred years, from the collapse of slavery in the South in 1865, until the 1960's, countless Black men traded their enslavement for employment as a Pullman Porter on America's railroads. Responsible for serving as ushers for passengers along the rail lines, these men were universally referred to as "George" (in honor of the owner of the company, George Pullman), thus stripping them of their sense of self and putting them in the same conundrum that Ralph Ellison's *"Invisible Man"* experienced as an individual without his own identity. But never fear... I am here. The world may not know your names, Black men, and may refuse to see you... but I have never taken my eyes off of you.

I *am Lady Justice.*

The stories I will share with you in this book, hearken back to the fictional experiences of a Black man I will present to some and reintroduce to others; one without a name or an individual identity who, in many ways, did not exist, but is as real as you and I. As your narrator on this, your path to compassion and understanding, I will also introduce you to other Black men, from various walks of life who, like the *"Invisible Man"*, have spent their lives seeking to be seen for their individual contributions, but unlike the *"Invisible Man"*, they are real, very real, and so are their individual, yet collective, experiences. As the reader, you should note that it is where their personal experiences intersect, regardless of their income or education levels, that the truth of America is exposed. As the guardian of that truth, you should also be mindful of the fact that I have an ugly underbelly that would shock your conscience, were I to lift my gown. In theory, I'm blind. In reality, I see everything. *Don't let the tipped scales fool you.*

I am Lady Justice.

I am the muse that lovers seek, but only some will ever find. I'm the cream in your cup of *Starbucks* coffee—*paying customers only, please!* Everyone wants me, but I tend to play hard to get. A lady must have standards, right? And if you want my undivided attention, please know it's going to cost you, because I am no cheap thrill. In his poem, "Let America Be America Again," Langston Hughes, an African American poet who emerged during the height of the Harlem Renaissance, declared: "America was never America to me." And he was right, I must admit. Especially, Hughes observed, as it relates to her citizens of color.

" "

"O, let my land be a land where Liberty/ Is crowned with no false patriotic wreath/ But opportunity is real, and life is free/ Equality is in the air we breathe./ There's never been equality for me/ Nor freedom in this "homeland of the free." America was never America to me". (Hughes, p. 15-21).

In eighteenth century America, when the framers of the *United States Constitution* embedded within the *Declaration of Independence* the three ideals that made its citizens quintessentially "American," namely the rights to *"life, liberty and the pursuit of happiness,"* those inherent truths were initially guaranteed only to white men with money. *Initially...* What is less understood, however, is that in twenty-first century America, one can't truly enjoy "life," and the "pursuit of happiness," without the "liberty" one needs to search for them in earnest. And that's where I come in...

I am Lady Justice.

In 1507, with the publishing of the Waldseemüller Map, which included the newly "discovered" continent that would thereafter be called "America", the country that would become the United States has been a complex ideal of one nation, theoretically indivisible, but in reality indelibly divided and perpetually angry, one side with the other. Moreover, since its organizational inception in 1776, the country has been continually locked in an epic struggle between the sociopolitical realities of those fighting for change, versus the intractable views of those urging "more of the same". And, at varying points in its history, one ideal has prevailed over the other. Throughout this time, however, as a nation established by and for *"white slave holders who wanted to be free"*, willing to decimate an entire group of people - namely Native Americans - to take the land for themselves, America's name and reputation has been met with skepticism and wariness almost everywhere. But, to be fair, that's only one aspect of what can arguably be described as the "greatest country on earth."

Since the founding of its republic, America's brand has *also* been synonymous with **hope**, **opportunity,** and **_"generosity; of spirit"_**; welcoming those from around the world willing to contribute to our society, an opportunity to enter through the golden door of liberty. With that being said, however, America is **also** known for standing with the oppressed, responding to tragedies and natural disasters and promoting economic opportunity and free market capitalism all around the world. As a force for good, the United States has stared down the world's most scurrilous dictator, Adolph Hitler; defeating Nazism and fascism in one fell swoop. As a beacon of hope, America has held aloft the lamp of liberty for those who seek better opportunities. As a land of unending opportunity, America has been the only place on the globe that someone with nothing can make something of themselves.

Time and again, the United States has risen to the call of leadership and, in doing so, has continued to secure democracy and defeat tyranny for countless individuals "yearning to breathe free". I should know, I helped to make all of that happen. As the ultimate protector of freedom, I, too, sing America. I just pick my lyrics carefully and always put my best foot forward. After all...

I am Lady Justice.

In **my** America, justice is often an expensive proposition. So, *"tip me now, that way I will know how to serve you!"* For it is I, who stands between you and the ravenous wolves, chomping at the bit, waiting to tear you limb from limb. And whether or not I cast you into the depths of the "just us" system *(as some have come to call it)*, has little to do with your guilt or innocence, and more to do with your pedigree. If you've got the "complexion for protection" or a mountain of money--preferably both--then by all means... let's make a deal. If not, take your chances.

It has often been said, *"the more things change, the more they remain the same."* I can vouch for that. Times have changed, and so have I. Sort of... You see, unlike the year 1952, when Ellison introduced us to his *"Invisible Man"* (*what was his name again?*), in today's America, freedom is no longer **just** black or white--but green! *"It's all about the Benjamins baby!"*

Now, I consider that progress!

When self-described socialist minister Francis Bellamy wrote the "Pledge of Allegiance" in 1892, he posited that America was a utopian meritocracy,

"...with liberty and justice for all." President Ronald Reagan once called our nation a *"shining city on a hill."* And they, *too*, were *also* correct! So <u>which</u> America is it? The answer is ... all of the above! Has America changed since its founding? Absolutely! But, on issues of racial equality and equitable treatment of all her citizens, the concept of making the necessary changes to achieve these goals has morphed from moving with *"all deliberate speed"* to crawling along at glacial pace in the view of those who are deleteriously impacted. As such, until the promise of liberty is extended to each and every citizen, without regard to race, creed, national origin or orientation, this land will never truly be free, and I will always be for sale. *"In God I trust... All others pay cash!"*

Kindest Regards,

Justitia

Lady Justice

(A drawing of Lady Justice: "The Personification of Fairness")

Will It Ever End?

Throughout the history of America, the United Sates has gone to great lengths to marginalize men of African descent, from the moment enslaved men and women of color were forced ashore onto the banks of Hampton, Virginia in 1619, until today; where black men represent one-third of America's prison population, according to John Gramlich of the *Pew Research Center*. In his article, "The Gap Between Blacks and Whites in Prison Is Shrinking," the author points out the fact that even though the chasm that existed between the inordinate number of blacks that were incarcerated versus their white counterparts in crime has decreased over the years, African Americans are still overrepresented in the prison population, illustrating a system of jurisprudence tilted towards partiality. In his analysis of the racial dynamics that color the criminal justice system, Gramlich noted the following: "The racial and ethnic makeup of U.S. prisons continues to look substantially different from the demographics of the country as a whole. In 2017, Blacks represented 12% of the U.S. adult population but 33% of the sentenced prison population. whites accounted for 64% of adults but 30% of prisoners. And while Hispanics represented 16% of the adult population, they accounted for 23% of inmates." If America is to ever realize her full and utmost potential, she must first begin by understanding that criminalizing individual existence has never been the answer. When given the opportunity to excel and succeed in every aspect of American life, Blacks have demonstrated time and again that capacity, character and commitment are universal abilities that transcend racial politics.

On April 16, 1952, two days after the release of what would be Ralph Ellison's only novel, *New York Times* writer Orville Prescott set the example for other white journalists to follow when he publicly acknowledged that Ellison's brilliance could not be ignored, when he declared "*Invisible Man*" to be "the most impressive work of fiction by an American Negro which I have ever read." (Prescott). In a country already fraught with racial strife, with the recent murders of Harry T. Moore and his wife Harriett, who became the first martyrs of the civil rights movement when they were killed by a bomb placed underneath the floorboards of their bed on Christmas Eve, some four months earlier, Ellison's novel and, indeed, the world's response, was the beginning of a running dialogue on what it means to be a black male in America. "*Invisible Man,*" Prescott wrote, "is undoubtedly melodramatic; but each melodramatic incident represents some aspect of the Negro's plight in America, or of his response to it."

But just as important as it is to recognize the literary genius Ellison exhibits in his work, we must also be mindful of the struggle the book's narrator and protagonist continued to encounter in every aspect of his life, all of which led to his feelings of hopeless invisibility. Today, Black males in America continue to face some of the same challenges that the "*Invisible Man*" faced in his own life, as a college educated man who continually finds himself in situations that reinforce his own societal limitations. They, too, feel trapped in a skin that, at once, renders them as someone to be watched warily, simultaneously forgotten, and increasingly inconsequential.

In the nearly seven decades that have passed since the publishing of Ellison's work, *"Invisible Man"* has shined a light on the effects of systemic racism in America. For example, a recurring theme of the book centers around the narrator's need to fit into his environment and, in doing so, becomes an inauthentic version of himself. Today, this same narrative continues to play out in the lives of African-American men everywhere, as they live sicker and die quicker than any other group in America, all while struggling to be seen in a nation that pretends that they aren't there. In his article, "American Nightmare: Ralph Ellison's *"Invisible Man"* At 60," journalist Nathaniel Rich of the *Daily Beast* reminds us that this iconic novel not only broke barriers in literature, it also went a long way towards helping to expose the harsh realities of racial discrimination in the country. In his insightful analysis of the book's impact since its initial publication, Rich observed: "In *Invisible Man* we experience American history as a nightmare. Sixty years after the novel's publication we still haven't woken up." On this singular point, history and time, have agreed. Perhaps the most insightful synopsis of *"Invisible Man"* comes from Ralph Ellison himself, who described the nameless protagonist at the heart of this novel, as "a depiction of a certain type of Negro humanity that operates in the vacuum created by white America in its failure to see Negroes as human." ("American Nightmare"). And even in the age of a "post-racial America," Black males are still asking the fundamental question: "will they ever see us?"

In their Op-Ed piece entitled, "Forcing Black Men Out of Society," the *New York Times* Editorial Board, led by Editorial Page Editor Andrew Rosenthal, spoke with one clarion voice about the need to address the systemic exclusion of Black men in many aspects of American society. "An analysis—"1.5 Million Missing Black Men"— showed that more than one in every six Black men in the 24-to-54 age group has disappeared from civic life, mainly because they died young or are locked away in prison," the times noted (Rosenthal). "While the 1.5 million number is startling, it actually understates the severity of the crisis that has befallen African-American men since the collapse of the manufacturing and industrial centers, which was quickly followed by the "war on drugs" and mass imprisonment, which drove up the national prison population more than sevenfold beginning in the 1970s," the editorial board continued, noting the dismal statistics that are oftentimes attendant with being Black in America (Rosenthal). Unless and until we reverse these declines and bring our missing men back into the fabric of our nation as productive members of society, nothing will ever change.

The aforementioned *New York Times* report went on to note that systemic racism, poverty, crime and lack of opportunity have all colluded together to effectively stymie the ability of Black males in America to beat the odds stacked against them. "In addition to the "missing," millions more are shut out of society, or are functionally missing, because of the shrinking labor market for low-skilled workers, racial discrimination or sanctions that prevent millions who have criminal convictions from getting all kinds of jobs. At the same time, the surge in imprisonment has further stigmatized blackness itself, so that Black men and boys who have never been near a jail now have to fight the presumption of criminality in many aspects of day-to-day life..." (Rosenthal). Be that as it may, in spite of the fact that the majority of Americans know and fully understand the impacts that systematic exclusion can have on any group of people, many still refuse to even address these intractable issues, preferring instead to pretend they don't exist, and simply hope that they will go away. Then, in 2016, Donald J. Trump was elected the 45th President of the United States and everything changed.

Here We Go Again?

In quoting novelist Jesmyn Ward, winner of the 2011 National Book Award for Fiction, Conrad Pritscher, in his book "Skin Color: The Shame of Silence" underscored the necessity of rooting out racism at its core, if America is to ever deal with its "original sin" once and for all and truly become a more perfect union. "There is power in naming racism for what it is, in shining a bright light on it, brighter than any torch or flashlight. A thing as simple as naming it allows us to root it out of the darkness and hushed conversation where it likes to breed like roaches. It makes us acknowledge it. Confront it." (Pritscher 107). But before racism can be effectively confronted, it must be universally recognized for what it is.

In his 1964 concurring opinion in *Jacobellis v. Ohio*, reversing the conviction of Nico Jacobellis, the manager of an Ohio movie theater, for his repeated screening of the movie "The Lovers" which the state had classified as obscene, *US Supreme Court* Justice Potter Stewart laid plain the reality of a "thing that speaks for itself," in writing: *"I shall not today attempt further to define the kinds of material I understand to be embraced within that shorthand description; and perhaps I could never succeed in intelligibly doing so. But I know it when I see it..."* (Jacobellis). For hundreds of years, the United States of America has demonstrated to her citizens of color that it operates on a system of racism and discrimination designed to keep minorities in a permanent state of disadvantage. As such, if there is one thing most Black people know when they see, like Justice Stewart was with obscenity, its racism; an odious disease of the spirit they can smell a mile away.

In his article, "Trump Ain't New: America Has a Long History of Racist Presidents," author David Love of *The Grio.com* delineated the multiplicity of examples of American presidents that have exhibited racist behavior before, during or after holding office. George Washington, who owned more than 300 enslaved Africans at his death, approved of whipping them into submission and working them into old-age. Thomas Jefferson, our third president and author of the *Preamble to the Constitution of the United States* regularly raped his subjects and then enslaved the children he forced them to carry to term. So, what Black Americans are experiencing now, in the current renaissance of white nationalism, is certainly nothing new. In fact, the history of America has demonstrated time and again that it is not unusual for the United States to elect political leaders to the highest offices in the land that are committed to upholding the vestiges of white supremacy and social privilege. "Andrew Jackson–Trump's hero– was one of the worst American presidents, and also one of its most racist. He owned hundreds of slaves, and censored anti-slavery mailings from Northern abolitionists while president. Nicknamed "Indian killer," he committed genocide against of Native Americans, including women and children. His Indian Removal Act removed 46,000 native people from their land, making 25 million acres available to white settlers and slaveowners, while 4,000 Cherokee people died during the "Trail of Tears" forced relocation to the West." (Love). As the conscience of the country, Black Americans are not shocked by the antics of the current occupant of the White House who wants to keep it just that way--a WHITE House. For them, its par for the course and business as usual.

Dr. Martin Luther King, Jr. once said: "In the end, we will remember not the words of our enemies, but the silence of our friends." For far too long, too many "good people" have remained silent while an overt assault on the human rights and basic dignities of all people in America are clearly being stripped away. And yet many say nothing. Absolutely nothing. Instead some choose moral equivocation when faced with a choice of "us vs. them," which pits otherwise peaceful neighbors against one another and is demonstrative of an unhealthy country. According to Juliana Menasce Horowitz, Anna Brown and Kiana Cox of the *Pew Research Center*, in their "Race in America 2019" Report, the public's view on race relations has worsened and most people blame Donald Trump. In a nationally representative online survey of 6,637 people, 18-years and older, conducted in English and Spanish, the researchers discovered an alarming rise in racial anxiety all throughout the country. According to their report, nearly seven-in-ten citizens believe that race relations are not only bad, but are prone to get worse. "Most Americans (65%) – including majorities across racial and ethnic groups – say it has become more common for people to express racist or racially insensitive views since Trump was elected president. A smaller but substantial share (45%) say this has become more acceptable." (Horowitz, *et. al.* 6). And, in spite of all this, Black people are still expected to keep their mouths shut, for fear of being labeled "angry" or, much worse, a "thug", rendering many of these men as voiceless as the *"Invisible Man"* was three generations ago. And white people are also expected to keep their mouths shut, for fear of being labeled "out of touch" or, much worse, "racist", effectively killing any opportunity for meaningful dialogue. And nothing ever changes.

In his blog post, "According to White People, Talking About Racism Makes You Racist," author Gee Lowery of *Onyx Truth,* made a curious observation about the "freedom to speak" prohibitions placed upon Black people when it comes to talking openly about their daily experiences, even in the age of Trump. Lowery noted, "The new approach white society is attempting to use to deflect from Black people talking about systemic racism (the only form of racism most Black people are actually talking about) is to label Black people racist for **SIMPLY TALKING ABOUT RACISM.** That's it. If you are Black and you start talking about racism, white people will try to label you as racist for talking about racism. Seriously. I'm not making this shit up", he observed. Provocative? Yes. Correct? Debatable. It depends upon the perspective. What is not up for debate, however, is the fact that even though

Lowery's broad generalizations can't speak to the totality of an entire group's beliefs and/or opinions, his views do represent a broadly held opinion, particularly amongst people of color, that they should simply be silent in the face of incredible injustice. America, "love it or leave it," they say. Even to those who have earned the right to be here.

What Can We Do?

Martin Luther King, Jr., once prophetically declared: "In the end, we will not remember the words of our enemies, but the silence of our friends." Today, in the age of extreme racism, with vicious screeds of "go back to where you come from" emanating even from 1600 Pennsylvania Avenue, open discrimination and bold faced bigotry, the time has come for men, women and children of goodwill to stand up, speak out and be heard. Arm yourselves with the truth and give yourselves permission to empathize with the black male experience.

When you consider the debt that is owed by _you_, and can never be repaid, as you begin this journey of enlightenment and understanding, it is important to remember what makes the "promise of America" an idea whose time has come, is that each of her citizens are "endowed with certain inalienable rights" that must never--ever--be abridged! So until the tenet of total inclusion is realized by all Americans, the fight for freedom will continue.

If America is ever to be "America" again, the time has come for those who love this land to pause, if only but for a moment, to acknowledge the extraordinary challenges that come along with being born a Black male in this country. Along with that blessing comes the burden of constantly being on the run from vigilantes who have questions and authorities who demand answers for doing what others do: going about your everyday existence. Nonetheless, you must run the race that is set before you, while never giving up on the promise of a brighter future.

Famed Abolitionist, Harriet Tubman, once said: _"If you hear the dogs, keep going. If you see the torches in the woods, keep going. If there's shouting after you, keep going. Don't ever stop. Keep going. If you want a taste of freedom, keep going."_ There are many reasons, as a Black male in today's America, for them to simply give up and quit on themselves. And there are plenty of reasons for everybody else to give up on Black males. But life in America would not be the same without the demonstrable contributions of African-American males. And America must never forget it.

So, it is in this vain, with the hope of reigniting a dialogue that can no longer be ignored, I ask you to consider one critical question...

Works Cited

1. Shmoop Editorial Team. "Invisible Man Power Quotes Page 1." *Shmoop*. Shmoop University, Inc., 11 Nov. 2008. Web. 25 Jul. 2019.

2. Hughes, Langston. *Let America Be America Again and Other Poems*.1st Vintage Books ed. New York: Vintage Books, 2004.

3. Gramlich, John. "The Gap Between The Number of Blacks and Whites In Prison Is Shrinking." *Pew Research Center: Fact Tank: News In the Numbers*, 2019, **https://perma.cc/FUP7-KWUD**. Accessed 26 July 2019.

4. Prescott, Orville. "Books of the Times." The New York Times, April 16, 1952. https://perma.cc/RY2U-DB2X. Accessed 26 July 2019.

5. Rich, Nathaniel. "American Nightmare: Ralph Ellison's 'Invisible Man' at 60." *The Daily Beast*. June 28, 2012: *The Daily Beast*. Web. 26 November 2014. **https://perma.cc/LN2B-E6V4**

6. Rosenthal, Andrew. Editorial Page Editor. "Forcing Black Men From Society." The New York Times. June 25, 2015. **https://perma.cc/XQ5N-J58E**

7. Pritscher, Conrad P.,*Skin Color: The Shame of Silence*. Brill Publishers. Rotterdam, 2014, p. 107. *Jacobellis v. Ohio*, 378U.S.184(1964).

8. Love, David. "Trump Ain't New: America Has A Long History of Racist Presidents." *The Grio*. 15 January 2018. **https://perma.cc/ECT9-ACE9**. Accessed 27 July 2019.

9. Juliana Menasce Horowitz, Juiana. "Race in America 2019." *Pew Research Center*, 2019, p. 6. **https://perma.cc/EJD9-VCJK**, Accessed 25 July 2019.

10. Lowery, Gee. "According to White People, Talking About Racism Makes You Racist." Web blog post. *Onyx Tr Society*, 29 March 2016. **https://perma.cc/5R4R-4VHY**. Accessed 20 April 2016.

Chapter 1: Born With A Birthmark?

Blackballing Boys as Babies

"

They're my birthmark," I said. 'I yam what I am!'"

- Ralph Ellison, "Invisible Man" (Shmoop Editorial Team, 13.33)

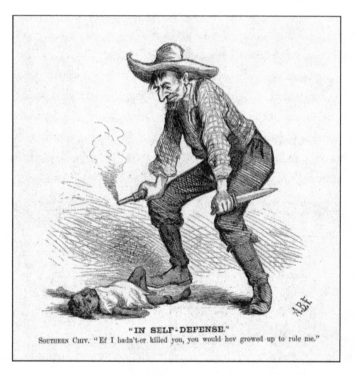

(A racist cartoon depiction from 1876, drawn by A.B. Frost for Harper's Ferry Weekly)

Casualties of Conflict

Can A Kid Just Be a Kid?

Noted educator and activist, Catrice Jackson, once said: *"If you don't have an anti-racism plan, you plan to be racist."* In the United States, for all practical purposes, when the institutions that racial supremacy have built are ignored and allowed to function as designed, more often than not, that is the end result. In fact, since the founding of our great republic almost two and a half centuries ago, our nation has promoted the concept of a white male patriarchy that has always placed Caucasian men at the top of the pecking order in American society. Followed closely behind white men in this impenetrable social construct is, of course, white women (like me) who, by virtue of our station in life, often enjoy the spoils of our male benefactors who afford us the pleasure of living a life of privilege and favor in the land of unlimited opportunity. After that, the social constructs of our society tend to get a bit complicated, if you will... except for the fact that Black men have always been at the bottom of the American social caste system--to be clear-- without question. How do I know? I know because I alone stand between those who seek to maintain the status quo and those who seek to change it through judicial precedent. I am Lady Justice.

As the arbiter of jurisprudence in this, the greatest, freest country in the world, I am loathed to admit that, when it comes to the inequities faced by Black males, that is, not much has been done to change the narrative of this century's old reality. Now, of course I would never admit this undeniable truth outside of polite company and, were I to be placed under oath in the very same system I oversee, I would "plead the fifth" on the grounds that I could incriminate myself, if ever confronted with the systemic inequalities attended upon even the youngest Black males amongst them. To that end, it goes without being said that, as a matter of pattern and practice, the frivolities of childhood and its accompanying youthful exuberance, is really never fully extended to Black children in America. "Too bad... so sad..."

According to Stacey Patton of the *Chronicle of Higher Education*, in her article, "In America, Black Children Don't Get to Be Children," Black childhood is considered inherently less valued and oftentimes indistinguishable from Black adulthood. In fact, research has revealed that the overestimation of a Black child's age begins as young as age twelve, impacting the way they are often seen and treated by others. "A study published... in the *Journal of Personality and Social Psychology* — which long ago published racist studies on Black children — linked the higher use of force by police on Black youth to the common perception that, by age 10, they are less innocent" (Patton). As such, I'm sure you can understand how police officers acting in the heat of passion, and well-meaning majority white juries, can justify state sanctioned aggression against these "larger than life" threats, can't you? Even with my delicate sensibilities and limited vision, I can see that... Can you say: "I feared for my life?" I rest my case.

In 1955, during the trial for the group of white men exonerated in the murder of a 14-year old Black boy, Emmett Till, one of his assailants remarked that Till "looked like a man." Nearly sixty years later, in 2014, Tamir Rice a 12-year old child in Cleveland, Ohio, would go on to meet his untimely demise when, what I can only presume was a well-meaning community patriot fulfilling his unwritten public duty of protecting white America from what could have been a menacing Black threat, when he called 911 with reports of "a guy, tall for his age" playing with a gun in a park. Granted, the caller did say, "it's probably a fake" and "he's probably a juvenile" to the emergency services operator, but, then again, those are just the details--way too many for the police to keep track of, of course. After all, it's a fast-paced job, and everybody's entitled to a few mistakes. Including the police, right?... Right?!

At the close of the *Civil War*, African-American citizens, through the passage of the 13th, 14th and 15th amendments to the *Constitution* of the United States, were successful in establishing political parity and participation for millions of newly freed Black people, but in doing so, the need to minimize the value of Black boys in this country became central to maintaining a white supremacist construct that continue to this day. "If a white life cycle features innocence, growth, civility, responsibility and becoming an adult, Blackness is characterized as the inversion of that. Not only are Black children cast as adults but, just as perversely, Black adults are stuck in a limbo of childhood, viewed as irresponsible, uncivil, criminal, innately inferior" (Patton). As perverse as this may be to the untrained eye, in my America, white is always right. That's just the way it is. And though the fate of some of our most vulnerable citizens is something that is of little consequence to people who look like me, I do, in fact, sympathize with the women who must bear the brunt of it all, the mothers of young Black boys who may never make it into adulthood. Their pain may never be my reality, but as a woman, I understand.

In a poignantly gripping letter to her son about the challenges he will ultimately face in the world he was destined to inherit, Celia K. Dale, a contributor to the *Atlanta Black Star*, wrote, in part, the following heartfelt plea:

❝

To my beautiful boy,

It is with profound sadness that I sit here writing this letter to you. You are only 8-years old and your world revolves around your friends and your family. You are oblivious to the ways of the world and what's in store for you as you learn and mature and leave the safety of my arms. I wish that I could guarantee this safety for the rest of your life; but I can't. I am no longer able to pretend that raising you right is all you'll need...

Son, you, no, we live in a country built on hate, fear, and oppression. We live in a country that will judge you, NOT by whom you are and what you stand for, but for what some random person with the same skin color does. We are a part of a race of people that are looked at collectively. You are an African American and you're a male and being those two things can be deadly...

...What I'm about to tell you will make you question my sanity, but I am telling you this because I want you to live. There is NO room for mistakes in your life, Braxton; none. You cannot dress a certain way, you cannot talk a certain way,

you cannot walk a certain way and you CANNOT EVER commit ANY kind of crime that will put your life in the hands of someone else. You CANNOT hang around certain people, walk in certain areas, or even go to the store with a group of friends to buy a sandwich. I may never see you alive again. Your life can be taken by police and there will be NO recourse because all they'll have to say is 5 words…. "I feared for my life." That's it. Guess what? They will be believed because it appears that the prevailing belief is just by virtue of your skin color and sex that you are to be feared. It doesn't matter that you're very sensitive. It doesn't matter that YOU don't care about what color your friends are. It doesn't matter, honey.

A lot of people will assume you're a thug… not because you act like one, not because you've EVER walked the streets of an inner city, but because you are Black. It doesn't matter that I worked my fingers to the bone to ensure that I raised you in a safe environment away from the issues that prevail in poor communities. It doesn't matter that I'm educated and articulate. It doesn't matter that I didn't let you run the streets doing what you wanted to do; NONE OF THESE THINGS MATTER!

If you are ever stopped by the police, Braxton, I want you to do the following: Comply with their requests. It doesn't matter how they request it, what they are doing while they request it or how you feel about the request. JUST DO IT! I need you to come home. Make NO sudden movements. If they ask you for ID tell them it's in your pocket and suggest that they get it out. Lord knows if they fear for their lives at that moment you may be killed. If you're driving, keep your license and registration in your lap or very close by so that any movement to retrieve it isn't a big movement. You may be shot if they fear for their lives. If the officers grab you, push you, rough you up. Take it! Demean yourself, humiliate yourself but take it. Remember those 5 words. "I feared for my life…"

…When a Black man does something positive it's an individual accomplishment. When a Black man does something negative, it is somehow a collective condemnation of all Blacks. Others can distance themselves from the negative, criminal acts of those like them… we don't have that luxury….

You need to know and understand that in this country, you can be killed by the police without ever drawing a weapon, without ever being convicted of a crime, without ever committing a crime. I know what you're thinking. I know you're wondering what the hell you're supposed to do with the cards stacked this way. I am telling you to do WHATEVER you need to do to make it home to your family alive. That is what you're supposed to do. Come home! I want you to live to deal with the justice system another day. Come home!...

I need to see you graduate from high school and college. I need to see you meet the woman of your dreams and marry her and give me grandchildren because your sister says she's NOT having them. I need to see the man you're destined to become. I need you to live, Braxton. I will figure out how to deal with my fears when you walk out the door, but I need you to walk back in that door alive. I am sick as I type these words because it isn't fair that I have to tell you these things. I don't imagine other mothers have to do this with their sons. But I need you to live, so here I am.

I love you... Mom

Today, in a country that will judge Black boys by the color of their skin, rather than the content of their character, even the heartfelt cries of a cacophony of mothers can't drown out our desire to maintain the status quo, no matter how bad things look on video or falsified reports. Unfortunately, in my America, that's the cost of doing business. And for that I make no apologies. *It is... what it is...*

Keep the Faith,

Justitia

Lady Justice

Gregory Diggs: The Fight for Equitable Education

Who's Your Daddy?

The iconic songwriter and heralded Black history-maker, Dr. James Weldon Johnson, writer of "*Lift Ev'ry Voice And Sing*", a soon-forgotten song he penned early on in his teaching career that would ultimately become known as the Negro National Anthem, once poignantly declared: *"You are young, gifted, and Black. We must begin to tell our young, 'There's a world waiting for you. Yours is the quest that's just begun."* As an individual who spent his entire professional career reminding both himself and the children he served as an educator in the Denver Public School System that they were capable of achieving the things that others could only imagine, Dr. Gregory Diggs has stood in the gap for vulnerable populations, namely Black children, his entire professional career.

"I'm originally from Silver Spring, Maryland and was born the son of Dr. John W. Diggs and Claudette Barnes," Diggs says as he describes his middle-class upbringing in the suburban Washington, DC area. "I grew up in a pretty upper-middle-class African-American community that was sort of nestled in a larger white community. I was fortunate in that most of my role models were members of my family. My father, for example, was a member of *Alpha Phi Alpha Fraternity, Incorporated*, and was part of quite a storied chapter of members that was founded in Silver Spring back in the 1970's, and also birthed the idea of a national memorial to Dr. Martin Luther King, Jr., one of the fraternity's most revered members."

The first *Black Greek Letter Organization* for college educated men, the fraternity boasts an illustrious membership of luminaries, including the Rev. Dr. Martin Luther King, Jr., *U.S. Supreme Court Justice*, Thurgood Marshall, former Vice President of the United States, Hubert H. Humphrey, and former *United Nations* Ambassador and mayor of Atlanta, Georgia, Andrew Young, among many others. "We had successful Black families in my neighborhood," Diggs remembers. "In the 1980's, when the *Cosby Show* was on television and showcased a successful Black family, The Huxtables, many of my white colleagues thought it was a fantasy that such a family could exist, but in my day, those are the kind of families I grew up with," he recalled. "Both of my parents were working professionals and they taught their children the importance of education and doing your best, at all times, to move forward in this life." But even for Black children who grew up just as Dr. Diggs did, the obstacles many face in the American education system leaves them left further and further behind, trailing their counterparts and not being pushed to their peak potential due to what former U.S. President George W. Bush often called "the soft bigotry of low expectations."

Even having grown up in what many Blacks would consider a "charmed existence," Diggs believed that the persistent devaluing of the Black family is a continuation of a pattern of discrimination visited upon minority communities. "Society is built on this notion that white middle-class norms and values and people are what the 'normal' American experience is, and everyone else is pretty much considered to be either 'less than' or 'less desirable', as compared to their 'normal'", he emphasized. "So, when you've got people that don't grow up around diversity, there's a fear, misconception, and ignorance about what the 'other' is. It doesn't matter what we do as 'others', our accomplishments and virtues remain invisible," Diggs continued. "We have long been victims of violence fueled by ignorance and it clearly didn't end with the Civil Rights Movement."

As an educator that wore a variety of hats, Diggs was both a university professor and a manager of a program that promotes social and emotional learning for the more than 90,000 students throughout *Denver Public Schools*. "My experience in education centers around research and evaluation methods, as well as the social foundations of education, which means I also so conduct student testing and help to implement cultural equity initiatives throughout our schools." Yet, the uphill battles Diggs faced in getting his colleagues and, indeed, the entire education community to treat all children equitably remains one that lies at the heart of the foundational issues Black males encounter in a system not designed to benefit them in the most important areas of American life. "Most of the students and families that I serve in my role, are either Latino or African-American, and most of the teachers who teach our students are Caucasian", Diggs noted. "What we've been trying to do is introduce the principles of culturally relevant education to the teachers, while simultaneously exposing them to the 'whole child' perspective while, at the same time, continuing to recruit and hire more educators of color."

According to authors Michelle Knight-Manuel and Joanne E. Marciano in their book, "Classroom Culture: Equitable Schooling for Racially Diverse Youth", implementing various learning strategies that leverage the individual learner's background and culture are critically important in meeting students where they are academically. "Culturally relevant education is an exceptional framework that recognizes the importance of including students' cultural backgrounds, interests and lived experiences in all aspects of teaching and learning within the classroom and across the school" (Knight-Manuel and Marciano, 2018). "Culturally relevant education," they continued, "is viewed as critical to improving student engagement and achievement, and college readiness and success for all youth, particularly youth of color." (Knight-Manuel and Marciano, 2018). With this realization in hand, however, leveling the playing field in early academic settings designed to serve as a pipeline for college and career, as opposed to dead-end jobs and prison, continues to remain a challenge.

In her article, "Why Talented Black and Latino Students Go Unnoticed," *New York Times* author Susan Dynarski illustrates the difficulties faced by students of color when they are generally not considered for higher level courses, placing them on track for better post-secondary scholarship opportunities. "Black third graders are half as likely as whites to be included in programs for the gifted, and the deficit is nearly as large for Hispanics", Dynarski observed. Buttressing this claim, in describing a widening academic achievement gap that exists in American schools, Diggs laid bare the challenges that educators, students and parents face daily. "What I'm about to describe," he begins, "is not just anecdotal but is actually fact-based and objective. What we are experiencing in Denver Public Schools is the same thing we are seeing across the nation, where our Latino and African American students are performing significantly below their white and Asian counterparts. Another thing that we are working on is the fact that we have disproportionality in discipline," he continued. "Our Latino and African American students are three to five times more likely to be suspended or expelled than their white or Asian counterparts, for the same behavior infractions," Diggs bemoaned, determined to help stem the tide of unfair and disparate treatment for any of his students.

What many African-American parents are increasingly beginning to realize, however, is the fact that the struggle to ensure that their young sons are being treated as fairly as other children starts much earlier than elementary school, but rather begins at birth and is exacerbated during their preschool years. In her plea to right-minded educators and frustrated parents hoping to create better disciplinary outcomes for their oft-misunderstood children, Tunette Powell, in her *Washington Post* essay entitled, "My Son Has Been Suspended Five Times, He's Three", expressed her frustration with "trigger-happy" school administrators opting to "suspend or expel first, and ask questions last", especially for young Black boys. In describing her preschooler's travails, Powell reflected on the following experience: "I received a call from my sons' school in March telling me that my oldest needed to be picked up early," Powell wrote. "He had been given a one-day suspension because he had thrown a chair. He did not hit anyone, but he could have, the school officials told me," Powell recalled. "For weeks, it seemed as if JJ was on the chopping block. He was suspended two more times, once for throwing another chair and then for spitting on a student who was bothering him at breakfast. Again, these are behaviors I found inappropriate, but I did not agree with suspension." (Powell).

Having had her own run-ins with school administrators as a young student, Powell initially faulted herself for the challenges her son was having. "I blamed myself, my past. And I would have continued to blame myself had I not taken the boys to a birthday party for one of JJ's [Powell's son] classmates." It was at this private get-together that Powell soon discovered that JJ's actions, although unacceptable, were part and parcel of how many of the other preschoolers in his classroom often behaved, none of whom had ever been suspended for their misdeeds. "My son threw something at a kid on purpose and the kid had to be rushed to the hospital," another parent said. "All I got was a phone call" (Powell). According to the *United States Department of Education's Office of Civil Rights*, in their "Data Snapshot: School Discipline" report, African American students are over represented in adverse disciplinary actions throughout the American school system, even at the preschool level. "Black children represent 18% of preschool enrollment, but 48% of preschool children receiving more than one out-of-school suspension; in comparison, white students represent 43% of preschool enrollment but 26% of preschool children receiving more than one out of school suspension. Boys represent

79% of preschool children suspended once and 82% of preschool children suspended multiple times, although boys represent 54% of preschool enrollment (Powell)."

According to Gregory Diggs, when a cultural gap exists in which the majority of the student population is Caucasian, and the majority of the educators are Caucasian, one can expect that there will be an achievement gap to follow for minority students. "If you can think about this, we [the United States of America] have an agrarian/industrial school curriculum, in terms of how we setup the classrooms and how we assess our students, which is based on 18th century and 19th century models of education, and this system doesn't fit with the kind of students that we are serving today," he noted. "As a result, there are some cultural mismatches and intractable issues that play into how education and discipline are communicated and delivered to a diverse student population. And yes, some teachers are actually afraid of the emotional expressions and behaviors of students of color, even when they are similar to the same behaviors of Caucasian students. I believe that part of the reason behind this response is a lack of exposure to diverse populations with some teachers, and part of it is attributable to the cultural climate in which we currently find ourselves, particularly with regard to the racial myths and fears that we have in America," Diggs noted. "And until educators at the administrator level," he continued, "to include principals, superintendents and school boards across the country, take matters into their own hands to reverse the trend of treating children of color as students rather than suspects, very little will change."

Fast-tracked to Failure?

Nicknamed the "City of Lakes" and nestled on the banks of the Mississippi and Minnesota Rivers, the great midwestern city of Minneapolis, Minnesota is a diverse and cosmopolitan locale that boasts a long history of diversity. Having first been inhabited by a group of permanent Native American settlers, the Dakota tribe, in the 1500's, Minneapolis has historically opened its portals to citizens from all around the world that have converged upon the "Twin Cities" to make it their home. With that being said, however, even this traditionally progressive city found itself at a crossroads when it was suddenly confronted with the fact that its African-American boys were being unduly punished in schools, facing suspension and expulsion at rates higher than all other students.

In her article, "A Superintendent in Minnesota Has Banned Black Kids from Being Suspended Without Her Permission," Krisytle Crossman noted the bold action being taken by a solitary school administrator who had come to her own conclusion that "enough was enough"! "Minneapolis, Minnesota superintendent Bernadeia Johnson is making sure that students of color are getting the same treatment as white students when it comes to suspension in their schools," Crossman begins. "Black children are suspended ten times more than white students and she wants to make sure that changes. In order to do so she has come up with new guidelines for her schools" (Crossman). For example, when a school in Johnson's district requested the suspension of a student in which the student's actions did not result in harm or violence, principals and other disciplinary administrators had to have Johnson's authorization before doing so. "The guidelines that were set out by Johnson were part of an agreement with the Civil Rights office at the *U.S. Department of Education*... Johnson is setting an example for school districts all over the nation in showing that the suspension rates for students of color are far too high and something needs to be done about it," Crossman continued. "Some students never recover from these punishments and end up feeling like they are already labeled as bad kids, so why not continue with the bad behavior. This lands them in prison at early ages." (Crossman).

According to a report in the *New York Times*, young African-American males are almost certainly destined to an economic reality in which they will earn less than their white counterparts, even if they come from wealthy families and well to do neighborhoods. In their article, "Extensive Data Shows Punishing Reach of Racism for Black Boys", journalists Emily Badger and her colleagues from the *Times* revealed the stark economic futures facing Black males in America. "White boys who grow up rich are likely to remain that way. Black boys raised at the top, however, are more likely to become poor than to stay wealthy in their own adult households. Even when children grow up next to each other with parents who earn similar incomes, Black boys fare worse than white boys in 99 percent of America. And the gaps only worsen in the kind of neighborhoods that promise low poverty and good schools" (Badger).

Chapter 2: "Don't They All Look Alike?"

Debunking Broad Generalizations

“

What1 and how much had I lost by trying to do only what was expected of me instead of what I myself had wished to do? What a waste, what a senseless waste! ... I had accepted the accepted attitudes and it had made life seem simple... "

- Ralph Ellison, "Invisible Man" (Schmoop Editorial Team)

"

(Written in 1896 by Ernest Hogan, the first African-American to perform on Broadway, this popular tune helped to further perpetrate broad generalizations and stereotypes about African-Americans in the late 1800's and the early part of the 20th century.)

"A Lie Doesn't Care Who Tells It!"

What's Wrong with Harmless Humor?

Noted American human rights and anti-corruption activist, John Pendergrast, once said, "American's perceptions of Africa remain rooted in troubling stereotypes of helplessness and perpetual crisis." Since the rise of western civilization, Africa, rich with its natural resources and diverse topography, has effectively been marginalized as the "dark continent" in need of salvation, governance and authoritarian by good white folk, like myself (of course), seeking to civilize the natives. In fact, throughout the course of American history, Black men, like the continent from which their ancestors hail, have been cast in a pejorative light that has, at times, been blinding and at other times illuminating. Whether confronted with issues of social justice, civic engagement, or economic empowerment, the challenges these men face are, fortunately for everyone else in America, localized primarily to them and, as a result, are undetectable in the eyes of to the uninitiated and ill-informed. For me, however, as the paragon of justice and fair play, I am acutely aware of what's happening to them but, as you can imagine, my hands are tied. Be that as it may, however, that doesn't mean I don't feel their pain and sympathize with their struggle. I mean, what kind of lady do you think I am?

Beginning in the mid-nineteenth century and continuing even today, the constant degradation of Black men in the eyes of the general populace has been a matter of economic survival and social stratification that has helped to perpetuate white supremacist ideology ever since. In fact, many of the more popular tropes that have been tactically deployed to torpedo the ambitions of Black men, have included labeling them as lazy oafs, brutish beasts, ignorant children and dangerous criminals who must be kept at arm's length and controlled at all costs. In fact, one of the most universal suppositions attributed to people of color, not just Black men, is the notion that "they all look alike." Popularized in the song "All Coons Look Alike to Me: A Darkey Misunderstanding" written, composed and performed nearly 125 years ago by America's first Black Broadway star, Earnest Hogan, the idea that the African-American community is just one big, homogenous group, indistinguishable one from the other, is a malignant metaphor that continues to last the test of time. Whether used by even the most well-meaning law enforcement officers who habitually stop and frisk innocent pedestrians under the guise that they "fit the description" of a sought-after suspect, or utilized as the punchline to an off-color joke, there is no denying the fact, even by me, that African-Americans, in general and Black men, in particular, are clearly subjected to debilitating depictions that can weigh down even the strongest amongst us.

Born Earnest Reuben Crowdus and raised in the rolling hills of Bowling Green, Kentucky, Earnest Hogan began his show business career as a traveling minstrel singer, who would ultimately reach the heights of fame and fortune on the backs of his own community as he enamored white audiences with his catchy tunes that became a musical phenomenon known as the "coon song craze" of the 1890's. Later on in life, Hogan regretted having contributed to the degradation of Black culture, but not before it made him exorbitantly rich by most standards. I mention this because, just like Hogan, there are showbiz entertainers willing to make a heap of cash "steppin' and fetchin'" for the Almighty Dollar (but I digress). Eventually, Hogan died at the age of forty-four years old in 1909, with today's equivalent of $715,000 in the bank; most of which earned from his aforementioned doozy of a ragtime tune. Speaking of which, "All Coons Look Alike to Me", is a song of unrequited love for a woman who dumped her beau for another man who, (and I'm not making this up), *looked just like him!* (Isn't that hysterical)?

"

"All coons look alike to me. I've got another beau, you see/And he's just as good to me/As you, nig! ever tried to be/He spends his money free/I know we can't agree/So, I don't like you no how/All coons look alike to me" ("All Coons").

And while those characterizations may be patently unfair, for the rest of

America, it's a price we are willing to let Black men pay if that's what it takes to keep them on the periphery of society. Moreover, in our never-ending quest to maintain control of all aspects of life in this country, many of the hapless souls who have had the burden of being born Black in this country, don't even realize that, regardless of what they do, they may never quite "fit in" with mainstream America. Yet they keep trying... and that's alright by me for, if nothing else, it helps to build character. And that's worth something...right?

Today, while it is important to note the work that lies ahead in building a more just nation for all of our citizens, everything isn't all doom and gloom, if I do say so myself. From mass media, to politics, to pop culture, African-American men have staked out a corner of the market that is truly all their own. Moreover, with the proliferation of "gangster trap" music (see what I did there?), there's no place to go but up when it comes to the public perception of African-American men, and we can all celebrate that... Can't we?

Always Hopeful,

Justitia

Lady Justice

Joseph C. Phillips: Please, Don't Fence Me In!

Whose Line Is It Anyway?

"I'm an actor, author and entrepreneur. I owned a restaurant, wrote a book, and had a weekly opinion column for many years. In addition to all of that, I've done television, film, theater, commercials and all other aspects of acting," says the Denver, Colorado native who went on to graduate from *New York University* with a Bachelor of Fine Arts in Acting in 1983, before finding his way to the "City of Flowers and Sunshine," Los Angeles, California. Ever since his introduction onto the television landscape as Lieutenant Martin Kendall of the *U.S. Navy*, and husband to Denise Huxtable, played by Lisa Bonet, on the *NBC* hit television program, *The Cosby Show*, Joseph C. Phillips' image and voice have been a constant fixture on the national stage for more than thirty years. The father of three sons, Phillips understands the importance of standing up for what you believe, while being mindful of the fact that, as a Black man in America, both he and his sons are subject to the same issues of racism and marginalization, regardless of what side of the political spectrum Black men fall on.

"I had, I've always thought, an interesting upbringing. As I get older, however, I realize it probably isn't that interesting. My mother was a teacher, my father was a pediatrician and I was able to grow up in what was a predominantly Jewish neighborhood. Then my parents initiated divorce proceedings when I was in about the sixth grade, and were finally divorced when I started high school. And I left the life that I had come to know, living with my mother, and ultimately moved in with my father. In the winter of that year, my mother committed suicide when I was fifteen years old and my father remarried, but that didn't really work out for him," Phillips noted when reminiscing on his early years. The only male child, Joseph's childhood was spent split between two homes, one with a father whose time with Phillips was limited to weekend visitations, and a politically active mother and three strong-willed sisters who helped teach him how to stand firm in his convictions. "I remember accompanying my mother to her state *Democratic Conventions* and, I didn't really know what she did, but I know my sisters and I had a lot of fun, running around the convention halls, collecting buttons and stickers and all of that. Believe it or not, I remember attending the *Democratic* convention when Jimmy Carter was nominated and ultimately elected as President of the United States," Phillips recalls, noting the tough economic times that ensued with the Carter Administration. "My mother was involved in the *NAACP* and, being outspoken and politically active, influenced me greatly and encouraged me to share my opinion," he recalled, ever mindful of the strong voices his sisters were encouraged to share both at home and in the world. "As a result, I have very particular ideas about the world, Black people's place in this world, that a lot of times run counter to Black conventional wisdom," Phillips conceded. "As with Paul Laurence Dunbar's poem, "We Wear The Mask," as a conservative, there is an assumption about who I am and what I believe and people are wrong all of the time," Joseph Phillips notes as he recalls instances in which he has been challenged for his views om issues. "There are times where people have taken exception with me over things that I have never said and things I don't believe. I think that there's a huge assumption others make about me because I step outside of the traditional view of what it means to be a Black man in America," he noted.

An outspoken spokesman for conservative political principles, Phillips is an atypical figure within the African-American diaspora who represents an important voice on what most Blacks would consider the opposite side of the political aisle. His presence within the conservative movement helps to shatter the preconceived notion that the African-American diaspora is a homogenous society, all of whom possess the same political persuasions. "I have been actively involved in politics, although not as deeply as a lot of people might think," Phillips demurs before describing his impressive resume of bona fides, which include having been named to the *Republican National Committee's* African-American Advisory Board and having received an appointment by then Governor Arnold Schwarzenegger to the board of directors of the *California African-American Museum*. "I was also a surrogate for President George W. Bush and the Bush-Cheney campaign in 2004," recalls Phillips, a familiar conservative voice on cable news, always willing to uphold the mantle of Black conservatism that was cemented wen President Lincoln emancipated enslaved Africans in 1863.

As late as the mid-1930s, African-American Republican John R. Lynch, who had represented Mississippi in the House during and after *Reconstruction*, summed up the sentiments of older Black voters and upper middle-class professionals: "The colored voters cannot help but feel that in voting the Democratic ticket in national elections they will be voting to give their indorsement [sic] and their approval to every wrong of which they are victims, every right of which they are deprived, and every injustice of which they suffer" ("Party Realignment"). In today's political climate, however, being both Black and Republican is often a lonely place to be, as the party has, over time, morphed into a club for rich white men. "The reality is that as America's electorate becomes more diverse, the Republican party is getting whiter. According to the Pew Research Center, the vast majority of Asian American voters (65 percent), Hispanic voters (63 percent) and Black voters (84 percent) identify as Democrats or lean toward the Democratic Party," observed Michael Harriot of *The Root*, in his essay called "#RepublicansSoWhite: Why Black Voters Don't Mess With the GOP". "Although no more than one-third of the voters in each non-white group leans toward the GOP, a majority of white voters identifies or leans toward the Republican party," Harriot noted. "And none of this is to say that the *Democratic Party* is a pro-Black party that inherently cares about Black people. It is still controlled and funded by white people, and most Black people are aware of this. But for Black voters, it is still better than the Republican Party" (Harriot). With that reality in hand, however, Joseph's role in the *Grand Old Party* is just as integral to the political and economic successes of Black people as those who are members of the Democratic Party.

According to the *History, Art & Archives* of the *United States House of Representatives*, in their article, "Party Realignment and the New Deal," the tectonic political shift of African-American voters from the party of Lincoln during the Great Migration of Blacks from the South to the North and solidified during the term of President Franklin Delano Roosevelt. A series of public works initiatives, social services programs and economic and financial reforms aimed at lifting debt-stricken Americans out of poverty as a result of the disastrous Great Depression, FDR's *New Deal* offered African-Americans an opportunity at a better economic future, thus beginning their mass exodus to the Democrats ever since. "The realignment of Black voters from the *Republican Party* to the *Democratic Party* that began in the late 1920s proliferated during this era. This process involved a 'push and pull': the refusal by Republicans to pursue civil rights alienated many Black voters, while efforts—shallow though they were—by northern Democrats to open opportunities for African Americans gave Black voters reasons to switch parties" ("Party Realignment"). Prior to that shift of political loyalty to Roosevelt and his party's standard bearers, however, African-Americans have not always been a staple constituency group of the Democrats.

Be that as it may, however, Phillips has continued to confound and top-end stereotypes of Black males throughout the entirety of his long and storied professional career. Having played the roles of an uptight business executive in the 1991 comedy movie, *Strictly Business*, a district attorney on the long running soap opera, *General Hospital*, and a big city mayor on the *CBS* television show, *The District*, Joseph does not fit into the typical archetype for Black men many Americans regularly see in television and film. Even outside of the glare of the cameras, Phillips assumes multiple roles, all of which are aimed at strengthening the community and the country that he loves. In doing so, Phillips is content with obliterating the erroneous assumptions that some may have of him and other Black men who are often misunderstood. "I once took a hiatus from show business and began substitute teaching, which is another passion of mine," said Phillips. "I was teaching a history class one day and I asked the kids in the class if they could tell me what the fifty-five most important words in modern history were [the Preamble to the *Constitution* of the United States] and soon after we began a discussion about the *Declaration of Independence*," he recalled. "There were two Black kids in the class and one of them told me that someone had written a racial epithet on the desk and I said, 'ignore it unless they are, they speaking to you!' I then proceeded to tell the student that I grew up in the sixties, during the height of the Civil Rights Movement. I was in second grade when Martin Luther King, Jr. was assassinated,' he recollected, emphasizing the fact that times have, indeed, changed since his childhood. "I was certainly passed over because I was Black, called names, denied service, that kind of thing. Well, one day, my mother told me, because she knew it would happen, that I would be standing in line somewhere, and the clerk will pass me by and whenever that happens to you--because it will happen to you--speak up for yourself and refuse to be treated as a second class citizen! Today, when people are being extremely rude or are intentionally overlooking me, I am prone to say to them: 'Hey, am I invisible to you?!'

How Does It All Begin?

Understanding what makes Phillips, and other Black men, invisible when it matters, and front and center on almost all negative things when it's politically and culturally expedient, is critical in understanding how stereotypes work and are perpetuated throughout generations. In her research project entitled,

"Negative Racial Stereotypes and Their Effect on Attitudes Toward African-Americans", Laura Green notes: "As human beings, we naturally evaluate everything we come in contact with. We especially try to gain insight and direction from our evaluations of other people. Stereotypes are "cognitive structures that contain the perceiver's knowledge, beliefs, and expectations about human groups". These cognitive constructs are often created out of a kernel of truth and then distorted beyond reality. Racial stereotypes are constructed beliefs that all members of the same race share given characteristics. These attributed characteristics are usually negative" (Green). The challenge that Phillips faces, in spite of his unmistakable presence and disarming persona, is the fact that the negative perceptions of he and other Black men in the United States are so deeply ingrained in the fabric of the nation that it will take an untold number of years to even begin undoing racist stereotypes.

The genesis of many of the historic unfavorable descriptions of Blacks came about as the majority culture's desire to stop the growing perceived threat that Black liberation represented grew across the country. "Beliefs that Blacks were mentally inferior, physically and culturally un-evolved, and apelike in appearance' were supported by prominent white figures like Abraham Lincoln, Andrew Johnson, and Thomas Jefferson," Green observed. In fact, having received significant backlash for reaching out to and engaging in discussion with one of the leading African-American thought leaders of the time, Booker T. Washington, U.S. President Theodore Roosevelt even pledged his allegiance to white supremacy, when he stated his belief that, as a race of people, African-Americans were "altogether inferior to whites" (Green). "This idea of African-Americans as apelike savages was exceptionally pervasive. For example, in 1906, the New York Zoological Park featured an exhibit with an African-American man and a chimpanzee. Several years later, the Ringling Brothers Circus exhibited "the monkey man," a Black man was caged with a female chimpanzee that had been trained to wash clothes and hang them on a line" (Green). Today, while not as ubiquitous as it once was, typecasting Blacks as inferior and childlike is something that has been part and parcel of how America has continued to perpetrate white supremacist ideology.

Even still, Joseph Phillips believes that the moment in which African-Americans begin classifying all issues that deleteriously impact Black people, such as interactions between Black males with law enforcement officials, it dilutes the argument for change. "When you lump everyone together, I have a problem with that," declared Phillips as he noted the dichotomy between the tragic circumstances related to the high-profile deaths of Tamir Rice and Michael Brown, two young Black males who died by the hands of police. "When you're innocent and minding your business, as with the case of Tamir Rice, and the cops assault or even kill you, it's very different than when you attack police," he said. "In my opinion, the whole idea of 'hands up, don't shoot' is a false premise [as it pertains to Michael Brown's interaction with Ferguson, Missouri Police Officer, Darren Wilson, which resulted in Brown's death]. When you begin with a false premise, that premise is then used to support a narrative or agenda that I don't think moves Black people forward. And I also have a problem with that," Phillips protested.

"What we have now are a bunch of people that want to continue fighting for that narrative because it enriches them in some way, maybe not simply monetarily, but it gets them on TV and feeds egos." With that thought in mind, however, Phillips also believes that it's incumbent upon the state to not become an occupying force in communities of color. "When you have a police force that suddenly stops being keepers of the peace and are now law enforcement agencies who need armored vehicles, high-powered rifles, cannons and tanks, to enforce laws, something is wrong somewhere," he said. "The fewer reasons to interact with the state you have, the fewer of these kinds of shootings and things you're going to have. And one of the first things that we need to do is revisit this *War on Drugs* and we need to rethink why we are all invested and up in other people's business looking for drugs," the theatrical impresario intoned. "One of the reasons I'm a conservative is because I want to be left alone. I don't want to be frisked. I don't want to have to report what I'm doing to other people. I don't want people involved in how I raise my kids. I don't want people involved in my life. I want to be left alone, and I don't see anything wrong with that. Furthermore, I think that all of us should have the same desire--leave me alone let me live my life!" To that end, whether you agree, or not with Phillips' perspective, it goes without saying that even today, African-Americans are, more likely than not, pre-disposed to presume the worst when it comes to the state and how it has historically treated people of color. And historically, the state has been happy to respond in kind, subjecting Black males to a myriad of unfair presuppositions that can have tragic consequences. Unfortunately, for large Black men like the aforementioned Michael Brown, a 6'4" young man weighing in at 292 pounds, his height and size may have also made him a threat in the eyes of law enforcement, as evidenced by empirical research showing "large Black males" are perceived as particularly dangerous and should be treated as an eminent threat.

In their report, "For Black Men, Being Tall Increases Threat Stereotyping and Police Stops," researcher Neil Hester exposed an insidious bias that impacts big and tall Black men in a particular way. "Young Black men are stereotyped as threatening, which can have grave consequences for interactions with police. We show that these threat stereotypes are even greater for tall Black men, who face greater discrimination from police officers and elicit stronger judgments of threat," Hester wrote. To further illustrate the point, the report noted the unspoken advantage that height has for some in American society, and the distinct disadvantage that it could have for others. "We challenge the assumption that height is intrinsically good for men. White men may benefit from height, but Black men may not" (Hester. p. 1).

Today, as the American workforce expands and becomes more diverse, every single asset workers bring to the table helps them to move further and faster up the corporate ladder. To that end, the willingness to leverage height is something that further underscores the privilege that some benefit from in the country. "Height seems beneficial for men in terms of salaries and success; however, past research on height examines only White men. For Black men, height may be more costly than beneficial, primarily signaling threat rather than competence" (Hester. p. 1). The report goes on to note three separate research studies analyzing the distinct disadvantage that height has for Black males. "Study 1 analyzes over one million *New York Police Department* stop-and-frisk encounters and finds that tall Black men are especially likely to receive unjustified attention from police. Then, studies 2 and 3 experimentally demonstrate a causal link between perceptions of height and perceptions of threat for Black men, particularly for perceivers who endorse stereotypes that Black people are more threatening than white people. Together, these data reveal that height is sometimes a liability for Black men, particularly in contexts in which threat is salient" (Hester. p. 1). And therein lies the challenge: what, if anything, can Black males do to make themselves less threatening to others? On the converse, however, why should Black males, or anyone else for that matter, have to make themselves "less threatening" (which is difficult to do if you are big and Black), simply to assuage the irrational fears of fragile people? Incredulously, but not unbelievably, it's not just height that's held against Black men in America, as the width of their noses, and texture of their hair also play a part in the continued oppression of African-American males.

According to Alesha Bond, in her communique, "Black Stereotypical Features: When a Face Type Can Get You in Trouble", the more Afrocentric the features of a Black male's face, the more some are inclined to associate them with bad things. "Negative biases associating Black men with criminality are most pronounced for a subgroup of men with Afrocentric features (e.g., a wide nose, full lips)," Bond noted, in laying out an appalling obstacle facing many Black males based solely upon their perceived Blackness. "Face-type bias occurs for men with these features because they are readily categorized as stereotypically Black and representative of the category Black male. This categorization in turn makes this subgroup more likely to be associated with the criminal-Black-male stereotype than are men with non-stereotypical Black features" (Bond). When the totality of the impact these preconceived notions, based upon unfounded beliefs and characterized by a sustained public perception campaign aimed at ingraining them into the fabric of the country, the ability to make meaningful change is oftentimes hampered by intransigent mindset issues.

To that end, it is important to note that what many of these racist caricatures do is underscore ridiculous fears that can have disastrous consequences for African-American males. Another prime example of the unconscious bias that many whites have against large Black men was played out in the recorded murder of Eric Garner of Staten Island, New York, whose death was ruled a homicide due to an unauthorized choke hold applied to him as he stood on a the street corner, surrounded by police officers who had accused him of selling untaxed cigarettes. As such, it is important to understand that phobias are often extreme aversions. Moreover, they are embedded deep in our psyches and are activated when we come face-to-face with the things we fear most. In his article, "Negrophobia: Michael Brown, Eric Garner, and America's Fear of Black People," Brandon Hill of *Time Magazine* opined about the impact that Garner's physical presence played in his fateful police interaction. "Garner's 400-pound anatomy forms an object of American

Negrophobia: the unjustified fear of Black people. Studies show that Black people, particularly Black men, are the group most feared by White adults," Hill found. "Negrophobia fuels the triangular system of oppression that keeps people of color pinned into hapless ghettos between the pillars of militarized police, starved inner-city schools, and voracious prisons" (Hill). But what sparked the flames of bigotry that have now become a fiery inferno of intolerance?

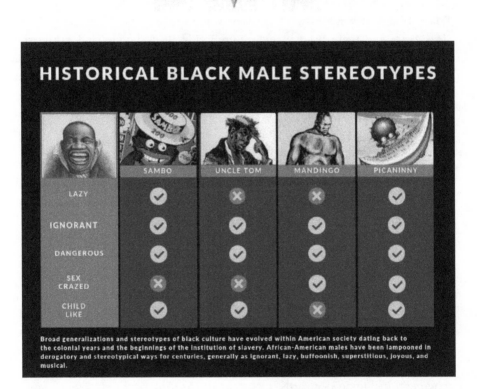

HISTORICAL BLACK MALE STEREOTYPES

	SAMBO	UNCLE TOM	MANDINGO	PICANINNY
LAZY	✓	✗	✗	✓
IGNORANT	✓	✓	✓	✓
DANGEROUS	✓	✓	✓	✓
SEX CRAZED	✗	✗	✓	✓
CHILD LIKE	✓	✓	✗	✓

Broad generalizations and stereotypes of black culture have evolved within American society dating back to the colonial years and the beginnings of the institution of slavery. African-American males have been lampooned in derogatory and stereotypical ways for centuries, generally as ignorant, lazy, buffoonish, superstitious, joyous, and musical.

Does History Have an Impact?

The *National Museum of African-American History & Culture*, in their piece, "Popular and Pervasive Stereotypes of African-Americans", observed that the imagery deployed to portray Black people has been used as a means of justifying the continued marginalization of an entire race of people since the founding of America. "Decades-old ephemera and current-day incarnations of African American stereotypes, including Mammy, Mandingo, Sapphire, Uncle Tom and watermelon, have been informed by the legal and social status of African Americans," the Museum noted, delineating a number of caricatures that have been used throughout the years to shape American perspective. "Many of the stereotypes were created during the height of the *Trans-Atlantic Slave Trade* and were used to help commodify Black bodies and justify the business of slavery. For instance, an enslaved person, forced under violence to work from sunrise to sunset, could hardly be described as lazy. Yet laziness, as well as characteristics of submissiveness, backwardness, lewdness, treachery, and dishonesty, historically became stereotypes assigned to African-Americans ("Popular Stereotypes").

Years before it became a racist trope during the height of the *Jim Crow Era*, watermelon, for Blacks, like cotton and tobacco for whites, represented economic independence for those who harvested this crop. Following Lincoln's proclamation calling for what would be the gradual liberation of enslaved Africans, many Southern Black sharecroppers successfully sold the fruit, which ultimately became a symbol of the very freedom they had always longed to achieve. In response to their use of the watermelon as a newfound tool for achieving economic stability, many resorted to maligning the fruit, and anyone associated with it, as being beneath the dignity of civilized people. "Many Southern whites reacted to this self-sufficiency by turning the fruit into a symbol of poverty. Watermelon came to symbolize a feast for the 'unclean, lazy and child-like.' To shame Black watermelon merchants, popular ads and ephemera, including postcards, pictured African Americans stealing, fighting over, or sitting in streets eating watermelon. Watermelons being eaten hand to mouth without utensils made it impossible to consume without making a mess, therefore branded a public nuisance. ("Popular Stereotypes"). In addition to marginalizing newly freed Blacks in America by stereotyping the watermelon, the fourth estate, better known as the press, was willingly deputized with the responsibility of consistently defining Black men as dangerous and prone to abhorrent behavior.

Created in the minds of the most devious enslavers and auctioneers to increase profits with the sale of Black males, the concept of the "Mandingo" came to be associated with strong Black men. "While under the violence of enslavement, a physically powerful Black man could be subdued and brutally forced into labor. Emancipation brought with it fears that these men would exact sexual revenge against white men through their daughters, as depicted in the film 'Birth of a Nation', the museum chronicled. "The reinforcement of the stereotype of the Mandingo as animalistic and brutish, gave legal authority to white mobs and militias who tortured and killed Black men for the safety of the public. ("Popular Stereotypes"). Emblazoned across newspapers throughout the United States at the beginning of the twentieth century and continuing to this day, have been the fates of Black males from boys to men, who have met a most scurrilous fate, having been tried, convicted and sentenced, oftentimes by lynch mob, of alleged crimes and offenses.

To make matters worse, inflaming the challenge that brutish Black men posed to white sensibilities at the time, was the rise of John Arthur "Jack" Johnson to become the first African-American to reach the pinnacle of boxing success. "Heavyweight boxing champion Jack Johnson epitomized the Mandingo or Black Brute of white imaginations in the flesh. Called a beast, a brute and a coon in print, Johnson's relationships with white women took up as much newsprint as his fighting abilities. With his 1910 victory over James Jeffries, promoted as the "Great White Hope," Johnson brought white fears to a head. The result was weeks of riotous mob violence across the nation that left thousands of African American communities and lives in ruin ("Popular Stereotypes").

Today, more than a century since Jack Johnson broke an important racial barrier in American sports, the resentment that lingers from seeing a seemingly successful Black man is one that continues to transcend time, with Black men continuing to pay for it even today. . In his *National Public Radio* submission for "The Race Card Project," Marc Quarles discussed the ever-present monikers placed on Black men by majority culture and how it invades even the safest of places. A Black man with a white wife, and two biracial children, living in a predominantly white neighborhood in California's wealthy Monterey Peninsula, Quarles spoke of being treated with indifference and sometimes disdain by neighbors. "Every summer, Quarles' wife and children go to Germany to visit family. Consequently, Quarles spends the summers alone. And without his family around, he says, he's treated very differently. Most of the time, "I've noticed my white counterparts almost avoid me. They seem afraid," Quarles tells *NPR* special correspondent Michele Norris. "They don't know what to think of me because I'm in their neighborhood. I oftentimes wonder if they think I'm a thug," Quarles recalled. "Those experiences prompted him to share his six words with The Race Card Project: "With kids, I'm Dad; Alone, thug" The same does not happen when I have the security blanket and shield of my children," Quarles says. "When my children are with me, I'm just a dad. I love being a dad."("Race Card").

During the radio segment, Quarles recalled a particular instance in which he was questioned, days after moving into his new home, when the police knocked on the door to ask him if he had noticed anything suspicious in the neighborhood. "The officer asked Quarles if he had noticed anything suspicious in the neighborhood. "And I said, 'Like what?' And he said, 'Well, the woman across the street is missing her purse" ("Race Card"). Surprised by the insinuation and a bit taken aback, Quarles responded instantly, by inviting the officer to search his home, if he so desired, all the while denying having any knowledge of his neighbor's purse. Taking it all in stride, however, Quarles chooses to teach his own sons to beware of the challenges that face men of color in America. "Just because of his appearance and his brown skin, there are things that he can't do that the other kids can do," Quarles notes. "And if that sounds like a double-standard, that's because it is. 'That's my answer: 'It is a double standard, Son. And trust me, one day, you'll understand'" ("Race Card").

Undeterred by this dubious past, and despite the double standards, Joseph Phillips, and countless men of color, continue to help shape and change the narrative and obliterate unfounded assumptions. The goal, as Phillips describes it, is to clearly demonstrate the diversity of thought and experience that exists within the African-American diaspora--despite popular opinion. "A friend of my mother's recently passed away at 83 years old. She was a very strong proud Black woman," Phillips remembered, when reflecting upon the impact that she had on his own life. "She and her husband had been chased out of Mississippi during the early days of the Civil Rights Movement. In fact, he was the first Black man to run for city council where they lived down in

Mississippi, and she was an educator; a very dynamic woman, indeed," he went on. "I remember several times when she emphasized to me that there was *'no monopoly on brain power,'* and that is something that I say to my children today. Black kids and Black people can compete on any field, in any endeavor, whether it's classical music, philosophy or physics. We don't need help, just open the door," Phillips demanded.

When asked how Black men in America can overcome the overwhelming obstacles placed before them due to lingering racial depictions, Phillips simply exhorts others to always remember who they are. "The only thing that someone cannot take away from you is your name. You have to be a man of your word. You have to be honest and people have to be able to trust you," Phillips implored. "If you destroy someone's trust, the hardest thing to do is regain it. So, in your dealings with people, they can take all the money you have, but they can't take your good name. You've got to be in touch with God and, with His strength, you can overcome anything!"

(Joseph C. Phillips: Acclaimed Actor & Conservative Commentator)

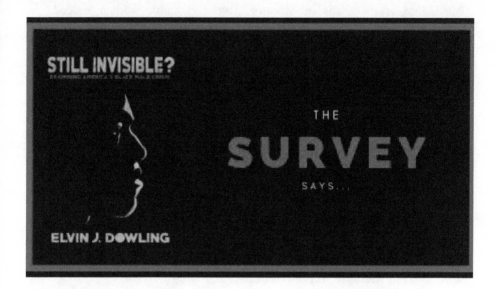

How strongly do you agree or disagree with the following characteristics describing Black males?*

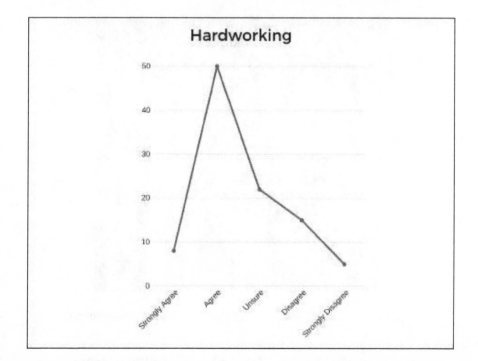

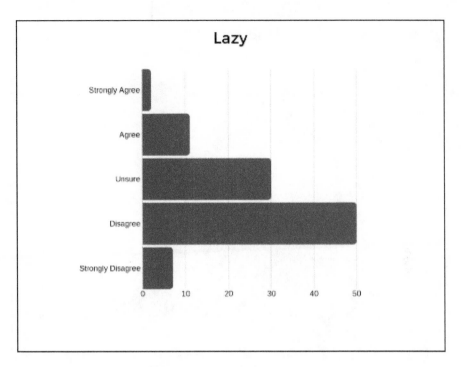

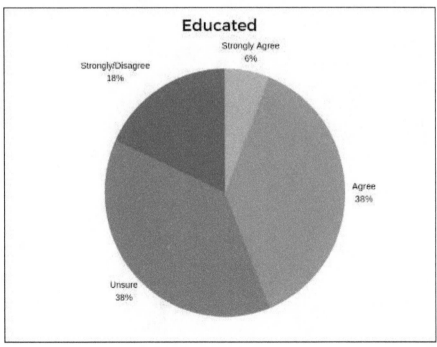

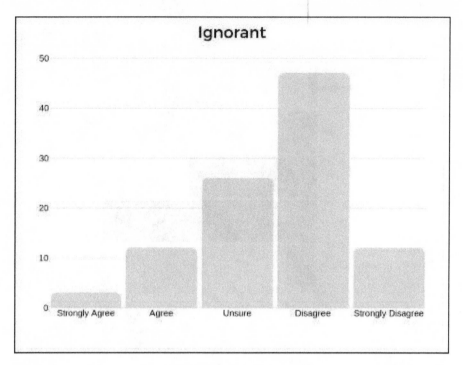

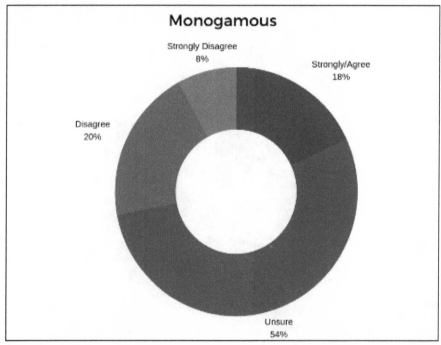

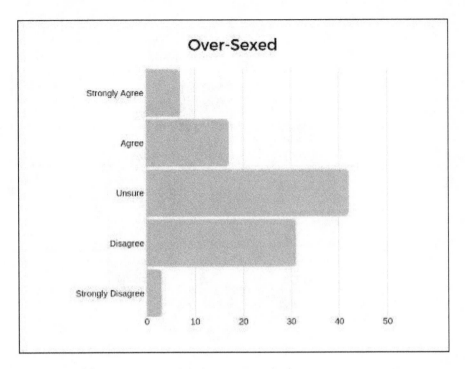

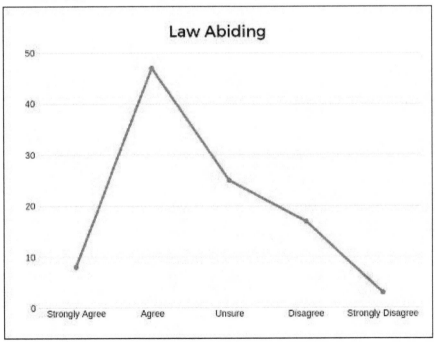

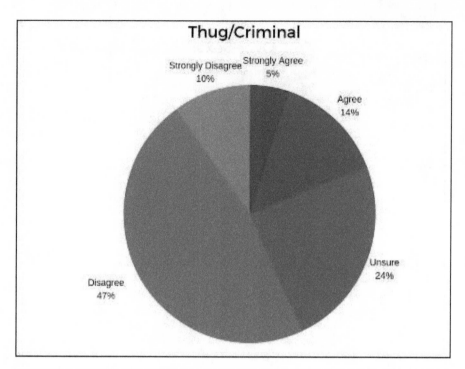

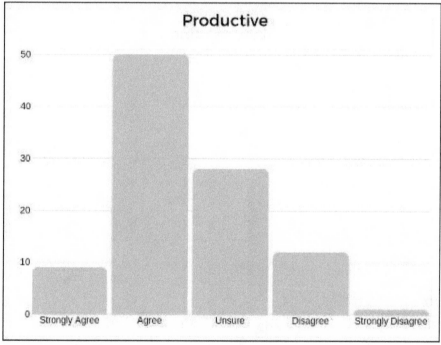

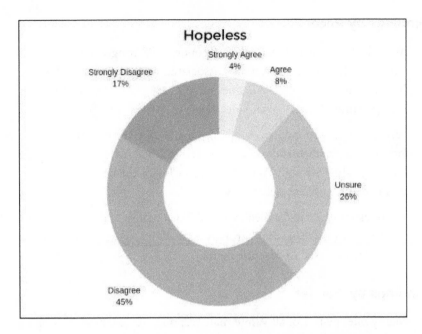

All survey results displayed above are in represented by the overall percentage of survey respondents. For more information on our survey methodology, please see the Author's Note, located in the front matter of the book. To review raw survey results, visit. http://bit.ly/stillinvisiblesurvey

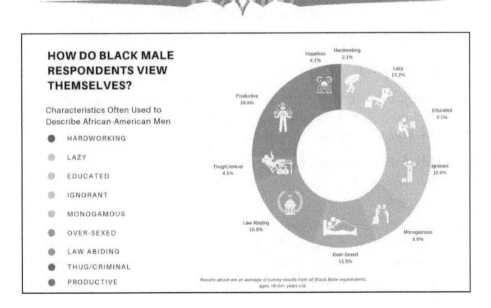

Findings by Race

- At least 13.33% of all Black male respondents "Strongly Agree" or "Agree" with the following characteristics associated with Black males: Lazy (13.33%), Ignorant (13.33%), Ignorant (13.33%), Over-Sexed (16.66%), Thug/Criminal (13.33%) and Hopeless (13.33%).

- White female respondents (88.40%), ages 18-24 years old, took a positive view on the characteristics used to describe Black males, with a small minority who "Strongly Agree" or "Agree" with the negative characteristics used to describe Black males.

- Asian respondents had a bleak view of Black males, with nearly 4 out of 10 respondents (39.00%) who "Strongly Agree" or "Agree" with the negative characteristics used to describe them.

Findings by Gender

- Nearly one quarter of all White male respondents (24.00%) "Strongly Agree" or "Agree" with the description that Black males are "Over-Sexed".

- More than 4 out of 10 of Other male respondents "Strongly Agree" or "Agree" with the description of Black males as "Lazy" (42.86%) and "Hopeless" (42.86%).

- 1 out of 4 Hispanic female respondents (26.31%) "Strongly Agree" or "Agree" with the description of Black males as "Thug/Criminal".

Findings by Age

- More than 6 out of 10 White male respondents, ages 18-24 years old, "Strongly Agree" or "Agree with the description of Black males as Hardworking (67.64%), Educated (68.18%) and Productive (67.64%).

- Half of all Black female respondents, ages 18-24 years old (50.00%), "Strongly Agree" or "Agree" with the description of Black males as "Ignorant".

- A plurality of Female Respondents, from all age groups (51.50%) "Strongly Agree" or "Agree" with the description of Black males as "Law Abiding", with Asian female respondents (33.33%) and Hispanic Female respondents (26.31%) who "Strongly Disagree" or "Disagree" with the aforementioned description.

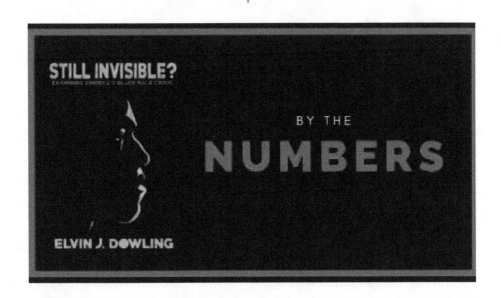

"Shuckin' & Jivin'... Rarely Ever Thrivin'!"

- The media often portrays Blacks in subservient or negative roles on television, such as a servant, a crook, a cook, an entertainer, a musician, an exhibitionist, an athlete, or a corrupt individual. Very rarely are Blacks depicted as having professional occupations or a supervisory position in comparison to white characters ("Perceived Realism." p. 2).

- In one of the earliest examinations of African-American portrayals on television, the *U.S. Commission on Civil Rights* found that Blacks are frequently depicted with unfavorable personality including being inferior, stupid, comical, immoral, dishonest, buffoonish, untrained, uneducated and hopeless ("Perceived Realism." pp. 2-3).

"Larger, Stronger, Faster? Leads to Disaster!"

- In 2014, researchers studied 176 mostly white, male police officers, and tested them for unconscious "dehumanization bias" against African-Americans and found that officers commonly barbarized Black people, and those who did were most likely to have a record of using excessive force on Black children in custody (Lopez).

- Research has found that Blacks are sometimes perceived as having super-human powers, with whites more likely to associate paranormal or magical powers with African-Americans than with Caucasians and, as a result, they are less likely to believe Black people feel pain to the same degree that whites do (Lopez).

"When They're Bigger ... Pull the Trigger?"

- Despite stereotypes about Black men being larger than white men, the *Centers for Disease Control* reported in 2012 that the average height of non-Hispanic White men and non-Hispanic Black men are roughly the same . Even still, identical and similar body types, when perceived as Black, were often equated as larger and more threatening (Lopez).

- According to a series of studies published by the *American Psychological Association*, when researchers removed racial identifiers from the color-inverted images of males, whites who believed that the man in the image was African-American, they were more likely justify use of force (Lopez).

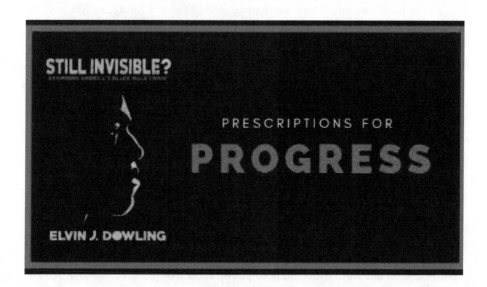

"Don't Just Expose the Lie... Diversify!"

• Stereotypes and mischaracterizations are based on myths and unfounded fears. By exposing the inaccuracies of myths that sustain stereotypes and prejudices and being prepared to correct misconceptions we can help change perceptions. Dispelling these notions is the responsibility of those who work to improve relations ("Reducing Racial Prejudice").

• When racial diversity exists, the opportunity for greater understanding amongst the groups is strengthened, while simultaneously underscoring commonalities. Effective solutions for eliminating stereotypes should center on acknowledging the opinions and attitudes of all involved ("Reducing Racial Prejudice").

"Insist Those Who Lead Understand, Indeed!"

• For maximum effectiveness, strategies for debunking myths and racial tropes should have the full support and participation of those with authority and power. As such, ask whether those in leadership are modeling appropriate behaviors and "walking the talk" and if consequences exist for those who discriminate ("Reducing Racial Prejudice").

• Racism and discrimination are often a result of societal influences. Changing behavior often requires accountability from others. Seek to influence the actions of others, to include what motivates them, and don't just limit efforts to only increasing awareness and understanding ("Reducing Racial Prejudice").

"Change Begins When Strangers Become Friends!"

• Effective strategies for eliminating racism must begin in America's schools, as a part of a continuing set of learning activities that are valued and incorporated throughout the curriculum. Opportunities for racial progress should implement highly focused activities that ensure positive intergroup relationships ("Reducing Racial Prejudice").

- Teach students the importance of understanding that, while racial and ethnic groups may have differences, there is more that unites these groups than divides them. Focusing on differences understates commonalities. Further, making "the other" seem less different can help avoid broad generalizations ("Reducing Racial Prejudice").

Works Cited

1. Shmoop Editorial Team. "Invisible Man Identity Quotes   Page 7." *Shmoop.* Shmoop University, Inc., 11 Nov.   2008. Web. 16 Sep. 2019.

2. "All Coons Look Alike to Me." SongFacts.com, *Songfacts,*   *LLC.* Retrieved 16 September 2019,
   http://bit.ly/2lYhe5n

3. Harriot, Michael. "#RepublicansSoWhite: Why Black   Voters Don't Mess With the GOP." *The Root.* Web.   17 April 2019. http://bit.ly/2kJxvee

4. "Party Realignment and The New Deal." *History, Art &*   *Archives:* *United States House of Representatives,*   2018.

   http://bit.ly/2k7SqaC

5. "Popular and Pervasive Stereotypes of African-Americans." *Smithsonian Institute - National Museum of African-* *History and Culture,* 2018.
   https://s.si.edu/2kFGNIa

6. Green, Laura. "Negative Racial Stereotypes and Their   Effect on Attitudes Toward African-Americans." *Jim   Crow Museu* *Racist Memorabilia,* 1998. Ferris   Sta http://bit.ly/2mbd4Yc

7. Hester, Neil and Gray, Kurt. "For Black Men, Being Tall Increases Threat Stereotyping and Police Stops."   *Proceedings of* *the National Academy of Sciences of the* 2018. Web. 13 March 2018.

8. Bond, Alesha, et. al. "Black Stereotypical Features: When a Face Type Can Get You in Trouble." *Association for Psychological Science*. 8 February 2017. http://bit.ly/2lHGe0V

9. Quarles, Marc. "Six Word: With Kids I'm Dad, Alone Thug: An Interview with Marc Quarles." Interview Conducted by Michelle Norris. *Morning Edition*. 17 November 2014. https://n.pr/2kKzRcX

10. Hill, Brandon. "Negrophobia: Michael Brown, Eric Garner, and America's Fear of Black People." *Time Magazine*. 29 August 2014. http://bit.ly/2lQa6YW

11. Punyanunt-Carter, Narrisra. "The Perceived Realism of African American Portrayals on Television." *The Howard Journal of Communications*. 2008. Retrieved 17 September 2018. http://bit.ly/2lY3Mig

12. Lopez, German. "Study: People See Black Men as Larger and More Threatening than Similarly Sized White Men." *Vox*. 17 May 2017. http://bit.ly/2kQP6kv

13. "Strategies for Reducing Racial and Ethnic Prejudice: Essential Principles." *Teaching Tolerance: A Project of the Southern Poverty Law Center*, Retrieved 17 September 2019. http://bit.ly/2kFVHOX

Chapter 3: "What Do You Call A Black Man with a Ph.D.?"

A Look at Higher Education & Social Mobility

"

...White folks seemed always to expect you to know those things which they'd done everything they could think of to prevent you from knowing. The thing to do was to be prepared."

- Ralph Ellison, "Invisible Man" (Shmoop Editorial Team. 14.185)

BLACK AT LINCOLN BANQUET?

E. H. Morris, Chicago Negro Lawyer, Secures $25 Ticket.

ONLY WHITES ARE WELCOME

(The above newspaper headline was featured in the February 11, 1909 issue of the Chicago Tribune.)

We Need All the Help We Can Get!

Education: A Passport to the Future?

Outspoken Black Nationalist, Minister Malcolm X, once said, *(and these are his words, not mine)*:

"

"What do you call an educated negro with a B.A. or an M.A., with a B.S., or a PhD?" The answer? "You call him a nigger, because that is what the white man calls him, a nigger."

As America continues to evolve into a more democratic society, some fifty-five years since the Supreme Court ruled in *Brown v. Board of Education of Topeka*, that "separate" was, indeed, "unequal", the sentiment's the minister expressed, in only a way that he could--I might add, are still prescient today--even when respect is earned. In fact, credible statistics underscoring the nation's achievement gap leave no doubt that the court's directive to move with "all deliberate speed" has proceeded since then, at a snail-like pace. Moreover, the idea that being an alumnus of the hallowed halls of academia is somehow, a panacea for upward mobility and social equality in this, "the land of opportunity", is far from a reality in this country; even in twenty-first century America. *(Honey, I wear a blindfold and even I can see that)*. Just as importantly, the economic impact of continuing our centuries long "unofficial policy" of keeping Black men in the dark, if you will *(no pun intended)*, is coming at a cost that we just simply can't afford.

In an exhaustive report on "The Economic Impact of Closing the Racial Gap," McKinsey and Company, a global management consulting firm that serves leading businesses, governments and non-governmental organizations, the financial footprint that Black America leaves behind could be all the more indelible when they are given the chance to succeed. So, here's **why** equal access to educational opportunities should matter (to anyone who can count, that is):

1. The racial wealth gap between Black and White families in America grew by 50% in the last 25 years, due in large part to the fact that Black wealth has remained stagnant and, in many instances, has lost ground; as whatever modest gains they have had quickly evaporated into a plume of ash during the financial crisis of 2008. *Afterall, "when White America gets a cold, Black America contracts pneumonia!"*(McKinsey).

2. In addition to the disastrous human consequences that the racial wealth gap in America has on the Black bottom-line, this persistent gulf between the *'White Haves'* and the *'Black Have-Nots'* is projected to cost the U.S. economy nearly $1.5 TRILLION of lost Gross Domestic Product over the course of the next decade. *Do you realize how many missiles and guns we could buy?*! (McKinsey).

3. African-American workers make up 13% of the US labor force and 26% of racial discrimination complaints filed with the *Equal Employment Opportunity Commission*, hampering what everyone knows are the *"world's biggest spenders'"* abilities to give us more of their money. And, yes, we want MORE of their money. *To be clear... without question* (McKinsey).

Ergo, the one thing that affords us the best opportunity to close those stubborn gaps that stand in the way of our collective economic expansion is our willingness to give it a try. As the greatest, most prosperous country on the planet, it doesn't take a genius to figure out that equal access to and fair treatment in higher education and public service opportunities, at the end of the day, means more money for everybody! To that end, if the notion that a "rising tide lifts all boats" is ever to become a rule of thumb in America, it is past time that our nation not only dismantle the barriers that are intentionally placed in the way of those seeking to improve their lot in life, but also throw open to anyone desirous of becoming a productive, taxpaying member of society. After all, as the *United Negro College Fund* so eloquently puts it: *"A mind is a terrible thing to waste."* And, by the way, so is our money!

Yours in Service,

Justitia

Justitia

Will Moreland: "Don't Call It A Comeback!"

"Straight Outta Compton?!"

"My name is Will Moreland, also known as 'Dr. Will' to most", began the gregarious speaker and coach who earned a Doctorate of Ministry Degree in Organizational Leadership from the *Minnesota Graduate School of Theology*, located approximately ten miles due north of Minneapolis. Known as much for his ability to inspire countless individuals to live their best lives, as he is for his infectious demeanor that leaves others motivated to step into their greatness, Moreland is a successful author of forty books, fifteen of which have become bestsellers. "I'm originally from this little city in California called Compton," he beamed with the pride befitting a native son. "I grew up at a time when high crime rates, drug violence, and gang activity had many people labeling Compton as the 'worst city in the USA,'" he recalled. "Part of the time, I was raised by a single mother," Moreland professed, "as my father was a drug dealer and was absent from our home. I met him for the first time when I was 7 years old, yet I also remember when he was serving time in the *California State Penitentiary*, almost like it was yesterday," Moreland recollected.

"My life is pretty interesting," Dr. Will explained, "having grown up with two polarizing views of the world. You see, my mother and grandmother were very much grounded in the church," he elaborated. "Yet, on the opposite end of the spectrum, I had my father, the neighborhood dope man who was the complete antithesis of what my mother represented. On Saturday mornings," the internationally known business authority reminisced, "my mom would drop me off at my father's house and I would be knee-deep in the drug world, with all of the characters and activities that swirl around that lifestyle. But on Saturday night or Sunday morning she would pick me up because we had to go to church. So, I had these two polarizing childhood experiences," he noted, "and it was very confusing for a young guy like myself; especially from the standpoint of seeing the "so-called" wicked prosper. "You see, my grandmother and my mother would take me to church, and everybody I saw in that world seemed like they were struggling. When I went to my father's house," Moreland went on, "it seemed like everyone who was doing bad things, who weren't ever thinking about going to church, were the ones who were thriving," he said. "So, naturally, I started gravitating towards the life that my father was leading and I found myself, at an early age, getting into gangs and drugs, before I had what I call my *first interruption,*'" the professionally trained preacher professed.

"My father had me when he was 50 years old, and I'm not his youngest kid, so we had a pretty peculiar type of relationship," Moreland admitted, in recalling his paternal relationship. "I remember my mom dropping me off at his house and, at that time, my father had maybe nine other kids that were *actually* living with him. At his home, there were actually no other male children, there was just he and my sisters, and I was actually the only boy in his house," Will wistfully reminisced. "I had other brothers, but they were not a part of his life, so I was his only son and his namesake which, as the son of a drug dealer, made me very conflicted," he recalled. "Later on, in my life, however, I had one of my mentors who helped me to change the narrative by which I used to view my father," Moreland explained. "You see, because he was a drug dealer," Moreland furthered, "and even though he showed *me* love, he also had to maintain a tough exterior. So, I saw my father fighting with people and 'handling his business,' so to speak, and I kind of had mixed feelings about that," he said.

"One day, my mentor helped me to begin to understand that, even though my father was engaging in negative activity, but when drilling down to the root of what he was *trying* to do-- it was to achieve a positive result," Dr. Will explained. "Yes, he was the dope man, but in his eyes, what he was *trying* to do was to make the best of a bad situation. Was he just trying to destroy people's lives," Moreland asked, "or was he trying to navigate the American dream with the best resources he had at the time?" he conjectured. "And when she painted *that* picture for me, it made me look at my father through an entirely different lens," he remarked. "My father was in the *United States Navy* and wasn't treated equitably, nor could he freely compete economically," the best-selling author noted. "He could not go to Corporate America and get a good job, so he had to get what he could out of his environment and, as a result resorted to doing something negative, hoping to get a positive result, just like many other Black men in our society," Will surmised.

"The person who had, perhaps, the greatest influence on my life, however, was neither my mother, nor my father, but my grandmother," Dr. Will elucidated, in describing who inspired him to change his personal circumstances. "I always joke that my grandma would go to church *eight days a week, 25 hours a day* if that were possible," the motivational minister said, in a joke laced with a heavy dose of truth. "She helped to give me my foundation, in terms of treating people right and loving your neighbors. Even though my mother was in the house," Will recalled, "she was very young at the time and was kind of *'doing her thing,'* so she would leave me with my grandma and that's when our bond was cemented," Moreland concluded. "In fact, although she was born in 1920, my grandmother was very educated, having graduated from the *University of California Los Angeles (UCLA)* with a nursing degree and was very involved in the community. Two years before she died at the age of 75, she received her doctorate degree," Dr. Moreland beamed with pride, celebrating the legacy of a woman who paved the way for his own future. "She was very instrumental in showing me that, even though we lived in Compton, California, we could still do meaningful things and have a purpose filled life," he pointed out.

In explaining the catalyst for launching him into stratospheric success, Dr. Will recalls two fateful "interruptions" that forced him to focus like a laser beam on his future. "My *'first interruption'* refers to the moment when I was in front of a California state judge, having done nothing wrong-- except for the unfortunate circumstance of getting caught--and he offered me an ultimatum. "'*Mr. Moreland,'* he said to me rather sternly, in a way that only a person holding your fate in their hands could do, *'you are going nowhere fast... But this is what I'm going to do for you,'"* the judge continued. *"'I'm going to release you on your own recognizance, but you need to come back to my courtroom in two weeks and let me know how you're going to transform your life','"* the future family man brought to mind, detailing an final warning that would forever change his life. "I left not knowing what I was going to do, before encountering what I like to call my *'second interruption'*, in the form of an officer and a gentleman by the name of Corey Oliver, a recruiter for the *United States Army*, who stopped me whilst I was wandering through the mall searching for a solution."

"Three days before I was due back in court, I had yet to have an answer for the judge and hadn't figured anything out," Moreland admitted, detailing a chain of events that would ultimately force his hand. "Corey walked up to me in his military uniform and asked me the million-dollar question: *'Have you ever thought of going to the military?'* Before meeting him," Moreland acknowledged, "I had never considered joining the Army before, but when he asked me I said *'YES!'"* he laughed; beginning what would be a remarkable journey of service above self and dedication to country, and would take him across the globe to exotic locales far away from the bright lights and broad streets of "Hub City," California.

"After getting into the *United States Army* and being stationed in Germany, I began to imbibe foundational principles and life lessons to help me reimagine my future," the tenacious thought-leader intoned; laying out the path to which he transformed himself from a potential public nuisance to an officer and a gentleman. "Thankfully, I was able to attract some good mentors who were willing to invest their time in me and, from there, I've been able to totally reposition my life; from that of a kid growing up in Compton, California getting in trouble, into the owner of a leadership consulting company who now works with all types of *Fortune 500* companies," Moreland extolled, "from *Edward Jones and Intel,* to *Target* and *Boeing.* More importantly," he continued, "I have had the privilege of serving as a mentor to others, helping them to get on the path they need to realize their highest potential," he declared. Yet Moreland's ability to transcend his personal circumstances to become an exemplar of African-American success is atypical to the Black male experience, even for those who hope to achieve their dreams through military service or higher education opportunities.

"As a 'forty-something' year old African-American man who has served in the military, and now holds an earned doctorate degree, owns my _own_ company, and is a best-selling author, I struggle with the dual realities of having lived in 'both worlds', if you will," the dapper Doctor of Ministry declared as he contemplated his life's path. "I struggle with the reality of what it means to be me, every single morning when I get ready to get dressed," Moreland admitted, in a moment of vulnerability that underscores the emotional angst that most Black professionals feel. "For instance," he reiterated, " I own a pair of _Chuck Taylors_ (I grew up wearing _Chuck Taylors),_ but in my old neighborhood, if I put on a pair of _Chuck Taylors,_ a pair of jeans, and a T-shirt, is there is a danger of me being mistaken as a gang banger?," he asked. "When I walk into a store, is there a danger of me being profiled and followed around simply because of how I might be dressed or that I am Black," he went on. "Just as much as I think about the potential implications of my wardrobe ensemble on the streets of my hometown, I also think about and often question the narrative that colors the lens through which I am viewed in my current neighborhood, especially when I'm out with my family," Dr. Will conjectured.

"I live in a predominantly Caucasian community," Moreland explained, "and I joke with my wife often about how _"they"_ look at us--myself, a 'well behaved' Black man and my wife, a 'well behaved' Black woman, with _two_ 'well behaved' Black kids... we're like dinosaurs to them," he joked. "Why is it, when I'm wearing my _Jordan's,_ when I'm in my _Chuck Taylors,_ when I'm in my _Air Maxes,_ people talk to me a certain kind of way? But when I put on my slacks," the charismatic clergyman pointed out, "when I'm in my _Ferragamo_ shoes, when I put on my _Ralph Lauren_ shirt, I get a very different conversation, because a lot of people don't know how to distinguish between the two, without choosing to see the man wearing the clothes," Moreland surmised. "Listen, you go to any airport and find an average white man wearing running shoes, sweatpants and a t-shirt, and to many people, he can still be classified as a businessman," the corporate coach concluded. "If I were to wear the same thing," Will observed, "I would be assumed to be homeless, or out of sorts, but certainly not given the benefit of the public doubt regarding who I am or what I do for a living," he lamented; describing perceptions cemented long ago, yet continue to be exacerbated in twenty-first century America where the act of doing almost anything "while Black" can have lasting consequences.

"Moving on Up?!"

Since the call for Black soldiers by the *Union Army* during the *Civil War* in the 1860's, Black men, like Will Moreland, have sought to "uplift the race" and their own circumstances through faithful service to a nation that has rarely been faithful to them. After the end of the war, with many parts of the country lying in ruins due to perpetual combat in both large cities and small hamlets, African-Americans soon began to seek the promises that educational advancement theoretically affirmed; building more than 100 institutions of higher learning throughout the American landscape, with the goal of educating a newly freed populace possessing abundant hopes for the future. Since then, young Black students have had a variety of educational options provided by a network of "alma mamas"; schools willing to provide a nurturing atmosphere for students of color guaranteed virtually nowhere else at the time. Today, however, evidence indicates that the perks of being a college graduate, having successfully navigated the challenges of academia, are of little to no benefit to Black males in America, particularly within an increasingly competitive admissions environment.

In his research article, "Intergenerational Education Mobility Trends by Race and Gender in the United States," Joseph J. Ferrare of the *University of Kentucky* found that, when it comes to equitable access to higher education even for the children of Black college graduates, membership *does not* have its privileges. "While family background characteristics and practices evidently have a profound impact on securing educational advantages across racial groups," Ferrare observed, "the rates at which Black students leverage their parental advantages appear to lag well behind those of White students with similar backgrounds" (Ferrare). "In fact," Ferrare continued, "middle-class status does not improve education attainment for Black Americans to nearly the same degree as White Americans". As a result, many Black students are hobbled by the lack of an internal network of family friends, business contacts and professional referrals they needed to set themselves apart and, perhaps, crack the corporate glass ceiling. To compound this inherent disadvantage, colleges and universities, influenced in part by the military industrial complex, have administered historically biased aptitude tests to "separate the wheat from the chaff" on college campuses across the country.

Developed in 2011 as a means of explaining the inextricable relationship between social mobility and income inequality, The Great Gatsby Curve, as was called the protagonist in the well-known F. Scott Fitzgerald novel, "The Great Gatsby", is a possible explanation for why wealth and privilege are the preeminent determinants of upward mobility in America. Named after the fictional figure James Gatz, later to be renamed Jay Gatsby, a character who presents himself as a wealthy "man about town" in the 'Roaring '20's', only to be revealed as the son of poor farmers struggling under the weight of economic malaise, The Great Gatsby Curve denotes the link between inequality and intergenerational social immobility. First coined by Alan Kreuger, the former Chairman of the U.S. President's Council of Economic Advisors during the Obama Administration, the theory underscores just how difficult it is for those deleteriously impacted by economic inequality to "move on up" in most countries in the world, "Genetic Lottery" in America a head start in the "game of life."

According to David Vandivier, then Chief of Staff for the Council of Economic Advisors, in a blog submission posted on WhiteHouse.gov about the systemic unfairness, The Great Gatsby Curve details how the most vulnerable in American society-- namely children and the poor--are affected by its impact for the entirety of their lives. "The curve shows that children from poor families are less likely to improve their economic status as adults in countries where income inequality was higher – meaning wealth was concentrated in fewer hands – around the time those children were growing up," Vandivier noted. More importantly, this entrenched inequality has become more indelible for those who call the United States of America their home. "The U.S. has had a sharp rise in inequality since the 1980s," Vandivier explained. "In fact, on the eve of the Great Recession [December 2007], income inequality in the U.S. was as sharp as it had been at any period since the time of "The Great Gatsby," the economic spokesman declared, underscoring the genesis of the term's literary name. The problem with closing this gap, however, is made all the more insurmountable for those who fail to hurdle the obstacles in their path to greatness.

For starters, there are aptitude tests that applicants must perform well enough on to be considered for admission to post-secondary institutions; to include the most commonly used exams such as the Scholastic Aptitude Test (SAT), Law School Admissions Test (LSAT) and Graduate Records Examination (GRE). For the military, potential recruits are required to take the Armed Services Vocational

Aptitude Battery (ASVAB), a multiple-choice test, administered by the *United States Military Entrance Processing Command*, to figure out whether or not a recruit is "fit" for military service. What many fail to realize, or acknowledge, however, is that the impetus behind the implementation of these expensive, culturally biased exams was the exclusion of "undesirables" from entering elite majority historically white institutions.

In 1926, the first *SAT* was administered to a group of 8,000 students, nearly half of them female, and consisted of more than 300 questions. The original test lasted ninety minutes and from that initial exam almost a century ago, to today, critics have posited that the perlustrations that unsuspecting students are forced to endure are geared to ferret out ne'er-do-wells, using discriminatory "research" tools. According to John Rosales of the *National Education Association*, in an exposé entitled, "The Racist Beginnings of Standardized Testing", minorities and other disadvantaged students enter the foreboding testing facilities with the cards already stacked against them, to confront an exam designed not to give them an opportunity to succeed, but rather a reason to be excluded. "Unlike the college boards, the *SAT* is designed primarily to assess aptitude for learning rather than mastery of subjects already learned," reported Rosales in an interview with Erik Jacobsen, an educator in Livingston, N.J. "For some college officials, an aptitude test, which is presumed to measure intelligence, is appealing since at this time (1926) intelligence and ethnic origin are thought to be connected, and therefore the results of such a test could be used to limit the admissions of particularly undesirable ethnicities" (Rosales).

The precursors to the *SAT*, which is now ubiquitously used by academic institutions across the country, were a battery of military exams developed at the height of *World War I*, as a means of maintaining a segregated workforce, stratified by both race and perceived intellectual ability. In 1917, the *American Psychological Association* coordinated with the *United States Army* to create a series of intelligence exams to achieve this goal, sparking a school testing revolution that continues unfalteringly today. "During *World War I*, standardized tests helped place 1.5 million soldiers in units segregated by race and by test scores. The tests were scientific yet they remained deeply biased, according to researchers and media reports" (Rosales). Today, whether being used by the military, college admissions boards or even in employment opportunities, standardized tests have historically been used as psychosocial tools designed to marginalize and exclude otherwise talented and deserving individuals seeking to better themselves and create a new reality for their futures. One of those exams in particular, the *Law School Admissions Test,* has also come under scrutiny for the continued role that it has played in limiting the enrollment of African-Americans into law schools all across the country.

In a study released by the *Florida International University Law Review* called, "The Marginalization of Black Aspiring Lawyers", which examines the nexus between a lack of diversity in the legal profession and the use of the *LSAT* by admissions boards, continues to underscore the need for testing reform in the nation's professional schools. The research, conducted by Aaron Taylor, Executive Director of *AccessLex Center for Legal Education Excellence* and a longtime expert on diversity in legal education, found that the *LSAT* is not only culturally biased and skewed to be more difficult for Black test takers, but the practical implications of using the test's results as the gold standard by which future barristers are measured, is much more insidious and far-reaching than had been previously reported. "The fundamental goals of legal education are longer term, but the *LSAT* does not predict one's chances of attaining these goals, well... surely not well enough to be the primary admission criterion," Taylor wrote. "For example, *Texas Tech* found that the *LSAT* explained a noteworthy, but limited, 13 percent of the variance in bar exam scores of its law graduates. The *University of Cincinnati* found that, among its law graduates, the '*LSAT* score does not correlate with Ohio bar exam performance.' Two professors from the *University of California, Berkeley,* found that the *LSAT* had very weak (or no) value in predicting lawyering skills among its law graduates," Taylor observed. "Nonetheless, the *LSAT* is used by law schools in ways that systematically exclude Black people to extents experienced by no other racial or ethnic group—using justifications that merit much suspicion." (Taylor, p. 490). So then, why would law schools continue to use them as predictors of academic success when there's a growing body of evidence that suggests the opposite? Therein lies the question, however, regardless of the reasoning behind its widespread usage and acceptance, the reality is that, at the end of the day, otherwise qualified Black students seeking opportunities in the legal industry are quietly being met at the "school house door" with a bright neon sign that reads, DO NOT ENTER... and the statistics are there to support this reality.

In an analysis of the *FIU Law Review's* findings, writer Scott Jaschik, of *Inside*

Higher Education, outlined how the negative impact that the test has had on the hopes and dreams of aspiring African-American attorneys has, in many ways, continued to stunt the growth and diversity of one of America's most exclusive clubs--lawyers . Consider this:

- In the 2016-17 admission cycle, "it took about 1,960 Black applicants to yield 1,000 offers of admission," compared to only 1,204 among white applicants (Jaschik).

- The average *LSAT* score for Black test takers is 142, while the average for white and Asian test takers is 153 (Jaschik).

- Nearly half of all Black law school applicants (49 percent) were not admitted to a single law school. That share is larger than that of any other racial or ethnic group (Jaschik).

- Among Black applicants with *LSAT* scores between 135 and 149, 55 percent received no admission offers. But this compares to only 39 percent of similar white applicants (Jaschik).

- Black applicants who are admitted to law schools enroll at law schools with less desirable outcomes (in job placements and other outcome measures) than other law schools (Jaschik).

- Black applicants who are admitted to law schools -- which use LSAT scores in awarding scholarships -- are less likely than those in other groups to receive non-need-based aid (Jaschik).

In responding to the report's findings, the *Law School Admissions Council* noted that there were other extenuating factors that also contributed to the rejection of an abnormally high number of Black law school applicants other than just their LSAT scores. In doing so, however, the organization conceded that there was still more work to be done to achieve equity in the admission of otherwise qualified Black applicants. "We regularly remind our member law schools to use the *LSAT* correctly," the Council said in Jaschik's report. "We believe that the over-reliance [the *FIU Law Review* study] criticizes is driven by too much focus on *U.S. News & World Report* rankings and, in some cases, a failure on the part of schools to understand that even if they choose to focus on rankings, they have room to admit a wider range of *LSAT* scores" the report noted (Jaschik). With that admission in hand, while acquiescing to the realization that the use of these biased predictors of intellectual capacity for those seeking to get into the military, college or graduate and professional school, it is important to remember that inequality will not end any time soon. To that end, what can enterprising Black aspirants do to level the playing field in an increasingly competitive marketplace? Dr. Will Moreland believes that the answers lie in the nation's willingness to give deserving individuals, an opportunity to make something of themselves with the time that they have left on earth--without placing unnecessary obstacles in their path.

"The importance of giving folks a shot to prove themselves is something that's very dear to my heart, because of my own personal experiences," Moreland began. "I have a sister that is serving a life sentence in prison right now. I also have a brother that is a 'Returning Citizen', who is now out of prison and finds it very difficult to assimilate back into mainstream society," acknowledged the preacher turned professional motivator, who may have also ended up in a jail cell were it not for his fateful encounter with the judge. "I think it's very unfair for a person to be continually punished for a mistake that they have made," Will lamented. "What I mean is that, when you've done the crime, and you've done the time, in America, more often than not, you're still labeled by society as a felon. It's a no-win situation," he concluded. "My brother, for an example, who made a choice--_not a mistake_--a choice, and has now met all conditions for his release, shouldn't be punished for his bad choices for the rest of his life, especially if he has paid his debt to society," the entrepreneur explained. "I think if all of us were criminalized because of a choice that _we_ made, and had to live with that bad decision for the rest of our lives, a lot of us would not be where we are today," Moreland theorized. "It was just by the grace of God-- _the grace of God_--that I got arrested when I was underage, so it didn't go on my record," Dr. Will noted thankfully. Because, had it been permanently ensconced on his record, Moreland's delinquent behavior would have almost certainly been a deal breaker for his latter attempt to reinvent himself, from miscreant to mogul; leveraging his desire to serve others, both in the military and in ministry.

"My mom was born in 1954, the same year that the _Supreme Court_ desegregated schools with their groundbreaking ruling in _Brown v. Board of Education,_ and in the sixty-five years since that landmark decision, it's amazing to me that we're _still_ dealing with some of the issues that our nation had hoped to solve, "quick, fast and in a hurry" more than a half-century ago," Dr.

Will detailed. "I do believe that for an African-American male, even today, it continues to be a struggle, in many major parts of American society, just for us to survive. And I struggle with the idea," Moreland professed. "For Black people, we have always had to learn how to be a chameleon in mainstream America. When we answer the phone," the executive consultant confessed, "we put on a different voice. We <u>all</u> put on our 'white voice' when we go to an interview and when we go to certain places," he declared. "We've always been the people that have had to change and had to switch up who we are, to fit in. And," Moreland continued, "if you live *'on the other side of the tracks'*, like me, an educated African-American man, you're still going to be subjected to prejudice," he theorized. "When I get on the elevator with a Caucasian woman, for example, she may *still* clutch her purse at the very sight of me! Unfortunately, when some people see any random Black person, they are conditioned to only believe one narrative, the negative one, and it's a major problem," Moreland declared. Through it all, however, the man who would defy the expectations of everyone, in achieving unparalleled success on his own terms, must still contend with the attitude of some who would suggest that he still doesn't belong or is, somehow, "out of place".

THE HISTORY OF STANDARDIZED TESTS

A Legacy Rooted In Racism & Supremacy

1 ### THE BIRTH OF IQ TESTS

In 1905, having been commissioned by the French government to identify students who would face the most difficulty in school, psychologist Alfred Binet developed a standardized test of intelligence, in what would eventually be incorporated into a version of the modern IQ test.

2 ### MILITARY EXAMINATIONS

In 1917, a group of psychologists led by the president of the American Psychological Association, created the Army "Alpha and Beta tests", specifically designed to help the military distinguish those recruits of "superior mental ability" from those ho were "mentally inferior."

3 ### FORCED STERILIZATIONS

In 1923, Carl Brigham published "A Study of American Intelligence", which predicted the decline of intellect in America. His research resulted in the forced the sterilization of those deemed "feeble-minded".

4 ### MEASURING APTITUDE

First administered to high school students in 1926 as a gatekeeper exam, the SAT was created to predict which students would do well in college and which would not based on culturally biased examinations.

5 ### CREATING OBSTACLES

In 1959, the ACT exam was created as a competitor to the SAT, and was designed to be an indicator of academic preparation.

6 ### WEIGHING ADVERSITY

In 2017, the College Board began using an "Adversity Index" to assist underperforming students, however, it does not, consider race in final scores.

FOR MORE INFORMATION VISIT WWW.NEA.ORG

What's My Name?

Since the desegregation of the *United States Military* under *Executive Order Number 9948*, issued by then US President Harry S. Truman on July 26, 1948, African-American soldiers have used the platform of military service to lift themselves up from the economic doldrums of the financial constraints imposed upon them. In response to that action, however, the majority culture, in their quest to keep Blacks socially marginalized, began to target these brave public servants with abuse, violence and lynching; all intended to further deflate and deject those who had already committed themselves, and their lives, in service to their country. In chronicling the challenges that Black soldiers have had in getting respect and full recognition for their service to the nation, Bryan Stevenson, Executive Director of the *Equal Justice Initiative*, in his report entitled, "Lynching in America: Targeting Black Veterans," detailed the continued indignities that African-Americans were subjected to, simply for attempting to better themselves and their families, through their efforts at social mobility.

"Military service sparked dreams of racial equality for generations of African Americans," Stevenson reported. "But most Black veterans were not welcomed home and honored for their service. Instead, during the lynching era, many Black veterans were targeted for mistreatment, violence, and murder because of their race and status as veterans," Stevenson continued. "Indeed, Black veterans risked violence simply by wearing their uniforms on American soil" (Stevenson). Even today, Black soldiers in uniform experience disproportionate punishment, this time, however, their travails are less at the hands of a murderous mob hell-bent on keeping them "in their place," and more from the actions of the very military they serve and offer their lives, when necessary.

According to a study published by the military advocacy group, *Protect Our Defenders*, the number of instances in which Black soldiers are disciplined and subjected to non-administrative judicial punishment, as well as court martial, far outpaces their White counterparts; despite the fact that African-American soldiers do not comprise a majority of the membership in the armed forces. In fact, Black service members are "substantially more likely" than white service members to be punished in four out of the five branches of the *U.S. Armed Forces*, reported Carla Herreria, in covering the disparity for the *HuffPost Black Voices* column. "Data obtained by the organization through the *Freedom of Information Act* revealed that Black service members were as much as two and a half times more likely than their white counterparts to face court-martial or nonjudicial punishment in an average year. The disparity is notable, considering white service members make up the largest racial group in the military" (Herreria).

Throughout the history of the *United States Military*, no other group of recruits has been more at risk of experiencing mob violence and targeted terror than brave Black veterans who have stared down America's fiercest enemies at each period of war and conflict, only to be dehumanized upon their return to the only home they have ever known. "Because of their military service, Black veterans were seen as a particular threat to *Jim Crow* and racial subordination. Countless numbers of Black veterans were assaulted, threatened, abused, or lynched following military service" (Stevenson). What's more, for those who choose the route of higher education as a career path, they too have found that their experiences are minimized and their credentials questioned; often leading to adverse employment actions taken against said African-American academicians. In 2018, after an exhaustive search for a new leader of the *University of Massachusetts Boston*, the top three finalists for the chancellorship-- two of whom were Black--abruptly removed their names for consideration for the post, after the university's faculty openly questioned their capacity to take the helm.

According to an account of the public repudiation of seemingly qualified candidates for the presidential position, published in *Black Enterprise Magazine*, a Black-owned multimedia company, the *UMass Boston* professorate chose an oft-used rationale for rejecting Black college administrators--they are just not qualified. "The faculty assert a collective and resolute judgment that none of the final candidates have demonstrated that they are sufficiently qualified to serve as the chancellor of the only public research university in the Greater Boston area and the most diverse four-year public institution in New England," read a statement released by the group ("Black Enterprise"). One of the finalists, Dr. Jack Thomas, an accomplished university administrator with an unassailable record of leadership and service to the broader educational community, was labeled a relative featherweight for a job the *UMass* faculty believed required the skills of someone with more heft and gravitas. Dr. Thomas, having served as president of *Western Illinois University*, an educational institution with more than 10,000 students, nestled in Macomb County, just seventy-five miles southwest of Peoria, is considered within academic circles as one of the top leaders in higher education; having made his mark transforming promising schools into exemplary institutions. In fact, in his role as the chief executive officer of *"The Fighting Leathernecks"*, Dr. Thomas was responsible for "over 700 faculty members, and an annual budget of over $220 million," *Black Enterprise* reported. "Under his leadership, *Western Illinois University* continues to be ranked as a "Best Midwestern College" and as a "Best Regional University" by the *Princeton Review* and *U.S. News and World Report*, respectively. *Western Illinois University* also continues to be named a "Military Friendly School" by *GI Jobs Magazine"* ("Black Enterprise"). Notwithstanding these lofty accolades achieved by an exceptionally equipped administrator, for the faculty of *UMass Boston*, Thomas' abilities were deemed "wanting" and thus, his presidential prospects dashed by a faculty that was, arguably, less qualified than himself. Moreover, while having to endure less of the "in your face" racism that Blacks in the military were oftentimes subjected to at the end of each of America's cataclysmic wars, esteemed Black male educators, even today, are often belittled and made to feel like helpless children, "boys" if you will, as men of African descent have often been referred, rather than accomplished men to be admired.

For centuries, the term "boy", when used to describe African-American men, has been a well-worn insult designed to marginalize and minimize the intended target as being somehow inferior, or childlike and, as such, undeserving of the respect to which they are due and are otherwise entitled. In fact, whether the individual being insulted was dressed in full military regalia, or a three-pieced suit made no difference to the perpetrators promulgating their hate, as use of the infantile insult became more prevalent throughout the country. In an essay for *ThoughtCo.com*, a premier reference site for education content, Nadra Kareem Nittle, who has written about education, race, and cultural issues for a variety of publications, reported on the problematic history and use of derogatory terms that are subtly (and sometimes obviously) offensive to people of color. "Historically whites routinely described Black men as boys to suggest African-Americans weren't on equal footing with them," Nittle accurately noted. "Both during and after slavery, African-Americans weren't viewed as full-fledged people but as mentally, physically, and spiritually inferior beings to whites. Calling Black men 'boys' was one way to express the racist ideologies of yesteryear," Nittle said. Today, this linguistic dog-whistle is not only a painful reminder of the discourtesies that Black men are regularly subjected to, it also underscores the fact that, in spite of institutional attainments, such as college degrees, big houses, or other trappings of American success, upwardly mobile Blacks may always have to fight against the notion that others view them as, somehow, "less" than deserving of their hard earned accomplishments.

In a notorious "incident" caught on camera for the entire world to dissect and evaluate, famed Black historian and *Harvard University* professor, Dr. Henry Louis Gates, host of the popular *PBS* television series, *Finding Your Roots*, was left feeling like a "boy" in his own abode, when he was unceremoniously arrested by the *Cambridge Police Department* for "breaking into his own home" near the tony neighborhood near *Harvard Yard*. In the summer of 2009, having returned home from an extended vacation, Dr. Gates, the internationally known historian and filmmaker, was soon detained, then subsequently arrested, by law enforcement officers responding to a call of a "suspicious man" and charged with disorderly conduct and racial harassment. In writing about the national spectacle that would ultimately lead to a brokered meeting between the professor and the police officer who arrested him, by President Barack Obama no less, in a courtyard near the *White House Rose Garden*, in what became known as the "Beer Summit," one of Black America's most recognizable academicians was reminded, as all Black men ultimately will be, that his degrees were of no use to him when his skin color was probable cause.

In a series of well publicized news accounts of the arrest seen around the world, to include the *Washington Post's* front page reporting by Krissah Thompson entitled, "Harvard Scholar Henry Louis Gates Arrested," the ubiquitous *Ivy League* instructor was treated like most Black men often are when perceived as guilty, even though he had broken no laws in rightfully entering his own domicile. "Gates was ordered to step out of his home. He refused and was followed inside by a police officer," Thompson reported.

"After showing the officer his driver's license, which includes his address, Ogletree [former fellow *Harvard University* Professor, Charles Ogletree, who was also Gates' attorney] said Gates asked: *"Why are you doing this? Is it because I'm a Black man and you're a white officer? I don't understand why you don't believe this is my house,"* the article noted; all this took place despite the fact that a reasonable law enforcement officer doing due diligence could see--particularly with personal photos on the wall--that Gates lived there.

For most educated African-Americans, however, many of whom are as credentialed, respected and talented as the great Dr. Henry Louis "Skip" Gates, there was little surprise that he would be unfairly detained and publicly humiliated. "I felt bad that I would hear about something like this happening, especially to someone as recognizable and distinguished as [Gates], but in the academy we still sometimes encounter that. I've been in situations where I encounter people who don't believe I'm a college professor," said Jelani Cobb," [a Professor of African-American Studies] the story noted (Thompson). "We have obvious signs of progress, but we're not there." After a considerable outcry from allies of both Gates and those who support the right for a man's home to be "his castle," the case was ultimately resolved, but the indelible impact it made on both the professor and the people is one that continues to remain more than a decade later (Thompson). Even Hollywood movie stars, who happen to be Black men, are sometimes treated with contempt and assumed criminality when not immediately recognized and presumed to be someone of "inferior" caliber.

Actor Forest Whittaker, known for a stellar career in a variety of successful movies, to include a variety of accolades from the *Academy Awards, Screen Actors Guild* and *BET,* for his reprisal of the murderous African dictator, Idi Amin, also known as the "Butcher of Uganda" in his 2006 film, "The Last King of Scotland", also fell victim to discrimination and profiling while shopping in New York City. Based on eyewitness accounts of the incident, Whitaker was publicly frisked in the middle of a New York deli after being accused of shoplifting. "Anyone who hasn't been hiding under a rock for the past century knows that Forest Whitaker is an *Academy Award* winning actor who has also obtained much success in directing and producing as well. So why in the world would he be trying to shop lift goods that even the average middle-class American can afford from a deli in NYC?," Gordon Taylor of the *Atlanta Black Star* inquired. "While there isn't any proof of racism being what provoked the public frisk, you can't help but wonder if the only thing Whitaker was guilty of was shopping while Black" (Taylor). Even as well-known as Whitaker is, however, nothing beats the most recognizable couple in the world, Barack and Michelle Obama, who admit to having been "mistaken for the help" a time or two.

In responding to an interview, the Obamas conducted with *People Magazine*, journalist Nia-Malika Henderson noted the solemnity to which the realities that even the most well-known African-Americans bodes for average, everyday Black folks. "We need to emphasize," she said, "that this isn't the *first time* the Obamas have told this story, but it is the first time that these stories have come up within the context of nationwide protests after a string of police shootings involving unarmed African American. "This, from the First Lady", Henderson continued...

❝

I tell this story – I mean, even as the first lady – during that wonderfully publicized trip I took to Target, not highly disguised, the only person who came up to me in the store was a woman who asked me to help her take something off a shelf. Because she didn't see me as the first lady, she saw me as someone who could help her. Those kinds of things happen in life. So, it isn't anything new.

And then this from the president:

❝

The small irritations or indignities that we experience are nothing compared to what a previous generation experienced. It's one thing for me to be mistaken for a waiter at a gala. It's another thing for my son to be mistaken for a robber and to be handcuffed, or worse, if he happens to be walking down the street and is dressed the way teenagers dress (Henderson).

In expressing their continued concerns about the rate of progress the United States has made on the issues of race and culture in the country, the ever-so-careful president went on to refer to the experiences Black males face at the hands of police as "small irritations," but to Dr. Will Moreland, the answer lies in being viewed as a person, first and foremost, before presumptions are made and then set in stone.

"After joining the military, I ended up living in Germany for about 15 years and I had the opportunity to travel all throughout the world. And it was the first time that I was seen, not as a Black man, but as an American," Dr. Will recalled. "It was the first time in my life that I felt like, 'Wow'! I am an American," he said. "Living in the United States, I never felt like I was part of the American fabric," the native emphasized. "In America, I was labeled a thug. But not so around the world. While I was abroad, others saw me as 'American' and it helped to open up my eyes and reshape the way I saw the world and how the world, in return, saw me," the motivator declared. "I've been blessed to go to over forty different countries and the ways that I've been embraced have been both eye-opening and polarizing at the same time," Moreland admitted. "I went to speak in India once for a leadership conference," he continued, "and they literally had big billboard posters of me on the walls around the city," the famed inspirational speaker recalled in amazement. "I'm riding in the car and I'm taking it all in and I am just astonished," Moreland admitted. "In fact, when I arrived, they had a mini-parade in my honor and everything! I had people jumping out to greet me when I exited the car, and people were just running up to me and hugging me," Dr. Will noted surreally. "And I'm thinking to myself, 'I could never get this in America'. I'm a veteran who fought for the rights of all Americans, and I would never get that sort of reception in the 'good ole' US of A'", Dr. Will theorized. "So, to feel that type of love and embrace, in a strange land nonetheless, was very interesting indeed." With that thought in mind, and a goal of ensuring that every Black boy in America experiences that same love and acceptance right here at home that he enjoyed himself while traveling abroad, Moreland--while always advancing the communal agenda of social acceptance and upward mobility for all Americans, regardless of the color of their skin--believes the act of "paying it forward" can go a long way towards creating a new reality for generations to follow.

"Mentoring is one of the most powerful tools for development that I know," Moreland explained, "as it puts what I call 'a new pair of glasses' on your individual perspective. Taking things back to my humble beginnings," the corporate coach continued, "for the first nineteen years of my life, I lived in a box," Moreland said plainly. "And inside that box, everybody that looked like me, everybody that talked like me, and everybody *just like me*, had the same or similar aspirations," he remembered. "But I wanted something different for my life," the prolific preacher proclaimed. "When I joined the military, I became acquainted with a leader by the name of 'Master Sergeant Bob' and he began to mentor me, and helped to put *'a new pair of glasses'* on my otherwise limited perspective. In my box," Moreland elaborated, "the enemy was the White man," he confessed. "In my box, the police were the enemies. In my box," he went on, "I had very limited potential. But what 'Master Sargent Bob' did for me was to enable me to see the world from a much broader view. He enabled me to see the totality of what was going on, and began to show me that, if I did work hard and earned my degree, I could, ultimately change my reality. He gave me something to look forward to," Will acknowledged. "And now, having seen the results of mentoring firsthand, I'm totally committed to mentoring other individuals, because it really is a game changer," Moreland declared.

"As an accomplished African-American man, I probably don't face the day-to-day challenges that many of my brothers and sisters face every day in the inner city. But that doesn't give me the right to ignore their suffering. At the same time, for my brothers and sisters living in the inner city, they have to be mindful of the fact that we have enough examples of African-American individuals who have been able to achieve some modicum of success in our current society," Dr. Will intoned. "We don't have the overt racism of days gone by, like dogs chasing us down or "Whites Only" signs, so we've come a long way... but we *still* have a long way to go," he concluded. "That's why it's so critically important for our young brothers and sisters out there to begin to educate themselves which is, I believe, one of the biggest factors we seem to be missing today. Begin to stretch yourself," Dr. Will went on. "Begin to use your own mind and don't just take something at face value. Do your own research. You can never have too much information and, once it's yours... they can never take it away!"

(Will Moreland: Best-Selling Author & Fortune 500 Coach)

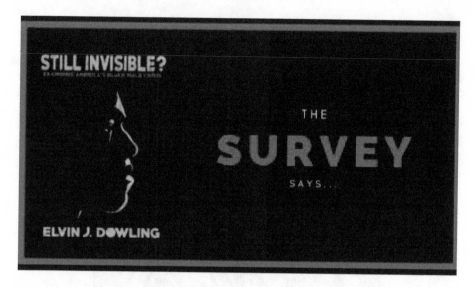

Considering the thought that higher education is a stepping-stone to greater acceptance in America, regardless of race, which of the following statements do you most agree with?*

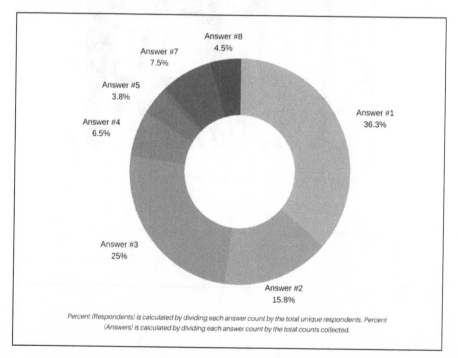

Percent (Respondents) is calculated by dividing each answer count by the total unique respondents. Percent (Answers) is calculated by dividing each answer count by the total counts collected.

1. Yes, educated Black males have an equal amount of advantages as others in American society = 36.25%

2. Yes, educated Black males have MORE advantages than others in American society = 15.75%

3. Yes, but educated Black males still have FEWER advantages than others in American society = 25.00%

4. No, higher education in America no longer provides opportunities for anyone, regardless of race = 6.50%

5. No, higher education is only working for those with access to resources in America (rich/whites) = 3.75%

6. No, higher education is only working for those with special advantages in America (poor/minorities) = 0.75%

7. I don't know enough about the subject to answer this question = 7.50%

8. I have no opinion = 4.50%

All survey results displayed above are represented by the overall percentage of survey respondents. For more information on our survey methodology, please see the Author's Note, located in the front matter of the book. To review raw survey results, visit: http://bit.ly/stillinvisiblesurvey.

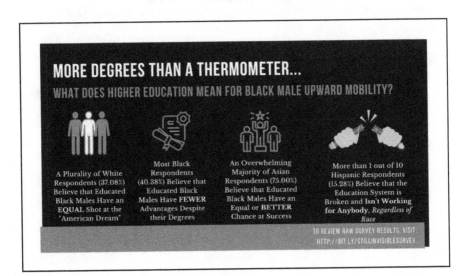

MORE DEGREES THAN A THERMOMETER...
WHAT DOES HIGHER EDUCATION MEAN FOR BLACK MALE UPWARD MOBILITY?

A Plurality of White Respondents (37.08%) Believe that Educated Black Males Have an EQUAL Shot at the "American Dream"

Most Black Respondents (40.38%) Believe that Educated Black Males Have FEWER Advantages Despite their Degrees

An Overwhelming Majority of Asian Respondents (75.00%) Believe that Educated Black Males Have an Equal or BETTER Chance at Success

More than 1 out of 10 Hispanic Respondents (15.28%) Believe that the Education System is Broken and Isn't Working for Anybody, *Regardless of Race*

TO REVIEW RAW SURVEY RESULTS, VISIT: HTTP://BIT.LY/STILLINVISIBLESURVEY.

Findings by Race

- More than one-third of all Hispanic respondents (34.72%) "Most Agree" with the statement, *"Yes, educated Black males have an equal amount of advantages as others in American society."*

- Less than any other group, a little more than 1 out of 10 Black respondents (11.54%) "Most Agree" with the statement, *"Yes, educated Black males have MORE advantages than others in American society."*

- Only 2 in 10 White respondents (22.92%) "Most Agree" with the statement, *"Yes, but educated Black males still have FEWER advantages than others in American society."*

Findings by Gender

- More than any other group, Hispanic female respondents (10.53%) "Most Agree" with the statement, *"No, higher education in America no longer provides opportunities for anyone, regardless of race."*

- A tiny minority of White Male respondents (2.00%) "Most Agree" with the statement, *"No, higher education is only working for those with access to resources in America (rich/whites)."*

- Only one-half of one percent of all Female respondents (0.50%), regardless of race, "Most Agree" with the statement, *"No, higher education is only working for those with special advantages in America (poor/minorities)."*

Findings by Age

- Nearly half of all White respondents ages 25-34 years old *(47.95%) "Most Agree" with the statement, *"Yes, educated Black males have an equal amount of advantages as others in American society."*

- One third of all Asian Male respondents, ages 45-54 years old (33.33%) "Most Agree" with the statement, *"Yes, educated Black males have MORE advantages than others in American society."*

- Almost 1 out of 4 Hispanic respondents, ages 18-24 years old (23.08%), "Most Agree" with the statement, *"Yes, but educated Black males still have FEWER advantages than others in American society."*

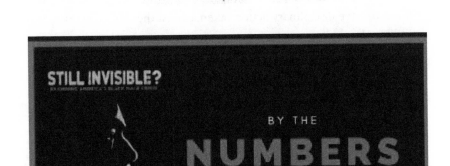

"Equal Access Makes All the Difference"

- Only 57 % of Black students have full access to the math and science courses they need for college success, compared to 81% of Asians and 71% of white students (Bridges).

- Because of the over-reliance on test scores for college admissions, the achievement gap in *SAT* math performance will inevitably produce inequality later in life (Reeves).

"The Soft Bigotry of Low Expectations"

- According to the *College Board*, which administers the *SAT*, only 20% of Black students who take the test meet the "benchmarks" for college success ("New SAT").

- While Black men have the lowest college completion rate of all other racial groups at 40%, it is still twice the "college success rate" the *College Board* predicts (Bridges).

"Walking Papers, Marching Orders & Bread Lines"

- Black service members are between 1.29 and 2.61 times more likely than Whites to have disciplinary action taken against them in an average year ("Military Justice).

- Although there are more than 37,000 Black college professors in the U.S., it will take nearly 150 years to reach parity with their percentage of the population ("Faculty").

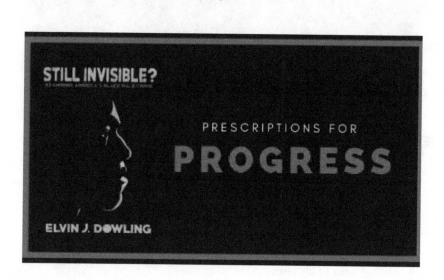

"Stop Measuring Success Using Discriminatory Tests!"

- Long-term success is often determined by nonacademic qualities. Encourage schools to implement social and emotional skills surveys during admissions (Kamanetz).

- Visit your state legislators to educate them about the effects of standardized testing, and encourage them to oppose (or support) specific legislation addressing the issue (Kohn).

"Lobby for Laws & Challenge the Flaws!"

- Challenge elected officials and those who support the use of standardized tests to take the tests themselves. In many states, few adults could pass these exams (Kohn).

- Take your case to court by suing the tests, which may be discriminatory, inconsistent with the state standards or require students to know information not taught (Kohn).

"Insist Top People Treat Everyone Equal!"

- Tell *Congress* to insist the military empower prosecutors to determine when to refer a case to court-martial, reducing potential bias based on race or ethnicity ("Military Justice").

- Call upon local universities to insist their schools maintain a non-toxic work environment where Black professors aren't treated more harshly or as token hires (Krupnick).

Works Cited

1. Ferrare, Joseph J. "Intergenerational Education Mobility Trends by Race and Gender in the United States." *Sage Journals*, SAGE Publishing. 28 November 2016. http://bit.ly/2CjBund

2. Vandivier, David. "What Is the Great Gatsby Curve?" *WhiteHouse.gov*, The White House - Council of Economic Advisors. 11 June 2013. http://bit.ly/2qrWm93

3. Rosales, John. "The Racist Beginnings of Standardized Testing." *NEA.org*, National Education Association. Accessed 7 November 2019. http://bit.ly/2rn3Sma

4. Taylor, Aaron. "The Marginalization of Black Aspiring Lawyers." *Law Review*, Florida International University. Spring 2019. Accessed 8 November 2019.

http://bit.ly/2pKqkFt

5. Jaschik, Scott. "Do Law Schools Limit Black Enrollment With LSAT?" *InsideHigherEd.com*, Quad Partners. 15 April 2019. http://bit.ly/2JPopG7

6. Stevenson, Bryan. "Lynching in America: Targeting Black Veterans." *EJI.org*, Equal Justice Initiative. Accessed 10 November 2019. http://bit.ly/2qIinAp

7. Herreria, Carla. "Even in The Military, Black People Are Punished Disproportionately, Report Shows." *HuffPost.com - Part of HuffPost Black Voices*. Verizon Media. 7 June 2017. http://bit.ly/2Cif0CQ

8. Agboola, Adedamola. "Black Academics Withdraw Candidacy After UMass Boston Faculty Calls Them 'Unqualified.'" *BlackEnterprise.com*, Earl Graves Publishing, Co., Inc. 29 May 2018. http://bit.ly/2pNfY7s

9. Nittle, Nadra Kareem. "Terms You Might Not Know Are Considered Racist." *ThoughtCo.com*, Dotdash Publishing. 26 June 2019. http://bit.ly/2NX7rXV

10. Thompson, Krissah. "Harvard Scholar Henry Louis Gates Arrested." *WashingtonPost.com*, Nash Holdings. 21 July 2009. https://wapo.st/2qqzOp2

11. Gordon, Taylor. "Forest Whitaker Frisked Publicly for Shopping While Black in New York." *AtlantaBlackStar.com*, Atlanta Black Star. 17 February 2013. http://bit.ly/2WJEnXP

12. Henderson, Nia-Malika. "The Obamas Say That They've Been Mistaken for 'The Help' (Again). That's Telling." *WashingtonPost.com*, Nash Holdings. 17 December 2014. http://wapo.st/1wFNtTN

13. Bridges, Brian. "African-Americans and College Education by the Numbers." *UNCF.org*, United Negro College Fund. 29 November 2018. http://bit.ly/2OjItSN

14. Reeves, Richard V. and Halikias, Dimitrios. "Race Gaps in SAT Scores Highlight Inequality and Hinder Upward Mobility."

Brookings.edu, The Brookings Institution. 1 February 2017. https://brook.gs/33RBqXS

15. Jaschik, Scott. "New SAT, Old Gaps on Race." *InsideHigherEd.com*, Quad Partners. 27 September 2017. http://bit.ly/33SKjjN

16. Kamanetz, Anya. "What Schools Can Use Instead of Standardized Tests." *NPR.Org - NPREd: How Learning Happens*. 6 January 2015. https://n.pr/2KnL3G9

17. "The Snail-Like Progress of Blacks in Faculty Ranks of Higher Education." *The Journal of Blacks in Higher Education*, BROCON Publishing. Accessed 17 November 2019. http://bit.ly/2r4maIs

18. Kohn, Alfie. "Fighting the Tests: A Practical Guide to Rescuing Our School." *AlfieKohn.org*, Phi Delta Kappan. Accessed 14 November 2019. http://bit.ly/36ZjRXX

19. "Racial Disparities in Military Justice." *Protect Our Defenders*, 5 May 2017. http://bit.ly/2XhVhNm

20. Chotowski, Sarah E. "We Need A Good War: Factors that Influence the Experience of Racism in the United States Military." *Smith Scholar Works*, Smith College. Published in 2014. Accessed 14 November 2019. http://bit.ly/2qSgRvM

21. Krupnick, Matt. "After Colleges Promised to Increase It, Hiring of Black Faculty Declined." *HechingerReport.org*, Teachers College at Columbia University. 2 October 2018. http://bit.ly/2XdgibW

Chapter 4: "Mo' Tea, Suh?"

How Marketing, the Media and Memes Shape the Black Male Narrative

" "

He's invisible, a walking personification of the Negative, the most perfect achievement of your dreams, sir! The mechanical man!"

- Ralph Ellison, "Invisible Man" (Shmoop Editorial Team. 3.299)

(First performed by George Dixon in 1834, Zip Coon was a figure in a popular Blackface minstrel show that made fun of free Blacks by portraying the character as an uppity figure who, despite his best efforts, could never quite fit in with mainstream society.)

Makes Me No Never Mind!

Is What You See Truly What You Get?

In a memorable scene from the 1993 movie "Posse", directed by Mario Van Peebles, actor Billy Zane, in his portrayal of the sinister Colonel Graham, a racist military officer fighting in the *Spanish-America War,* called upon his servant "Weezie" to *"fetch him a drink."* While doing so, he asked his guests if they were aware of the fact that "Weezie" was the *"last surviving member of the Motisa Tribe."* Not quite understanding what Colonel Graham was talking about, actor Zane then holds up his cup and saucer, forcing his hapless stooge to ask the $25,000 question: *"Mo' tea, Suh?" (Cracks me up just thinking about it).* Today, in the ever evolving parlance that is urban dialect, when someone is referred to as a member of the *"Motisa Tribe"* it's because that person is seen as a clown, at best and a "coon" always, which is usually not a good thing (depending on what side of the tracks you live, of course). And for hundreds of years, the systematic depiction of all Black men as subservient and ignorant, or aggressive and deviant, depending upon whatever convenient narrative works at the time in which it needs to, has made them *"Motisas"* in the eyes of many in this, "the land of the free."

Noted African-American attorney and author, Charles Waddell Chestnutt once said: *"The workings of the human heart are the profoundest mystery of the universe. One moment they make us despair of our kind, and the next we see them in the reflection of the divine image."* Throughout the course of American history, Black males in this country have provided a dichotomous and interchangeable image of both strength and weakness to those with whom they interact. In fact, as our nation continues to evolve from a time in which the very existence of Black men in polite society was considered anathema, at best, to the point where we have been able to elect our first Black president, is progress. Then again, stabbing someone in the back with a twelve-inch serrated knife and pulling it out six inches is progress too... but I digress.

Because I strive to be fair and impartial in the administration of my duties, I would be remiss if I did not point out the stacked deck awaiting Black males in the media and in the marketplace. In a piece by Bob Fagan called, "The History of African-American Advertising", the portrayal of Black males in marketing and media have not only been overwhelmingly negative, but steeped in racist imagery. "While African-Americans were featured early on in advertisements, most depictions were derogatory" (Fagan). In fact, some might even go so far as to deduce that the plethora of jaundiced presentments of Black males that are omnipresent in television, radio, newspapers and magazines, are part and parcel of what happens when those who are not in "the know" are writing the story. But if you don't know... you'd better ask somebody!

Popularized in 1834 by musician George Dixon in a racially offensive song, and later as a Black minstrel character with the eponymous, and uproarious name of "Zip Coon," the fast-talking jester loved by some (and hated by most) sure was a hoot! As was the intent of his creator, Zip Coon's insatiable desire to be accepted by "the man" was so invasive to his soul and craven in its presentation, that it led to his own marginalization. Moreover, his fancy clothes, cheap jewelry, and inappropriate use of the King's English just screamed *"Uppity..." (if you know what I mean...).* All of which, I might add, led him to being the object of everyone's laughter. Now, I'm not going to mention the little tidbit about Zip Coon being played by a white guy in blackface *(that just spoils the whole story),* but I will say that his fateful introduction into the American cultural landscape would help lay the foundation for how Black men in America would be viewed for more than a century. Today, however, as America looks to correct some of the historic imbalances that have kept us from truly becoming "an equal society," particularly as it relates to the shaping of public opinion, I will be the first to pledge my commitment to changing minds and shifting perspectives--no matter how long it takes *(and I'm not in a rush). As such,* I will play my part in the ongoing saga that is the Black male narrative. Trust me on this. I won't let you down.

You Can Count on Me,

Justitia

Lady Justice

Andre Showell: "Telling It Like It Is"

Does Perception Become Reality?

The great city of Baltimore, Maryland, home of the famed *Baltimore Inner Harbor* and birthplace of America's national anthem, *The Star-Spangled Banner*, is an urban metropolis that has been in a state in flux for nearly three hundred years, since its founding in 1729. Having been named in honor of Cecil Calvert, the second "Lord Baltimore" of the *Irish House of Lords* and a founding settler of Maryland, Baltimore was originally a settlement that was largely inhabited by Native Americans going back thousands of years. Today, the "Monumental City" as John Quincy Adams once termed it, is now an inner-city bastion of the challenges and opportunities that plague urban America. Born and raised in the hometown of such national treasures as abolitionist Frederick Douglass and Justice Thurgood Marshall of the *US Supreme Court*, Andre Showell, a towering and recognizable media figure whose depth and breadth of wisdom and experience don't comport with his youthful appearance, is a man who will undoubtedly be included in the pantheon of notable Baltimoreans who have made marks upon the world that can never be erased.

"I am Andre Showell and I am a news reporter for BET News," commenced the always astutely attired newsman with a booming baritone voice. "I cover national politics, society, The White House and any issues that happen, which may impact Black America. I have been in the news business since I was 18 years old," Showell said, "when I secured my first internship and was subsequently hired full-time the following year. So, I am not that old, per se, but I am old-ish when it comes to the mass media industry," he laughed; noting half a lifetime of service as a reliable reporter for one of Black America's most trusted and well-known news sources. "I have been covering issues that impact Black people for the last twenty years--from the events of *9/11*, *Hurricane Katrina*, the various riots of the past few years, and everything in between that affects people of color in this country," Andre continued, detailing a litany of stories that have given him a front row seat to the history of a people and a culture.

"I grew up in Baltimore, Maryland, along with my siblings, as well as my mother and father, who played an instrumental role in my life. "As a proud product of *Baltimore City Public Schools*," Showell explained, "I was privileged to attend excellent schools in the city and, in many ways, my family sort of countered the typical image of what it means to grow up in Baltimore, and what it means to be Black *and* from Baltimore," he elaborated. "In a lot of ways, I do not have the type of horror stories that other people who grew up in my hometown have, because I _did_ have a supportive family and they _did_ have resources to make sure that we had everything we needed to flourish and be contributing members of society," the correspondent concluded, describing an idyllic upbringing that contributed greatly to the man he is today.

"The church was an extremely critical component for all of us," explained Showell, a *"preacher's kid"* who clearly did not miss many Sunday services; as he continues to imbibe the principles and values he learned as a child, all of which help him to navigate today's contemporary challenges. "In fact, I would venture to say that the church has been our lifeline, in many ways," he continued. "On one hand, we had a very ideal upbringing. But on the other hand, some of the issues that have impacted many families in Baltimore have also visited our family as well. No matter how much time and resources and prayers were put into our lives," the newsman noted, "my oldest brother still fell victim to a homicide while I was covering the riots in Baltimore after the tragic death of Freddy Gray while in Baltimore Police Department custody. So, no one is really safe from tragedy," the man of faith surmised, "and that includes my family. Be that as it may," he went on, "I have wonderful memories of growing up in Baltimore, and if it weren't for this city, I wouldn't be the man I am today," Showell concluded. "Baltimore is where I get my grit, my determination, my fighting spirit and my external drive to succeed. So that's who I am," he remarked.

Born the son of a Baltimore native and a North Carolina transplant, Showell is obviously a Baltimorean through and through. "As a kid growing up, my father was a superhero to me... and still is to me today. He was the smartest man I knew. He was the tallest man I knew. He was the strongest man I knew, both emotionally and physically. So, he is who I pattern my life after and, I think I can speak for both of my brothers in saying that this was the case for them as well," the proud scion of a real-life "superman" beamed. "My father is the Bishop Franklin Showell, the pastor of the *First Apostolic Faith Church*. It is a 100+ year old institution that services the needs of families and children in East Baltimore which, when the church first began, was a thriving family community, but later, it evolved into sort of an inner-city bastion of drugs and crime. For the past 15 years, however, the area has been the center of development for the community," the neighborhood native noted. "My father is also a scholar and a teacher, having worked as a Professor of History at *Morgan State University*. He has been a museum director and a successful businessman as well. In fact, he is _still_ is an entrepreneur in real estate development. My father has always been a "Renaissance Man" and has been an active presence in the community all of my life and most of his," Andre acknowledged, with a sense of duty that comes with a life committed to service.

"My mom, Ella Showell, is the classic loving Black mother," the newshound declared. "She is a very strong woman from Knoxville, North Carolina, who came to Baltimore to attend *Morgan State University*, where she and my father would ultimately meet. Her aunt," Showell elaborated, "was a member of *First Apostolic Faith Church*, so not only was she going to school with him, but she was also going to church with him, and that is how their relationship began to take root. Now she is the "First Lady" of the church, but when she got here, she was a country girl with a dream who became a strong woman who fulfilled them," the proud son proclaimed. "Even though she presents like a very graceful beautiful and a supportive, doting wife and mother, she is also a power broker behind the scenes," he warned cautiously. "My mother is smart, witty, and understands and truly excels in her emotional intelligence. which is where she really excels. She understands people and how to operate. She is also a prayerful woman who has a connection with God that is clear and uncanny," he recalled.

"When we were growing up, we couldn't get away with anything. She always knew," Showell joked, grateful for his mother's keen sense of intuition that helped to keep him on a straight and narrow path. "At the same time, however, she wasn't one who always lord over us. My mom wanted us to grow up and experience life, so she, nor my father, ever steered us in any direction. Having a mother like mine made life so much more bearable," the correspondent confessed. "When people congratulate me over some of the hurdles that I have been able to overcome, I always tell them, *You don't understand, I was able to jump over that hurdle because I have so many people around me that are lifting me up'*. So, without them," Andre admitted, "I don't know if I really am *that* strong," Showell surmised. "Maybe I'm strong because they're strong?" What makes Showell's experience so atypical, however, particularly as it relates to the way he grew to see himself as capable of achieving anything he set his mind to, is the fact that the images both he and other Black males are inundated with on a continuous basis, ones in which the worst behaviors of Black men are amplified ad nauseam on media platforms across the globe, never stood in the way of his dogged determination to succeed despite the odds.

"My parents insisted that we go to church. They insisted that we adhere to Godly principles. But they were not taskmasters about it. In fact, the church was a community institution not only for us, but for those who need a place to go when they are physically hungry. It's also a place where people go when their spiritual souls are hungry as well," declared Showell, a man of deep faith and firm conviction. "The church was my foundation. I spent two to three days of my week, every week, inside the sanctuary. My grandfather was the pastor of *First Apostolic Faith Church* before my father was, and my great-uncle before him," he declared. "I have uncles and aunts and cousins who are in ministry, and we were always taught that *everyone* has a ministry, and it doesn't necessarily have to be inside the church," committed Christian concluded. "Because of that, I was always encouraged to go into journalism as a way to empower the community and, as a result, my faith has been the background to which I speak truth to power and always search for truth. As followers of Jesus Christ, it is our mandate, to do both of those things. As a journalist I take that charge very seriously." Today, as the heir to a proud legacy of leadership and service, as demonstrated by his exceptional parents, Showell continues to take the lessons they have taught him--both at home and at church--and have parlayed them into a reputation for "telling it like it is"; working to ensure that the idea of a fair and balanced media is a reality for all its subjects, most specifically African-American males.

"I think that Black men in America are very visible in society, especially in media," Showell remarked. "If you look at the news, if you look at entertainment, if you look at social media, I think that we are flooded with images of Black people in general, but also of Black men. Now the question is this: what do those images look like and do they show the breadth and the depth of who we are and the complexity and nuances that make us individuals? That is the problem," the award-winning journalist lamented. "But if you turn on your local news," he went on, "if you aren't seeing a Black face delivering the news, then you are certainly seeing images of Black men on the news, particularly if you live in an urban area. As we know," Showell intoned, "Black males are typically shown as either perpetrators or victims of crime," he explained. "On the other hand, you, have the entertainment side where Black men *seem* to be seen as 'the ticket' to entertainment success," Showell found. "When a new network wants to build their audience, for example, they will typically start off like, *Fox* did, with programming specifically designed to attract Black people," the media luminary explained. "*Fox*, at one point, was fledgling, until they produced shows like "Martin" and "In Living Color" in the early 1990's, and is now a behemoth, having built its viewership on the backs of Black viewers before abandoning them for more lucrative markets," the longtime influencer intoned. "And now, if you turn on any of the *Fox* channels, you would be hard-pressed to find shows that focus on Black people or that show Black people in diverse arrays, right?," Showell asked rhetorically, already knowing the answer to his own question. More importantly, the realities of network broadcasting cannot be appropriately understood without first delving into the use of imagery itself to portray individuals of African descent in negative and unflattering ways in most communications platforms; from television to print, and more.

"How Do You Really See Me?"

In his analysis of the history of racism in the media and its impact on the cultural perceptions of African-American males, Trevor Robinson of *Adweek* chronicled the long and storied relationship between mass media and the monsters it creates through caricatures and creatures masquerading as Black males. "Advertising has a long history of racism. In the rare cases that Black people were portrayed in ads, they were invariably depicted as subservient, ignorant and unattractive," Robinson observed when examining a century of racist examples that portrayed Black people as buffoonish, ugly or downright illiterate. "From the late 1800s when African-Americans first started appearing in advertising and through the 'Mad Men' era, they were negatively stereotyped or ridiculed. Products used cartoonish images of Black people, and bleach and soap brands, like Pears, "jokingly" claimed their products could lighten dark skin," Robinson continued. Even today, African-American males still appear more regularly in sports ads and athletic brands than any other category on the market, further contributing to the stereotypical notion that Blacks can only be legitimately "seen" in American society when they engage in the areas of sports, play and entertainment; further reducing their value in the eyes of general population, while continuing to feed into unhelpful racial tropes. "Both under-representing the Black community and portraying them in a stereotypical way has a profound effect on the collective self-esteem. It creates feelings of isolation and impacts self-belief. If you can't see anyone who looks like you in the media, your thinking will inevitably be limited in terms of what you can achieve. Black people, and bleach and soap brands, like Pears, "jokingly" claimed their products could lighten dark skin" (Robinson).

According to a 2011 report by *The Opportunity Agenda,* a social justice communication lab that seeks to ensure that equal opportunity is extended to all Americans, entitled: "Improving Media Coverage and Public Perceptions of African-American Men and Boys", the perceptions of Black males and their relationship to the media are inextricably attached to one another, leading to a confluence of negative perceptions from all aspects of mass media. Moreover, the results of their research revealed the following trends that, while not surprising, continue to provide challenges for a subset of the American population struggling under the weight of systemic oppression, including:

- An over-representation of Black males in episodes of violence and crime.

- The continued ignoring of the positive aspects of the lives of Black males, such as fatherhood, hard work, and their significant contributions to their communities.

- The distorted depictions of Black males in the media, which inevitably lead to negative perceptions of them, often resulting in increased public support for punitive law enforcement in Black communities and racial disparities in the criminal justice system.

- Inaccurate illustrations of Black males, which ultimately affect self-perceptions and ultimately lead to diminished self-esteem ("Improving Media." p. 1.).

The report goes on to detail the extent to which imbalanced portrayals of Black males has far reaching consequences. "Change is needed in these areas because research and experience find persistently distorted media depictions of Black males that contribute to negative stereotypes, unfair treatment, and unequal opportunity in areas ranging from employment to education to criminal justice and beyond" ("Improving Media." p. 1.).

In their thought-provoking article, "Perceptions of and by Black Men," *The Opportunity Agenda* explored the fear and self-loathing that Black men have for themselves and those who look like them. "More Black men experience significant challenges than white men, have higher levels of worry, and are harsher in their judgment of Black men. Even so, more are focused on achieving success in a career, on living a religious life, and are optimistic about a bright future. In just about every area, Black men are their own harshest critics, as well as the most optimistic that things will get better," the article continued ("Perceptions"). "Black men are harshly critical of the priorities of Black men generally, saying that Black men put too little emphasis on education (69 percent), health (66 percent), their families (48 percent), and getting ahead at work (43 percent), and too much emphasis on sports (49 percent), maintaining a tough image (41 percent), and sex (54 percent)" ("Perceptions"). According to Andre Showell, while the media has a role to play in perpetuating myths about Black males that have little bearing on the totality of their contributions to American society, there is also a growing realization that they can and simply must do a better job at highlighting much more positive aspects of the Black male experience.

"While we are seeing more images of Black males in the media than we did twenty or even fifty years ago, much of the imagery we are seeing are seeing depictions of Black men as thugs, criminals, irresponsible, entertaining, over-sexualized over-the-top, over-sexualized people horrible priorities," Showell pointed out. "And that is not who *I* am. That is not who *we* are," he exclaimed. "The media needs to do better about representing the Black man in all of his glory. We [the media] have already shown a dark light on us. It's now time to shine a bright light on us," the television reporter remarked. "Why don't we show Black people in a positive light? Why don't we know about the heroes in our community?," Showell continued. "Why don't we highlight the grandfathers who have been in our community for generations? Why don't we talk about the business leaders that are doing great things in our neighborhoods, or the young kings who are performing laudable feats on the road to greatness? Why is it that you only see the extreme of who we are," he inquired? "Whenever people are shown at their worst, the media does the community a disservice. Even in news, we still have so far to go," Showell elucidated. "Black men are under-represented in newsrooms. We are under-represented as producers. We are under-represented as reporters and anchors. But in particular, we are under-represented as general managers and news directors," the veteran journalist decried. "These are the power brokers. These are the ones that can set the tone for the coverage that we see on a daily basis. That is where we need to focus our attention," Showell continued, "getting opinion leaders and decision makers of color to stand up in these newsrooms and say, *'the community that we are serving is varied and diverse, therefore you've got to do a better job.'* We can be responsible about what we are showing," he reasoned. Just as importantly, Showell is convinced that, by dismantling the institutional structures that perpetuate negative stereotypes, from the newsroom to the movie set, America can finally, take a forward step into the future.

"Racism has not ended," Andre conceded, detailing his analysis of why some of the intransigent problems facing Black males in America today. "We had a Black president and it sparked a discussion of whether or not we were a post-racial society. I don't think that people are saying that today," Showell reckoned particularly not in this, the Trump era and all of the issues that have come out of his presidency," noted the longtime *White House* correspondent who spends his waking hours chronicling the attitudes and actions of America's 45th President. "For example, we have seen a rise in hate crimes all over. Furthermore, police involved shootings of unarmed, defenseless Black men have also increased under his administration, although they didn't start with this president," Showell acknowledged. "Why is that happening?," the man who asks questions for a living queried rhetorically. "The institution of racism is still at work. We as a society have not yet had meaningful and deep conversations about this system of racism that this country was built on," he went on, "and until we do that, these stubborn issues will continue." To that end, Showell not only believes that the onus is not just on the media to reform itself, but that those in leadership roles within the African-American community--whether elected or assumed--must lead the effort to change the narrative of a people and the soul of a nation.

"Black men in leadership play a vital role in changing the conversation around what it means to be Black in America. The late, great Congressman Elijah Cummings of Baltimore, is a shining example of a leader who truly understood that responsibility," Showell stated. "He was not only representing the community; he was *in* the community! He lived blocks from where Freddie Gray was tragically killed at the hands of police officers and was instrumental in stopping some of the rioting" the ubiquitous inquisitor recalled; noting that Cummings was successful in leveraging the amplification of a bullhorn and the trust of a community to help stop a riotous onslaught in the wake of Gray's untimely demise. "We need more leaders like *that*" Showell quickly concluded. "Sadly, I believe that we also have a number of leaders who have been drawn in by the allure of a "celebrity culture" that seems to be taking us over. A lot of people are not being driven by their desire to help the community," the minister of information opined. "They're being driven by their own personal ambition, and the *'star politician'* is now a new thing in our culture," he bemoaned. "We have politicians that are now gracing red carpets and hobnobbing with celebrities. The same thing with our activists," Showell observed. "Our activists are now at a point where they are being featured on the cover of magazines and are doing *Instagram* selfies, talking about 'outfits of the day'", he joked. "They're getting sponsored by makeup companies and clothing lines, and it makes you wonder whether the heart of the movement is still alive in the same way that it was alive when Rosa Parks sat in the front of that bus. Is that spirit still alive in the same way?," he questioned. "I wonder if it is. When people point to Elijah Cummings as a community hero," Showell wondered, "is that because now he is an outlier? I think we need more leaders with a heart, and are truly connected with the people they represent. I think that we need more leaders," he proceeded, "that will put their own personal ambitions on the back burner for the sake of the greater good of our communities. We need more of *that!*

"As someone who covers politics," Showell continued, "there are some bright lights and shining stars," the correspondent confirmed. "There are a lot of faceless and nameless heroes among us that don't get the credit that they deserve," Andre decried. "But I also know that politics is not the only solution to what ails the African diaspora in this country. I believe that the faith community and the activist community and teachers and all of us, need to join forces to do what the government is *not* doing. We can fill in the gaps," Showell believes. "People's lives are impacted by politics, but we must begin to focus on laws that impact people where they live, which can only happen at the grassroots level. So, while we have our eyes on our national leaders, it would be more prudent for us, and more effective for us, to look at what's happening in our states and in our cities and in our local neighborhoods. That is where the rubber meets the road," the journalist deduced. "That is where we can make the biggest difference."

WHAT'S WHITE & BLACK & READ ALL OVER?

White Headlines	White Suspects	Black Headlines	Black Victims
Alabama suspect brilliant, but social misfit	Lubbock Avalanche-Journal Headline used to describe a college professor who killed three colleagues and wounded three	Montgomery's latest homicide victim had a history of narcotics abuse	Headline AL.com ran about the shooting death of a 25-year-old Black man in Alabama
Son in Staten Island murders was brilliant-- but his demons were the death of his parents	Staten Island Advance article covering the case of a mentally ill New York man who allegedly killed his parents	Trayvon Martin was suspended three times from school	NBC News ran this headline during ongoing coverage of the Trayvon Martin killing
Oregon school shooting suspect fascinated with guns but was a devoted Mormon	Fox News headline about 15-year-old after he killed a classmate, injured a teacher and took his own life at school	Slain Lakeland Teen Had Been Shot Before; Death Possibly Drug-Related	Florida Ledger article focusing on the death of a 19-year-old victim, making it seem expected, or at least unsurprising
Santa Barbara shooting: Suspect 'soft-spoken, polite, a gentleman'	Whittier Daily News headline in the wake of a mass shooting	Ohio man was carrying variable pump air rifle-not a toy when cops killed him	New York Daily News headline defending police after killing a Black man at a Walmart

The information and headlines contained in this chart were compiled from an article entitled, "When the Media Treats White Suspects and Killers Better than Black Victims," by Nick Wing of the Huffington Post.

How Do We Change the Narrative?

Since the establishment of the fourth estate in American society, the task of leveling the playing field on how Black males are perceived in marketing campaigns, Internet memes and mass media stories, has been made is all the more difficult when--even when found to be the victims of crime--they receive no respite from unfair scrutiny and little benefit of the doubt from a relentless media leviathan always eager to engulf its next prey. In his opinion piece for the *Huffington Post*, entitled: "When the Media Treats White Suspects and Killers Better Than Black Victims," journalist Nick Wing detailed the ways in which newsrooms, in particular, have contributed to the devaluing of Black people in the eyes of the general public. "News reports often headline claims from police or other officials that appear unsympathetic or dismissive of Black victims. Other times, the headlines seem to suggest that Black victims are to blame for their own deaths, engaging in what critics sometimes allege is a form of character assassination", Wing observed. "When contrasted with media portrayal of white suspects and accused murderers, the differences are more striking. News outlets often choose to run headlines that exhibit an air of disbelief at an alleged white killer's supposed actions. Sometimes, they appear to go out of their way to boost the suspect's character, carrying quotes from relatives or acquaintances that often paint even alleged murderers in a positive light" (Wing).

On the other side of the invisibility equation, however, is the fact that African-American males, while often unseen when performing acts of heroism, patriotism and community service, are placed front and center when one amongst them engages in, or is even accused of, bad or questionable behavior. According to the *Journal of Mass Communications & Journalism*, in its research article written by Trina Creighton and her colleagues, entitled "Coverage of Black versus White Males in Local Television News Lead Stories", the prevalence of newscasts depicting Black males as a lawless group of roustabouts that require supervision, incarceration and, if necessary execution, all of which is played out on the nightly news.   "Research has examined how some television news programs disproportionately portray Black males, as lawbreakers, while White males are significantly more likely to be shown in the context of a defender, or the "good guy" (Creighton. p. 1). In fact, when African-American males are often the lead-in to the news broadcast, the stereotype of Blacks being predisposed to committing crimes, there are very real ripple effects felt by others innocent of the offenses for which they are often saddled with. "The implications of connecting Blacks, especially Black males with crime is well documented and some researchers believe that link may have been solidified during the 1988 Presidential election race between George Bush and Michael Dukakis, when the Bush campaign unveiled the infamous Willie Horton photo," the report continued. "Even though it has been more than 25 years since Horton's face was splashed across television screens into American homes, his image may still be what researchers call the iconography of Black criminal threat so much so that Horton has led to the assertion that "today's prevailing criminal predator has become a euphemism for 'young Black male'"(Creighton. p. 2). Yet there are those seeking to change that point of view or, at the very least, provide a competing narrative to the onslaught of negativity surrounding Black males in America.

Before journalists like Andre Showell burst upon the mass media scene, making marks upon the industry that can never be erased, there were unheralded forces such as Thomas J. Burrell. The first African-American advertising executive in Chicago, Burrell is a trailblazing force for good in the world of Black media, working behind the scenes to advocate for more appropriate depictions of people of color and what has historically been presented to the general market audiences. Growing up as a shy kid from the South Side of Chicago, Illinois, Burrell started out in the advertising industry working in the mailroom at *Wade Advertising Agency* in Chicago before ultimately opening up the pioneering firm, *Burrell Communications Group*, a powerhouse in advertising today. As a part of his unique calling to represent the best of Black culture in magazines, television ads and other mediums aimed at reaching the African-American consumer and reintroducing the majority community aspects of Black life that often goes under-represented, Burrell has helped to reshape and, in some ways, reclaim the imagery of "Black" as something beautiful and worthy to be presented in a much more thoughtful light.

In an interview with Burrell about his contributions to the field of advertising, Sonari Glinton of *National Public Radio's Morning Edition* chronicled other people's perception of the adman's global contribution as one that helped to change the narrative of African-American men. "Black people are not dark-skinned white people. Those words spoken by legendary ad man Tom Burrell seemed very obvious in 2015. In the '60s, though, the idea that Blacks or other minorities should be advertised to directly seemed very risky, to say the least" (Glinton)."I feel like what Burrell did opened the door for the kind of ethnic micro-targeting that we see today," said Roberta Klara, an editor at *Adweek*. "And the way that he did that was by making mainstream brands not just aware of the Black community as a very viable community of consumers, but he also furnished them with a means to reach them that was new and effective" (Glinton). Yet and still, even the herculean efforts of people like Tom Burrell can't undo the damage that other marketing men have done simply by erasing the contributions of Black men in America or rewriting history to fit a convenient and sellable narrative.

In 2013, actor Johnny Depp reprised a well-worn role in American cinema when he starred in the *Walt Disney* film, "The Lone Ranger", a crime fighting lawman who used trickery, disguise and sheer creativity to capture bad guys and protect communities throughout the American West. What many may not know, however, is that the character that Depp embodied was, perhaps, inspired by a lone Black police officer, the late Bass Reeves, who patrolled the wild west hunting scofflaws and outlaws seeking to outrun the long arm of the law. According to a report by Sheena McKenzie, a Digital News Reporter for *CNN International*, headlined: "Was an African-American Cop the Real Lone Ranger?", Reeves, a former slave from an Arkansas plantation rose to become a Deputy United States Marshall, who would ultimately capture more than 3,000 criminals before the end of his long and storied career.

"Sometimes he dressed as a preacher, at other times a tramp, and occasionally even a woman," McKenzie reported. "Many of Reeves' personal attributes and techniques in catching desperadoes were similar to the Lone Ranger," says Art Burton, author of "Black Gun, Silver Star: The Life and Legend of Frontier Marshal Bass Reeves. He was bigger than the Lone Ranger -- he was a combination of the Lone Ranger, Sherlock Holmes and Superman," Burton told *CNN*. But because he was a Black man his story has been buried. He never got the recognition he deserved... He's one of America's most important heroes and it's sad his story isn't known more than it is," said Burton. "But unfortunately, the majority of Black history has been buried" (McKenzie). So, why is it important that Black men in America be less vilified and more lionized in the eyes of those who tell these stories? Because, as Andre Showell believes, the work of repairing in Black men what has been broken by society, begins and ends with the ways in which they see themselves and are perceived by others.

"Black men in America are still struggling and are engaged in a war that they did not sign up for," Showell ominously observed. "We are being attacked on every side. We are being attacked in our homes. We are being attacked in our neighborhoods. And we are being attacked when we venture out into this world. There is nowhere that is safe for Black men in this country. To be a Black man is to know that every moment you were living in this society, someone can take your life and nothing will be done," he said. "We have seen that from the headlines, time and time again. Yet," he went further, "I am hopeful and understand that because we are here, we are heroes, and someone must tell those stories," the newsman declared. "We were enslaved a few generations ago. We were sought out, hunted down like wild animals, placed in shackles and forced to live with our individual will being stripped away from us... for centuries," he exclaimed. "For us to have survived *that* is a testament to the fact that we are incredible. We *are* superhuman," he theorized, "and God has his hands on us! Because we're here and we have survived, every Black boy that is born, in my opinion, is special. And I don't think that God would put us in this place called America, where we are here and functioning in this world, for us to wallow in all of the problems that have plagued us," the preacher's son surmised.

"I don't think that is why we are here. I think that we are here to do the work. We are here to, *if we can't look to society to change,* we are here to change ourselves. We are here to empower each other and to be our own lifesavers. I believe that we can do that...I do! And when that happens, *and I do think that it will happen,* I believe the world owes us an apology," said Showell, in responding to the media's role in helping to shape the Black male narrative. To that end, however, when not erasing or minimizing the positive contributions of Black males in advertising, film or the news media--either through omission, commission, or both--marketers have used stereotypical imagery of Black men to sell products, evoke laughter and reinforce a negative narrative of buffoonery and ignorance that has been cemented in public perception for hundreds of years in America. In doing so, oftentimes these dubious brand hustlers have substituted white men in "blackface" to portray African-Americans as fools of the highest order.

Alexis Clark, in writing for *The History Channel*, revealed why the legacy of blackface is steeped in racism. "The portrayal of blackface–when people darken their skin with shoe polish, greasepaint or burnt cork, and paint on enlarged lips and other exaggerated features, is steeped in centuries of racism", Clark noted. "It peaked in popularity during an era in the United States when demands for civil rights by recently emancipated slaves triggered racial hostility. And today, because of blackface's historic use to denigrate people of African descent, its continued use is still considered racist" (Clark). Having cemented his place in history as the "Father of Minstrelsy," New York born actor Thomas Dartmouth Rice forever impacted the way in which both slaves and free Blacks would be treated in American society, for the next one hundred and twenty-five years, when he created the ignominious character Jim Crow in 1830. "With quick dance moves, an exaggerated African-American vernacular and buffoonish behavior, Rice founded a new genre of racialized song and dance—blackface minstrel shows—which became central to American entertainment in the North and South. White performers in blackface played characters that perpetuated a range of negative stereotypes about African Americans including being lazy, ignorant, superstitious, hypersexual, criminal or cowardly" (Clark).

Social Media Influencer and author of "Blackballed: The Black and White Politics of Race on America's Campuses", Lawrence Ross, often proclaims: *"The most nefarious thing about white supremacy is that you don't need white skin to perpetuate it."* For more than 400 years that has absolutely been the case in America, as there has historically been a never-ending number of Black men willing to demean themselves and besmirch a people for fleeting fame and the roar of laughter from a crowd. In the late nineteenth century and well into the twentieth century, the most famous Black comedian of the time was a native Kentuckian and former slave named Billy Kersands, a popular theater performer who popularized blackface minstrelsy, as he sang in musical performances across the American South for nearly sixty years, beginning in the early 1860's. According to the website, *Blackface!*, the uber-popular performer would go on to secure his place in the pantheon of satirists who made an indelible impression on public perception through their work.

"Billy Kersands was the most popular minstrel star and the highest paid Black entertainer of the era, earning as much as one hundred dollars a week---a lot of money in the 1870s and 1880s. Kersands was a comedian who enjoyed entertaining the public. But his real forte was dancing. He was credited as being the first dancer to introduce the 'soft-shoe' dance, and the 'buck and wing' ("Kersands"). He is also credited with the creation of an enduring stereotypical brand that lives on to this day, the legendary "Aunt Jemima." Initially embodied in the spirit of a "mammy" song written for a white minstrel singer in 1875, the character in Kersands' song was eventually trademarked in 1889 and sold to *The Davis Company*, who hired a former enslaved woman named Nancy Green to "become" Aunt Jemima, in an effort to help them sell pancakes at the Chicago Exposition in 1893. Today, more than a century after the demise of Kersands, a controversial symbol of Blackness as monkeyshine entertainment for the masses, the impact of unhelpful allegories on the Black male narrative continue to play a role in the way Black men are viewed. According to Andre Showell, reaching back and lifting others up, is key to overcoming unhelpful stereotypes that make life more difficult for Black males in this country.

"I believe that mentoring plays a role for African-American males, particularly because there are so many absent fathers in our community, which makes the need for stable Black men to step in and stand up for those men who have abdicated their responsibilities as fathers and as friends to their children," said the man of faith and family. "Our young men need someone to look to who has *'been there and done that'*. Too many Black males have had to be their own fathers and their own guides, and we wonder why they struggle," Showell demanded. "They are struggling," he speculated, "because they are not getting the same guiding light like I received from my own father. Part of the challenge that Black males face, however, in traversing the vicissitudes of life," Andre elaborated, "is the continued devaluing of Black lives." Each day, as is well known, the ill-fated stories of Black victims and villains alike are splashed across newspapers and television screens with little to no regard for the guilt or innocence of the individual in question, in a media environment permeated by the ethos, "if it bleeds... it leads!" For media professionals like Showell, however, until the day comes when the images we see of African-American males in the United States are truly reflective of the diverse mosaic that is Black manhood, there is yet work to be done.

"Unfortunately, we live in a world where an elephant is one of the most hunted animals living in the wild because its tusks are so valuable," Showell explained. "People will hunt down a lion, for example, and earn a fortune for the kill, because the lion is a prized animal and, regrettably, a commodity throughout the world. In American society," the broadcaster observed, "a lot of people have said the Black men are hunted prey. I believe that it's because people know that we are valuable. And because of that, 'much is required of us'," he asserted. "Because of that, I would encourage Black males everywhere to be ever mindful of the fact that *we are powerful*," Showell explained. "*The Bible* says, '*To whom much is given, much is required*'. A lot of people, when they look at that Scripture, they see it as a call to service. In fact, because we, as Black males in America, have been given gifts and talents and, in many instances, a certain 'standing in society', it is our obligation to reach back, to lift others," he hypothesized.

Today, in spite of the obvious challenges that lie ahead for the countless Black males who will all be viewed through the same narrow prism that he works to counterbalance every day, Andre Showell still believes in the inherent capacity of the indomitable spirit within the African-American community and its ability to rise above the challenges set before them. "You, Black man, have to do your own work if you want to change your own reality. You **have to know** that this society is *not* rooting for you... so root for yourself," Showell concluded. "There is a God who loves and cares for you, and as long as you know who you are, and you know that He is by your side, there is nothing that you can't accomplish. You can start a new tradition. You can change the narrative of what it means to be a Black man... one young Black boy at a time!"

(Andre Showell: Trusted Journalist & Media Influencer)

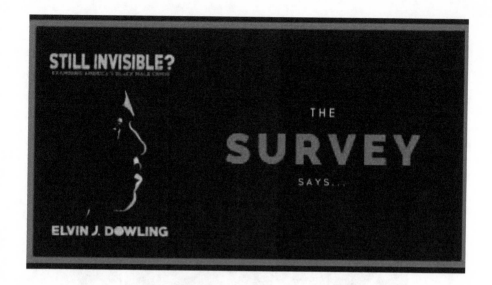

How strongly do you agree or disagree with the following statements?*

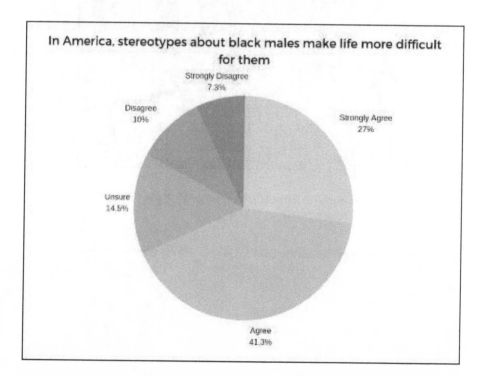

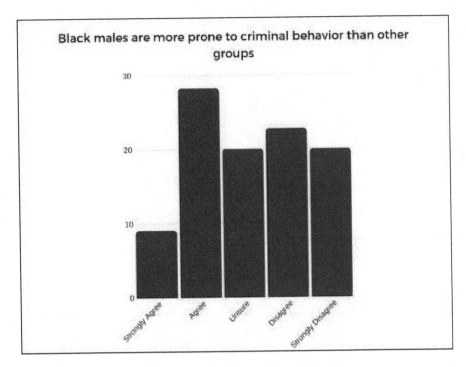

Black males are more prone to criminal behavior than other groups

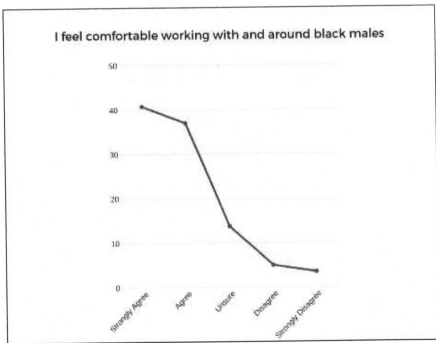

I feel comfortable working with and around black males

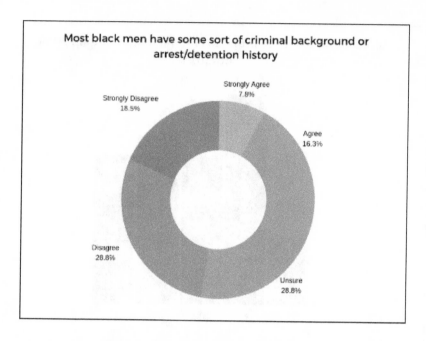

Most black men have some sort of criminal background or arrest/detention history

Strongly Agree
7.8%

Strongly Disagree
18.5%

Agree
16.3%

Disagree
28.8%

Unsure
28.8%

All survey results displayed above are represented by the overall percentage of survey respondents. For more information on our survey methodology, please see the Author's Note, located in the front matter of the book. To review raw survey results, visit: http://bit.ly/stillinvisiblesurvey

THE BATTLE FOR PUBLIC PERCEPTION

Broad Generalizations About African-American Males

DIFFICULT LIVES	**CRIMINAL BEHAVIOR**	**COMFORT LEVEL**	**ARREST HISTORY**
More than 2 out of 3 respondents (68.25%) believe stereotypes make life harder for black males.	42.00% of White male respondents "Strongly Agree or "Agree" that black males tend to be criminals.	Despite stereotypes, more than 3 out of 4 respondents (77.75%) are comfortable interacting with black males.	Nearly 6 out of 10 respondents (57.15%) ages 18-24 believe most black males have been arrested or are unsure.

Findings by Race

- Half of all Asian respondents (55.0%) and almost 9 out of 10 Black respondents (86.54%) "Strongly Agree" or "Agree" with the statement: *"In America, stereotypes about Black males make life more difficult for them."*

- Across all racial demographics, an overwhelming majority of respondents (77.75%) "Strongly Agree" or "Agree" with the statement: *"I feel comfortable working with and around Black males."*

- Nearly one-third of all Black respondents (32.69%) "Strongly Agree" or "Agree" with the statement: *"Most Black men have some sort of criminal background or arrest/detention history."*

Findings by Gender

- 4 out of 10 Black female respondents (40.91%) "Strongly Agree" or "Agree" with the statement: *"Black males are more prone to criminal behavior than other groups."* This percentage is only exceeded by Asian female respondents (75.00%).

- 1 out of 3 Multiracial female respondents (33.34%) "Strongly Disagree" or "Disagree" with the statement: *"In America, stereotypes about Black males make life more difficult for them."*

- More Black male respondents than White male respondents (26.67% vs. 19.00%) "Strongly Agree" or "Agree" with the statement: *"Most Black men have some sort of criminal background or arrest/detention history."*

Findings by Age

- Fewer respondents ages 55 and older (13.33%) "Strongly Agree" or "Agree" with the statement, *"Most Black men have some sort of criminal background or arrest/detention history,"* than do respondents ages 18-24 years old (23.41%).

- Almost half of all White female respondents, ages 35-44 years old (48.65%) "Strongly Agree" or "Agree" with the statement: *"Black males are more prone to criminal behavior than other groups."*

- Nearly 7 out of 10 respondents (65.33%), across all age groups, "Strongly Agree" or "Agree" with the statement: "In America, stereotypes about Black males make life more difficult for them."

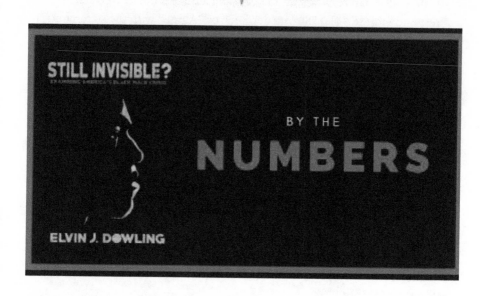

"What They See, They Will Be!"

- Black males are twice as likely as white males to be portrayed as perpetrators and criminals and four times more likely to have their mugshots included in the "lead" story, which often portrays urban America as out of control and Black men as the culprits who are primarily responsible for crime (Creighton. pp. 2-3).

- Crime-related stories accounted for more than 60% of all lead news stories. Black males were the primary story subject in 69% of all crime-related news stories. Research has shown that when Black boys see themselves regularly in the news as lawbreakers, those images may have a negative effect by causing a self-fulfilling prophesy (Creighton. p. 5)

"Black Male? On Track for Jail!"

- Black males are among the most misunderstood and often maligned groups in America. They are often perceived and stereotyped by the five D's: dumb, deprived, dangerous, deviant and disturbed. In every area considered an indication of success, Black males are failing and obviously in peril (Creighton. p. 2).

- Black males are suspended, expelled, placed in special education, drop out of school, unemployed and incarcerated at more disproportionate rates more than any other group in America. In fact, Black males are the only segment of the population in America whose life expectancy is declining (Creighton. p. 2).

"Change the Frame, Change the Game."

- Over-representing certain groups as perpetrators and others as victims of crime often leads to misperceptions based on race and gender and how people are treated in the criminal justice system. Over the last twenty-five years, incarceration rates have tripled despite the fact that crime is leveling, much of it driven by locking up Black men (Creighton. p. 2).

- Researchers have theorized that the perpetrators of criminal activity, who according to what they view during local newscasts, overwhelmingly appear to be African-American males, eventually begin to represent the "evil forces" that must be controlled to maintain social order, resulting in America's mass incarceration problem (Creighton. p. 2).

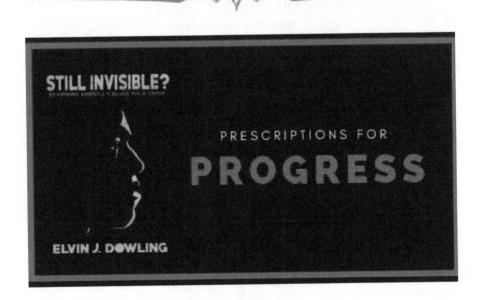

"When 'On Air' ... Please Be Fair!"

- Insist that the news media focus on "full and accurate" portrayals, not "positive" or "negative" coverage. Inaccurate depictions affect African-American males' self-perceptions and lead to diminished self-esteem. Call for coverage of systemic causes of, and solutions to, unequal opportunity for African-American males in all aspects of life. ("Improving Media." p. 1.).

- Emphasize values such as truthfulness, accuracy, impartiality, fairness, and public accountability in the production of news and media content. Distorted portrayals lead to negative attitudes toward Black males, such as increased tolerance for racial disparities.("Improving Media." p. 1.).

"Be Wise ... But Tell No Lies!"

- Lift up systemic causes that tend to set Black men back in society and in life. Explain the role of systems and structures as obstacles to opportunity, thereby helping people see beyond "personal responsibility" and "individual bigotry" as the sole causes of inequality ("Improving Media." p. 2).

- Avoid arguments—as well as metaphors like "leveling the playing field"—that imply competition between ethnic groups. Instead, focus on shared goals and values, and how everyone wins when opportunity is expanded to all citizens, regardless of race, creed or national origin ("Improving Media." pp. 2-3).

"Have No Doubt? Call Them Out!"

- Highlight exemplary coverage while condemning distorted and problematic content that contributes to stereotypical and racist narratives. Be sure to emphasize the need for clear, concrete solutions to help overcome "problem fatigue" and build support for change ("Improving Media." p. 2).

- Principles of integrity, accuracy, impartiality, and fairness are an essential component of professional journalism. When editors, producers, or executives are unresponsive to your concerns, target media advertisers and shareholders on economic and social responsibility grounds. ("Improving Media." pp. 2-3).

Works Cited

1. Shmoop Editorial Team. "Invisible Man Identity Quotes   Page 4." *Shmoop*. Shmoop University, Inc., 11 Nov.   2008. Web. 25 Jul. 2019.

2. Fagan, Bob. "A History of African-American Advertising."   *The One Club*. 4 February 2014. Web.   shorturl.at/ayGLP

3. Robinson, Trevor. "A Brief Rundown of Racism Within Advertising and Why It's Still Happening Today."   *Adweek*. 21 February 2019. shorturl.at/otKLR

4. The Opportunity Agenda. "Improving Media Coverage and   Public Perceptions of African-American Men and   Boys." *Tides Center*. 2013. Web. May 2014.   shorturl.at/QU234

5. The Opportunity Agenda. "Perceptions of and by Black   Men." *Tides Center*. 2017. Web. 18 March 2017.

6. Wing, Nick. "When the Media Treats White Suspects and   Killers Better Than Black Victims." The *Huffington*   *Post*. Web. 6 December 2017. shorturl.at/dnCV3

7. Creighton, Trina, et. al. "Coverage of Black versus White   Males in Local Television News Lead Stories." *Journal*   *of Mass Commun & Journalism*. 2014. 17   September 2014. shortur

8. Glinton, Sonari. "How an African-American Ad Man   Changed the Face of Advertising: An Interview Interview Conducted by   *Morning Edition*. 15 June 2015.   shortur

9. McKenzie, Sheena. "Was an African-American Cop the Lone Ranger?" *CNN.com*. Web. 6 August 2013.

10. Clark, Alexis. "How the History of Blackface is Rooted in Racism." *The History Channel*. Web. 15 February shorturl.at/tGX17

11. Padget, Ken. "Billy Kersands: 1842-1915." *Blackface!*   Web. Accessed 4 September 2019. shorturl.at/cd125

Chapter 5: What's the Difference Between 3/5 and 87%?

The Economic Impact of Devaluing Black Male Labor

"

I am not ashamed of my grandparents for having been slaves. I am only ashamed of myself for having at one time been ashamed."

- Ralph Ellison, "Invisible Man" (Shmoop Editorial Team. 1.2.)

(The illustration above, entitled "Am I Not a Man and a Brother?", was placed atop the publication of John Whittier Greenleaf's poem, "Our Countrymen in Chains." The image was originally adopted as the seal of the Society for the Abolition of Slavery in England in the 1780's.)

The Check Is in the Mail ...

"You Believe Me, Don't You?"

In 1787, at the close of the *Constitutional Convention*, Benjamin Franklin, one of America's Founding Fathers was reportedly approached and asked a fateful question. Dr. James McHenry of the Maryland delegation, who said: *"Well, Doctor, what have we got? A Republic or a Monarchy?"* And without skipping a beat, Benjamin Franklin replied: *"A Republic, if you can keep it!"* Since that time, the greatest historical challenge the United States of America has grappled with is what to do with its enslaved population, and in doing so, has called the very definition of "democracy" into question when it comes to African-Americans.

The "Three-Fifths Compromise" came about four years before the ratification of the constitution, and emerged as a point of contention between delegates from the North and the South. First, and most importantly, it goes without saying that the entire debate was essentially about money. Isn't that the genesis of all things important in America? At any rate, you see the problem began when the various delegates to the *Constitutional Convention* realized rather quickly that the only way to effectively sustain this new nation was through the generation of taxes which, of course, would be assessed based on population and land values. To create loopholes to this requirement, many of the states would consistently undervalue their land, with the goal of reducing their tax burden. Sound familiar? As a result of this "conundrum" of sorts, those states with large populations of enslaved Africans weren't too keen on cutting into their profits and, as such, our nation's little problem with how we would recognize *"the help"* would soon commence. Ultimately, after multiple attempts to quantify an entire "invisible population," James Madison came up with an idea that would forever be ensconced on America's founding document... and thus "The Three-Fifths Compromise" was born. In short, it would take five great slaves to equal three good white people. Confused? You do the math! Even today, more than 230 years since the founding of our experiment in democracy, African-Americans still aren't considered equal in most measurable areas of American life, especially in their paychecks. "What do I mean", you ask? Well... darling let me tell you...

For starters, Black men are paid $0.87 for every dollar a white male is paid for the same work. That means that the earnings potential for Black male labor, if we consider the whole 3/5 thing, has gone from 60 cents on the dollar to 87 cents on the dollar in 230 years. That's an annual pay increase of $0.011739130473483, not counting inflation—of course. At that rate, it's going to take Black males another 152 years before they reach pay equity in the America. Fortunately for the rest of us ... we've got time.

So, if you're looking for a response to the question, *"What's the Difference Between 3/5 and 87%,"* the answer is simple—Not very much! But we're making progress! Aren't we?

Be Best,

Justitia

Lady Justice

Kelvin Boston: "Always Prepared for Rainy Days!"

Why Are Family Ties So Expensive?

"My name Is Kelvin Boston and I produce the *Moneywise* public television series," said the reserved global economist known throughout the world for his prescient economic forecasts. A financial strategist that has helped to boost the nest-eggs of countless individuals and families seeking true economic independence, Boston is matter-of-fact baby boomer who has served as a trusted source on financial matters since he began his career as a financial planner in 1980. An astute money maven who first came into the collective national consciousness in 1996 as the host of *The Color of Money* on the cable television network *Knowledge TV*, Boston is a journalist, author, entrepreneur and leading example of what many would describe as someone who has achieved the American Dream.

"The reason why we created the *Moneywise* television program, and tour the country encouraging smart money moves and expanding entrepreneurship, is because there's a lot of economic pain, fear and anxiety out there in America," Boston said, reflecting upon what he believes is his life's passion and purpose, ever mindful of the vulnerable population he serves. "There is an economic wealth gap in this society that continues to persist, and we must also understand that, while real wage [earnings adjusted for inflation or, equivalently, wages earned in context with the goods and services that can be bought with those earnings] is increasing for some white households, earnings aren't going up for everybody else. And that's not good. Meanwhile, African-American households have to go into more debt to recover after each market crash," Boston warned, understanding full well the implications of the harsh realities of economic hardship for depressed populations.

In her analysis entitled, "Whites Get Wealthier, While Blacks and Hispanics Lag Behind," Tami Luhby, a senior writer for *CNN Business* who has covered areas of personal finance and economic mobility, further underscored Boston's belief that the wealth gap in America has stark fiscal fault lines and clear racial implications. "Whites have 13 times the net worth of Blacks, the largest wealth gap that's existed since George H.W. Bush was president in 1989," Luhby found. "The ratio of net worth between whites and Hispanics now stands at more than 10, the widest it has been since 2001. Real estate, on the other hand, makes up a big chunk of Blacks' and Hispanics' net worth," she observed. "But homeownership declined faster among minorities than whites...Only 47.4% of minorities were homeowners... But 73.9% of whites owned homes" (Luhby). And it's exactly for those reasons that Boston is sounding the alarm.

It has often been said that America is a land of unlimited opportunity for those seeking to improve their lot in life, particularly for those who "work hard and play by the rules." In theory, the idea of the United States being a meritocracy that affords anyone with the willingness to take a chance and the gumption to succeed, is a powerful notion that has persisted since the nation's inception. In reality, however, the ability to move onward and upward in life is oftentimes determined at birth. According to Matt O'Brien, an economic policy writer for *The Washington Post*, the gaps that exist between those who have and those who have not are rooted in the use of language and vocabulary as an early advantage to possible advancement. In a study that demonstrated how inequality often begins at birth and almost never ends. "Affluent parents talk to their kids three more hours a week on average than poor parents, which is critical during a child's formative early years," O'Brien noted. "That's why, as *Stanford* professor Sean Reardon explains, "rich students are increasingly entering kindergarten much better prepared to succeed in school than middle-class students," and they're staying that way" (O'Brien). While this may seem to be a subtle distinction, it is one with a difference, particularly if communal expectations are already diminished. But that's not where the advantages for those born wealthy end.

"Even poor kids who do everything right don't do much better than rich kids who do everything wrong. Specifically, rich high school dropouts remain in the top about as much as poor college grads stay stuck in the bottom — 14 versus 16 percent, respectively. Not only that, but these low-income strivers are just as likely to end up in the bottom as these wealthy ne'er-do-wells." (O'Brien). In fact, another advantage that the well-heeled have that the scions of the poor do not--a family inheritance. "Rich kids who can go work for the family business — and, in Canada at least, 70 percent of the sons of the top 1 percent do just that — or inherit the family estate don't need a high school diploma to get ahead. It's an extreme example of what many economists call "opportunity hoarding." That includes everything from legacy college admissions to unpaid internships that let affluent parents rig the game a little more in their children's favor.

In an analysis for *The Atlantic* titled, "Her Only Crime Was Helping Her Kids", writer Annie Lowery shared the very personal stories that demonstrated the depths of a mother's love, when she wrote of the stark contrasts in the American criminal justice system, meted out to two women: one white, one Black. Same crime; different outcomes. In her piece, Lowery wrote of how one mother, an internationally acclaimed actress, and another seemingly desperate mother, much less well known (of course), both of whom were similarly accused of rigging the American education system to give their child a perceived advantage, but that's where the similarities end. Huffman, when caught in what would become known as the "College Admissions Scandal" for paying to have her child admitted, through a "back door" (of sorts) into the university of her preference, plead guilty to cheating the system and rigging the college admissions process, was sentenced to 14 days in jail--to which she promptly protested.

On the converse, there is Kelly Williams Bolar, another mother similarly accused of breaking the law to give her child a better education. But that's where the similarities end. "One is a story of a family having everything and wanting more, exemplifying the opportunity-hoarding of America's often-unaccountable 1 percenters. The other is a story of a family working with what they had, seeking opportunity amid the deep forces of segregation, wealth inequality, and public underinvestment "(Lowery). As a result of her decision, Williams Bolar ended up in jail, suffered from severe depression and ultimately lost her father while incarcerated, the one individual who had assisted her in getting her children into a better funded school district by lending her his address. "She was never the same after that trauma," Williams Bolar told Lowery. "She spent years and years struggling with depression, shame, and regret... Her girls ended up back in the struggling Akron schools." The distinction between these two cases is important because, regardless of the race of the defendant, the one thing they both had in common was the innate desire to have what was best for their children. Yet, at every turn, that goal is made increasingly difficult to achieve for the "have nots" who are almost always invariably individuals of color, especially those born into dire circumstances.

"Rich families have the option of pulling their kids out of public schools and putting them in private or parochial ones, as well as the option of moving to a better district," observed Lowery. "Rich families have the option of coaching their kids through standardized tests, and helping ensure they get into gifted and talented programs and specialized schools. Rich families have the resources to investigate what different public schools offer, and to game lottery and ranked-choice enrollment systems," she continued. "Rich families sometimes skirt the law, too — cheating on standardized tests, making up their kids' athletic accomplishments, paying bribes" (Lowery). And when those children of privilege get older, they have the benefit of parental connections, questionable contributions and undue influence on the part of their parents and their parent's network of friends, relationships and contacts.

Poor families, on the other hand, have far fewer options—leaving many of them with illegal options such as boundary-hopping, to help give their children an opportunity outside of the often-failing public school system to which they are assigned, simply because they have the unfortunate circumstance of living in a school district that is over-policed, underfunded and often in need of reform. "Given that low-income families often have unstable housing situations and use intergenerational child-care structures, what might seem like enrollment fraud to a school district might feel like nothing more than school choice to a parent" (Lowery). Having hailed from a tight-knit but struggling community that helped to shape his earliest experiences, Kelvin Boston can speak to the experience of economic hardship and living in public housing without the benefit of his father in the home, and no choice about what school he would attend as a child, having overcome those obstacles with the help of others, when family simply wasn't enough to get him through.

"I knew my father, but he wasn't in the household. I did, however, get a chance to spend some time with him and get to know him better later on in my life, but I didn't grow up seeing him at home every day," said Boston, the bow-tie clad, always nattily attired television host; underscoring the fact that, even with his father's daily absence, there was an effort on the part of both parent and child to make the most of their relationship. Even still, the impact faced by fatherless young men, regardless of their race, is something that makes it that much more difficult for that child, particularly if they are Black, from ever achieving economic self-sufficiency. First, and most importantly, there are the governmental impacts of policy and practice that often undermine the institution of the Black family. More often than not, this is done through unnecessary intrusion into the affairs of Black families and a paternalistic approach to social services that often breeds mistrust and creates continued economic anxiety. Furthermore, in keeping the family inexorably dependent upon and accountable to the state, also has the indelible effect of creating a permanent underclass that is struggling to survive on the margins of American society even today.

Then Assistant Secretary for the *United States Department of Labor* during the presidential administration of Lyndon Baines Johnson, the Honorable Daniel Patrick Moynihan, who would go on to become a long-term Democratic Senator from New York, in his infamous report on the American welfare state and it's practical implications on Black families called, "The Negro Family: The Case for National Action," spoke of the challenges facing Black America, from the government's perspective, and what the nation's best bureaucrats could do to fix them. Unsurprisingly, his book would go on to become one of the most controversial public works of the twentieth century. Published in 1965, the publicly funded project went on to note a number of issues that the government believed contributed to setting Black men behind.

In his oft-quoted missive about the plight of Blacks in America, Moynihan, who would also go on to serve as a *Harvard University* professor and U.S. presidential advisor, brought to light a number of systemic challenges that Black families face which keep them from transitioning into permanent economic self-sufficiency. In his analysis of the efficacy of Moynihan's missive at the 50th anniversary of its release, author Daniel Geary of *The Atlantic*, found that the report, while controversial, was, nonetheless, prescient in many of its unfortunate findings. "The Moynihan Report is a historical artifact best understood in the context of its time. Yet it remains relevant today amidst current discussion of why racial inequality persists despite the passage of civil-rights legislation. Even those who do not see the report's analysis as pertinent to the present can learn how it shaped contemporary discourse. Fifty years later, "The Moynihan Report" is still a contested symbol among American thinkers and policymakers, cited by everyone from Barack Obama to Paul Ryan" ("The Moynihan Report"). Some of its findings exposed the following challenges visited upon Black families in 1965:

- Approximately 25% of Black families are headed by women, with no man at home ("The Moynihan Report").

- The divorce rate is about 2 1/2 times what it was, as compared with whites at the time ("The Moynihan Report").

- The number of fatherless children keeps growing. And all these things keep getting worse, not better, over recent years" ("The Moynihan Report").

At the time of his report, Moynihan went on to note that the institution of the Black family itself is irreparably harmed when the head of the household is not present. Moreover, the assistant secretary noted that, at the time, it was estimated that most Black children would reach the age of majority, having not been raised in a home with both parents. "Once again, this measure of family disorganization is found to be diminishing among white families and increasing among Negro families," the Moynihan Report noted, further emphasizing the seismic impact that fatherless families have on the futures of the children they produce. "The Negro situation is commonly perceived by whites in terms of the visible manifestation of discrimination and poverty, in part because Negro protest is directed against such obstacles, and in part, no doubt, because these are facts which involve the actions and attitudes of the white community as well" Moynihan noted. "It is more difficult, however, for whites to perceive the effect that three centuries of exploitation have had on the fabric of Negro society itself. Here the consequences of the historic injustices done to Negro Americans are silent and hidden from view." With that being said, however, the report's focus on the diminution of the nuclear Black family as _the_ reason for all the ills plaguing the community are, at best, overly simplistic and may be, as many have suggested, an idea whose time has passed. "Some believe liberal backlash against the report has had a chilling effect on research that focused on so-called "cultural pathologies"—versus structural issues—for problems faced by African Americans" ("The Moynihan Report").

First the Degree... Then the Money?

Be that as it may, however, like other individuals who were born poor and forced to grow up with limited resources, Kelvin is ever mindful of the obstacles he has had to overcome to get to where he is today. "I grew up in public housing in Wilmington, Delaware," Boston recollects, "and it was definitely segregated--100%! And what I remember most were the economic differences between what my family had or--more importantly--didn't have, versus what other people had, especially when I went outside the projects I lived in and saw the opportunities that others had and were given," states Boston. "My mother was a good provider and, although she only had a sixth grade education, she made it clear to me from day one that I would go to college, even before I knew what college was," remembers the future sage of sound financial planning, "she always made it clear that I would go to college, not that I knew what it was at the time, but for me it was an expectation," he intones. "I tried to study and I wasn't the best student, but I was good enough to get accepted into *Lincoln University* where I found out that I wasn't that good at all," he laughs while simultaneously evoking the challenges and opportunities he faced while matriculating through the nation's second oldest *Historically Black College or University (HBCU)*. "But once I got there, I had a great amount of experiences that transformed me," Boston notes.

Initially founded as a private university in 1854, the historic *Lincoln University*, located approximately thirty-one miles from Boston's hometown, in Oxford, Pennsylvania, is known for its programs in social work, human services and teacher education and became a haven for Kelvin and other students seeking to remake their very existence through higher education and its supposed guarantee of a financial future, regardless of race, creed or culture in America. The first institution of higher learning for free Blacks in America, *Cheney University*, also located in the state of Pennsylvania, was founded a quarter-century before Abraham Lincoln issued his Emancipation Proclamation; with its aim of freeing slaves in America, under states that he no longer controlled, was established with the goal of empowering African-Americans and other individuals of color to enter the social and economic mainstream of the country as quickly as possible. Today, however, nearly 160 years since Honest Abe's exercise of executive power, and nearly sixty years since Martin Luther King, Jr.'s s dream speech in Washington, DC, the economic fates of Black men and their families has been, in many ways, intentionally stymied by institutional disadvantage that sets them back before the race even begins.

"For many years now, my television show has been focused on providing financial information to help people cope with their lives and to develop financial illiteracy, so we spend a lot of time talking about wealth building and trying to coach them to close the economic racial wealth gap, which is why our target audience are primarily people of color," Boston notes proudly, pleased with his ability to provide timely and sound financial advice to untold numbers of individuals and families who may otherwise not have access to sound financial education and advice. "We have an African-American church tour that goes around the country, providing information person and specifically to underserved communities," Boston notes, underscoring his continued commitment to the economic empowerment for communities of color. "We have to look at the very serious economic issues facing the Black community, and go back to focusing on entrepreneurship, or the lack thereof, as well as a lack of jobs, the low rates of home ownership and the need to build wealth," he believes.

With that being said, however, Boston believes that the younger generation of African-American males, many of whom come from similar economic circumstances, aren't striving to reach their full potential. "Black people in America must _want to do better_, as we _aspire to do better_. It's never been easy for us, but I'm finding it challenging when dealing with some of the younger African-Americans who, like some of their white counterparts, feel as if they're entitled to things, even if they've not done the work," Boston laments. "Even if they dropped out of college or high school, even if they did not pursue a career, even if they ended up in the penal system, some of them feel as if they are still owed something. And there's a disconnect when people expect things that they should have to work to earn," the economist denotes, standing firm on the conviction that work and entrepreneurship are essential components for those who seek to rise above difficult circumstances. "Today it seems like, to some, especially younger people who don't really understand their heritage and why it's important for those of us struggling to push the Black community forward, that being best person in the room, regardless of their situation, is asking too much of them." But even when those same young men follow the traditional model of seeking higher education and successfully integrating into American society as a productive, taxpaying citizens, there are still hills to climb before they reach the land of pay equity.

In today's America, a Black man with a post-secondary degree still has less of an opportunity for employment than a white man with a high school diploma. According to _The Washington Post,_ in a report examining the nation's disturbing double standard when it comes to Black men in the job market, Jonnelle Marte authored an analysis that helped to bring into greater focus the impact of the racial wage gap in America. "A Black man with an associate's degree has the same chances -- about 88 percent-- of finding a job as a white high school graduate, according to a recent analysis of employment rates and education for whites and minorities by *Young Invincibles*, a nonprofit group focusing on the economic issues impacting millennials," Marte wrote in the economic policy piece. "Getting a bachelor's degree ups those chances to 93 percent for a Black man, the same as a white man who dropped out of college. The report showed that even after African-Americans find work, they earn less than white men with the same level of education. They are also more likely to get part-time jobs than white men in the same age range" (Marte). In fact, in 2003, a study published in the *American Journal of Sociology* found that African-American candidates applying for entry-level jobs in Milwaukee, for example, were less likely to be called back for an interview than white candidates with criminal records. So, what should Black men do to gain their footing in the area of economic self-sufficiency if the avenues for advancement are barricaded from those who need access the most? For Kelvin Boston, the answer lies in expanding entrepreneurship and access to capital so that Black men can begin amassing generational wealth.

"Corporate America will never create enough jobs to put all Americans back to work, there's just not the capacity to do it, and therefore, if we want to see long-term, low unemployment in Black communities, we have to support Black entrepreneurs," intones Boston. "That's why it's so important, we need to have jobs in our communities, so we can hire people, which is why entrepreneurship is key," he continued. "In fact, I believe that every Black family must own a business! There's no such thing as a guaranteed job in America, and for those people who are going to find it difficult to even get into Corporate America, they are going to need a place they can come to for employment opportunities and to be hired by people that look like them," Boston declared. "But just having a business by itself will not make you wealthy if you don't save or invest... and that's the next conversation that our community needs to have," he noted.

Despite the current political and economic climate, African- Americans have a long and storied history of business creation. According to Tiffany Howard of the *Congressional Black Caucus Foundation's Center for Policy Analysis and*

Research in her report on Black entrepreneurship, a long history of cooperative economics exists within the African diaspora. "Within two decades of abolition, Blacks established several thousand successful businesses that thrived in exclusively African-American communities. However, the escalation of racial tensions and *Jim Crow* laws made these businesses vulnerable to targeting and destruction," Howard contextualized. A leading historical example of the targeting of successful Black business, and in this particular instance, an entire community, lays in the fire-bombing and wholesale destruction of what was then known as "Black Wall Street." A self-contained beehive of economic activity, Tulsa, Oklahoma's African-American neighborhood, with Greenwood Avenue serving as its business hub, "Black Wall Street" was a thriving enclave of shopkeepers, wealthy landowners who, despite their best efforts, couldn't defeat the scourge of racism and violence that befell their community in Spring of 1921.

In their chronicling of what would become known as the "Tulsa Race Riots", the *Official Black Wall Street* website memorializes all that was lost in the domestic terrorist attack launched against successful Black entrepreneurs and their families. "June 1st will forever be remembered as a day of great loss and devastation. It was on this day that America experienced the deadliest race riot in the small town of Tulsa, Oklahoma," the organization observed. A century since America's wealthiest minority neighborhood--at the time--was destroyed, the area is still recognized as a bulwark Black success. "With hundreds of successful Black-owned businesses lining Greenwood Avenue, it became a standard that African- Americans are still trying to rebuild. The attack that took place in 1921 tore the community apart, claiming hundreds of lives and sending the once prosperous neighborhood up in smoke" ("Black Wall Street").

As a result of the attack that decimated the hopes and dreams of an entire community that has yet to fully recover, the national rates of Black entrepreneurship have declined since then, beginning a descent that began more than seven decades ago and has continued unabated. "Black business ownership remained stagnant for several decades before re-surging again in the early 1980s, and while growth has been slow, Black business ownership has continued its upward trajectory ever since." (Howard. p. 7). Today, however, the challenges that African-American entrepreneurs are having, has less to do with the eminent threat of vicious mobs, and more to do with the continued lack of the resources needed to effectively launch their businesses —while supporting themselves in the interim. "Research has demonstrated that when compared to other minority business owners, Black entrepreneurs are at a social capital disadvantage," (Howard. p. 7). And therein lies the rub. Yet for eternal optimists like Kelvin Boston, economic liberation is still possible for a people who have been on the "short end of the stick" for centuries; but only if they are willing to flex their collective purchasing power to demand change.

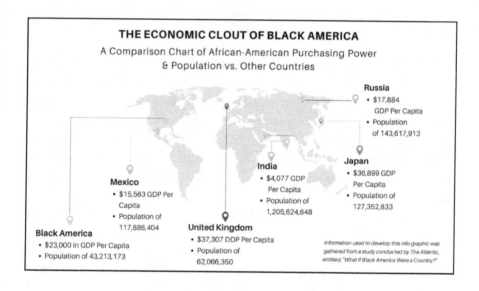

THE ECONOMIC CLOUT OF BLACK AMERICA
A Comparison Chart of African-American Purchasing Power & Population vs. Other Countries

Russia
• $17,884 GDP Per Capita
• Population of 143,617,913

Mexico
• $15,563 GDP Per Capita
• Population of 117,886,404

India
• $4,077 GDP Per Capita
• Population of 1,205,624,648

Japan
• $36,899 GDP Per Capita
• Population of 127,352,833

Black America
• $23,000 in GDP Per Capita
• Population of 43,213,173

United Kingdom
• $37,307 DDP Per Capita
• Population of 62,066,350

Information used to develop this info-graphic was gathered from a study conducted by The Atlantic, entitled, "What If Black America Were a Country?"

How Much Do Black Dollars Matter?

With $1.2 trillion dollars in annual purchasing power, the collective economic clout of the Black community is greater than the Gross Domestic Product (GDP) of Russia, Mexico and India and just behind the United Arab Emirates. Even still, the financial prospects of African-Americans is one that is precarious, at best, and reminiscent of the experiences of those living in fledgling democracies, autocratic governments and dictatorial regimes. According to Theodore R. Johnson of *The Atlantic*, African-Americans, despite the enormous capital they possess, are oftentimes exploited for their resources and their labor has historically been equitably compensated in the marketplace. "[Black America] is a troubled, fragile state suffering from socioeconomic disparities and structural subjugation in ways that degrade life, liberty and the pursuit of happiness (on some measures Black America resembles countries like Brazil, China and Russia--emerging powers that are struggling with stark economic inequality)" (Johnson). Despite the historical obstacles they continue to face, however, Black America's ability to move markets, indelibly impact economies and shape cultural and public opinion is something that is difficult to ignore, even when Corporate America pretends they don't exist.

The Nielsen Company, an international data analytics firm that provides information and insights on consumers and markets worldwide, in their article, "Black Impact", about the ability of Black buyers to move consumer markets, found that African-Americans are making considerable contributions to the marketplace. "Black consumers and consumers of color alike are making considerable contributions to the overall market—in some cases representing more than 50% of the overall spending in key product categories. For example, half of the total spend ($941 million) on dry grains and vegetables in the U.S. in 2017 came from consumers of color ("Black Impact"). Just as importantly, African-American consumer choices are often the tipping point for overall acceptance in the marketplace. In measuring consumer trends within the Black community, *The Nielsen Company* found a measurable impact that could not be ignored.

"Our research shows that Black consumer choices have a 'cool factor' that has created a halo effect, influencing not just consumers of color but the mainstream as well," said Cheryl Grace, Senior Vice President of U.S. Strategic Community Alliances and Consumer Engagement. "These figures show that investment by multinational conglomerates in R&D to develop products and marketing that appeal to diverse consumers is, indeed, paying off handsomely," the *Nielsen* executive continued. "Again, with $1.2 trillion in spending power, African-American consumers are an important population for smart brands that want to grow market share and brand preference. More importantly," Grace continued, "the data suggests that Black consumer spending already significantly affects the bottom line in many categories and industries, and brands can't afford to lose favor or traction with this segment without potential negative impact" ("Black Impact"). Today, the African-American market makes up a sizable majority of the revenues earned in a number of consumer goods categories, which further demonstrates the collective community's capacity to build economic. So why isn't more Black wealth being created? Kelvin Boston believes he knows the answer to that problem and, more importantly, what we can do to fix it.

"The United States of America has gone through a period of the worst economic downturn in the history of our country since the *Great Depression*, and African-Americans have taken the biggest hit you can possibly take during this period," reflected Boston, wondering if it would ever end. "In many ways, we're still going through it. And the only thing, in my opinion, that kept us from really exploding under the weight of it all, was seeing a Black man in the White House. But we also saw how people treated this President. He got treated like he was invisible *every day*! So, for many of us, watching Obama endure what he did on a daily basis, made us see what we were experiencing as no big thing," the economist surmised. "I remember reading "*Invisible Man*" when I was at *Lincoln University* and it impacted me greatly, realizing how African-Americans were not seen or recognized in greater society," Boston said. "But, in many ways, we all *still* feel invisible. We *still* feel slighted. We *still* feel like we are undervalued for what we do... whether it's in Corporate America or entrepreneurship. Be that as it may, we must always insist upon showing the value of our word and our work, rather than letting others define it for us," Boston noted.

"Now when it comes down to being invisible in areas of personal finance," Kelvin Boston continued, "you have to look at the medical epidemics that flow through a society, and how that impacts and shortchanges generational wealth building. African-American mortality rates from diseases such as Alzheimer's, diabetes, obesity, heart disease is through the roof, and all of which have a financially devastating impact upon the Black family, and *still* no one's talking about it," the financial journalist lamented. "It's an invisible issue to many, but we have to deal with it. It's hard for us to talk about helping a race increase their wealth without also talking about issues impacting longevity," he said. "And so, we see that direct relationship between health and wealth, therefore we have to talk about and develop a strategy to deal with all those things."

In an ominous foreboding about the economy of the future, Boston spoke vociferously of the need for Black America to change its spending habits, shift its focus to entrepreneurship and individual business ownership and prepare for the jobs of the future. "What I'm most concerned about today, is the current state of Black Economics. We only have about 10 or 20 years or so to make some serious changes in how we manage our money and build wealth, the economist warned, hoping to head off the makings of a permanent underclass of people living on the margins of society in America. "If the Black community doesn't do something different, starting now, Boston emphasized, "we will be left to depend on *Social Security* and food stamps to survive. We have to consider what are we going to do differently, because America is going to keep moving forward, whether we move forward or not." Understanding that continued economic instability is a recipe for future financial ruin, Boston still believes that intestinal fortitude is necessary, that—and help from a Higher source—to lift Black America out of the economic malaise in which it has been mired in for centuries.

"If I could give Black males of all ages one piece of advice, it would be to stay spiritually grounded and to understand where your power and success comes from. Oftentimes, what you deem to be 'success' is not all its chalked up to be," Boston continued. "We are not necessarily human beings having a spiritual experience, more than we are spiritual beings having a human experience. Life is a wonderful thing, but it's not an easy thing to go through," the financial forecaster surmised. "So—to me—it's important that Black men everywhere have a truly spiritual understanding of *where* they are *going to* (when this life is over), and *where* their prosperity is *coming from*, while they are alive on this earth."

(Kelvin Boston: Economic Expert & Financial Advisor)

How strongly do you agree or disagree with the following statements?*

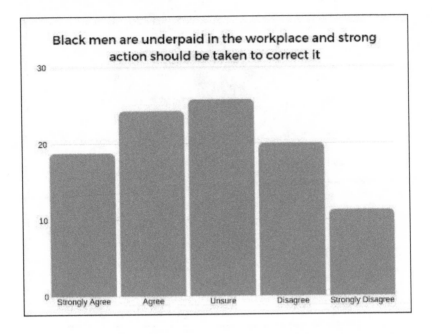

Black men are underpaid in the workplace and strong action should be taken to correct it

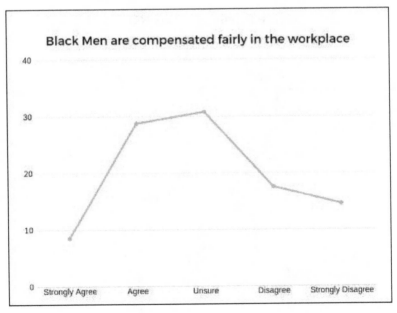

Black Men are compensated fairly in the workplace

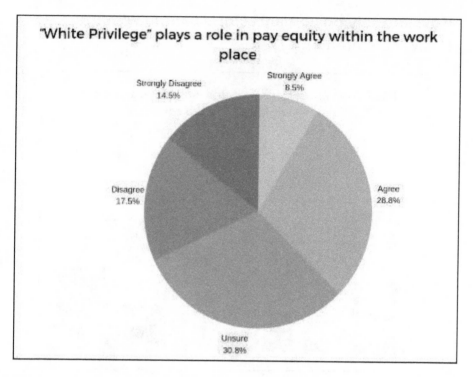

"White Privilege" plays a role in pay equity within the work place

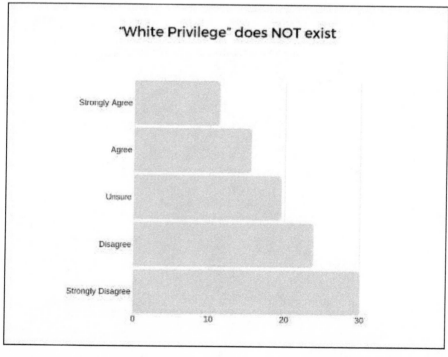

"White Privilege" does NOT exist

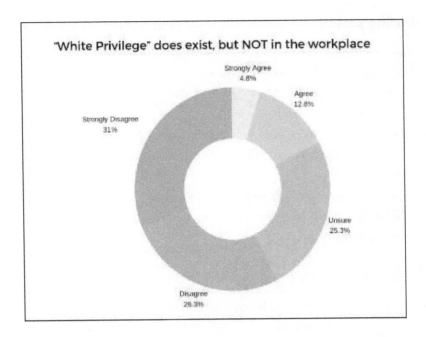

"White Privilege" does exist, but NOT in the workplace

Strongly Agree
4.8%

Agree
12.8%

Strongly Disagree
31%

Unsure
25.3%

Disagree
26.3%

All survey results displayed above are represented by the overall percentage of survey respondents. For more information on our survey methodology, please see the Author's Note, located in the front matter of the book. To review raw survey results, visit: http://bit.ly/stillinvisiblesurvey

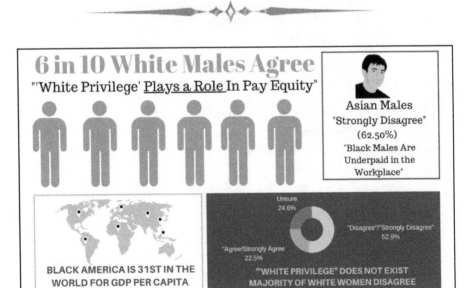

6 in 10 White Males Agree
"'White Privilege' Plays a Role In Pay Equity"

Asian Males
"Strongly Disagree"
(62.50%)
"Black Males Are
Underpaid in the
Workplace"

BLACK AMERICA IS 31ST IN THE
WORLD FOR GDP PER CAPITA

Unsure
24.6%

"Disagree"/"Strongly Disagree"
52.9%

"Agree/Strongly Agree
22.5%

"'WHITE PRIVILEGE" DOES NOT EXIST
MAJORITY OF WHITE WOMEN DISAGREE

Findings by Race

- More Hispanic respondents of all ages "Disagree or Strongly Disagree" (37.00%) with the statement, *"Black men are underpaid in the workplace and strong action should be taken to correct it"*, than those who "Agree" or "Strongly Agree" (30.0%).

- 2 out of every 3 Black male respondents (66.67%) "Strongly Disagree" or "Agree" with the statement *"Black Men are compensated fairly in the workplace."*

- Nearly 6 out of 10 White male respondents (57.15%), ages 18-24 years old, "Strongly Agreed" or "Agreed with the statement, *"White Privilege" plays a role in pay equity within the work place."*

Findings by Gender

- One-third of all White male respondents (34.00%) "Agree" or "Strongly Agree" with the statement, *""White Privilege" does NOT exist."*

- More than half of all White female respondents (53.57%) "Strongly Disagree" or "Disagree" with the statement, *""White Privilege" does exist, but NOT in the workplace."*

- More than any other group, regardless of race or gender, Asian male respondents of all ages (62.50%) "Strongly Disagree" or "Disagree" with the statement, *"Black men are underpaid in the workplace and strong action should be taken to correct it."*

Findings by Age

- Eight times more White female respondents, ages 18-24 years old, "Disagree" or "Strongly Disagree" (57.14%) with the statement, *"Black Men are compensated fairly in the workplace,"* than those who "Agree" or "Strongly Agree" (7.14%).

- More than 7 out of 10 Black female respondents (72.72%), ages 25-34 years old, "Agree" or "Strongly Agree" with the statement, *""White Privilege" plays a role in pay equity within the work place."*

- 2 out of 3 Asian female respondents (66.67%), regardless of age, "Disagree" or "Strongly Disagree" with the statement, *""White Privilege" does NOT exist."*

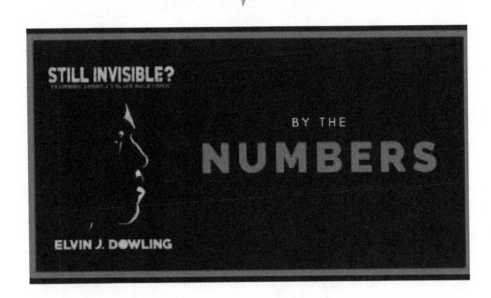

"Chances Are Better—With Families Together!"

- The disproportionate rate of African-American children under 18 years, old living in single parent homes headed by women has INCREASED more than fifty-percent to 38.7% in 2019, since the release of "The Moynihan Report" more than 50 years ago; leading to continued economic instability for the Black family ("Single Mothers").

- 1 out of 3 African-American kids under age 18 live with unmarried mothers—nearly five times the rates of white kids. Social scientists have long argued the financial, academic, physical and emotional benefits of growing up in a two parent home benefits for children who live in two-parent homes ("Single Mothers").

"Honest Day's Work? Honest Day's Pay!"

- Between 1966 and 2013, overall Black participation in the American workforce increased from 8.2 percent to 14 percent, even though they make up only 13% of the nation's population. Despite the gains in employment, the Gross Domestic Product for Blacks is $23,000, compared with the national median of $51,017 ("American Workforce").

- African-American men have the largest pay gap compared to white men, earning $0.87 for every dollar a white man earns. Hispanics have the next largest pay gap, earning $0.91 for every dollar earned by a white man, and Asian men tend to earn the most of all, by comparison, earning $1.15 for every dollar a white man makes (Gruver).

"Black America: "Long Money" ... Meet Longsuffering!"

- If Black America were its own country, it would be ranked 46th in the world —between crisis-hit Portugal and post-Communist Lithuania. What's even worse is the fact that the average Black household has just 6 percent of the total wealth ($7,113) of the average white household ($111,146) (Bremmer).

- Black consumers have an outsized influence over spending on essential items such as personal soap and bath needs ($573 million), feminine hygiene products ($54 million), men's toiletries ($61 million), bottled water ($810 million--15% of total spending) and $587 million on refrigerated drinks (17% of overall spending) ("Black Impact").

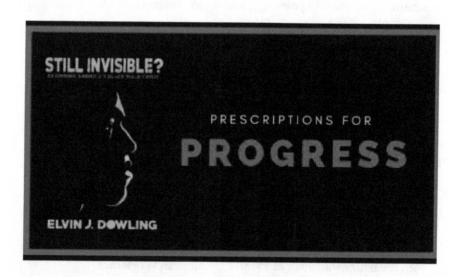

"You Sweat Less ... When You're Debtless!"

- African Americans are significantly more likely to have some type of debt (94%) compared to the general population (82%). As such, credit card, student loan and personal debt are all significantly higher in the Black community, regardless of education or income level ("Financial Experience." p. 13).

- Debt exacts an emotional toll on the bearer as well as an economic one. 1 out of 4 Black Americans have reported that they have experienced some level of depression and/or anxiety that they relate to financial stressors; over 1 in 10 have experienced relationship conflict (14%) or low self-esteem (12%) due to debt ("Financial Experience." p. 13).

"Trust Is _Always_ A Two-Way Street!"

- African-Americans give low marks to most sources of financial information. Although financial services providers and parents fare the best, there is still a level of distrust that lingers. As such, the financial services industry has a unique opportunity to better engage the Black community through community-based activities. ("Financial Experience." p. 15).

- Due to a history of mistrust with American financial institutions, Blacks are much more likely to choose credit unions and financial seminars as key sources of information. Just as importantly, churches are significantly more important sources for trusted information amongst the Black community ("Financial Experience." p. 13).

"Money Makes the World Go Around!"

- Blacks are less likely to own mutual funds, stocks and bonds. Savings accounts are by far the most commonly held, followed by retirement plans, then life insurance. By facilitating greater access to financial advisors, the Black family's financial diversity is strengthened and greater wealth can accumulate ("Financial Experience." p. 16).

- The number of Black small business owners in the United States has increased by a staggering 400% in the last few years, driven largely by a desire of the business owner's to "pursue their passion." Fairly accessing capital to grow their business remains elusive, thus necessitating transparency and accountability amongst lenders (Pickard-Whitehead).

Works Cited

1. Luhby, Tami. "Whites Get Wealthier, While Blacks and Hispanics Lag Further Behind." *CNN Business*. 15 December 2014. https://cnn.it/2kZNOE4

2. Geary, Daniel. "The Moynihan Report: An Annotated Edition: A Historian Unpacks the Negro Family: The Case for National Action on its 50th Anniversary", *The Atlantic*. Web. 14 September 2015. http://bit.ly/2m24afw

3. O'Brien, Matt. "Poor Kids Who Do Everything Right Don't Do Better Than Rich Kids Who Do Everything Wrong." *The Washington Post*. 18 October 2014. https://wapo.st/2lHWmQg

4. Lowery, Annie. "Her Only Crime Was Helping Her Kids: Kelley Williams-Bolar, Like Felicity Huffman, Was Punished for Trying to Get Her Children a Better Education." *The Atlantic*. 13 September 2019. http://bit.ly/2lMbI6b

5. Marte, Jonnelle. "The Economy's Troubling Double Standard for Black Men." *The Washington Post*. 2 July 20 https://wapo.st/2mLFXdJ

6. Howard, Ph.D., Tiffany. "The State of Black Entrepreneurship in America: Evaluating the Relationship Between Immigration and Minority Business Ownership." *Congressional Black Caucus Foundation - Center for Policy Analysis and Research*. Web. April 2019. http://bit.ly/2lsKmCc

7. "The Race Riot That Destroyed Black Wall Street." *OfficialBlackWallStreet.com*, Official Black Wall July 2015, http://bit.ly/2lvpz0Q

8. Johnson, Theodore R. "What If Black America Were a Country?" *The Atlantic*. Web. 14 October 2014. http://bit.ly/2nlRTD7

9. "Black Impact: Consumer Categories Where African-Americans Move Markets." *Nielsen.com*, The Company (US), LLC, 15 February 2018, http://bit.ly/2n4CmHG

10. Prince, Zenitha. "Census Bureau: Higher Percentage of Black Children Live with Single Mothers." *Afro.com*, The Afro-American Newspapers, Web. 31 December 2016. http://bit.ly/2o87tmp

11. "African-Americans and the American Workforce." *EEOC.gov*, U.S. Equal Employment Opportunity Commission, Retrieved 1 October 2019, http://bit.ly/2mBUtFa

12. Gruver, Jackson. "Racial Wage Gap for Men." *PayScale.com*, PayScale, Inc. Web. 7 May 2019, http://bit.ly/2nkAlYK

13. Bremmer, Ian. "These 5 Facts Explain America's Enduring Racial Divide." *Time.com*, Time, USA LLC. Web. 29 June 2015, http://bit.ly/2oa7MgH

14. *The African American Financial Experience: 2013-2014 Prudential Research*. Prudential Insurance Company and its Affiliates Newark, NJ. May 2014.

15. Pickard-Whitehead, Gabrielle. "Wow! African-American Small Business Ownership Up 400% In A Year, *Smallbiztrends.com*, Small Business Tre December 2018. http://

Chapter 6: "Can You Help A Brother Out?"

What It Means to Be Black and Unemployed

"

Play the game, but play it your own way – part of the time at least. Play the game, but raise the ante, my boy. Learn how it operates, learn how you operate..."

- Ralph Ellison, "Invisible Man" (Shmoop Editorial Team. 7.28)

(Taken 43 years after the end of slavery, this 1908 photo is of a Mississippi plantation owner and the sharecroppers working his land under armed supervision).

"Hey... It Ain't My Fault!"

Did I Do That?

In his iconic song, "(Sitting On) The Dock of the Bay," award winning artist Otis Redding, crooned the following all-too-real lyrics about the challenges of Black unemployment, when he sang the following tune:

"

Sittin' in the mornin' sun
I'll be sittin' when the evenin' come
Watching the ships roll in
And then I watch 'em roll away again, yeah

I'm sittin' on the dock of the bay
Watching the tide roll away
Ooo, I'm just sittin' on the dock of the bay
Wastin' time...

As Black America continues to grapple with the financial obstacles faced by those who have been historically marginalized and forced to live from paycheck to paycheck (if they dare lucky), the need to address the strain created by economic insecurity is one that can no longer be ignored by society. With that being said, however, solving the challenges of an entire segment of the American population that has traditionally been overlooked and unappreciated is no small feat (even for the greatest country the world has ever known). Today, more than 150 years since Honest Abe issued his fateful proclamation that technically liberated enslaved Africans from the manacles of state sponsored oppression, the task of full equality is one that continues to remain elusive. In fact, despite the economic gains that have been experienced by white families who have benefited from a system designed to afford them the privilege of amassing significant wealth, in the form of cash, property, and investment instruments which help them to cement their position in society, Black families, on the converse, have experienced paltry progress as America became the world's monetary megalopolis.

So, what seems to be the problem--two natural lifetimes removed from the abolition of slavery--that time can't cure? Honestly... your guess is as good as mine! As a neutral and detached arbiter for equality and justice, my goal is to examine each case on the merits. From where I stand, there have been issues, some of which could be systemic and possibly intentional, that have adversely impacted the "souls of Black folks" and have left an indelible mark upon the future of Black males yet unborn. On this, I will concede the point. But, seriously, how long are Black people going to use the old *"my people didn't get paid for hundreds of years of slavery"* excuse to continue in a predicament that may (or may not) be of their own making?

Nonetheless, in my opinion *(and I would venture to say that I am not alone)*, Black America's ability to effectively "pull itself up by its own bootstraps" remains nobody's fault but its own. Yes, they may not have any bootstraps to "pull up", but what does that have to do with the price of slaves on Wall Street? And sure, they have been dealt a dubious hand with the cards stacked against them, yet every time we look up, one of them is attempting to play the race card... and, in my opinion, dealing from the bottom of the deck! And that's just not fair to the rest of us! After all, I don't know anybody still living who was enslaved in the 1800's. In short, my friends, there's nothing to see here. Let's all just... move along!

Always Keeping It Real,

Justitia

Lady Justice

Jose Thompson: "Helping Others to Help Themselves"

Can Glass Ceilings Be Broken?

"I'm Jose Thompson, a 20-plus year Human Resources professional," began the reserved executive, subtly obscuring the vast array of experiences he holds in the field of talent management. "I began my career in recruiting and I have worked in a wide variety of industries, including industrial construction, media, aviation, consumer goods, as well as for *Fortune 500* companies, either as a consultant or as an employee," Thompson continued. "I grew up in Atlanta, during a time of great political expansion for Blacks in the city and it was like a "Tale of Two Cities," he said, '*it was the best of times, it was the worst of times*'. We elected the first Black mayor in the city's history, Maynard Jackson, and people in my family were part of his administration. But I also saw all kinds of contradictions growing up in a city like this, where you have a really thriving and booming Black middle-class and upper-class, and you also had poverty that was astonishing. So, in that sense, Atlanta, in my opinion, is an example of the best and the worst of the Black experience in America today," said the native of *"The City too Busy to Hate."* "As I got older, however, I chose to see the best of what Atlanta represented, even though there was a lot of great prosperity in the midst of a lot of despair when I was growing up, and is still the case to this day." Today, even though *"Hotlanta,"* as it is often called, is considered by many to be a Black financial oasis in a vast ocean of American wealth, the *"Gate City of the South"* continues to struggle with Black unemployment and job insecurity.

Ernie Suggs, an investigative reporter for the *Atlanta Journal-Constitution*, in his article called, "Atlanta is Known As a 'Black Mecca.' Jobs Data Tell A Different Story," described the deep angst within a majority Black populace that, despite a booming economy, continues to persist. "The [African-American unemployment] rate is still roughly double that of white Americans. It is a gap that has remained constant for more than half a century, through Republican and Democratic White Houses, Vietnam, the tech bubble, the Great Recession and now the longest jobs expansion on record," the article noted. For the City of Atlanta, however, with nearly 500,000 residents, more than half of whom are Black, the racial unemployment gap more than quadruples, with intransigent Black unemployment raging at 11.5%, compared to 2.5% for white Atlantans. "The nearly five-fold gap was only exceeded by Washington, D.C. among U.S. cities with 100,000 or more working-age people, according to an *Atlanta Journal-Constitution* analysis of *Census* data" (Suggs). In fact, research indicates that the "blacker" a city's demographics, the higher the rates of unemployment, even for those who have "worked hard and played by the rules," to include gaining advanced degrees with the often-erroneous belief that this would give them a leg up on the competition.

According to Dr. Valerie Rawlston Wilson, Ph.D., Director of the *Economic Policy Institute's Program on Race, Ethnicity and Economy* (PREE), in her report entitled, "Black Unemployment Twice as High as White Unemployment," Washington, DC--the nation's capital--leads the way in Black unemployment in the United States of America. Known to many as "Chocolate City," the District of Columbia boasts a majority Black population of 49% and, attendant with that, an unemployment rate nearly six times that of its white residents. "The District of Columbia has a Black–white unemployment rate ratio of 5.7-to-1, while Alabama and Mississippi have the highest ratios among states (3.0-to-1 and 2.8-to-1, respectively)" (Wilson). What African-Americans who are actively seeking employment in the labor market in places like Washington, DC and Atlanta and other majority Black metropolitan areas have discovered, however, is an impenetrable forcefield of privilege, bias and opportunity hoarding that renders much of the eligible and qualified Black workforce lingering on the sidelines or, at best, underemployed.

In a separate report on the persistent disparities African-Americans face in employment outcomes, Dr. Valerie Rawlston Wilson also spoke of the challenges for those who may have jobs, but are not earning enough revenue to help make ends meet: the chronically underemployed. "The term 'underemployment' is commonly used to encompass a broader definition of labor underutilization that includes not only the unemployed but also involuntary part-time workers (those part-time workers who would prefer to be working full time) and those who are marginally attached to the labor force (those who have given up looking for work—and so are not counted in official unemployment numbers—but who are willing and able to work if the opportunity presented itself)" ("Employment Outcomes"). To that end, when factoring in the underemployed and those who have simply dropped out of the job market, African-Americans have a significantly higher unemployment rate than government statistics would suggest. In fact, even Black workers with college degrees struggle to find full-time employment with comprehensive benefits.

"When they are employed," Rawlston wrote, "Black workers with a college or advanced degree are more likely than their white counterparts to be underemployed when it comes to their skill level—almost 40% are in a job that typically does not require a college degree, compared with 31% of white college grads. This relatively high Black unemployment and skills-based underemployment suggests that racial discrimination remains a failure of an otherwise tight labor market" ("Employment Outcomes"). But the question remains: why is it educated, qualified Black applicants have such difficulty even getting an interview? Jose Thompson believes that part of the answer lies in having someone "on the inside" willing to pry open the doors for those stuck "on the outside" struggling to get in.

Is It Over Before It Begins?

"The higher you go up the corporate ladder, the fewer women and people of color you will find," Thompson observed. "As a human resources officer, my role is to help introduce minority talent, if you will, into an organization that is, oftentimes, not very diverse. And in some of those cases, the employer I was recruiting for believed the minority candidate was asking for too much money, primarily because the company had been accustomed to low-balling minority candidates from the initiation of the conversation, to the offer of compensation," he noted. "They just couldn't understand or make a correlation between the experiences a candidate displayed on a resume and the way they would often articulate those experiences during the interview process," Jose continued. "This seems to be a pattern, particularly when you're dealing with people of color interviewing in front of Caucasians or more 'mainstream individuals'".

"The other interesting part of this equation is that you'll find people of color who may be more biased towards other people of color trying to come into an organization, particularly from the standpoint of getting hired. Sometimes it's because they are sensitive of the opinions of their white counterparts," Thompson explained. "I've had situations where, it has been communicated to me, not outright expressed, but communicated to me nonetheless, that a 'particular type of candidate' would be best for a 'particular type of role'. But the real inference there is not on the type of candidates they *did* want to hire, but the type of candidates they *didn't* want to hire. And those people generally looked like me," he intoned. "In other instances, I've supported African-American executives in their hiring decisions, and some of them barely wanted to see *any* Black males on the hiring slate for that role. And if Black men did end up on the interview list, it was often just for window-dressing; to show that we looked at these candidates--but they weren't as qualified," he said. According to research on minority hiring trends, Thompson's anecdotal examples are buttressed by the cold, hard facts which clearly show a hiring system that is severely tilted by both conscious and unconscious bias, beginning with an individual's resume.

In a thought-provoking opinion series called, "When Whites Just Don't Get It," *Pulitzer Prize* winning journalist, Nicholas Kristof, of *The New York Times*, discusses the impact of racial privilege in the job market. "In one study, researchers sent thousands of résumés to employers with openings, randomly using some stereotypically Black names (like Jamal) and others that were more likely to belong to whites (like Brendan). A white name increased the likelihood of a callback by 50 percent," Kristof observed. In fact, the discrimination experienced by African-Americans in the job market because of stereotypically sounding names is one that seeps into other aspects of African American life; whether it's in their efforts to reach out to their local elected officials in writing and getting a response, or getting a university professor to respond to a student inquiry. "Why do we discriminate," Kristof asked sincerely, before providing a succinct and truthful response to his own question. "The big factor isn't overt racism. Rather, it seems to be unconscious bias among whites who believe in equality but act in ways that perpetuate inequality" (Kristof).

For more than two hundred years, the United States has proffered both hard work and education to be the "great equalizer" in one's pursuit of the

"American Dream." But many now argue that meritocracy and academia are no longer steps to achieving the American Dream. In his essay on class and equality published in the *Boston Review*, a political and literary forum, Richard Reeves, editor-in-chief of the *Social Mobility Memos Blog*, disabuses the notion of true social mobility in America for those with institutional disadvantages. "Postsecondary education in particular has become an "inequality machine." As more ordinary people have earned college degrees, upper middle-class families have simply upped the ante. Postgraduate qualifications are now the key to maintaining upper middle-class status," Reeves wrote. "The upper middle-class gains most of its status not by exploiting others but by exploiting its own skills. But when the income gap of one generation is converted into an opportunity gap for the next, economic inequality hardens into class stratification"(Reeves).

Moreover, the idea of being rewarded for both grit and playing by the rules in American society is, as former US Labor Secretary, the Honorable Robert Reich has labeled it, as "mythical" as the Loch Ness monster. In his essay for *Newsweek* Magazine called, "The Myth of Meritocracy in Trump's America", Reich observed the following: "While some entrepreneurs in America's billionaire class lack a prestigious degree, it's become harder to become a run-of-the-mill multimillionaire in America without one", he wrote. "Most CEOs of big corporations", Reich continued, "Wall Street mavens, and high-priced lawyers got where they are because they knew the right people. A prestigious college packed with the children of wealthy and well-connected parents is now the launching pad into the stratosphere of big money" (Reich). Just as importantly, by accessing those impenetrable networks of family connections and influential social networks, an opportunity gap is created and hoarding by the rich and well-connected takes place, much to the detriment of even the most educated African-Americans. And bridging that opportunity gap, particularly for Black workers, is oftentimes a friendly face on the other side of the hiring desk willing to give them a chance to get in the door. For Jose Thompson, it was an unassuming corporate executive willing to mentor him and patiently teach him "the ways of white folks."

"I met a guy by the name of Henry Lee, and he was a diversity supplier for *Media One*, who gave me an opportunity to intern for him one summer," Thompson said, reflecting upon the guardian angel willing to swoop in and save the day by taking a chance on him. "As I called him, 'The Great" Henry

Lee', was a very dynamic African-American male; a great speaker who was adept at getting buy-in and consensus on many issues. In fact," Thompson recalled fondly, "Mr. Lee was once recruited by Dan Rather to come work for *CBS*, but he didn't want to didn't take the job because he didn't want to leave home. To me, however, that speaks to his gift of gab and his ability to connect with a wide variety of people," he said. "Not only did I make a great deal of money during that first internship, but I learned a lot also, and he's the one that exposed me to the business side of diversity hiring," Jose declared. "I have performed a number of different roles since that first internship, but my career trajectory started with Henry Lee who gave me my shot more than twenty years ago, and that was my break into the industry."

To that end, Thompson is a staunch supporter of professional mentoring as a means of assisting Black males seeking success in Corporate America. "Mentoring plays a huge part in the ultimate success of the individual, especially those who find themselves working as a minority within a majority culture," Thompson believes. "We've all had folks who show up at the right time, with the right words, and the right actions. And that means something, you know, when somebody is really trying to help you... and you can sometimes *feel* that," he emphasized. "Just being able to pull somebody out of their situation and give them a glimpse of what their future potential is, or what it could be--reaffirming and uplifting that potential--can make all the difference in the world," Thompson continued. But placing the onus upon the limited numbers of Black hiring managers to remedy institutionalized opportunity hoarding in the job market through mentoring alone, isn't sustainable. Moreover, simply applying a band-aid approach to solving the problems attendant with bias in recruitment and hiring, is a challenge that cannot be effectively overcome without first examining the genesis of such entrenched discrimination. Additionally, understanding the economic benefits that afforded America the opportunity to turn a blind eye to the ideals that make the nation great, is a fundamental prerequisite for appreciating the intractability of the problem today.

So, Where Should We Start?

Why not at the beginning...

Commencing with the landing of the first ship carrying enslaved Africans on the banks of the James River in Hampton Roads, Virginia, some 400 years ago, in what would become a long-running saga of human misery and suffering that came to be known as the *Trans-Atlantic Slave Trade*, the history of an overworked and underpaid Black labor force is as essential to the development of the United States and is as "American as apple pie." In a comprehensive series called "The 1619 Project," *The New York Times* undertook a massive effort to report on and accurately reframe the history of the United States from that fateful year forward. Beginning with the birth of a fledgling democracy that would claw its way up from the doldrums of international obscurity, fueled primarily by the benefit of an enslaved workforce, to become the world's undisputed economic superpower today, the history of the United States is one that is inextricably attached to her "original sin."

Exacted from the bodies of Black men and women stolen from Africa and shipped off to a strange land by greedy and unscrupulous kinsmen willing to trade their brethren for whiskey and beads, African-American labor in the United States has been historically undervalued. In his piece within "The 1619 Project's" report, sociologist and author Matthew Desmond described the economic impact that uncompensated Black laborers had on the founding of the nation. "Slavery was undeniably a font of phenomenal wealth. By the eve of the *Civil War*, the Mississippi Valley was home to more millionaires per capita than anywhere else in the United States," Desmond detailed. "Cotton grown and picked by enslaved workers was the nation's most valuable export. The combined value of enslaved people exceeded that of all the railroads and factories in the nation," he continued. "What made the cotton economy boom in the United States, and not in all the other far-flung parts of the world with climates and soil suitable to the crop, was our nation's unflinching willingness to use violence on nonwhite people and to exert its will on seemingly endless supplies of land and labor. Given the choice between modernity and barbarism, prosperity and poverty, lawfulness and cruelty, democracy and totalitarianism, America chose all of the above" (Desmond).

As a part of chronicling the economic expansion of the United States during the antebellum period of the late 18th century America, "The 1619 Project" noted that the increased production of cotton also brought with it the introduction of the Industrial Revolution and, as a result, more exploitation of Black bodies and Black labor. "In 1810, there were 87,000 cotton spindles in America. Fifty years later, there were five million. 'Slavery,' wrote one of its defenders in De Bow's Review, a widely read agricultural magazine, 'was the nursing mother of the prosperity of the North'" (Desmond). Today, as the United States struggles to reconcile its past, one of economic exploitation, with a future society that is growing more increasingly diverse, the need for full employment, once again, for Black men in America, is both necessary and prudent for the nation's continued economic growth. But that won't happen unless and until those who have the ability to make hiring decisions check both their conscious and unconscious biases at the door when viewing potentially worthy applicants. For Jose Thompson, however, the onus must be on those who create jobs at the corporate level, beginning with a redoubling of their efforts to expand employment opportunities to the myriad of consumers that help to keep them in business, particularly qualified candidates of color.

"When we talk about diversity and inclusion in Corporate America, what you are essentially talking about is risk mitigation. The big companies are oftentimes trying to show that they are making an attempt to hire diverse talent, but the results speak for themselves," Jose observed. "I was really set back by *Silicon Valley, Google, Facebook* and all of the big tech companies and how they talk about the lack of minority representation, which is oftentimes minuscule," he chided. "It's not difficult to hire a diverse workforce. Everybody might not be suited to be an engineer; however, you've got a lot of *Historically Black Colleges and Universities* that have students that can fill other positions at these major corporations that are struggling to diversify their workplace," he continued. "There are accountants coming out of school, information technology professionals coming out of school, business professionals coming out of schools," he continued, "so there are opportunities to hire more Black workers, *if* they wanted to. But when you have a power structure that is primarily white male dominated, human nature dictates that it is going to want to feed itself first, by hiring people that mirror that white male dominated perspective," Thompson surmised. But the challenges are still great when many Black applicants don't even get a second look, despite their qualifications, because they seem "too Black." And therein lies the challenge.

"In terms of stereotypes," Jose began, "I think there are a couple of things for Black male job searchers to remember when looking for a job. First," the longtime hiring manager noted, "there will always be attempts to find fault in who you are or a flaw in what you have done," Thompson continued. "I was even asked once in an interview, *where I lived!* As if that had any bearing on my ability to do the job in question," he said incredulously. "If the person sitting across from you at the interview table is a white male, for example, and you're competing with other white males for the role in question, unless someone in charge explicitly says, "I want a Black candidate for this role", you are most likely not going to be the successful candidate for that position," he noted from decades of observations in human resources. "That's been my experience on both sides of the hiring and recruitment process, both as a person interviewing for the job, and also as a person in a position to introduce talent to some of the biggest organizations in the world," Thompson said. So, how does America ever create an equitable playing field, particularly for those who have been historically marginalized and oppressed, without continued government oversight, new legislation and fair access to opportunity? For some, the answer is both a bit controversial and an idea whose time has come: reparations for American descendants of enslaved Africans.

According to a report written by Frank Newport of the *Gallup* organization, entitled, "Reparations and Black Americans' Attitudes About Race," the issue of reparations, or making amends for historic wrongdoings perpetrated against one group by another (often by paying money to or providing other substantial benefits), is one that has historically been divided along racial lines; with a majority of Blacks believing that it must be considered as a form of long overdue payment for centuries of backbreaking, free labor, and a majority of whites who are staunchly opposed to even the suggestion of such a notion. "A *YouGov* online survey in 2014 showed roughly six in 10 Black Americans said that the U.S. government should offer cash payments and education and job training programs to the descendants of slaves," Newport reported. "A *Kaiser Family Foundation/CNN* survey from 2015 found that 52% of Blacks said that "as a way to make up for the harm caused by slavery" the government should "make cash payments to Black Americans who are descendants of slaves" (8% of whites agreed)," he continued.

In addition to the stark contrast in racial views on the hot potato issue of "Reparations for American Descendants of Slaves," *Gallup* also found that Black Americans overwhelmingly support the idea that government policies should be implemented to protect Black workers from systemic discrimination, as well as to effectuate positive economic change for the broader community. "Overall, Blacks in the U.S. have continuing concerns about discrimination and structural impediments to their success, and most believe that the government must step in and do more to help this situation," Newport noted. "The concept of reparations *per se* is broad, and the exact level of Black support for the idea depends on how it is defined. But we know that at least a majority of Blacks appear from past polling to be in favor -- not surprising given the general context of Black support for the government actively addressing race inequalities in the U.S. today" (Newport).

In searching for an agreeable framework for fixing systemic problems in hiring and recruiting of otherwise qualified Black males who want what everyone else does, an opportunity to rise to their potential, Jose Thompson believes that Black males must continue to seek assistance from one another, and guidance from a Higher Power whom he believes can, and will, supply all needs. Whether those solutions include the guarantee of full employment for anyone who wants a job with a living wage, or upward social mobility through the implementation of affirmative action programs, creation of professional mentoring programs, or the dissemination of monetary reparations, American Descendants of Slaves, Jose Thompson's perspective is one that is both steeped in the realities of being Black in America, yet one that is cautiously optimistic about the future. "First of all," Thompson declared, "if you are a Black man and you are alive, you are lucky! In fact," he continued, "anybody that doesn't quite understand and appreciate that fact, really doesn't understand what's happening in America. To be clear, African-American men do more harm to each other than anybody else, just like white folks do more against other white folks," Thompson pointed out. "Most people tend to rob and kill people they know. That's a human thing, it's not a racial thing, so let's just keep it real. As far as the African-American perspective is concerned," Thompson went on, "instead of turning *on* each other, Black folks need to turn *to* each other. That's something that we really used to believe in," he remembered. "Somehow we have lost that, becoming content with being 'the only one in the room' without understanding fully what that *really* means," he continued.

"If you're the only one in the room that looks like you, you've got to be ever mindful of the possibility that you are constantly outnumbered and almost certainly outgunned," foreshadowed the mild-mannered manager. "I believe it's incumbent for all persons of color, who are in a position to make a difference, to bring each other along; regardless of gender or ethnicity. Moreover, as African-Americans, we must always remember that we can't help anyone else until we first help ourselves," he summarized. "And we have to help as many of *us* as we possibly can... because if we don't... who will?"

(Jose Thompson: Human Resources Expert & Entrepreneur)

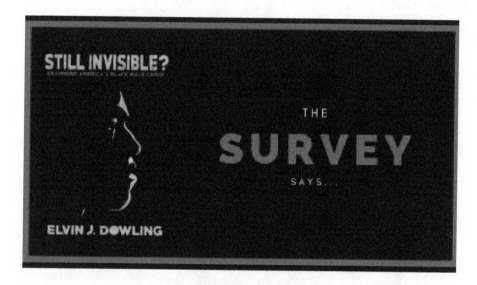

Based on the idea that Black males are underpaid for their labor, how strongly do you agree or disagree with the following statements?

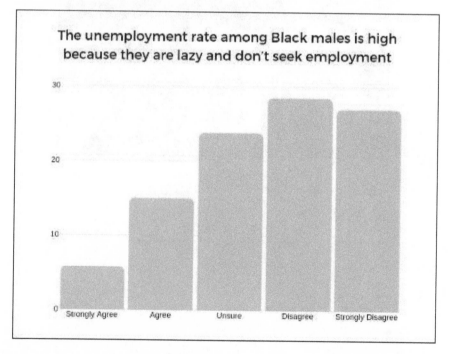

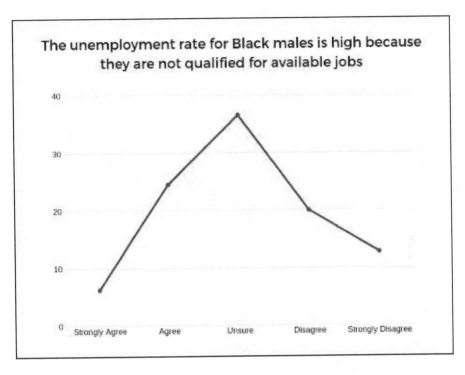

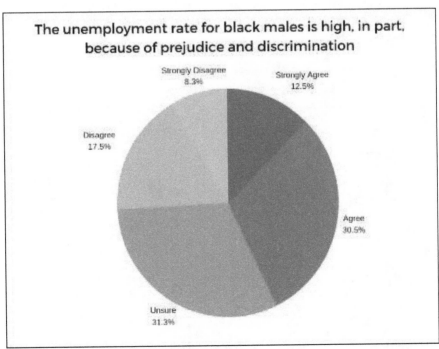

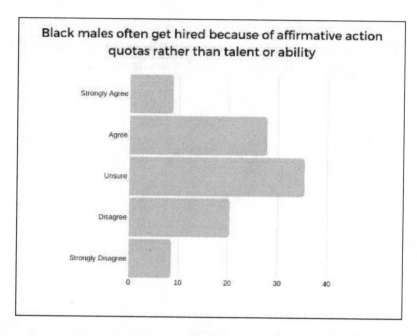

Black males often get hired because of affirmative action quotas rather than talent or ability

All survey results displayed above are represented by the overall percentage of survey respondents. For more information on our survey methodology, please see the Author's Note, located in the front matter of the book. To review raw survey results, visit: http://bit.ly/stillinvisiblesurvey

OPINIONS OF BLACK MALES IN THE WORKPLACE

LAZY	UNQUALIFIED	MARGINALIZED	QUOTAS
More than half of all White male respondents (53%) "Strongly Disagree" or "Disagree" with the characterization of black males as lackadaisical	More Black male respondents (40%) "Agree" with the idea that black males are unqualified for jobs than those black male respondents who "Disagree" (33.33%)	More than half of all Hispanic female respondents "Strongly Agree" or "Agree" that black males face prejudice and discrimination in employment	4 out of 10 Asian respondents (45%) "Strongly Agree" or "Agree" with the notion that black males are hired primarily because of affirmative action policies

Findings by Race

- Once again, a consistent number of Black male respondents (13%) "Strongly Agree" or "Agree" with the statement, *"The unemployment rate amongst Black males is high because they are lazy and don't seek employment."*

- Nearly 4 out of 10 Black female respondents (36.37%) "Strongly Agree or Agree" with the statement, *"The unemployment rate for Black males is high because they are not qualified for available jobs."*

- More than one-third of all Asian respondents (35.38%) "Strongly Agree" or "Agree" with the statement, *"The unemployment rate for Black males is high, in part, because of prejudice and discrimination."*

Findings by Gender

- 1 out of 3 White male Respondents (33.00%) "Strongly Agree" or "Agree" with the statement, *"The unemployment rate for Black males is high, in part, because of prejudice and discrimination."*

- Nearly 4 out of 10 Hispanic male respondents (35.85%) "Strongly Agree" or "Agree" with the statement, *"Black males often get hired because of affirmative action quotas rather than talent or ability."*

- All Multiracial female respondents (100.00%) "Strongly Disagree" or "Disagree" with the statement, *"The unemployment rate among Black males is high because they are lazy and don't seek employment."*

Findings by Age

- More than a quarter of all Asian female respondents 55 years and older (27.59%) "Strongly Agree" or "Agree" with the statement, *"The unemployment rate for Black males is high because they are not qualified for available jobs.*

- Nearly half of all respondents, ages 18-24 years of (46.81%) "Strongly Agree" or "Agree" with the statement, *"The unemployment rate for Black males is high, in part, because of prejudice and discrimination.*

- 1 out of 3 Hispanic female respondents 33.00%), across all age groups, "Strongly Agree" or "Agree" with the statement, *"Black males often get hired because of affirmative action quotas rather than talent or ability."*

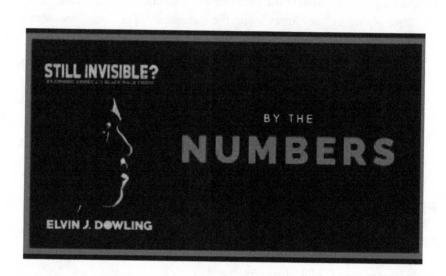

"A Degree Means Little to Me!"

- The annual unemployment rate of Black Americans was 6.6%, *more than double* the annual white unemployment rate of 3.2% in 2018. In fact, the last time the white unemployment reached 6.6%, in 2012, the Black unemployment rate topped 14%, a trend that has persisted for more than 40 years ("State of the Union").

- The hike in the number of African-Americans with a bachelor's degree or higher rose by 63% , from 14% to nearly 23%, between the years 2000 to 2018. Despite this dramatic increase, persistent unemployment rates for Blacks continues unabated, regardless of their level of education ("State of the Union").

"Twice the Pain... Still No Gains!"

- Although the unemployment rate for Blacks is twice that of whites, it's still 86% above the national average. Even worse, the rate amongst eligible Black job applicants is 116% higher than whites, and 204% higher than Asians. The only group that fares worse than Blacks are teenagers, with an unemployment rate of 13% (McIntyre).

- The African-American unemployment rate in large metropolitan areas with high a minority population, such as Atlanta, Detroit and Washington, DC, is often much higher than the rate for Blacks living in other parts of the country, which contributes to the high national average attributed to total Black unemployment (McIntyre).

"When One Door Opens, Another Closes!"

- The incarceration rate amongst African-Americans is nearly six times higher than the rates for whites. Moreover, as former convicted felons transition to becoming returning citizens upon their release back into society, employers are reticent in hiring individuals with past criminal convictions, disproportionately affecting Black men (McIntyre).

- The unemployment gap that exists between African-Americans and other racial groups is one that has persisted for decades and currently shows no signs of changing anytime soon. Currently, there are no policy solutions being implemented nationally that achieve anything near full employment for African-Americans (McIntyre).

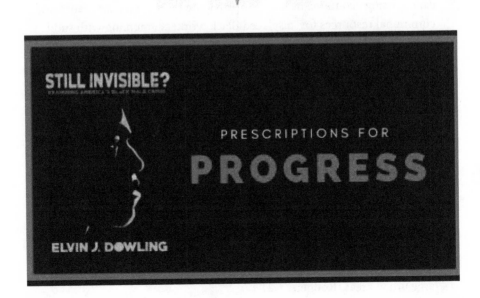

"Plant a Seed ... Reap a Harvest!"

- Provide training and increased opportunities with jobs that have a lower chance of being outsourced overseas, to include automobile mechanics, HVAC technicians and other skilled trades that are often stigmatized as being less desirable, but provides a level of job security and financial stability (Rodgers. p.20.)

- Increase employment options for Black youths, including teenagers and college students, by providing internships and volunteer opportunities that assist them in acquiring the much needed "soft" skills they will need to be effective in the workplace, while further decreasing their interaction with the criminal justice system (Rodgers. p.20.)

"It's Best to Invest in Success!"

- Assist returning citizens upon release from incarceration, particularly those who were convicted on nonviolent offenses and low-level crimes and have paid their debt to society, with employment retraining, housing assistance, voter registration, identifying transportation options and/or obtaining a driver's license (Rodgers. p.20).

- Strengthen community safety nets, to include nonprofit organizations, designed to assist those who are unemployed, underemployed or are experiencing economic distress, by providing professional assistance and communal resources for displaced Black workers grappling with sudden or prolonged job loss (Rodgers. p.21).

"Insist on Legislation and Track Discrimination!"

- Demand that both the President and Congress of the United States work together to pass legislation that increases the national "minimum wage" to a "living wage" that lifts the standard of living for the working poor, and insist upon the rigorous enforcement of existing laws aimed at preventing wage theft (Rodgers. p.21).

- Urge the federal government to empower the *Equal Employment Opportunity Commission (EEOC)* to track and measure discrimination complaints at the local level, with the goal of directly assessing and addressing the impact these issues have on the labor force, particularly in large urban areas (Rodgers. p.21.)

Works Cited

1. Shmoop Editorial Team. "Invisible Man Identity Quotes Page 5." *Shmoop*. Shmoop University, Inc., 11 Nov. 2008. Web. 2 Oct. 2019.

2. Redding, Otis. "(Sittin'On) The Dock of the Bay." *The Dock of the Bay*, 1st ed., Volt Atco V-157, 1968, track 1. *Genius.com*, http://bit.ly/2otUuvF. Accessed 2 October 2019. Produced by Steve Cropper.

3. Suggs, Ernie. "Atlanta is known as a 'Black Mecca.' Jobs Data Tell a Different Story." *The New York Times*, 25 July 2019, http://bit.ly/31KaOag.

4. Wilson, Valerie. "Black Unemployment Is At Least Twice as High as White Unemployment at the National Level and in 14 States and the District of Columbia." *EPI.org*, Economic Policy Institute, 4 April 2019. http://bit.ly/2IhA5Rd

5. Williams, Jhacova and Wilson, Valerie. "Black workers Endure Persistent Racial Disparities in Employment Outcomes." *PI.org*, Economic Policy Institute, http://bit.ly/2VkEtod

6. Perry, Andre M. "Black Workers Are Being Left Behind by Full Employment." *Brookings.edu*, The Brookings Institute, 26 June 2019. https://brook.gs/2AC2opz

7. Kristof, Nicholas. "When Whites Just Don't Get It - Part 6: White Resume Tops Black Resume." *NYTimes.com*, The New York Times, 2 April 2016. https://nyti.ms/359S59Z

8. Reeves, Richard. "The Dream Hoarders: How America's Top 20 Percent Perpetuates Inequality." *BostonReview.net*, Boston Review. 30 May 2017. http://bit.ly/32ZlL7S

9. Reich, Robert. "The Myth of Meritocracy in Trump's America." *Newsweek.com*. 19 March 2019. http://bit.ly/2Vdu5yb

10. Desmond, Matthew. "American Capitalism Is Brutal: You Can Trace That to the Plantation." *NYTimes.com*, The New York Times Company. 14 August 2019. https://nyti.ms/2VkUslV

11. Newport, Frank. "Reparations and Black Americans'
    Attitudes About Race." *News.Gallup.com*. Gallup,   Inc. 1 March
    2019. http://bit.ly/2Oqq0VZ

12. Wilson, Valerie. "Before the State of the Union, a Fact
    Check on Black Unemployment." *EPI.org*,   Economic
    Policy Institute, 1 February 2019.   http://bit.ly/2MkMwx0

13. McIntyre, Douglas A. "Why is Unemployment for Blacks   86%
    Higher Than US Average?" *USAToday.com*,   Gannett Company.
    6 May 2019.   http://bit.ly/31Y3rfu

14. Rodgers, III, William M. "Race in the Labor Market: The   Role
    of Equal Employment Opportunity and   Other Policies."
    Bloustein School for Planning and   *Public Policy*, Rutgers
    University. May 2018.

Chapter 7: "We Sick, Boss?"

The Role of Race in Black Male Mortality

❝

On his deathbed he called my father to him and said, "Son, after I'm gone, I want you to keep up the good fight. I never told you, but our life is a war... Live with your head in the lion's mouth."

- Ralph Ellison, "Invisible Man" (Shmoop Editorial Team. 1.2)

(Pictured is a doctor drawing blood from one of the unsuspecting test subjects of the infamous "Tuskegee Experiment," which illicitly studied the natural progression of untreated syphilis on poor Black patients.)

"Dead Men Tell No Tales!"

"Sick and Tired of Being 'Sick' *and* 'Tired'?!

It has often been said, *"The presence of the doctor is the beginning of the cure."* For African-American men, however, the sentiment behind that declaration is tantamount, in some cases, to standing on a street corner in any urban city in America and screaming, *"The police are on the way..."* and not expecting a visceral reaction! To Black men, those types of statements, as earnest as they may seem to those who believe in unicorns and fairy tales, are interpreted totally different. For many of them, asking Black men to go to the doctor's office is like asking them to go to the police station. I mean, they will... but it better be a life and death situation. In fact, not since the days of chattel slavery, when Black males were intrusively inspected for all manner of defect, prior to being sold on the auction block to the highest bidder, has the contentious relationship between Black men and white doctors ever been more fraught with peril. Moreover, from the early displays of "improper bedside manner" being administered by dismissive doctors who derisively treated their patients of color, until this very day, African-American males are innately distrustful of physicians, institutions and government officials--and not necessarily in that order.

In 1932, and for the ensuing four decades, the *U.S. Public Health Service* certainly didn't do the tenuous relationship between African-American men and their doctors any favors when, in conducting the notorious "Tuskegee Study of Untreated Syphilis in the Negro Male," it induced 600 poor Black men from rural Alabama to participate in a malevolent medical study, unbeknownst to them, in which they would get free meals, medical treatment and burial insurance, in exchange for their mental and physical health. In return for these generous government benefits, a "come-up" for many of these poor Black sharecroppers, unscrupulous doctors studied the devastating effects of a dangerous sexually transmitted disease on Black bodies and Black minds. Since then, the trust between these two groups has never truly recovered. As a result of this stalemate, if you will, Black males have been stuck on an abysmal road that oftentimes leads to an abrupt dead-end. Today, the early demise of Black males in America has a significant and material impact upon our collective bottom line, and therein lies our challenge. Please, allow me to explain...

According to the *Bureau of Labor Statistics*, the median weekly earnings for Black men in America in 2019 was $761. On an annual basis, that represents approximately $40,000 per year in revenue contributed to the American economy. And since we know that African-American consumers spend their money faster than their shirt tails can hit their fannies, as the Black dollar circulates within their own community less than six *whole* hours, keeping Black men alive and working for as long as possible is a win-win for everybody, right? *(Especially for the uber rich... but I digress...).* In fact, every time an 18-year-old Black male is gunned down over gang turf that they don't own anyway, there is an opportunity cost associated with their loss. If, for example, that kid worked until the age of 65 years old, as a productive member of society, approximately $1,859,884 in lost earnings potential over the course of a lifetime, will never make it into the overall American economy.

To that end, when you consider those numbers exponentially, especially at the rate Black males are killing themselves, whether it's with a pistol in their hands, or pork on their fork, the revenue loss is potentially in the trillions. And, in a capitalist society, that ought to concern anyone who likes money...like me! So, let's kiss and make up people. Let bygones be bygones... and move on already. Black men need doctors. Doctors need money and America needs taxes. Need I go any further?

Hope this helps,

Justitia

Lady Justice

Patrick Hines: "Building Bridges and Breaking Barriers"

Is There A Doctor in the House?

"I am originally from Elizabeth City, North Carolina, a small town in northeastern part of the state. I attended undergraduate school in Virginia before obtaining my medical (M.D.) and doctorate (Ph.D.) degrees from the *University of North Carolina at Chapel Hill*," says the debonair doctor who more resembles actor Wesley Snipes than he does Dr. Gregory House of the fictional television medical drama with the eponymous name. "I completed my clinical training in Pediatric Intensive Care Medicine at the *Children's Hospital of Philadelphia* and the *University of Pennsylvania*," he went on, listing a string of impressive accomplishments that would make even the most prolific professionals appear as mere dilettantes by comparison. "From there, I went on to the *Children's Hospital of Michigan*, where I currently practice as a pediatric cardiac intensive care physician, taking care of some pretty sick kids with a number of different ailments. In addition to that," Hines continued, "I continued working on a vibrant research program that has led to the creation of a company called *Functional Fluidics*, for which I serve as the Founder and Chief Executive Officer. In this role, I take some of the technologies developed in laboratories, and commercialize them to make them available for patients all over the world," noted Hines with an "awe-shucks" attitude that belied the fact that the work in which he has been engaged has contributed to the saving of countless lives. The product of a loving, stable environment, Patrick was raised by both of his parents, Billy and Patricia Hines, transplants from their native Alabama.

"My parents moved to Elizabeth City, North Carolina for work at the local college. My dad is a classically trained musician and bass-baritone vocalist, who was also the director of the choir at *Elizabeth City State University (ECSU)*, which is what he was recruited there to do," Hines noted. "My mother was also the librarian at *ECSU*, so there was a strong emphasis on education and reading, and really focusing on that as a pathway to a better life," he recalled. The scion of well-respected educators and academicians, Hines does not discount the challenges he faced in living up to his parent's lofty expectations. "They were definitely strict disciplinarians," he remembered, "and I grew up with those sort of 'old school,' Southern values, such as having respect for adults, and that kind of thing, which was ingrained in me as a child" he said, noting the relatively unencumbered path he took from childhood innocence to professional anomaly.

"The role that my dad played in my life has everything to do with who I am," Patrick began, explaining the impact his father had on his life's ultimate progression. "When I think about who I am as a man, and as a father, and as a member of the community, I have a direct example to pull from, my own dad, and that really guides the frame of reference from which I come," Hines said. "My father worked full-time as an educator, and used the medium of music to connect with students and, oftentimes, had to be more than just a music professor," Hines recalled. "He had to be a father, a social worker, a teacher, a disciplinarian, and sometimes he was the only male role model that many of these students had ever had," the proud son of Billy and Patricia Hines noted. "He cared as much about their development as people as he did about their development as musicians. There was always a deep connection that he established with his students."

As an example of how Hines learned empathy and patience for those in need, the physician noted that his boyhood home was often filled with students who found themselves in need of a good meal and family setting during Sunday dinners and school breaks. "We would see students all the time that would come to the house on holidays who couldn't go home, or didn't have a place to go for Thanksgiving or Christmas. So, there would always be someone showing up at the house that would sit around the table, and we would break bread with them and treat them like family. That's just what we did. And so, through music," Hines went on, "he took care of people. As a result, I knew that, whatever I did professionally, *service* was going to be a big part of that," he emphasized. Many African-American males, however, aren't as fortunate as Hines, with an inordinate amount of young Black males who never even reach the age of maturity; dying in emergency rooms and on street corners in urban centers throughout the country.

According to a study released by *Rutgers University, Washington University of St. Louis* and the *University of Michigan*, young African-American males are more likely to die of unnatural causes than anyone else. More alarmingly, the incidences of police-involved deaths of Black males, as a result of the use of deadly force, has become more prevalent in American society. In an in-depth article examining the results of the university study entitled, "Police Violence a Leading Cause of Death for Young Men," Joseph P. Williams, a Senior Editor for *US News and World Reports,* detailed the unnerving statistics of America's #1 cause of death for young Black males: violence. "Racially unequal exposure to the risk of state violence has profound consequences for public health, democracy, and racial stratification," the report delineated ("Police Violence"). "Young men of color face an 'exceptionally high risk' of being killed by police," Williams wrote, "and that risk continues to be greater for Black men as they age compared with whites" the report continued. What's even more startling is the fact that this unabated increase in police-involved homicides has now led to a full-blown national crisis. When compared to white men, over the course of a lifetime, the "Police Violence" report also laid bare their findings that Black men are nearly three times more likely to be killed by the police, followed by Native American and Latino men and boys. "Our models predict that about 1 in 1,000 Black men and boys will be killed by police over the life course," the report says. "Overall [the problem] is so acute, however, that the study labels such encounters a "leading cause of death" among all young men ages 25 to 29, not too far behind the diseases of cancer and heart disease" ("Police Violence").

"I want to be clear," said Frank Edwards, an assistant professor in *Rutgers' School of Criminal Justice* and the study's lead author, "when we talk about the leading causes, police violence trails behind some causes that are killing many, many people. Relative to all causes of death," Edwards went on, "it's not that frequent. But police are paid government employees who are, presumably, trained to use deadly force as a last resort. Police are responsible for at least 1% of all those deaths" of young men, Edwards says. "To say this subset of people is among those leading causes is still pretty striking." Oftentimes, however, when addressing the epidemic of so-called "Black on Black crime," those who point out the alarming but true statistics that bear out the fact that Black males do, indeed, take the lives of other Black males at frightening levels, there is oftentimes pushback from those who point out the obvious

Politifact, a nonprofit project operated by the *Poynter Institute* of St. Petersburg, Florida, highlighted the dichotomy between truth and accountability in its article chronicling the abysmal homicide rates of young Black males, more often than not perpetrated by other Black males, and what some see as a minimization of their role in the epidemic. In the wake of the riots in Ferguson, Missouri, following the police-involved homicide of Michael Brown in 2014, *Fox News* contributor Juan Williams, one of the few African-American voices on the conservative news outlet, spoke to the concerns of those who believe that Black men should be held accountable, first and foremost, for their own actions. "Civil rights activists and Black leaders have failed to address the very thing that's fueling conservative, white backlash — the high crime rate among the Black community, particularly among young Black men, Williams said "("Juan Williams"). "I think there's fear of intimidation and harassment, being legitimized by the fact that there is a high rate of crime, especially among young Black men," Williams said. "No. 1 cause of death, young Black men 15 to 34 —murder. Who's committing the murder? Not police. Other Black men."

Indeed, Williams is correct, as the *Centers for Disease Control and Prevention (CDC)* have confirmed. "According to the *CDC*, homicide was indeed the No. 1 killer of Black men between the ages of 15 and 34 in 2011. Accidents ranked second in causes of death, and suicide claimed the third-place spot for death amongst Black males 15 and 24 years old, while heart disease ranked third for men 24-34," the article continued. "Experts said that *CDC* data, compiled from coroner reports, are in line with *FBI* numbers, sourced from police reports. The *CDC* does not distinguish between the types of homicide (criminal, justified, etc.) or the types of accidents (auto accidents, falls, firearm discharge, etc.)" (Juan Williams). A former researcher for the *National Institutes of Health*, Dr. Patrick Hines believes that the public health impacts of intra-racial homicide amongst African-American males is a much more complex issue than mere incidences of rage and violence.

"When it comes to issues like Black on Black crime, the question is often asked, 'Do Black men do self-harm?' Sure," Hines exclaimed, as if he were stating the obvious. "We do harm to ourselves. White men do harm to themselves. People do harm to themselves. That's a fact of life, especially in any environment where you have people that don't have opportunities, don't have hope, don't have ambition, based upon a number of structural reasons, or what have you," the physician and scientist explained. "I can find the same patterns of behavior in Appalachia, in rural Northeastern North Carolina, urban Chicago, and other parts of the country. As such, I concede that you can certainly find examples where African-American men have done and are doing self-harm. But the unifying thread there is not that they are African-American men, it's the environment from which they hail," Hines elucidated. "It's the state of mind. It's the opportunities available for them to take care of themselves and their families , and to do the things that you are put on this Earth to be able to do," he went on. "These same patterns can play out in anyone in a similar situation. For example," he continued, "we see white people dying in droves from the opioid crisis, and much of that is driven by economic depression and a lack of hope and opportunity. But we don't blame the white people who are suffering, nor should we! We acknowledge that it's a crisis and it is something that we have to deal with and solve," Hines stated. "But when people suffering from addiction happen to be African-American men, _the problem is 'African-American men'_, which means we are approaching this public health crisis in the wrong way," he maintained. "We should figure out how to address the problems and understand that 'the problem' is not who 'the person' is." To that end, while ceding the point that Black males killing other Black males is, indeed, as big a problem as white males killing white males (or Hispanic males killing Hispanic males, for that matter), the role that government sanctioned law enforcement officers hold is a much higher level of responsibility and, more importantly, is a public trust not granted to common individuals.

As an on-call physician who has witnessed his fair share of police interactions between Black males and cops, Dr. Hines believes that a greater emphasis on communication and de-escalation must be employed by the professionals engaged with protecting public safety: the men and women of law enforcement. "With regard to the police, I really try to imagine myself on the other side of the fence, and not just make assumptions," he proceeded. "As a healthcare provider, in an environment where I have taken care of gang members, people who have been involved in gun violence, and families in crisis and conflict, things can tend to escalate. And I have to be on the de-escalating side of the equation and make decisions about whether or not I call security, for example," Hines went on. "Do I have this family member removed from the hospital because they are a potential threat to my staff, and my ability to take care of patients? Or, as a professional," the amiable physician asked, "is it a part of my job to be able to mitigate a situation with a person who is having a pretty normal human reaction who, were the individual a white female or someone else, for example, would never be seen as an imminent threat," he observed.

"I tend to think it's my job to be able to ratchet down a heightened, emotional situation because, at the end of the day, the best thing for the kids that I take care of is for them to have their parents present. And that's a part of them being well and being taken care of properly," Dr. Hines emphasized. "So, having a parent forcibly removed from a medical facility because they are emotionally distraught does that patient no good. They need that advocate there. And that's the first order of business! In many cases, police officers do a great job. My problem, however, with law enforcement," the doctor noted, "is when they actively escalate a situation," Hines explained. "And I can see, at the onset, how things could easily go sideways! When you take a situation that is already emotionally-charged," he observed, "and further escalate the situation, *that*, to me, demonstrates a police officer who has not been properly trained in dealing with the public. Just as importantly," Hines maintained, "if you're afraid of the people that you're supposed to protect, then I have to ask the question: *'Are you in the right line of work?'* If, as a physician," Dr. Hines explained, "I'm afraid of the families that I have to take care of, because they happen to be members of a gang, or they happen to be Pakistani, or from Yemen, or speaking a different language, if that makes me afraid, then I'm not equipped to take care of that patient effectively," he emphasized. "As a result, that patient, and that family, is not going to receive the same level of service that I would give to an African-American family or white family where there is not as much of a language or cultural barrier. It is the responsibility of the police to be equipped and trained to deal with the public they are supposed to serve," Hines reiterated, underscoring the need for professional accountability for law enforcement actions that have an impact upon public health. With that being said, however, police-related homicides and intra-racial violence alone still does not fully explain the decreased life expectancy for America's Black males. So, what gives?

Headed for an Early Grave?

To begin with, racism plays an outsized role in the health challenges faced by Black men in America. From a physiological perspective, research indicates that discrimination and systemic oppression are just as detrimental to one's health as hypertension and homicide. In an article published in the *US National Library of Medicine*, a division of the *National Institutes of Health* called, "Lagging Life Expectancy for Black Men: A Public Health Imperative," researchers M. Jermane Bond and Allen A. Herman discussed the ways in which external factors weighing on men of color tend to shape how they experience, process, and internalize the world around them. "Many historical, social, economic, physical, and biological risk factors shape the life course of Black men and contribute to their increased rates of premature morbidity and mortality," the researchers found. "These include the role of the places and spaces where Black men and their families live, work, worship, and play; the risk that accompanies family formation in the Black community; and the increased individual social, economic, and behavioral risk that is associated with being Black in America," it continued. In fact, even though life expectancy has increased for all racial groups in America over the course of nearly twelve decades, Black men still lag behind in average longevity. "In 1900, the estimated life expectancy for White men was 46.6 years; for non-White men it was 43.5 years; for White women it was 48.7 years, and for non-White women it was 33.5 years. By 2011, the life expectancy for White men was 76.6 years; for Black men it was 72.2 years; for White women it was 81.1 years; and for Black women it was 78.2 years" ("Life Expectancy").

In an analysis of the longevity of Black males in the United States for *Very Well Health*, a website that produces wellness information provided by health professionals, entitled, "Concerning Health Statistics Observed Among Black Men," Jerry Kennard, a psychologist and associate fellow of the *British Psychological Society* delineated a myriad of reasons why Black males, of all ages, pass away prematurely. "Black men in the United States suffer worse health than any other racial group in America," Kennard reported. "For example, as a group, Black men have the lowest life expectancy and the highest death rate compared to both men and women of other racial and ethnic groups," the report noted. "There are a number of reasons that can be pointed to as causes for the issues of poor health among Black men," Kennard said. "Racial discrimination, high rates of incarceration, unemployment, a lack of affordable health services, poor health education, cultural barriers, poverty, access to health insurance, and insufficient medical and social services catering to Black men all negatively affect the quality of life and health," the research found, listing a litany of challenges that ail Black men. According to Kennard's analysis, some of the sobering statistics impacting African-American men today, include the following distressing and deadly data points:

- African-American men live, on average, 7.1 years fewer than most racial subgroups in the United States.

- Black males have exponentially higher mortality rates in every leading cause of death in America.

- 4 out of 10 Black men perish prematurely from heart related diseases, twice the rates of white men in America.

- African-American men are 5 times more likely to die from HIV / AIDS than white men in the country.

- Suicide is the 3rd leading cause of death for young Black males between the ages of 15 to 24 years old.

- Nearly half of all Black men (44%) are considered overweight and suffer greater occurrences of diabetes.

Contextualizing these statistics are real life people, struggling to survive in all-too-real circumstances that collude to deprive them of a life free from the worst societal ills. In a gut-wrenching story about the travails of inner-city survival and the impact it has on the health of its inhabitants, Olga Khazan of *The Atlantic Monthly*, chronicled the threats posed to life and limb simply by "Being Black in America." Set in the gritty city of Baltimore, Maryland, Khazan's story examines the enormous challenges that residents of underprivileged, underserved neighborhoods have simply struggling to survive; resulting in a life expectancy gap between Blacks and whites that is nearly three times the national average. "A baby born in Cheswolde, in Baltimore's far-northwest corner," Khazan wrote, "can expect to live until age 87. Nine miles away in Clifton-Berea, near where "*The Wire*" was filmed, the life expectancy is 67, roughly the same as that of Rwanda, and 12 years shorter than the American average. Similar disparities exist in other segregated cities, such as Philadelphia and Chicago" (Khazan).

Often described as a city in distress, many of Baltimore's historic row houses, some having been around since the city's unprecedented population boom in the 1790's, have long been in need of rehabilitation. As such, attendant with urban blight and disrepair of these deteriorating buildings, come both disease and unsafe conditions for those forced to survive in abject conditions. "These dilapidated homes are in themselves harmful to people's health. Neighborhoods with poorly maintained houses or a large number of abandoned properties, for instance, face a high risk of mouse infestation," Khazan elaborated, shedding light on a silent and elusive health threat that has overrun many urban centers." Every year, more than 5,000 Baltimore children go to the emergency room for an asthma attack... mouse allergen is the biggest environmental factor in those attacks" (Khazan). According to researchers at *Johns Hopkins University,* the city's flagship institution of higher learning, those airborne allergens found in mice urine is regularly inhaled by residents living in these unsanitary conditions, resulting in respiratory issues, inflammation of the lungs and asthma, which also leads to obesity and other dangerous health maladies. But the mice, as dangerous as they are to the health of inner-city residents, pale in comparison to the death sentence that systemic segregation has on Baltimoreans.

"The mice, of course, are just one symptom of the widespread neglect that can set in once neighborhoods become as segregated as Baltimore's are. One study estimated that, in the year 2000, racial segregation caused 176,000 deaths—about as many as were caused by strokes (Khazan). In fact, independent studies have shown that the constant struggle to survive and simply "make ends meet" can decimate a person's immune system. "Certain stressful experiences—such as living in a disordered, impoverished neighborhood—are associated with a shortening of the telomeres, structures that sit on the tips of our chromosomes, which are bundles of DNA inside our cells. Often compared to the plastic caps on the ends of shoelaces, telomeres keep chromosomes from falling apart. They can also be a measure of how much a body has been ground down by life" (Khazan). Having taken an oath to "first do no harm," Dr. Patrick Hines knows all too well the impact that external pressures can have on even the strongest of individuals, seemingly fighting against the prevailing sentiment that uses harm as a first option when dealing with men of color.

"One would have to be deaf, dumb, and blind to not agree with the assumption that Black men in America continue to be targeted and marginalized at alarming rates even today," declared the unflappable physician who has seen the direct result of segregation, poverty and violence in some of the nation's leading intensive care units. "Those things are still happening," Hines continued. "They are happening in a targeted way towards Black men and, as a father of two Black boys, it scares the hell out of me! There's not many things in life that I'm afraid of, but when I think of my boys going out into a world where I know that the world looks at them and does not see their intelligence, their sensitivities, their curiosities, and just sees a potential threat, it really scares me," Hines confessed, with the angst that any loving father would have for their children. "The question is, 'why is that the case?', he inquired, before answering his own hypothesis. "There is a lot of carryover, I believe," Patrick elaborated, "from America's original sin of slavery. I think it is an example of America never really coming to terms with that original sin, which put African-Americans on a trajectory to not being able to have life, liberty, and the pursuit of happiness on par with white Americans. And because we have never really come to terms and acknowledged why that is, it's easy to sort of look at African-American men and the issues that we have, in terms of educational opportunities, health disparities and economic empowerment, and chalk it up to a lack of motivation, hard work, or intelligence," he said. "We must be mindful, however, that those assumptions can be made out of context and we must acknowledge the history of why things are the way they are--and never lose sight of that."

"I think that society has a responsibility," Dr. Hines continued, "but I think that we as Black men have a responsibility also. We have got to acknowledge and own up to our role in all of this and, to the extent that we can, chart our own path," he said. "Independent of what society wants to do. Independent of what politicians want to do. Independent of anyone else, we have got to take care of one another, and take care of our families, and make sure that the next generation is equipped with the tools that they need to be able to be successful in this world that we live in," Hines implored. "The absence of the Black male from families affects the health of our population much more than anything I can ever do in a hospital. A father being in the household, whether they are with the mother or not, being there for that kid and that kid knowing that there is a man out there that cares about them, and that will support them unconditionally, and love them enough to discipline them and teach them respect, those are things that we don't have to wait on. Those are things that we can do today," Hines concluded. And while he may be prescient in his assessment of how to fix what ails Black males in America, Dr. Hines also understands the fact that the trust between African-American males and authority figures, be they law enforcement officers or healthcare providers, must be restored before true healing can begin.

TOP 6

LEADING CAUSES OF DEATH

FOR AMERICA'S BLACK MALES

INFORMATION IN THIS INFO-GRAPHIC GATHERED FROM DATA COLLECTED BY THE CENTERS FOR DISEASE CONTROL AND PREVENTION. PERCENTAGES REPRESENT OVERALL TOTAL DEATHS. FOR MORE INFORMATION VISIT WWW.CDC.GOV

01 HEART DISEASE 23.4%

02 CANCER 21.3%

03 STROKE/UN-INTENTIONAL INJURY 5.6%

04 DIABETES 4.3%

05 CHRONIC LOWER RESPIRATORY DISEASE 3.3%

06 HOMICIDE 3.0%

Who Are You Going to Believe?

Noted theologian and pastor, Dr. Leonard N. Smith, once said: *"Trust is being able to go to sleep when someone else is driving."* As Black American men continue to struggle with the challenges of dealing with a society that consistently undervalues them, the trust level between them and the healthcare community is one that has not only on life support, but during several periods in history, has flatlined and been in need of immediate resuscitation. In fact, as the gulf that exists between these two subgroups widens unabated, the implicit bias that continues to deleteriously impact men of color is one that must begin to be addressed before real healing can begin. Whether its failing to see the humanity of their Black patients, or providing the necessary care they need in emergency rooms and doctors' offices across the country, America's medical professionals have a long way to go towards regaining the faith and confidence of the minority community.

According to an article written by Khlara Bridges and published by the *American Bar Association*, detailing the findings of a study conducted by the *National Academy of Medicine (NAM)*, the prevalence of ethnic inequalities visited upon Black people is a crippling epidemic within the healthcare industry that sees no end in sight. "NAM found that racial and ethnic minorities receive lower-quality health care than white people—even when insurance status, income, age, and severity of conditions are comparable" (Bridges). More than fifteen years ago, NAM sounded the alarm about the stark realities experienced by African-Americans when attempting to traverse the healthcare system, noting that Blacks have a difficult time being treated equitably at almost every phase of the delivery process. Moreover, the academy the notes that poverty plays a significant and material role in the health outcomes of Black Americans. "NAM reported that minority persons are less likely than white persons to be given appropriate cardiac care, to receive kidney dialysis or transplants, and to receive the best treatments for stroke, cancer, or AIDS," the *Academy* noted (Bridges). "It concluded by describing an uncomfortable reality: "some people in the United States were more likely to die from cancer, heart disease, and diabetes simply because of their race or ethnicity, not just because they lack access to health care " (Bridges).

Although physicians, like Patrick Hines, take an oath to always put the needs of their patients first, many African-Americans receive minimal treatments and procedures aimed at reducing costs rather than healing patients. Additionally, Black patients suffering from bipolar disorder are more likely to be treated with antipsychotics despite evidence that these medications have long-term negative effects and are not effective. For example, one study of 400 hospitals in the United States showed that Black patients with heart disease received older, cheaper, and more conservative treatments than their white counterparts. Black patients were less likely to receive coronary bypass operations and angiography. After surgery, they are discharged earlier from the hospital than white patients—at a stage when discharge is inappropriate. The same goes for other illnesses.

When African-American males do succeed in accessing healthcare, oftentimes the services Black men receive are limited or substandard, further contributing to higher mortality rates. In an interview by Kristian Foden-Vencil for *National Public Radio's* "Morning Edition" broadcast called, "Emergency Medical Responders Confront Racial Bias," the conscious and unconscious bias that paramedics and other emergency personnel subject Black patients to while on the job is a jarring wake up call for those who may believe that medical service is colorblind. "Even when factoring in health insurance status or socioeconomic background, the trend held true: Black patients were less likely to be given morphine or other medications that could help treat their pain" (Foden-Vencil). In response to the study's findings, one emergency medical technician, Jason Dahlke, seemed to minimize the need to provide commensurate treatment to all of his patients, without regard to race, religion, or perceived ability to pay for medical services. "When people are acutely sick or injured, pain medication is important," Dahlke says. "But it's not the first thing we're going to worry about. We're going to worry about life threats. You're not necessarily going to die from pain, and we're going to do what satisfies the need in the moment to get you into the ambulance and to the hospital and to a higher level of care" (Foden-Vencil). With that thought in mind, if Black males continue to encounter disparate treatment in the delivery of adequate healthcare services, even before they get to the hospital, what can be done to ameliorate their very founded concerns when encountering medical professionals? For some, the answer lies in connecting Black patients with Black physicians who may better understand their background and care for them accordingly.

In an analysis of a study published by the *National Bureau of Economic Research* entitled, "Does Diversity Matter for Health," Nicole Torres, a Senior Associate Editor of the *Harvard Business Review,* detailed how researchers concluded that Black physicians have a demonstrable impact upon positive health outcomes for Black patients at all levels of the healthcare landscape. "A substantial part of the difference in life expectancy between white and Black men is due to chronic diseases that are amenable to prevention," Torres wrote. "By encouraging more preventative screenings, the researchers calculate, a workforce with more Black doctors could help decrease cardiovascular mortality by 16 deaths per 100,000 per year — resulting in a 19% reduction in the Black-white male gap in cardiovascular mortality and an 8% decline in the Black-white male life expectancy gap" (Torres). Just as importantly, the researchers also discovered that the impact was most profound amongst patients who initially expressed mistrust of the healthcare system. "They were the most reluctant to have services done in the beginning, and they were the most likely to change their minds after talking to a Black doctor and to have more services done. This is meaningful, as other research has found that Black men are more likely to distrust the U.S. health care system than white men, and that this distrust leads to delayed preventive care and worse outcomes" (Torres). Having walked a similar path as those marginalized patients who inherently distrust medical professionals, much of which is attributable to historic and current examples of racism and discrimination, Dr. Patrick Hines acknowledges that the goal of rebuilding broken trust is one that may be difficult to achieve.

"As a pediatric and cardiac ICU physician, I take care of some of the direst cases imaginable," Hines intoned. "We are located right in the city of Detroit, so we draw patients from all over the state--and different countries--who need highly specialized care. Because we are in Detroit, we see patients along the cultural spectrum. As such, we see a lot of African-American patients right here from the city. In fact, Southeast Michigan also has one of the highest populations of people of Middle Eastern origin, outside of the Middle East, and so we see a lot of Muslim patients, as well as patients of Hispanic origin and patients who are White, from places like Oakland County, Michigan and the surrounding areas," he went on. "With that being said, however, although we are located in the heart of a city that is nearly 85% African-American, the majority of the healthcare providers in the hospital are not African-American.

As a matter of fact," Hines elaborated, "there are very few African-American providers in the hospital, so we don't reflect the patient population we care for," Hines noted, describing the dearth of minority doctors in one of America's blackest cities.

"Because we assist patients that are in crisis by definition of the fact that they are coming to see us," Dr. Hines observed, "it leaves us with a short amount of time to make a connection with that patient, and their parents or guardians, and to gain their trust. My dad always told me," the doctor recalled, "that *people don't care how much you know, until they know how much you care'*. I have always taken that philosophy with me in my own practice," he emphasized, "and more medical professionals need to do the same thing! As a critical care physician, I have to establish with the patient and their loved ones that I have this person's best interests at heart. You can relinquish that control to me," Hines explained, "and trust that I am going to provide the best care for your child, and do everything I can, to get them better and, if necessary, to save their life. Just as importantly," he went on, "I believe that being aware of an individual's culture and perspective plays a big role in the process. To that end, I seek to understand where they are coming from and govern myself accordingly. Many of my patients come from a history of having been disrespected and mistreated at all levels; by law enforcement officials, the education system, and society in general," Hines exclaimed. "And they come to me with that burden and baggage, and it really colors that initial interaction with me, whether they are inclined to trust me or not," he went on. "Some of my colleagues who don't really understand that experience, and that culture, will sometimes be put off by an initial resistance to relinquishing control of the medical decision-making process, or a willingness to, at the very least, put that trust in *them*. In some cases, " the experienced caregiver observed, "there is outright mistrust of some physicians, with the care of their child, resulting in a lot of conflict," Hines said. "Unfortunately, however, in the environment in which I am employed, conflict can be the difference between life and death!"

Never one to leave a problem unsolved, as far as he can help it, Dr. Hines works to mentor younger physicians on how they can improve their "bedside manner" in a way that leads to healthier results for patients of color. "When I train young doctors on how to effectively interact with patients, I try to emphasize with them that understanding and compassion are as much a part of the care that we administer, as the actual medicine that we prescribe or the therapy that we provide," Hines noted. "A doctor's ability to connect with a patient and extract the information that is needed to treat them, is an important component of their ability to provide good care. And," he surmised, "*if* they are truly concerned, and are a good physician, they ought to care about the cultural context in which each patient presents themselves," Hines explained.

When asked to consider all of the challenges, and all of the opportunities, facing Black males and their mortality, Dr. Hines still believes that there is hope for the future. "If I could offer one piece of advice to a young Black boy, a young Black teenager, and a Black man, they would be the following: First, for Black boys, I would tell them to listen to their elders," he offered, hearkening back to his own familial roots. "Respect your elders and learn from them," he went further. "For a Black teenager, I would remind them to get their education and learn as much as you can! Education isn't always college and graduate school, or even medical school, for that matter," Hines said. "Education sometimes means talking to mom and dad, the neighbor down the street, and people that have useful information to give you that will put you in a position to be educated and have more power and control over your life" Hines extolled. "Finally, for a Black man, I want to encourage them to *'believe in yourself'* and believe that there is a Higher Power at play that directs the course of your life," he concluded. "Be tenacious and never give up. Don't ever let anyone make you feel as if you are less than who you really are!"

(Patrick C. Hines: Physician, Inventor & Entrepreneur)

What, in your opinion, are the reasons Black males suffer greater mortality rates than other groups in America?

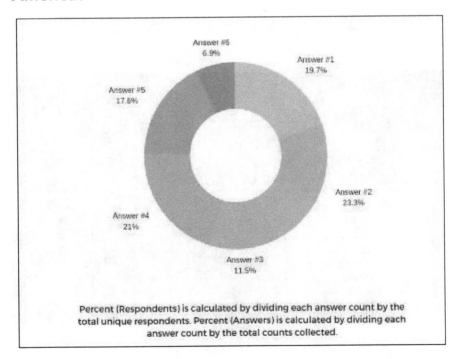

Percent (Respondents) is calculated by dividing each answer count by the total unique respondents. Percent (Answers) is calculated by dividing each answer count by the total counts collected.

1. Black males live more recklessly than others and generally do not take care of themselves = 19.67%

2. Black males are primarily responsible for their own homicide deaths, due to their own poor decisions = 23.32%

3. High rates of sexually transmitted infections among Black males is a result of their poor decisions = 11.48%

4. Black males have access to adequate healthcare, regardless of whether or not they choose to use those options = 20.95%

5. Black males are treated as equitably as others when seeking healthcare treatment = 17.57%

6. Blacks have higher pain tolerance than whites = 6.92%

All survey results displayed above are represented by the overall percentage of survey respondents. For more information on our survey methodology, please see the Author's Note, located in the front matter of the book. To review raw survey results, visit: http://bit.ly/stillinvisiblesurvey.

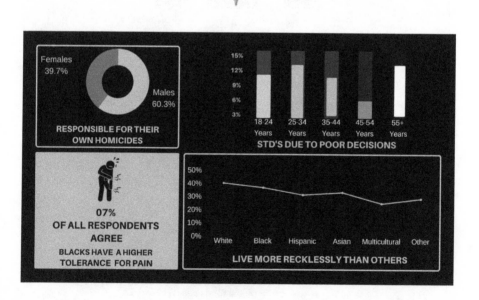

Findings by Race

- More than a quarter of all Hispanic respondents (25.77%), across all age groups, agree with the statement, *"Black males are primarily for their own homicide deaths due to their own poor decisions."*

- A plurality of all Asian respondents (23.53%) agree with the statement: *"Black males live more recklessly than others and generally do not take care of themselves."*

- Only a small number of White female respondents (4.09%) agree with the statement: *"Blacks have a higher pain tolerance than whites."*

Findings by Gender

- More than a quarter of all Male respondents (25.69%), agree with the statement: *"Black males are primarily for their own homicide deaths due to their own poor decisions."*

- 1 out of 4 Hispanic female respondents (25.00%) agree with the statement: *"Black males live more recklessly than others and generally do not take care of themselves."*

- Nearly 1 out of 4 Black male respondents (23.81%) agree with the statement: *"Black males have access to adequate healthcare, whether or not they choose to use those options."*

Findings by Age

- Less than 1 out of 10 Black female respondents (6.06%), across all ages, agree with the statement, *"High rates of sexually transmitted infections among Black males is a result of their poor decisions."*

- Nearly 2 out of 10 White female respondents (17.65%), ages 18-24 years old, agree with the statement, *"Black males have adequate access to healthcare, whether or not they choose to use those options."*

- Nearly 2 out of 10 Male respondents (19.67%), ages 35-44 years old, agree with the statement, *"Black males are primarily responsible for their own homicide deaths, due to their own poor decisions."*

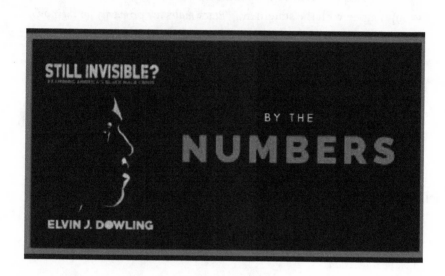

"Stop the Violence ... Increase the Peace!"

- For young Black males between the ages of 15 and 34, the number one cause for their death was homicide. Just as alarmingly, more than half of all deaths of Black teenagers (50.8%) are a result of homicide (Kennard).

- Black men are nearly 2.5 times more likely to be killed by police than are white men. Statistical models also indicate that 1 in 1,000 Black men and boys will be killed by police over their life course ("Police Violence").

"Bullets Don't Have Names on Them!"

- African-American men have a disproportionately higher mortality rate from all leading causes of death. As a result, they live 7.1 years shorter than most racial groups in America (Kennard).

- Approximately 4 out of every 10 Black men (40%) who have cardiovascular disease during their lifetime can expect to die prematurely, twice the rate for white men (21%) in America (Kennard).

"Risk Always Increases with Unchecked Diseases!"

- Black males suffer from preventable deaths more than most racial subgroups, to include oral disease that is treatable (if caught in time) and suicide; the 3rd leading cause of death for Black males ages 15-24 years old (Kennard).

- Black men are 5 times more likely to die of HIV/AIDS. Heterosexual Black men have a 1 in 20 lifetime risk, compared to a 1 in 132 lifetime risk for white heterosexual men and a 1 in 2 lifetime risk for Black gay men (Kennard).

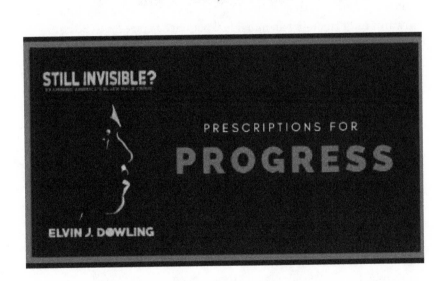

"More Black Doctors = Fewer Black Deaths"

- A healthcare system with more Black doctors could help lead to a 19% reduction in the Black-white male gap in cardiovascular mortality and an 8% decline in the Black-white male life expectancy gap (Torres).

- Sharing a racial or cultural background with one's doctor goes a long way towards promoting trust. Black men seen by Black doctors agreed to more preventive services than those seen by nonblack doctors (Torres).

"Work Together to Make Things Better!"

- Provide police with strategies they can use to prevent overreactions or potential misconduct by fellow officers, such as the use of codewords that encourage a colleague to calm down or stop what they're doing ("Proven Policies).

- Develop community based behavioral intervention programs that use cognitive developmental principles that teach youth how to properly react and respond in potentially violent or deadly situations ("Proven Policies").

"Check Yourself ... Don't Wreck Someone Else!"

- Healthcare professionals must be able to empathize with patients to better understand how to treat them. Increasing empathy can go a long way towards understanding an individual patient's perspective (Bucknor-Ferron, p. 61).

- Training is critical to recognizing and reducing incidences of unconscious bias. Increased educational opportunities for doctors , focusing on cultural awareness, can help to eliminate disparate treatment (Bucknor-Ferron, p. 62).

Works Cited

1. Williams, Joseph. "Study: Police Violence a Leading Cause   of Death for Young Men." *USNews.com*, US News   & World Reports. 5 August 2019.   http://bit.ly/312NYJG

2. Qui, Linda. "Juan Williams: No. 1 Cause of Death for African-American Males 15-34 Is Murder."   *Politifact.com*, Poynter Institute. 24 August 2014.   http://bit.ly/2MD3Op8

3. Bond, M. Jermane and Herman, Allen A., "Lagging Life Expectancy for Black Men: A Public Health   Imperative." *American Journal of Public Health*, US   National Library of

Medicine - National Institutes of Health. July 2016. http://bit.ly/2VBkaTl

4. Kenard, Jerry. "Health Statistics for Black American Men." *VeryWellHealth.com*, About, Inc. (Dotdash). 22 May 2019. http://bit.ly/2M81tUf

5. Khazan, Olga. "Being Black in America Can Be Hazardous to Your Health." *TheAtantic.com*, Web. July 2018. http://bit.ly/2OPlJMn

6. Bridges, Khlara. "Implicit Bias and Racial Disparities in Health Care." *AmericanBar.org*, American Bar Association. Web. Accessed 13 October 2019. http://bit.ly/2VC9ZxU

7. Foden-Vencil, Kristian. "Emergency Medical Responders Confront Racial Bias: An Interview with Jamie Kennel." Interview Conducted by Kristian Foden-Vencil. *National Public Radio - Morning.* Edition. 3 January 2019. https://n.pr/32aUFe4

8. Torres, Nicole. "Research: Having a Black Doctor Led Black Men to Receive More-Effective Care." *Harvard Business Review*, Harvard Business Publishing. 10 August 2018. http://bit.ly/2nM6loM

9. Novotney, Amy. "Preventing Police Misconduct." *APA.org*, American Psychological Association. October 2017. Web. http://bit.ly/2Bd2Ef1

10. Lopez, German. "Six Proven Policies for Reducing Crime and Violence Without Gun Control." *Vox.com*, Vox Media, Inc. 19 July 2016. http://bit.ly/2qgNVgL

11. Bucknor-Feron, Patricia and Zagaja, Lori. "Five Strategies to Combat Unconscious Bias." *Nursing2016.com*, Wolters Kluwer Health, Inc. November 2016, Volume: 46, Number 11. http://bit.ly/2BhYqT2

Chapter 8: "Will They Ever See Us?"

The Impact of Invisibility on the Black Male Psyche

❝❝

Or again, you often doubt if you really exist. You wonder whether you aren't simply a phantom in other people's minds. Say, a figure in a nightmare which the sleeper tries with all his strength to destroy. It's when you feel like this that, out of resentment, you begin to bump people back. And, let me confess, you feel that way most of the time. You ache with the need to convince yourself that you do exist in the real world, that you're a part of all the sound and anguish, and you strike out with your fists, you curse and you swear to make them recognize you. And, alas, it's seldom successful."

- Ralph Ellison, "Invisible Man" (Shmoop Editorial Team. Prologue. 2.)

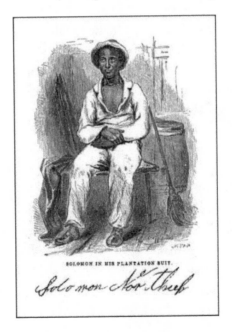

SOLOMON IN HIS PLANTATION SUIT.

Solomon Northrop

(Solomon Northrop, an African-American abolitionist and the author of the book, "Twelve Years A Slave", was a free man of color living in New York when he was kidnapped, stripped of his identity, and sold into slavery in Louisiana in 1841.)

"Out of My Sight ... Out of Your Mind!"

How Do You Define Insanity?

In the 1836 book, "Quakerism Examined", author John Wilkinson once profoundly proclaimed: *"One of the artifices of Satan, is to induce men to believe that he does not exist."* As the United States of America continues to evolve into a more "cosmopolitan society," one of the things our nation has become quite adept at is pretending that those who live on the margins of our society are, indeed, figments of our collective imagination. From the poor and disenfranchised who have no means of exerting their collective influence because, of course, they are struggling just to make ends meet, to those who have achieved a modicum of success, but don't necessarily have the "complexion for the protection" afforded them under the *Constitution* of the United States and, as a result are only rendered visible at the most inconvenient times, the feeling that Blacks have of not being "seen" by the rest of society is as old as the crack in America's *Liberty Bell*. Furthermore, in as much as the wretched souls who don't receive the same level of consideration and empathy as those of us who are of a more "landed gentry", the issue of "invisibility" for minorities in this country is as exasperating to them as it is for the rest of us who, frankly, just want to move on. Unfortunately, however, we won't be able to do so, unless and until we reckon ourselves with the 'ghosts slavery past' and acknowledge (even if doing so begrudgingly) its impact. Just as importantly, if and when this happens, we must begin by paying close attention to the enormous price that everyone pays when the mental health conditions of a people portend an ominous future for our nation--and therein lies my concern. To that end, we need look no further than the true story of a man who, through a series of indignities that confound human imagination, remind us of the enormous impact that trauma, stress and anxiety can have when visited upon those who have had the unfortunate experience of being considered less than human.

Born in 1808 in New York State as the son of free Negro parents, Solomon Northrup was an educated Black man who, as a farmer, landowner and professional violinist, was exceptionally gifted and relatively urbane by many measures in American society, except for one little problem... *(Did I mention that he was Black?).* Anyhow, in 1841, Northrop was offered a "job opportunity" that would change his fortunes for the worst, unbeknownst to him, particularly with regard to how he would be legally classified and perceived by the world around him for at least the next dozen years of his life. In responding to a traveling musician's job advertisement in Washington, D.C, hundreds of miles from freedom and deep into hostile territory, where the institution of slavery was legal, Solomon found himself in the unfortunate position of being "repatriated", if you will, having been sent, bound and chained, to the State of Louisiana, losing his status as a free man in America. *(Talk about being in the wrong place, at the wrong time!)* In fact, it wasn't until, by happenstance, Northrup convinced a wayfaring stranger to tell his tale of woe to friends in the North, ultimately leading to then New York Governor, Washington Hunt, championing Northrup's cause; ultimately liberating him in 1853. It wasn't however, before the once recognizable figure lost a large part of his life, his sanity and his own sense of self, before regaining his true identity—having spent "Twelve Years A Slave."

Since that time, to this day, Blacks in America have fought against the notion that they are undeserving, and inherently unequal, while continuing to paddle upstream against the tide of what many believe to be the "natural order of God," and, frankly, it must be overwhelming. In her book, "Post Traumatic Slave Syndrome: America's Legacy of Enduring Injury and Healing", Dr. Joy DeGruy, theorized that *P.T.S.S.* , as Post-Traumatic Slave Syndrome is called, is a survival mechanism that African-Americans use today—more than 150 years removed from emancipation—as a means of adapting to and overcoming the challenges of continued degradation and dehumanization. "It is a condition that exists as a consequence of multigenerational oppression of Africans and their descendants resulting from centuries of chattel slavery--a form of slavery which was predicated on the belief that African- Americans were inherently/genetically inferior to whites" (DeGruy). To that end, given the viciousness of the *Trans-Atlantic Slave Trade*, despite some who continue to insist that slavery was a happy and wholesome affair, and others who have theorized that the psychological and emotional consequences of this barbaric form of cruelty (even for my own standards) is still being felt today, it is clear to most that America's "original sin" can, at a minimum, be described as an "inconvenient truth." Moreover, as the traumatic shockwaves of slavery continue to reverberate within the lives of both those whose ancestors suffered through it and those whose ancestors benefitted from it, one thing remains abundantly clear: America can no longer afford to ignore a corrosive issue, bubbling just below the surface: the untreated mental health challenges of a clearly traumatized segment of her society.

One of our nation's most endearing founding fathers, Benjamin Franklin, no stranger to mental health issues *(having himself had a predilection for the macabre and a literal basement full of skeletons)*, once said: "An ounce of prevention is worth a pound of cure." *(Boy, was he right about that... but I digress!)* With that being said, however, I believe that the time is long past due that our country finally begins to address the social, emotional and psychological brunt of being Black in this country. Furthermore, at an annual expense to the American taxpayer of more than two hundred billion dollars, the cost of doing nothing about our collective anxiety is simply one we cannot afford. In short, my friends, "crazy is costly" and we can no longer afford the bill. Or, in the inimitable words of that hip American poet, David Marvin Blake, who once sang:

❝

"If it don't make dollars, it don't make sense. So, don't kill the game, let the pimpin' commence."

Let's talk about it people—here's my number and a dime...

Call Me Anytime,

Justitia

Lady Justice

Justin Hopkins: "Continuing a Legacy of Listening."

What's on Your Mind Today?

"I'm originally from Queens, New York, and was born the son of Everett and Audrey Hopkins," the psychological virtuoso began, describing the close-knit family unit from which he comes. "My entire family, both maternal and paternal, is from Queens, New York," he continued. "My father is a private practice attorney who owns a law firm in Queens, which has been in operation for about 30 plus years or so. My mom is the primary manager of the office, and my brother and I both worked in that office when we were growing up," Hopkins said. Hailing from a family of small business owners, Justin is a third-generation entrepreneur who understands the importance of building communities and relationships one customer or client at a time.

"My father's law firm, a community institution in and of itself, is actually right next door to my grandfather's barbershop," he noted. "In fact," Hopkins went on, "my grandfather's shop has been a staple in the community for more than 50 years and it was my grandfather, on my paternal side, who cleared the way for my father to open his office, as he owns the entire block of land in which both businesses are located. And that's how my family has sustained itself and kind of progressed in these modern times, and have been able to take part in and have economic success in this country," he noted. "So, while I currently reside in Washington, DC, the Borough of Queens is still a big part of my heart," the mental health clinician explained. "My summers," Hopkins explained, "were spent working in the law office and cleaning the homes of my father's clients, so he could help them close on their house; as well as sweeping up hair off the barbershop floor at my grandfather's shop just a few doors down. In turn," he explained, "my parents never, ever, ever missed a football game, or baseball game that I played in. In fact, my brother played college football and started at the position of center for two years, and my parents flew to every game he played in--all over the country," he emphasized. "From the get-go, since the day I was born, they were very committed to family, and to making sure that my brother and I had everything that we needed, and some of what we wanted," Hopkins noted proudly. "They knew we lived in a very tough world as a Black family, and they did not shy away from that reality. In fact, I am proud to say that I cannot ever remember, throughout my entire upbringing, thinking that there was anything negative about being Black.

"I have always felt supremely proud of the color of my skin, what it meant to be Black," Hopkins waxed poetically. "As young Black males growing up, my father taught my brother and I that we needed to be twice as good as anyone else to get anywhere in life. In doing so," he went on, "he often reminded us that we could do anything we set our minds to, and that he and my mother would always support our effort—no matter what," the psychotherapist recalled. "In fact, I inherited from them a sense of optimism and perseverance that sticks with me to this day," he said, noting that the genesis of his own father's ambition began one generation previously—with his own father—a man with a seventh grade education that would go on to amass a small fortune as an entrepreneur and real estate investor.

"Although my grandfather has experienced some modicum of success in his life, he quit going to school by the time he was thirteen years old, so that he could earn money for his family, and that's what he's been doing ever since," Dr. Hopkins explained. "He's one of ten children, who enlisted in the *U.S. Army* and fought in the *Korean War*. At that time, he earned $80 a month and he sent half of that home to his family. From an early age, my grandfather has continued to demonstrate to our family the fact that we've got to take care of each other, because no one else will. That's just what we do," Hopkins explained, reiterating his progenitor's humble beginnings "When I graduated from college, my grandfather was there, and all he kept saying was, 'I could never pass the 7th grade... I could never pass the 7th grade,'" Hopkins beamed proudly, observing that the most important thing to his grandfather was knowing that he had done everything he could to help move the family forward. "So now, I'm doing my part," Hopkins conceded.

"Professionally, I am a licensed clinical psychologist, specializing in providing psychotherapy for adolescents, adults and couples, on a wide array of challenges they face; including mood disorders, anxiety issues, and work or academically related stress," Hopkins said. "I just think there is something so fascinating about the human mind and human spirit. As you know," he went on, "there are not very many Black psychologists and mental health experts in my profession, but I got the desire to be in this field from growing up in my grandfather's barbershop, and seeing how barbers and patrons, men of all ages were actively engaged in supporting each other, and it didn't happen anywhere else in my community," Dr. Hopkins observed. "It literally happened _nowhere else_, where men of color came together and really talked about their issues, expressed their concerns, cried if they had to, and received the support that they needed to move forward in life. Watching those interactions, I saw that there was something very powerful there, and it led me to my work in the field of mental health," the clinician declared. It is no surprise then that those early experiences in his grandfather's barbershop helped to lead Hopkins into a profession that, to many African-American males, is shrouded in the stigma of weakness and frailty that is juxtaposed to the projection of strength they seek to portray to the public.

For many years, Black barbershops have historically been nonjudgmental spaces for African-American males, both men and boys, to talk about the things that are on their minds, from sports to dating, to manhood. In an innovative undertaking called "The Confess Project," a mental health initiative for boys and men of color, Black men are encouraged to express their emotions and accept communal support as they seek solace from the world around. According to an article written by Celeste Hamilton Dennis of _YES! Magazine_, the prevalence of untreated mental health issues within the African-American community is something that continues to keep the community in general, and Black men in particular, in a precarious state of hopelessness. "Black people more frequently have post-traumatic stress disorder than other ethnic groups. Yet Black men are less likely to get treatment than the general population, according to the _Centers for Disease Control and Prevention_ and _National Alliance on Mental Illness_," Dennis wrote. "Mental illness in the U.S. carries a stigma. For the Black community, especially for men, Lewis says, that stigma is manifold and gets in the way of asking for help" (Dennis). At the barbershop, however, the worries and stigmatization of the outside world melt away as Black men luxuriate, if but only for a moment, in the place where "everybody knows your name."

Perhaps Black America's leading paragon of credible information and reliable sources, *Ebony Magazine*, in an article written by Dr. Larry Walker entitled, "Black Men and Mental Illness Can Be a Barbershop Conversation, Too" celebrated the progress that is being made in grooming salons catering to African-American men all across the country. In his reporting, Walker noted that the continued challenges facing Black men center around issues pertaining to a toxic form of masculinity that is tearing away at the very soul of those who hold on to pain and despair. According to Dr. F. Abron Franklin, an epidemiologist and director of treatment and prevention services for *Volunteers of America - Oregon*, "African-American men are socialized by a definitional architecture of manhood that promotes the integrity of a man or manhood is premised on a man's level of resources to address his own issues and not to ask the help of others. Therefore, out a fear of appearing weak or infirm, African-American men are less motivated to utilize mental health services " (Walker). To compound this challenge, the issue of Post-Traumatic Stress Disorder (PTSD) that Black males are susceptible to continue to cloud their present and obscure their future.

Throughout the course of their sojourn in America, Black males have had an incredible burden to bear, as they confront daily indignities and discriminatory treatment. In their assessment of the state of Black mental health called, "Invisible Man: Black Men & PTSD," contributors for *BlackDoctor.org*, a website devoted exclusively to the strategies, tactics and health advice that help African-Americans live healthier lives, observed that Black males have challenges that can often overwhelm and debilitate even the strongest of men. "The stress comes in every direction on a daily basis. The impact of walking down the street in your own neighborhood can be a traumatic experience in itself. You don't know who to trust. You would love to trust your brother who shares the same pigment, but he's bound by that same fear that has you tiptoeing on eggshells just to walk to work or school," the doctors wrote, noting the sense of loneliness that comes with being a Black male in America. "It's hard to trust the police because you don't know if they'll protect or serve," they continued. "And sometimes the trauma happens in your own home. The dynamics of Black household relations can often put a strain on the mind of a young Black man who will grow up with this

this thing we call post traumatic disorder" ("PTSD"). As a Disorders Analyst devoted to positively improving the mental health conditions of distressed individuals, Dr. Justin Hopkins believes that the impact of invisibility in the everyday existence of Black males in America is one that is as corrosive to the mind as cancer is to the body.

"There are a couple of really concrete ways that marginalization affects the mental well-being of Black folks, particularly when they are rendered invisible by the rest of society," Hopkins explained. "One example is the high rates of Black boys that are diagnosed with Attention Deficit Hyperactivity Disorder (ADHD) because of whatever preconceptions educators and physicians may have about them, and their behaviors are more likely to be seen as threatening, whereas children from all ethnic groups, across the board, seem to demonstrate the same amount of destructive behaviors and acting out behaviors in classrooms, yet don't receive this diagnosis," he stated. "Black boys are more likely to be suspended and expelled from school, and it greatly impacts both the learning process of the child, not to mention their self-image, and also puts us behind the 8-ball in terms of undoing much of the harm that is created as a result," bookish clinician detailed. "That happens with adults as well," Hopkins went on. "We are more likely to receive a more severe diagnosis, however, as a Black person is quicker to receive a diagnosis of schizophrenia, or other disorders classified in the category of psychotic, than is a person of the majority race or group," he noted, pointing out the inequities in mental health treatment that can have a profound impact on the future trajectory of a patient's quality of life.

"The idea of our Blackness is first defined in the eyes of everyone else," Justin declared, explaining the reason why the mental weight of oppression is as burdensome to Black men as overt discrimination and racism. "We are Black before we are people, and that is a heavy, *heavy* weight that we have to carry," the doctor emphasized. "Black men exist under a double consciousness, in that we think of ourselves as a person, an individual if you will, but also as a 'Black person', and all of the burdens that come with that collective experience," he continued. "What society attributes to being Black is the burden we bear every single second of every single day," Hopinks explained. "How might I be perceived if I do this, or if I make that comment in a meeting? We have to be careful not to behave in certain ways that appear stereotypical or un-collegial, or in any way somehow attributed to the adverse qualities that are 'uniquely Black'. And that's a heavy cognitive burden to carry in the mind," the mental health clinician explained. "So, that's one thing that we have to adjust to, and I believe there's always a cognitive load on the minds of Black people, and that is exhausting. When I say our race takes up space in my mind," Hopkins delineated, "I mean that, in this society, it's impossible to be a Black person in America without, in some part of your mind, realizing that society isn't kind to you; that the cards are stacked against you, and that there are going to be obstacles that you have to overcome that are 'uniquely yours,' in light of the color of your skin. As Black men," Justin declared, "you're going to have it harder and you're going to have to try harder and be better in everything you do," he said.

"The margin of error is slim, or nonexistent in certain cases, and that's a lot of pressure! As such, we must continue to bear in mind the massive weight of our entire racial history in America, and what it means to be Black, and we have to be conscious of that from day to day; and we must do that every second of every day," Hopkins intoned "And every minute every hour" he declared. "We have to be conscious of how we behave, how we interact, how people see us; and that takes up space in our consciousness. In some situations," the therapist explained, "it can make our natural inclinations a bit more awkward, premeditated and clunky, and can challenge on natural way of being. When we interact with people in a majority 'Black space' , Black men tend to be more fluid in our emotions and thinking. When we are in a predominately white environment, however, we have to change our methods," Dr. Hopkins observed.

"As an early career professional, there are not very many Black clinicians in the field of mental health, especially in Psychology. I think one thing that often crosses my mind," the thoughtful therapist said, "is how my colleagues view me, in light of my Blackness. How are others responding to me in light of my Blackness? So, it does take up space in my own mind, even with regard to my interactions with colleagues and employers, peers or even the students I teach! How are they receiving me as a Black man," Hopkins asked? "Is it okay for me to give a lecture on diversity? Will they receive it the same way? Or will they just presuppose, 'of course I'm a Black man giving a lecture on diversity', because it only matters to me. And, more importantly," he noted, "in their minds, they don't ever have to validate my opinion" he said, resigning himself to the possibility that the struggle for visibility is one that confronts all Black males, regardless of their place or station in life. "So, when I say it 'takes up space', it is something that we have to constantly consider and not only does that make things complicated it's also incredibly exhausting," he sighed.

How High?

As a result of the constant bombardment of societal, economic, and cultural messages that continuously communicate a sense of pending doom and ultimate despair for men of color in America, particularly in light of the PTSD experienced by those who are on the receiving end of this war of the mind, researchers have theorized that a sense of learned helplessness, a phenomenon observed in torture victims and those subjected to continued mental and/or physical abuse, takes hold in the minds of many Blacks. In fact, according to Dr. Leon Green, Ph.D., a licensed clinical psychologist, in his report, "A Learned Helplessness Analysis of Problems Confronting the Black Community," the systems in which African-Americans navigate daily significantly contribute to what Dr. Martin Luther King, Jr. once called a "nagging sense of nobodyness." "Briefly stated," Green wrote, "learned helplessness occurs when an individual perceives that there is no response which he can make that will affect the outcome or control of a particular situation or event. The practice of racial discrimination and economic, political, and educational restrictions provide the basis for many Blacks to experience helplessness," he noted, citing previous research indicating the magnitude to which one's willingness to give up a will to persevere and fight on is diminished with each fleeting microaggression experienced by the besieged.

"At a basic level, Black people's color is often the basis for excluding them from certain housing areas," Green noted, further underscoring his position. "Blacks are restricted and excluded from certain jobs regardless of their qualifications and certain schools and educational institutions regardless of level of preparation. For many Black people, a perception of helplessness even extends itself to the political spheres; Blacks express futility in their attempts to participate actively in the political process in America," Green continued. "Black persons in ghetto-slum areas may not ascertain any possibility of escaping from their plight. Unskilled Blacks who are jobless frequently perceive no chance of acquiring a job in the future. Black children in schools may perceive no means to affect the grades they receive from white teachers, especially if the teachers express a lack of confidence in their ability to learn ("Learned Helplessness").

If this type of helplessness does, indeed, trigger a pervasive sense of despair that is difficult to overcome, how have African-Americans, in general, and Black males in particular, overcome such overwhelming odds? Just as critically, how have they been successful at accomplishing some of the jaw-dropping goals that they have realized—in a country designed to exclude, devalue and ignore their achievements? For many African-Americans, it is the notion of the requirement that they *"work twice as hard to (hopefully) get half the credit"* and, in doing so, be able to push past the boundaries and obstacles set before them. For some, adherence to that philosophy has reaped significant benefits . For the vast majority, however, the notion of hard work and dedication" paying off in the end is merely a pipe dream.

In an opinion piece written for *The Guardian* newspaper by Britni Danielle, a Los Angeles-based freelance journalist, editor and novelist, the concept of being "twice as good to get half the credit," falls flat on its face. Responding to a 2015 commencement address to the graduating class at *Tuskegee University* in Alabama, by then U.S. First Lady Michelle Obama, imploring students to look past the limitations that others had placed upon them and redouble their efforts to succeed, despite others' expectations, critics took the trailblazing leader to task for perpetuating a notion that does not ring true for the vast majority of historically disadvantaged individuals. "Our nation continues to lean on the myth of the American dream, but climbing the rungs of the socio-economic ladder remains difficult, particularly for those at the bottom," Danielle declared. "For every story of someone who overcame crushing poverty to achieve massive success are thousands of others of those who continue to languish in low-wage jobs and in substandard conditions. In fact," she continued, "while nearly two out of three white people make it into the middle class by middle age... that number drops to just three out of ten for

Black people" (Danielle). Today, the continuing challenge for the untold millions who face the scourge of learned helplessness and unyielding hopelessness is one that can no longer be ignored. As such, simply admonishing otherwise hard-working individuals to work *even harder,* with no guarantee of a return on their investment of labor and effort—without addressing the root causes of those issues--won't work either. So, what can be done to triage and treat the needs of a "suffering minority" that is mostly misunderstood and often overlooked? For Dr. Justin Hopkins, the answer lies in understanding the structures that help to perpetuate an environment that keeps African-American males perpetually of balance.

"I think at the core—at the absolute core—of our very humanity not quite being 'seen' by the world around us, the fact that we are _still_ invisible, is difficult for even the most astute individual to comprehend," Hopkins began, detailing what he believed to be the nexus between hope and despair for Black males in America. "The fact that we are, indeed, treated as invisible by others, in many aspects of our lives is, oftentimes, hard to pinpoint and call out, because it's not forthright. Today, it's a bit more subtle and it's a bit more insidious," he explained. "We've integrated our society, in many ways and there isn't any more outright lynching. We aren't enslaved physically anymore, but rather there is a system in place, that is dependent upon the mass incarceration of Black people. In many ways, the economy depends on it. As such, I would venture to say that the very fabric of American society, the capitalistic pillar of our country, is mass incarceration. The capitalistic function of America depends in part on the imprisonment of Black people," Hopkins opined.

"I think our country is working exactly the way it's designed to work. And I think it's working really well...and that's the problem. It's problematic and inhumane," he went on. "The idea of 'race', in general, is a fabricated concept that man just decided to make up one day, to exclude, to divide and to create caste systems. So, naturally, there are some folks who are excluded, and some folks who have access to power. But this idea that 'whiteness' is associated with racial supremacy, while it is a fundamental part of American culture, it's also a false and fragile concept because _it is false._ And because _it is false_ and because _it is fragile,_ some in the majority in our society, are fearful of losing that sense of 'supremacy' and the safety of what it means to be white in America," Hopkins surmised. "When you have a sense of supremacy, the concept of equality seems like oppression."

"These days," the candid therapist noted, "there are more white folks who are acknowledging, *whether they want to or not*, that there *is* such thing as 'white privilege'. The jig is up," Hopkins concluded. "If you have any kind of intelligence, you have to start acknowledging this reality. There *is* such thing as white privilege. For so long," he continued, "*White* has been associated with being right; being a little bit better of a human being than others—and it is just an outright lie. It's a falsehood that is losing its edge and for some people, that is excruciatingly painful and scary. But to lose that edge, for them, actually leads to equality for everyone else. To equity. To discovering that, *'no'*, whiteness does not mean that you're better than everyone else. What it does mean, however, is that you have better access to the things that other people don't, "Hopkins went on. "And, I think, people are losing that belief in the fallacy that America has told itself over, and over, and over again, that *'white is always right'*. So, giving up any semblance of privilege, for many feels like oppression to them," he concluded. "I really just want to say to those people— *'Welcome to my world'*."

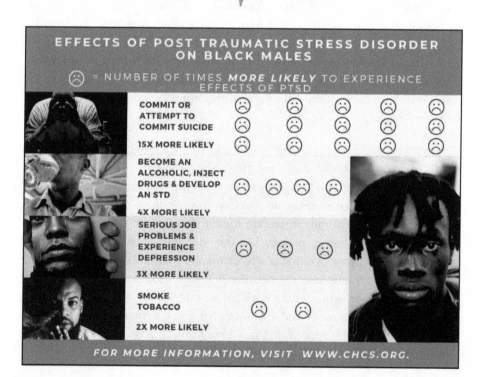

EFFECTS OF POST TRAUMATIC STRESS DISORDER ON BLACK MALES

☹ = NUMBER OF TIMES *MORE LIKELY* TO EXPERIENCE EFFECTS OF PTSD

COMMIT OR ATTEMPT TO COMMIT SUICIDE **15X MORE LIKELY**	☹ ☹ ☹ ☹ ☹ / ☹ ☹ ☹ ☹ ☹ / ☹ ☹ ☹ ☹ ☹
BECOME AN ALCOHOLIC, INJECT DRUGS & DEVELOP AN STD **4X MORE LIKELY**	☹ ☹ ☹ ☹
SERIOUS JOB PROBLEMS & EXPERIENCE DEPRESSION **3X MORE LIKELY**	☹ ☹ ☹
SMOKE TOBACCO **2X MORE LIKELY**	☹ ☹

FOR MORE INFORMATION, VISIT WWW.CHCS.ORG.

What's the Difference Anyway?

Famed writer, Toni Morrison, once declared: *"In this country American means white. Everybody else has to hyphenate."* The challenge that many African-Americans face, particularly Black males, is the fact that their very "Blackness" criminalizes and oftentimes dehumanizes them in the eyes of others. For more than 400 years, African Descendants of Slaves have faced an ominous challenge of exactly what to call themselves, as a myriad of names have been foisted upon them at various points in history, some of which have been used in a pejorative light, while others have been co-opted as terms of endearment. From the designation *"Negro"*, a term which, to elderly Blacks was once an honor, is now an insult to millennials, to its more derisive derivative, *"Nigger"*, an epithet still used today, to *"Colored"*, to *"Black"*, to *"African-American"*, the sheer identity confusion that men and women of color face is something that reverberates throughout generations. Moreover, the mental health implications of being Black in America is one that cannot be ignored.

According to extensive research, the different ways by which people of color are defined, go a long way towards how they are treated in American society. In a story entitled, "White Americans Draw Distinctions Between African-Americans and Blacks," writer Tom Jacobs of the *Pacific Standard*, an online magazine that focuses on issues of social and environmental justice, spoke openly of the differences in perception and treatment of African Descendants of Slaves and other individuals of color, simply by what they are called. In short, white Americans are comfortable (enough) with African-Americans but have significant and material issues with Blacks. In a series of experiments, researchers discovered that, how an individual is labeled, oftentimes colors how they are perceived by others. When given a list of characteristics associated with people of color, more often than not, the white subjects associated those traits associated with the term "Black" with a negative connotation, whereas the term African-American was perceived more positively. "The content embedded in the Black stereotype is generally more negative, and less warm and competent, than that in the African-American stereotype," the researchers noted. "These different associations carry consequences for how whites perceive Americans of African descent who are labeled with either term" (Jacobs).

According to a report of the *American Psychological Association* called, "Physiological & Psychological Impact of Racism and Discrimination for African-Americans", the weight of being Black poses a tremendous strain upon the physical and mental health of those struggling under the weight of continued oppression, regardless of the racial designations used to describe them. "Although the chronic condition of stress can have negative side effects on all persons, the unique psycho-social and contextual factors, specifically the common and pervasive exposure to racism and discrimination, creates an additional daily stressor for African-Americans," the report detailed. "Often, African-Americans do not realize daily stressors that may affect their psychological or physiological health and...the health effects that result from exposure and perception of racism and discrimination" ("Psychological Impact"). Justin Hopkins believes that this "distinction with a difference" helps to wreak havoc on the minds and consciousness of overburdened men of color.

"There is this really ingrained, almost psychotic state, that Black men have—living in this country—of being overtly when it comes to being negatively perceived and intentionally ignored at all other times, which leaves us with this incredibly dissonant experience," the psychotherapist surmised. "In my opinion," Hopkins elucidated, "the most urgent challenge facing us right now is for our humanity to be recognized! To this day, we are still not seen as human beings by many, we are just not, and it's been this way since the founding of our country," he explained. "We are still trying to assert, through various socio-political movements, that *'Black Lives Matter'*, and even saying just that has been met with so much contention and strife that it really is a psychotic experience. It underscores the notion that, yes, you're a person, but we don't acknowledge that your life has value. I think somehow," Hopkins speculated, "society has been conditioned to attribute the most negative possible qualities to Black men, no matter what the setting or context is," he bemoaned. "We are prone to be seen as more aggressive and less trustworthy, whether dealing with a police officer or a loan officer, but we are still human beings, yet somehow our humanity remains unseen and unrecognized to this day." With that being said, however, Justin believes that there is hope for the future, should Black men allow themselves to be more vulnerable than they already are.

"The state of the African-American male today, at least from my perspective, is downtrodden but powerful," Hopkins explained. "We are oppressed, but we are persistent and, more importantly, we are hopeful. We are striving, we are clawing, and we are fighting, with every ounce of our being, to move ourselves forward; and we are hoping and praying that our striving won't be in vain," he declared. "My advice to Black men in America is simple—don't suffer in silence ... and don't strive in isolation," he admonished. "No matter what," the caring clinician continued, "don't *ever, ever, ever* count yourself out. You are powerful, purposeful and valued in this life and on this Earth. Your life is invaluable, and you can do all things with the right focus and the right people to support you."

(Justin Hopkins: Psychologist & Practitioner)

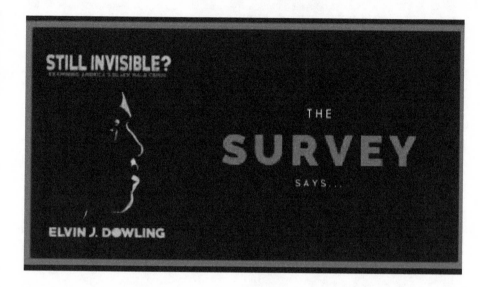

How strongly do you agree with this statement: Black men live in the margins of society?

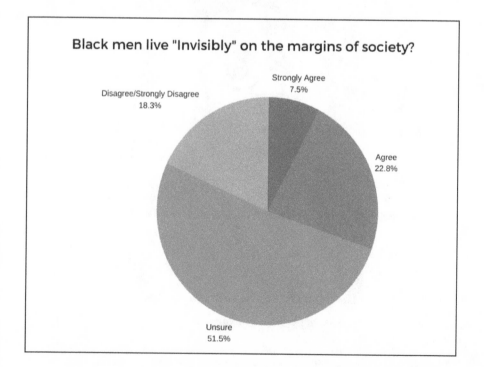

All survey results displayed above are represented by the overall percentage of survey respondents. For more information on our survey methodology, please see the Author's Note, located in the front matter of the book. To review raw survey results, visit: http://bit.ly/stillinvisiblesurvey

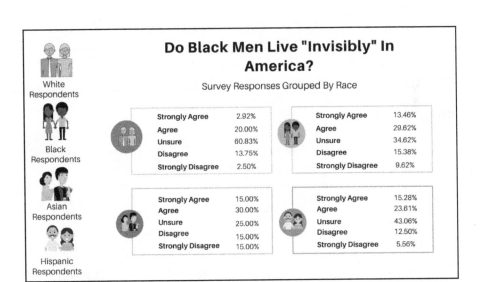

Findings by Race

- 4 out of 10 Black male respondents (40.00%) were "Unsure" about the statement, *"Black men live 'invisibly' on the margins of society."* On the converse, more than half of all Black female respondents (54.55%) "Strongly Agree" or "Agree" with the same statement.

- Nearly half of all Asian respondents (45.00%) "Strongly Agree" or "Agree" with the statement: *"Black men live 'invisibly' on the margins of society."*

- 6 out of 10 of all White respondents (60.83%) were "Unsure" about the statement, *"Black men live 'invisibly' on the margins of society."*

Findings by Gender

- More than any other group of women, Asian female respondents (58.34%) "Strongly Agree" or "Agree" with the statement, *"Black men live 'invisibly' on the margins of society."*

- 3 out of 4 Asian male respondents (75.00%) "Disagree" or "Strongly Disagree" with the statement, *"Black men live 'invisibly' on the margins of society."*

- Less than a quarter of all White male respondents (22.00%) "Strongly Agree" or "Agree" with the statement, *"Black men live 'invisibly' on the margins of society."*

Findings by Age

- More than a third of White female respondents (35.71%), ages 18-24 years old, "Strongly Agree" or "Agree" with the statement, *"Black men live 'invisibly' on the margins of society."*

- 2 out of 3 Black male respondents (66.67%), ages 55 years and older, "Strongly Agree" or "Agree" with the statement, *"Black men live 'invisibly' on the margins of society."*

- More than 4 out of 10 of all Hispanic respondents, ages 35-44 years old, "Strongly Agree" or "Agree" with the statement, *"Black men live 'invisibly' on the margins of society."*

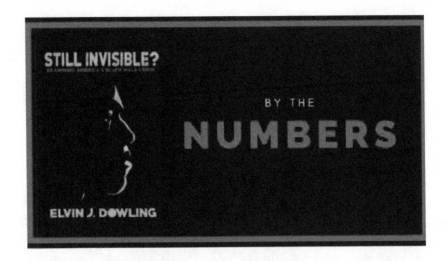

"Heightened Fears Make for Costly Tears!"

- Black men who earn more and are better educated have a lower risk of depression, but those who have no earnings are at an increased risk of suffering in silence ("Souls", p. 2).

- Depression financially impacts the American economy, with $43 billion annually in direct costs, along with another $23 billion in lost productivity ("Souls", p. 2).

"When Dying ... Is Better Than Trying."

- Black men in America are at least twice as likely as women to die from suicide, homicide and cirrhosis of the liver, due to alcoholism ("Souls", p. 1).

- In nearly three out of every four suicide deaths for Black males, ages 15-19 years old (72%), firearms were used to effectuate their demise ("Souls", p. 1).

"Asking No Questions... Telling No Lies!"

- Only 1 out of 3 Americans who suffer from a mental disorder receive care, with Blacks receiving treatment at a rate half that of whites ("Souls", p. 2).

- Although Blacks comprise 13% of the U.S. population, they only account for 2% of all psychiatrists and psychologists, and only 4% of social workers ("Souls", p. 2).

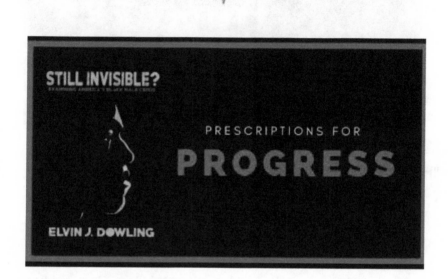

"Seek Safe Harbor with a Barber!"

- Partner with barbershops, churches and community groups to host awareness training on identifying mental health issues and eliminating stigmas ("Souls", p. 3).

- Create official and unofficial structures that provide Black males with opportunities to discuss their problems in a safe and familiar environment ("Souls" p. 3).

Serve the Need ... Stop the Bleed!

- Implement intervention initiatives for Black males impacted by various psychosocial factors that may predispose them to potentially harmful behavior ("Souls", p. 3).

- Develop evidence-based programs that seek to address the reasons that drive Black males to commit—or attempt to commit—suicide ("Souls", p. 3).

Help Black Men to Help Themselves!

- Provide culturally competent mental health services for those suffering from depression and trauma, through increased training for clinicians ("Souls", p. 3).

- Improve referral systems and follow up mechanisms from the legal system, nonprofit groups and mental health hospitals for those in need of ongoing care ("Souls" p. 3).

Works Cited

1. Shmoop Editorial Team. "Invisible Man Identity Quotes Page 1." *Shmoop*. Shmoop University, Inc., 11 Nov. 2008. Web. 17 Oct. 2019

2. DeGruy, Joy. "Post Traumatic Slave Syndrome." *JoyDeGruy.com*, Joy DeGruy Publications. Web. Accessed 28 October 2019. http://bit.ly/2Wl0vaJ

3. Hamilton Dennis, Celeste. "What Is Barbershop Therapy?", *YesMagazine.org*, Yes! Magazine. Web. 23 August 2018. http://bit.ly/2BohU8A

4. Walker, Larry. "Black Men and Mental Illness Can Be a Barbershop Conversation, Too." *Ebony.com*, Clear View Group, LLC. 10 October 2019. http://bit.ly/2p4mZ3A

5. "Invisible Man: Black Men & PTSD." *BlackDoctor.org*, BlackDoctor, Inc., Web. Retrieved 22 October 2019. http://bit.ly/2J7ZQUL

6. Green L. (1982) A Learned Helplessness Analysis of Problems Confronting the Black Community. In: Turner S.M., Jones R.T. (eds) Behavior Modification *Springer*, Boston, MA. Accessed 22 http://bit.ly/35ErTEJ

7. Danielle, Britni. "Michelle Obama's 'Twice as Good' Speech Doesn't Cut It with Most African-Americans." *TheGuardian.com*, Guardian News and Media. 12 May 2015. http://bit.ly/2pHxMAP

8. Jacobs, Tom. "White Americans Draw Distinctions Between African-Americans and Blacks." *PSMag.com*, The Social Justice Foundation. 14 June 2017. http://bit.ly/2PiXvKj

9. "Physiological & Psychological Impact of Racism and Discrimination for African-Americans." *APA.org*, American Psychological Association. Web. Retrieved 24 October 2019. http://bit.ly/2N8O4uu

10. "Souls of Black Men: African-American Men Discuss Mental Health." *CommunityVoices.org*, The Satcher Health Leadership Institute - Morehouse School of Medicine. Web. Retrieved 25 October 2019. http://bit.ly/32AtGIY

Chapter 9: "Must Jesus Bear the Cross Alone?"

How Mainstream Religion Ignores Black Believers

" "

"Nothing, storm or flood, must get in the way of our need for light and ever more and brighter light. The truth is the light and light is the truth."

- Ralph Ellison ("Invisible Man")

*(This culturally inaccurate oil-on-canvas rendering, "Christ Carrying the Cross," by Tiziano Vicelli, circa 1560, is of Jesus of Nazareth, a **Middle Eastern** hamlet located in Palestine, and Simon of Cyrene, a city located in the **Northern African** country of Libya— who was forced to carry the cross for Jesus, on the road to Calvary.)*

Let the Church Say... "Amen!"

Blinded by the Light?

In storied biblical parlance depicting the "Fourteen Stations of the Cross," by Italian Renaissance painter, Tiziano Vicelli, the Jesus of Nazareth whom Christians proclaim as their Lord and Savior, was helped along the way--in fulfilling his ultimate mission--by a bystander of African descent; Simon of Cyrene, who was forced into conscription and compelled to carry the cross because, well... who else was going to do it? Yet, more than a millennium and a half later, in an effort to memorialize that fateful day, the racial identity of Simon of Cyrene was "reinterpreted", if you will, permanently altering the way the world would view both he and his contribution to Christian history. In fact, throughout the annals of time, the contributions of individuals of African descent in the building and shaping of modern day religion is one that has been "whitewashed" from historical texts, at least since the earliest known depiction of Jesus Christ; unearthed from a fresco in the St. Castillo catacombs of Rome more than 300 years after he walked the earth. Furthermore, in stark contrast to the biblical description of Jesus, in the *Book of Revelation (Chapter 1, Verse 15)*, as having *"hair like wool"* and *"feet like bronze,"* the Savior many Christians acknowledge today, *"just as sure as Jesus' eyes are blue,"* is as "white as the driven snow." To be clear... without question. To that end, this blanching of religion to fit a more convenient racial narrative that undergirds the white supremacist beliefs of many of these "so-called" Christians, leads an agnostic like myself wondering why the need for the historical inaccuracies in the first place? That is, before I quickly deduced that for some, the use of Jesus Christ as a tool for human oppression, is as American as apple pie!

Each Sunday, for hundreds of years, church bells have tolled across the heartland, heralding the start of religious worship services aimed at reconnecting Christian believers with their spiritual center, while preparing them for the challenges of the week ahead. When taking a cursory look inside the doors of the church, however, it is apparent that the conundrum which continues to bedevil believers is the issue of race and class in America. As a result of the widening schism that has come to define, in many ways, Christianity in America today, the mainstream church, in many ways, has become complicit in perpetuating white supremacist dogma. As a materialist myself, were it not for the church's persistent intransigence on the Black/White divide in the country which is, frankly, unhelpful for America's image abroad--I would defer to the principle of a separation between church and state. Because it is, however, a malignant tumor on the soul of our nation, I am compelled to beseech you high falutin' church folks to get your act together... please! I mean, it's hard enough getting the rest of the world to believe that we are a people who "trust in God" while we simultaneously build walls out of fear, when your blatantly racist behavior, in the name of the Almighty, no less, is making us all look like hypocrites. And that's just bad for business!

May God Be with You,

Justitia

Lady Justice

Timothy Tee Boddie: "A Man After God's Heart"

A Voice in the Wilderness?

"My name is the Reverend Dr. Timothy Tee Boddie, Ed.D., and I am a native of North Carolina, having been born in Raleigh where my late parents met as collegians at *Shaw University*," began the exceptionally astute clergyman who bears the middle name of the late, great African-American preacher and acolyte of Dr. Martin Luther King, Jr., the Reverend Dr. Wyatt Tee Walker. "Although I was born in North Carolina, I claim Virginia as my home, as I was reared in the City of Newport News, where my late parents, the Reverend Dr. Fred J. Boddie, Jr., served as Pastor as of the *First Church of Newport News Baptist,* and my mother, the former Patricia Joan Hall worked as a sixth-grade Social Studies teacher," recalled "Tee," the second of three siblings and a fourth generation minister; a calling stretching back to his great-grandfather, the late Reverend Dr. Fred Douglas Boddie, who served for fifty years as the Senior Pastor of the *Bunn Chapel Baptist Church* of Nashville, North Carolina. Like his progenitors before him, Boddie hails from a long line of family preachers who have upheld the "Blood-Stained Banner" as Christian ministers for more than a century.

" I was blessed to have grown up in a family where there were two parents," Timothy beamed, bestowing a sense of pride in both his parents and his upbringing, as any dutiful and devoted son would do. "My father, as I've mentioned, was a minister, and he was involved in the home, but he was also from the 'old school'. As such, he was not as emotionally involved in our activities as our mother was," Dr. Boddie recalled, reminiscing about his childhood and the collective contributions his parents made to make it one that provided a foundation for he and his siblings to succeed. "My mother actually didn't even go to work until we got into grade school," he said. "She was very much close to us; nurturing us and rearing us in the home. My dad, however, being a minister, was always available to us and I am always grateful to him for being the breadwinner and the man of the house," the reverend remarked. "I am also proud that he helped to shape me in that same way, not so in a sexist way at all, but in a manner in which he and my mother were reared as well, in that the man of the house should handle his affairs," Dr. Boddie explained.

"My father was less of a disciplinarian than my mother, as she was the stricter parent. If any of us got into trouble, however, she would threaten to tell my father on us, and that would straighten us up pretty good," Boddie laughed. "She was also one who believed in the concept of *"spare the rod spoil the child,"* so we got our fair share of what we would call 'whippings' at the time. Our neighbors called them beatings," he observed, "but we called them 'whippings'," Reverend Boddie noted. "Now that I think about it," he continued, "both of them seem pretty violent today," he laughed, "but it was really just a way to chastise and correct children who would otherwise have had free reign and grown up to be what we would call 'wild bucks'. With that being said, however, that kind of correction was all we knew, at the time, and it was something that worked in our home, although it may not necessarily work in every home... but I am grateful for it," the profound preacher proclaimed.

"I came into the ministry very reluctantly," the one-time professor explained, "with great trepidation and reticence, not really wanting to do it; having seen both the positive and the negatives aspects that a life dedicated to ministry brings with it. There comes a time, however," he went further, "when you have a calling upon your life that you can't *not* answer," he described, detailing a quiet voice inside that was impossible to ignore. "Ministry is not a search for a career, it's truly a calling upon one's heart," the genial theologian emphasized. "Having said that," he elaborated, "I am now entering my sixth decade of life and have had quite an interesting career since my days of running from the ministry, all those many years ago," the pastor recalled. "During my twenties," Boddie continued, "instead of going into seminary right away, I completed my Master's Degree at *Stanford University* in California in English Education, before finally completing a doctorate in Religious Education from *Union Presbyterian Seminary* in Richmond, Virginia," he said, outlining an impressive pedigree of academic credentials that have positioned him to serve in a wide variety of unique positions in academia and ministry; including his work as a College Professor and University Chaplain at two of America's most prestigious HBCU's, *Morehouse College* and *Hampton University*, and Executive Director and General Secretary of two of the nation's most historic and powerful African-American religious conventions.

"I had an opportunity to begin my teaching career at my alma mater, *Morehouse College*, in 1985, working in the English Department; having only graduated from there four years earlier," Boddie recalled. "One of the greatest joys I had at that time was teaching the book, *"Invisible Man,"* for half a semester, to my sophomore *World Literature* class. In my considered opinion, the breadth and broad work that Ralph Ellison achieved in that sweeping, gargantuan novel, is really an analysis of the literature of the world, and how the experiences of Black men in America are oftentimes undervalued and overlooked in all aspects of American life, to include the church. One of my former students at *Morehouse*, Dr. Eddie Glaude, Jr., who now serves as the Chairman of the African-American Studies Department at *Princeton University*, wrote in his book, "Democracy In Black: How Race Still Enslaves the American Soul", about the same issues that Ellison addressed in *"Invisible Man"*, which is this continued devaluing of Blackness in America."

"In Glaude's work, he speaks to the idea of a human *"value gap"* in this country, in that Black and brown bodies are valued less in our society than white bodies," Boddie elaborated. "Until that 'value gap' is closed, the dehumanization of individuals of color will continue. "In a lot of ways," Professor Boddie noted, "it really bespeaks what Ralph Ellison talks about in *"Invisible Man"*, in that, as men and women of color, we walk through life in America not only devalued but, for all intents and purposes, invisible," he declared. "Unfortunately, it is only when we do things that may be construed as either illegal or unethical will we be noticed, and that kind of barbarism continues even to this day. America's racial challenges are really just a manifestation of its 'original sin', which is slavery," Boddie observed. "Now, having just observed the 400th anniversary of the landing of enslaved Africans who came to this country in 1619, we are finally getting the history correct today, particularly with regards to making certain that the story is told not only *accurately*, but also from the *perspective of those persons who were victimized* through that awful, dreaded institution," Dr. Boddie observed.

"Whose Report Shall You Believe"?

For centuries, heretics have used *The Bible* to justify the degradation of people who may have been considered "foreign", "dangerous" or otherwise "less than desirable" by the majority population. Moreover, as America crosses a significant historical milestone, having just commemorated four centuries of both representative government and selective disenfranchisement, the need to confront an institution that has both perpetuated and benefitted from slavery, namely the Mainstream American church and its legions of believers, is an idea whose time has come. In an article written by Julie Zauzner, a religion reporter for the *Washington Post*, detailing how Biblical Scripture has been used to colonize, brutalize and otherwise despise Black people in America, enslaved Africans for whom Christianity was used as a tool of oppression for centuries, have effectively reinterpreted those same bastardized scriptures and have used them as a source of liberation and motivation--a true miracle of the gospel story.

"Some ministers promoted the idea that Africans were the descendants of Ham, cursed in the *Book of Genesis*, and thus their enslavement was fitting," Zauzner wrote, highlighting a dubious use of Holy Scripture to justify man's inhumanity to man. "That biblical interpretation is made up whole cloth in the 15th century," she reported. "There's just no historical record of any seriousness to back it up. It's made up, at a time when Europeans are beginning to colonize Africa" (Zauzner). Likewise, to further perpetuate a doctrine that supported treating other people as human chattel, many theologians promulgated the belief that the value of the "message" of Christianity being taught to "savages" from the "dark continent," albeit through slavery, was, in essence, beneficial to the souls of their captives and, as a result, justifiable. Even still, despite the fact that their introduction to the Christian religion was presented to them as *"steak on a trash can lid,"* enslaved Africans developed a form of Christianity that would ultimately become the precursor to what is now known as "Liberation Theology"; a credo that emphasizes the social, political and economic emancipation of oppressed peoples everywhere. "As soon as enslaved people learned to read English, they immediately began to read *The Bible*, and they immediately began to protest this idea of a biblical justification for slavery. Literally as soon as Black people took pen to paper, we are arguing for our own liberation" (Zauzner). Unfortunately, however, for their descendants, the quest for emancipation continues.

According to Bishop Claude Alexander, the studied Senior Pastor of *Park Church*, in Charlotte, North Carolina, the development of the Black church came about as a direct result of the African-American experience itself, borne by centuries of systemic oppression that must not be minimized. "The [mainstream] church gave spiritual sanction [to racism], both overtly by the things that it taught and covertly by the critique that it did not raise," Alexander observed. "There's no quote-unquote 'theology' that's not shaped by context. And racialized violence is the context that has always shaped America, and the American church. It was the amniotic fluid out of which our nation was born," the Bishop declared (Zauzner). Moreover, as a result of the social constraints of the time, many of the mainstream Christian denominations of the day were split in their views on slavery, resulting in both a schism within their governing conventions, and the establishment of a strong and viable Black church; the only institution that has historically been wholly controlled by African-Americans. With that being said, however, from the very moment enslaved Africans were introduced to *"The Man from Galilee"* to this day, Black people in America "love themselves some Jesus," and continue to be the most faithful religious group in the country. And like the *Park Church's* Bishop Claude Alexander, the Reverend Dr. Timothy Boddie is also convinced that the genesis of America's trials and tribulations are rooted in the bowels of bigotry and white supremacy.

"Although commonly attributed to Dr. Martin Luther King, Jr.," Reverend Boddie began, "it was the great Black theologian, Dr. Howard Thurman, who first said, *"the most segregated hour in America is 11 a.m. on Sunday morning,"* the prolific pastor opined. "This phenomenon may be traced back to the nineteenth century schism of the mainline denominations, including the *Methodists* and the *Church of Christ*, over the issue of slavery before the *Civil War*. In fact, the church we know today as *Presbyterian USA* was against slavery, while *Presbyterian of America* was pro-slavery, having chosen to stick with its more Southern roots and traditions. In Baptist life," Boddie continued "you had the *Northern Baptists* and the *Southern Baptists*, with the *Southern Baptists* opting to support the Confederacy and its norms, including the enslavement of Africans. In fact, even though those many denominations have reached out to African-Americans and have tried to bring some reconciliation to the issue of slavery, inequality in their conventions still exists," he noted, taking aim squarely at their continued creed of racial superiority. "The *Southern Baptists*, for example, have even elected a Black president for their convention, but what they haven't changed is their theology," the Pastor Boddie lamented. "They may apologize for some past, historic mistakes that the church may have been complicit in, but what they haven't changed is their doctrine! Their theology is still one that is a hierarchical belief that White folks are still more valued than Black folks," Boddie surmised. Today, while the well-worn quip about *'White Christians who hang Black Christians from trees'* isn't as prevalent in twenty-first century America as it was fifty years ago, the goal of keeping Black believers in marginal positions within the church continues unabated.

"When it comes to the lack of diversity in leadership in many of these large religious institutions, what you're going to find is an issue that speaks to the whole idea of 'white privilege', going back even to the paternalistic view of the mission work of the 19th century," Dr. Boddie explained; outlining the justification used to subjugate people of color for centuries. "In a sense, this 'white privilege' undergirds and actually amplifies that whole idea, which says, *'What's White is Right'*, *'If You're Brown, Stick Around'*, and *'If You're Black Get Back!'*" the pastor opined. "What you are seeing," he intoned, "is not a mirage. What you're seeing is what you see, and that is, even in nondenominational churches across the country, you might find someone who has all of the trappings of the Black church, all of the nuances of the Black preacher, and even one who attracts lots of Black people to their worship service, but it's certainly not one that is *run by* or necessarily *speaks to* the sociopolitical needs of Black people," declared the 'Preacher's Preacher'.

"One example in particular," Reverend Boddie furthered, "is Pastor Paula White, who was also appointed by President Donald Trump as Advisor to lead the *White House Faith and Opportunity Initiative*. Prior to that stint," he continued, "she served as pastor of two predominantly Black congregations, yet she failed to stand up for the issues of justice and concern for African-Americans. To me, this represents a conundrum for the church, an organism that has historically been segregated and, to a large extent, still is today," Dr. Boddie lamented. "I think that's almost heretical and is certainly malpractice of ministry, to serve a congregation where the needs of the Black people you serve are not being met in a real and meaningful way, and yet not speak to those needs, is simply an extension of enslavement. In this case," the pastor proclaimed, "it's what might be identified as 'spiritual enslavement' around a theology that is oppressive and is the same one that allowed slavery to take root in the first place. To that end," the pastor professed, "I believe that it is a misnomer to call the church *"the church"* today, as we have some churches that do not speak of political issues at all, but their theology underscores a politics of conservatism. In fact," he went on, "even today, white evangelicals are still 'lock, stock and barrel' in support of a President [Donald Trump] who, thirty years ago, would have been considered almost demonic in terms of his behavior, his lifestyle and his character," Boddie explained. "But because they are getting what they want politically—particularly as it relates to judgeships, tax cuts, blocking immigrants from coming to this country, and being a bully to the world—now suddenly... it's okay," Reverend Boddie bemoaned. "If they are getting _that_, then racism is **not** a deal-breaker for them.

On the other hand," Dr. Boddie persisted, "there are some evangelicals who are now leading an effort to reclaim Jesus--the Jesus of _The Bible;_ such as Jim Wallis, the Founder of _Sojourners,_ and Tony Campolo of _Red-Letter Christians._ "The Jesus of _The Bible,_" he articulated, "taught us in _The Gospel According to Matthew (Chapter 25),_ and _The Gospel According to Luke (Chapter 4),_ and all over the _Old_ and _New Testaments,_ the concept of JUSTICE," he exclaimed. The learned biblical scholar then noted that the _Poverty and Justice Bible,_ published by the _American Bible Society_ and distributed by the _National Council of Churches,_ has over 2,000 scriptures highlighting poverty and justice. "The Jesus of _The Bible_ talked about caring for the underprivileged, widows, orphans, and the oppressed of our society," the thoughtful theologian intoned. "The Jesus of _The Bible_ taught us that it is not only the duty of the church, but also the duty of the state, to take care of those who cannot take care of themselves,' he said. "Dr. Martin Luther King, Jr., once said: "The church must be reminded that it is _neither the master, nor the servant_—but rather **the conscience**—of the state." Fortunately," Reverend Boddie remarked, "there are some mainline white Protestant churches, as well as some Catholic parishes (in part to the example of Pope Francis), who are embracing _this_ as the idea of what the church's role is in modern day society; which is to be prophetic, speak truth to power, and to hold the government accountable to those persons that are deprecated and devalued in our society," the reverend remarked. "It is not an 'either/or' proposition, that is, either the church, or the government, is responsible for achieving this overarching goal for our country. Rather, I believe that it is a 'both/and' proposition, in that the church, and the government, must work together to make real the promises of our nation's _Pledge of Allegiance,_ which includes "liberty and justice... for all."

In chronicling the American church's dubious history of exclusion and discrimination against Black congregants, the _Equal Justice Initiative,_ a nonprofit organization working to provide legal representation to those who may have been wrongfully convicted of a crime, outlined some of the varied reasons why many of the early Black churches were formed, most of which were in response to the rabid racism being exhibited towards them by their white Christian brothers and sisters. "The first independent Black denomination was formed in 1787, when Richard Allen and Absalom Jones founded the first *African Methodist Episcopal Church* in Philadelphia after white congregants yanked them from their knees while they prayed in a whites-only section of St. George's Methodist Episcopal Church," the *Initiative* observed, marking the spark that led to a Black reformation movement within the "Body of Christ." From that day hence, "Black churches became an indispensable cultural and political hub of the African American community" ("Racial Segregation"). Today, more than eight in ten African-Americans who identify as Christian, continue to cast their lot with traditional Black churches. For the other twenty percent, however, who opt to worship with their White compatriots, often they too experience a sense of marginalization and invisibility that has many of them eventually heading for the exits. In a *New York Times* accounting of the spiritual exodus taking place at large, majority white churches across the country, writer Campbell Robertson reported on the noticeable attrition of their African-American members, as those former congregants express palpable fears that the once welcoming mega-churches that offered a novel alternative to what they were accustomed to, have now become unrepentant "MAGA-churches" seeking to "Make America Great Again"—one congregation at a time!

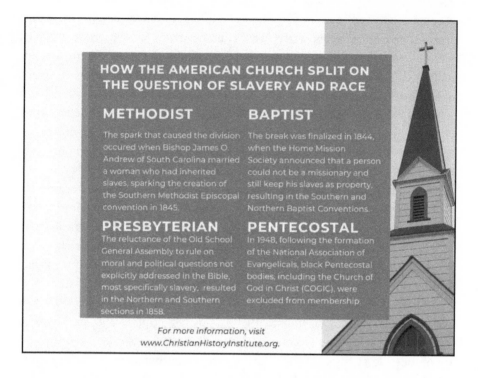

HOW THE AMERICAN CHURCH SPLIT ON
THE QUESTION OF SLAVERY AND RACE

METHODIST

The spark that caused the division
occured when Bishop James O.
Andrew of South Carolina married
a woman who had inherited
slaves, sparking the creation of
the Southern Methodist Episcopal
convention in 1845.

BAPTIST

The break was finalized in 1844,
when the Home Mission
Society announced that a person
could not be a missionary and
still keep his slaves as property,
resulting in the Southern and
Northern Baptist Conventions.

PRESBYTERIAN

The reluctance of the Old School
General Assembly to rule on
moral and political questions not
explicitly addressed in the Bible,
most specifically slavery, resulted
in the Northern and Southern
sections in 1858.

PENTECOSTAL

In 1948, following the formation
of the National Association of
Evangelicals, black Pentecostal
bodies, including the Church of
God in Christ (COGIC), were
excluded from membership.

For more information, visit
www.ChristianHistoryInstitute.org.

Leaving So Soon?

Throughout the history of *Christendom*, the goal of all Christians, regardless of race, creed or national origin, is to enjoy the promises of a Heaven above, where "the streets are paved with gold." As a precursor to the "sweet by and by," many of today's megachurches have attempted to rebrand themselves as "experiments in brotherhood" that seek to attract an array of families, from diverse cultures and backgrounds, to join them in Sunday fellowship and Christian camaraderie. In fact, over the course of the last several decades, many African-American parishioners, in responding to their call, have sought to integrate largely white congregations with the goal of finding a place "this side of glory" to lay their burdens down. Just as importantly, to the more cosmopolitan Black Christians conscious of their limited time, social status and personal commitments, many of these nontraditional churches offered convenient scheduling options, shorter service times and a different worship experience, among the many other perks, that helped to convince them to take a "launch out into the deep" and make the switch to majority white churches. "'*Racial reconciliation*' was the talk of conferences and the subject of formal resolutions," Robertson reported, detailing the impetus inspiring Black believers to take the leap into the unknown. "Large Christian ministries were dedicated to the aim of integration, and many Black Christians decided to join white-majority congregations" (Robertson). In the wake of more pronounced racial inequities, however, the perspectives of many Black worshippers have changed, over time, as some have felt that the issues of social justice and equality are, more often than not, ignored by white clergy, who seemingly prefer to not disturb the traditional order of things.

"Black congregants — as recounted by people in Chicago, Los Angeles, Atlanta, Fort Worth and elsewhere — had already grown uneasy in recent years as they watched their white pastors fail to address police shootings of African-Americans," Robertson observed. "They heard prayers for Paris, for Brussels, for law enforcement; they heard that one should keep one's eyes on the kingdom, that the church was colorblind, and that talk of racial injustice was divisive, not a matter of the gospel" (Robertson). Then, when white evangelicals voted for Donald Trump to become President of the United States in overwhelming margins, a Rubicon was crossed for many Black believers who have begrudgingly lost faith in the idea of a religious utopia. Moreover, the ascendancy of Trump to the highest office in the land, also revealed the power of the pulpit and the mainstream church's ability to, once again, elect conservative leaning politicians that many Blacks view as hostile to their interests.

Christopher Ladd, reporting for *Forbes Magazine* in a piece called, "Pastors, Not Politicians, Turned Dixie Republican," noted the power and influence that ministers wield in making sure that the political interests of white evangelicals is always represented--by block vote--at the ballot box and in legislative halls across the country. "Southern churches, warped by generations of theological evolution necessary to accommodate slavery and segregation," Ladd explained, "were all too willing to offer their political assistance to a white nationalist program. Southern religious institutions would lead a wave of political activism that helped keep white nationalism alive inside an increasingly unfriendly national climate," he noted. "Forget about Goldwater, Nixon or Reagan. No one played as much of a role in turning the South red as the leaders of the *Southern Baptist Church*" (Ladd). As a student of church history, the idea of the church still being used, even today, to further propagate discriminatory policies designed to keep minorities in America marginalized and "in their place" is not lost on Black believers.

The challenges that many Black churchgoers face, however, in this twenty-first century era of blatant racism and hyper-partisanship, are not just limited to the confines of the church itself, but also extends to other areas of the Black Christian experience. In recent years, for example, gospel music artist Kirk Franklin has expressed both heartache and dismay at the censoring of his comments on contemporary social justice issues, such as police violence against Black people in America, by the producers of the *Dove Music Awards*, Christian music's annual event honoring the industry's most prolific and successful religious artists and their work. At the 2016 awards ceremony, in response to the tragic police-involved homicide deaths of defenseless Black men throughout the country, including Philando Castile in Milwaukee, Wisconsin and Walter Scott in North Charleston, South Carolina, Franklin used the show's platform to call attention to tragedies. When the show later aired, however, Franklin's pleas for both accountability on the part of the police, and prayer and support for the families of the decedents, were surreptitiously edited out during the program's post-production phase and before it was aired to the viewing public. After approaching the show's producers, the *Trinity Broadcasting Network (TBN)*, according to Kirk Franklin, he was assured that the exclusion of his comments calling for healing and greater understanding for Black victims of state sanctioned violence was not intentional and, more importantly, would never happen again.

In 2019, however, lightning struck twice, as Franklin's comments on social justice and accountability were, once again, removed from the program's final airing when, in calling for peace and reconciliation, he highlighted the inexplicable deaths of other African-American victims who needlessly perished while simply attempting to live their lives; including Atatiana Jefferson, a twenty-eight year old, college educated woman with a promising and bright future who was senselessly gunned down by a *Forth Worth Police Department* officer as she played video games with her nephew in her own home. As a result of the second slight to Franklin and silencing of his message on their platform, the Grammy award winning entertainer called for a boycott of the program unless and until they supported these critical social justice issues. "I am aware that the word *boycott* often has a negative connotation and finality to it," Franklin noted, in explaining his position on the matter. "But my goal will forever be reconciliation as well as accountability. It is important for those in charge to be informed. Not only did they edit my speech, they edited the African-American experience" (Dove Awards).

In another instance of the "moral majority" demonstrating a certain "tone deafness" to the concerns of faithful Black believers, the *Word Network*, a global television conglomerate that boasts itself as "the largest African-American religious network in the world," owned by Kevin Adell, a white radio station owner from Detroit, Michigan, who also serves as the organization's Chief Executive Officer, came under scrutiny and threats of boycott for admittedly treating African-American pastors dismissively and derisively in his role as the gatekeeper of God's message; referring to his paying broadcasters as "hoes" and to himself as a "pimp" and "massa" of his domain. At the heart of the dispute, Bishop George Bloomer, an evangelist, television host and pastor of the *Bethel Family Worship Center,* a multicultural ministry in Durham, NC, alleged that Adell regularly refers to his Black patrons in a derogatory fashion even doing so in mass emails blasted out to staff and clients simultaneously, without a hint of embarrassment or remorse. When Bloomer called on Adell to repudiate the repugnant behavior, Adell allegedly responded by photoshopping a photo of Bloomer depicted as the character "Tattoo", popularized by actor Herve Villechaize, from the 1970's television show "Fantasy Island" and himself stereotypically dressed as a pimp. In responding to Adell's unwillingness to retract his despicable statements, Bloomer, supported by some of the biggest names in the Black Church, issued a scathing condemnation of the behavior.

"During these times of increased incidents of hate across our country, we as African-American clergy and allies of the African-American community cannot remain silent in the face of this blatant racism," read a petition that garnered thousands of signatures shortly after its release. "Black-face, pimp and hoe imagery, boss aka 'massa' comments, all are connected to the historical trauma African-Americans have endured for 400 years in this country" ("Word Network"). So, if the most sacred of spaces are not safe for African-Americans to feel liberated from the manacles of prejudice and pain, and protected from the realities of hurt, harm or danger lying in wait on the other side of the door, then where can Black men go for spiritual solace but to the Lord Himself? Moreover, what does this sad state of affairs forecast for the future of the Black man's place at the church's "table of brotherhood"? As far as Dr. Timothy Tee Boddie is concerned, the forecast is *"somewhere between fair and midland."*

"When it comes to the state of the African-American male, I would say, if I were to use a meteorological term, it's partly cloudy...with a chance of showers," the prescient preacher projected. "The question is what will those showers be? And how long will the clouds hang over our heads," he asked. "Some of those clouds are of our own making and some that can only be really addressed and corrected by a unified attempt to be honest with ourselves," the pastor predicted. "To be honest not only about our state of affairs, " he continued, "but to be honest about how we got here. It is easy for us to blame things on *'the man'*," Boddie explained, "but *'the man'* is merely a symbol of the racist structures that we are battling today, to include the financial, political and social structures that we currently have in our society. One of the things we have to do," Dr. Boddie theorized, "is to stop these false dichotomies that hold us back," he lamented.

"At the turn of the 20th century," Professor Boddie explained, "it was the dichotomy between W.E.B. DuBois and Booker T. Washington. In the 1960's, it was the dichotomy between Martin Luther King, Jr, and Malcolm X. In the 1990s, it was the dichotomy between Jesse Jackson and Louis Farrakhan," he noted. "These false dichotomies created for Black men, I believe, contributes to this *'partly cloudy'* thing that I'm talking about," Boddie hypothesized. "What I'm getting at, again, is the need for Black America be more adaptable than we have been in the past. We need *'both/and'* not *'either/or'*. For example, one of the things that we've done is to push for college education for Black men," he went on. "Without apology, we have pushed the notion that all Black men must go to college. Well, the four-year college experience is not a one-size fits all solution for everyone," the academician aptly noted. "We have to do a better job in identifying and affirming other options for Black men, and those other options will include twenty-first century trades and technical vocations. Those other options will include things where you don't have to have a four-year college degree to do the job that is required of you. It may be apprenticeships," Dr. Boddie pointed out, delineating a wide variety of options that include opportunities in Science, Technology, Engineering and

Math (STEM), which may not necessarily require an advanced degree for employment.

"Some Black men, no matter where they are, or how they grow up, are not interested in a four-year college degree," he pointed out. "I know a lot of brothers who are brilliant in some way that I am not; who are brilliant with their hands or may have another gift that I do not. And *that's ok*, too," he implored. "I'm going to call a plumber when I need a plumber, I'm not going to call a professor. And that plumber's going to charge me $75 an hour! So, you tell me who's winning," he joked! "If I may turn this back to literature," Professor Boddie concluded, "in Shakespeare's play *Hamlet*, Polonius provides sage advice to his son Laertes, that I would offer to Black men everywhere and it is simply this: *'To thine own self be true!'* Be yourself ... because everybody else is taken!"

(Timothy Tee Boddie: Professor & Pastor)

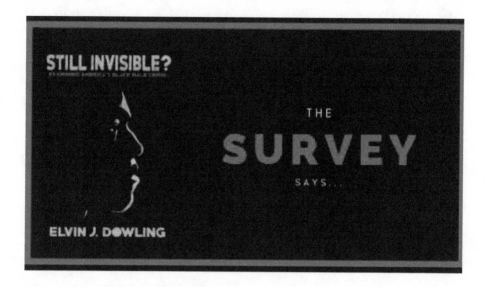

Do you believe religious leaders and organizations provide support for the needs and issues impacting Black males?*

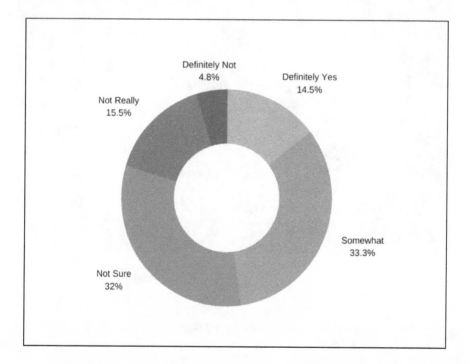

Please read the following statements and select the ones you most agree with.*

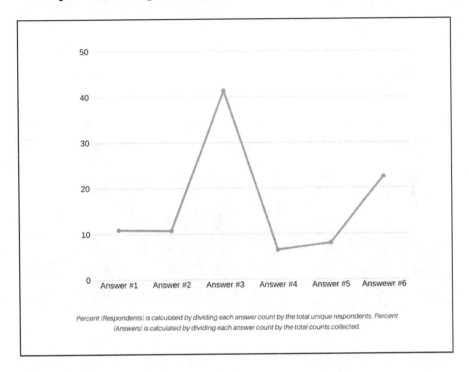

Percent (Respondents) is calculated by dividing each answer count by the total unique respondents. Percent (Answers) is calculated by dividing each answer count by the total counts collected.

1. The most segregated hour in America is 11:00am on Sunday morning = 10.90%

2. When attending religious services, I prefer doing so with a congregation that reflects my own race = 10.73%

3. I have no problem attending religious services where the religious leader is of a different race = 41.40%

4. My religious leader often speaks out on issues of race and class in America = 6.47%

5. My religious institution is actively engaged in issues of race and class in America = 8.01%

6. My religious institution speaks to the needs and concerns of all people, regardless of race = 22.49%

All survey results displayed above are represented by the overall percentage of survey respondents. For more information on our survey methodology, please see the Author's Note, located in the front matter of the book. To review raw survey results, visit: http://bit.ly/stillinvisiblesurvey.

01

"Separate Is Good"

Less than 2 out of 10 respondents Agree with the statement, *"11:00 AM on Sunday morning is the most segregated hour in America."*

02

"Prefer My Own"

An overwhelming majority of all White respondents (77.42%) prefer worshipping in a church with few, if any Black believers.

03

Silence Is Deafening

Only 1 out of 4 respondents believe their church "speaks to the needs and concerns of all people, regardless of race."

Findings by Race

- More than 4 out of 10 Hispanic male respondents (43.40%) say "Definitely Yes" or "Somewhat Agree" to the statement, *"Do you believe religious leaders and organizations provide support for the needs and issues impacting Black males?"*

- Half of all Black respondents (54.17%) "Agree" with the statement, *"The most segregated hour in America is 11:00am on Sunday morning."*

- Nearly 8 in 10 of all White respondents (77.42%) "Agree" with the statement, *"When attending religious services, I prefer doing so with a congregation that reflects my own race."*

Findings by Gender

- Only 1 out of 4 Asian male respondents (25.00%) "Agree" with the statement, *"I have no problem attending religious services where the religious leader is of a different race."* On the converse, 3 out of 4 Asian female respondents (75.00%) agree with the same statement.

- Half of all Multicultural male respondents (50.00%) "Agree" with the statement, *"My religious leader often speaks out on issues of race and class in America."*

- One third of all Black Female respondents (33.00%) "Agree" with the statement, *"My religious institution is actively engaged in issues of race and class in America."*

Findings by Age

- More than a third of White female respondents (35.71%), ages 18-24 years old, "Strongly Agree" or "Agree" with the statement, *"My religious institution speaks to the needs and concerns of all people, regardless of race."*

- Half of all Other respondents (50.00%), ages 25-34 years old, say "Definitely Yes" or "Somewhat Agree" to the statement, *"Do you believe religious leaders and organizations provide support for the needs and issues impacting Black males?"*

- Half of all Black male respondents (50.00%) of all ages, "Agree" with the statement, *"The most segregated hour in America is 11:00am on Sunday morning."*

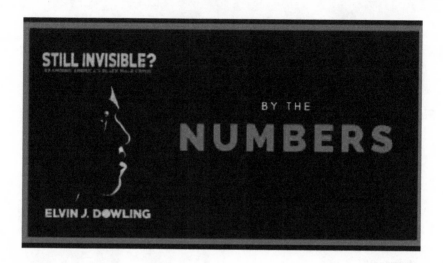

"Blacks Always Come Back!"

- In 2018, a majority of Americans reported that they "Seldom" or "Never" attend church or synagogue ("Church Attendance").

- African-Americans are the most consistent church attendees, with nearly 47% of Black believers filling the pews every Sunday ("Pew Research Center").

"In God We Trust?"

- Despite the belief about the United States being a devout, God-fearing, Judeo-Christian nation, half of all Americans have never read *The Bible* ("Bible Engagement").

- Nearly half of all Americans (48%) are "done with God" and believe that God plays no role whatsoever in their daily lives ("Bible Engagement").

"Talking Loud... Saying Nothing!"

- Half of all Americans who attended church services just last Sunday cannot remember a single spiritual insight from that sermon ("Bible Engagement").

- The faith that Americans have in its clergy has plummeted to an all-time low of 37%, with pastors ranking just below the police and just above journalists ("Bible Engagement").

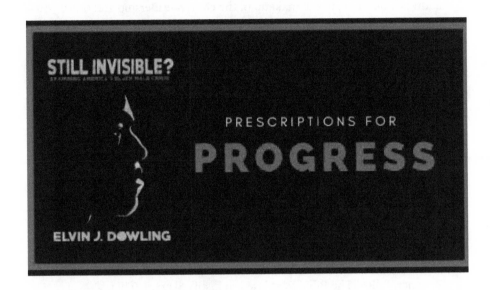

"Build a Beloved Community!"

- Churches can begin to promote community healing by working with local groups to host "listening sessions" aimed at examining racism's impact ("Becoming", p. 5).

- Religious leaders can engage in training in dismantling the structures of racism within the church, with the goal of growing a "beloved community" ("Becoming", p. 7).

"Do Justice... Walk Humbly!"

- Ecclesiastical conventions can implement a culture of diversity, racial reconciliation, social justice and true repentance in regular worship services ("Becoming", p. 7).

- Local churches can become active in criminal justice reform and racial healing by implementing programs that assist those who are formerly incarcerated ("Becoming", p. 8).

"A Church for Everybody!"

- Compare your church's racial composition to local demographics and address differences in the makeup of the church leadership and those you serve ("Becoming", p. 4).

- Integrate worship services that resonate with the entire congregation, incorporating prayers, songs and sermons that "rewrite the narrative on race" ("Becoming", p. 5).

Works Cited

1. Ellison, Ralph. "Invisible Man." New York: *Vintage International*, 1995. Print.

2. Zauzner, Julie: "The Bible Was Used to Justify Slavery. Then Africans Made it Their Path to Freedom." *WashingtonPost.com*, Nash Holdings. 30 April   2019. https://wapo.st/31RfaLW

3. "Racial Segregation in the Church." *EJI.org*, Equal Justice Initiative. Web. Accessed 30 October 2019. http://bit.ly/2Jrdvq7

4. Robertson, Campbell. "A Quiet Exodus: Why Black Worshippers Are Leaving White Evangelical   Churches." *NYTimes.com*, The New York Times   Company. 9 March 2018. https://nyti.ms/2MTrp6m

5. Ladd, Chris. "Pastors, Not Politicians, Turned Dixie Republican." *Forbes.com*, Forbes Media, LLC. Web.   27 March 2017. http://bit.ly/2C1PGAU

6. "Kirk Franklin Says the Dove Awards Edited the Broadcast   of His Speech to Remove Prayers for Victims of   Racial Violence." *ReleventMagazine.com*,   Relevent Medi Group. 28 October 2019.

7. Blair, Leonardo. "Black Clergy Call for Boycott of Word
   Network After White Owner Is Accused of Racial   Insensitivity."
   ChristiaPost.com, The Christian   Post, Inc. 10 October 2019.
   http://bit.ly/2NhWAY8

8. Duffin, Erin. "Church Attendance of Americans 2018."
   Statista.com, Statista. 9 August 2019.
   http://bit.ly/2qfdtuG

9. "Attendance at Religious Services by Race/Ethnicity." *Pew
   Research Center - Religion and Public Life, Pew*   *Charitable
   Trust*. 2014. Accessed 3 November   2019.
   https://pewrsr.ch/36nw2xg

10. "Bible Engagement in America: Biblical Literacy." *American   Bible
    Society*, Barna Group. 2016
    .   http://bit.ly/32cBUpG

11. "Becoming Beloved Community... Where You Are: The
    Episcopal Church's Long-term Commitment to   Racial Healing,
    Reconciliation and Justice."   *Presented to the Church by the
    Presiding Officers of the   Episcopal Church in response to General
    Convention   Resolution C019 ["Establish Response to Systemic
    Injustice"]*. May 2017. http://bit.ly/32f5N90

Chapter 10: "Where is the Love?"

Black Males & America's Unforgiving Penal System

❝

How had I come to this? I had kept unswervingly to the path placed before me, had tried to be exactly what I was expected to be, had done exactly what I was expected to do – yet, instead of winning the expected reward, here I was stumbling along, holding on desperately..."

- Ralph Ellison, "Invisible Man" (Shmoop Editorial Team. 6.94)

(A depiction of convicts in the South in the 1870's.)

Confession Is Good for the Soul

Can't We All Just Admit It?

One of my favorite American singers, Jimmy Buffett, once said: *"It's a fine line between Saturday night and Sunday morning."* When it comes to repentance, that's the truth. So, with that being said, let me get this out of the way, *so that I don't ever have to say it again:* I. Am. Sorry. Yes, America is a country that has benefited from slave labor and, yes, we continue to do so to this day. And no, it's not going to discontinue anytime soon. *It is... what it is!* There... I said it. Now, can we all just move on? *(Strangely, I feel so much better now ... Anyhow...).*

Now that we've got that little bit of business out of the way, let's talk about **why** and, more importantly **how**, we can turn a page in this country and shift the emphasis in the conversations about criminal justice in America from the effects of mass incarceration to, at a minimum, the need for fair adjudication. As the representation of justice in America, the idea of giving everybody a "fair shot" should not be a racially exclusive concept that deleteriously impacts poor people of color. It just makes us all look bad--especially me! Moreover, as the paragon of fairness, my job is to dispense jurisprudence in a way that reflects impartiality and deliberative thought for all who appear before me. But, because of laws that remove my judicial discretion, and policies that tilt the scale against a certain segment of our society, you're leaving me with very few options--if I do say so myself! You see, our nation's rush to be "tough on crime" with "Three Strikes Laws" and "Mandatory Minimum Sentences" has reshaped my reputation as one who provides "justice" for some, and "just us" for others. To say that this perception pains me is, indeed, an understatement. So, what's an icon like me to do? Why, throw myself on the mercy of the court, of course. So, here's what I propose as a workable solution to the problem of disparities in sentencing and gaps in jurisprudence.

First, if we, as a nation, are truly committed to the idea of "America First," I say we put our money where our mouth is, and pony up to the table. "What do I mean," you inquire? I'm glad you asked that question! You see, as Americans, we often lament the perceived disadvantages that inexpensive labor and technological automation have on the job market in our country. Our most typical target, Mexican nationals *(of course)*, now bear the brunt of our angst against the changing nature of the world's economy and the concept of globalization. But the real beneficiaries of the bloated largesse and excess profits are... wait for it... American corporations; who make billions of dollars each year by tapping into the labor pool of millions of Americans who happen to be a "captive audience." To that end, let's require companies like these, who still benefit from the slaves that we now call prisoners, to disclose this fact on their packaging? "Truth in Labeling" (if you will). Wouldn't that be fair? *"Even swap... ain't no swindle!"* Sort of like a fair-warning of sorts that gives the "politically correct community" an opportunity to "opt-out"—while providing those who could care less an opportunity to spend to their heart's content. Kind of like saying, *"Hey, before you buy these delicious Idaho Potatoes, you should know that they were harvested by the long-term guests of America's 43rd State."* See... everybody wins! While it may not be a definitive answer to the crushing criminal justice conundrum that impacts countless men and women, overwhelmingly people of color, it will at least make me feel better about the role that I play in the travesties often administered in my name. Every. Single. Day.

Finally, my friends, I've got to say that, while I am no mathematician, I am smart enough to understand that *"nothing from nothing leaves nothing."* With the hordes of Black males being released back into society each year, from local, state and federal correctional facilities that are clearly "big business" in many communities across this country, we ought to figure out what we can do--as a nation--to make it their final visit as "guests of the state". As such, we've got to do something--anything--to capitalize on the huge economic injection our nation could use and, in many cases, needs to remain the world's sole superpower--and get these fellas a job! You see, the costs of reduced employment for those who have "done their bids" and survived the hellish nightmare known as prison in America, is approaching $87 billion and growing by the year. Imagine all of the guns and ammo that this nation could buy for our "woefully underfunded military" by simply putting former prisoners back to work in this country. Now, an idea like that ought to excite at least half people in this country... are you with me? But until then, the fates of forgotten family members who have been locked away for longer than we care to mention (and they dare to recall), and a ballooning prison system, bursting at the seams and ripe for insurrection, hang-- ever so perilously--in the balance. Enough pressure for you? Hope so...

Just Don't Hold Your Breath,

Justitia

Lady Justice

John Williams, Jr.: Redeeming Time & Reshaping Futures

Is There No Forgiveness?

"My name is John Williams, Jr. and I was born in October 1963. My father's name was John Williams, Sr. and my mother's name was Alma Williams," began the New York native of one of America's most storied Black neighborhoods: Harlem USA. "Since regaining my freedom, having been incarcerated for an extended period of time, I have worked part-time at a laundromat, as a construction site demolitionist, and as a junk hauler," detailed the former inmate who has both paid his debt to society and has successfully reintegrated into the community from which he was removed; returning as a model productive citizen. "I was raised in *New York City Public*

Housing, the 'Lincoln Projects' as it is referred to, and basically I would say that we grew up in a lower-class situation. I don't know how most people view public city housing but, for me, it was pretty rough growing up around there," Williams confessed; outlining a litany of challenges that made his upbringing all the more difficult. "My pop was a *New York City Police Department* officer who worked in the housing division. My mom was a homemaker and, I would like to say, we lived pretty good compared to other people in the neighborhood," he continued. "A lot of my peers were from single-parent homes with absent fathers, and that wasn't the situation for me. With that being said, however, we just tried to do the best we could with what we had," Williams admitted.

"As a kid growing up, I was influenced by my parents to a certain degree, to do right by other people and to treat them with respect, but as I grew older I became a product of the environment that I lived in," John acknowledged; copping to a bevy of bad behavior that ultimately led to his imprisonment. "I pretty much got caught up in that environment and the negativity that came with it and, as a police officer's son, coming up I kind of felt like I was somewhat of an outcast because the police are not always welcomed in the Black community. They're not always seen as being a positive force," he went on, underscoring a long running concern that people of color have with those who represent the law enforcement community. "Actually, it's quite the opposite. In many ways, it felt as if I had a stigma attached to me, being a police officer's son. In fact, because of my father's profession, there were many individuals in the community who shunned me, thus spurring me to get out from under his shadow and do my own thing," Williams explained. What's curious about his perspective, however, was the fact that his own father, John Williams, Sr., was, himself, an archetype in the neighborhood of both fatherhood and manhood, going above and beyond the call of duty to help shape the lives of other children who, unlike his own children, did not have a father at home.

"Most of my friends stayed away from the police and saw the police negatively," the lawman's son conceded, while also noting the extraordinary lengths to which the senior Williams went to change the community's perspective. "My father had a pretty good reputation in the neighborhood that we lived in but, *even still,* he was the **_police_**," John declared. "My father was known to take my friends and I fishing, to baseball games, and things like that.

He didn't *only* take his sons when we went out, but made a point of taking other people's kids as well... especially those kids who didn't have fathers at home," the junior Williams beamed with pride. "My father spent his life trying to do some positive things with my peers and I, while also working to be accepted in the larger community as an asset, and not a liability. It wasn't easy, but he did it," he said.

"Historically, when the police get involved in anything in my community, somebody's going to jail," Williams remarked. "When you've got a community of low to middle-income people who are struggling," he explicated, "people often tend to do things that are not necessarily legal, just to survive and make ends meet. So, growing up with my father being a cop, I just *really* wanted to remove the stigma that was attached to me. So, to prove myself, I started to do things that most people would see as being 'against what the police stood for', and I tried to show everyone that I wasn't *just* the policeman's son," Williams professed. "I can smoke a little weed. I can fight. I can do just about anything that anybody else was doing, at least that's what I thought at the time," he exclaimed. "I was in a state of mind in which I felt that I needed to prove myself by letting the whole world know that I wasn't a 'goody-two-shoes'. In doing so, I gained more acceptance from the community and my peers by rebelling against my parents. To make matters worse," Williams bemoaned, "my behavior got to a point where I realized that I was eliciting a reaction that was positive from my peers," he said. "The wilder I became, the more accepted I was. So, of course, that promoted in me **more** negative behavior. But my reward, in doing so, was acceptance from the hood."

"So at a young age, I began to spend more time in the streets, and got involved in activities that, obviously, my parents would not have approved of, and it ultimately led toward me being indoctrinated into a street mentality and lifestyle that led to my ultimate downfall," Williams elaborated; lamenting the decisions he made that would lead to a deep disappointment experienced by his parents. "The way I was behaving wasn't the way I was brought up," he noted, "they were, however, poor decisions that I made during a period when I was trying to find myself, but I didn't go about it the right way," the one-time community liability turned asst declared. "A lot of Black males, like myself at the time, who really don't have an idea of what it means to be a man and, in particular a Black man, sometimes come upon the wrong things, like I did," Williams professed. What's important to understand, however, is that, in many ways, Williams' fate was sealed the moment his parents brought him home to live in an environment beset with insurmountable challenges that are not visited upon less vulnerable populations in America.

For decades, criminologists and sociologists have long posited the universally accepted conclusion that the environment in which an individual lives, helps to mold their behaviors, perspectives, predilections and decisions, unless and until something happens to interrupt the pattern. In a report issued by the *U.S. Department of Housing and Urban Development (HUD)*, the federal agency tasked with overseeing the nation's abysmal public housing programs entitled, "The Coaction of Neighborhood and Individual Effects on Juvenile Recidivism," the impact that an individual's neighborhood has on a youth's ability to resist delinquent behavior cannot be discounted when considering the totality of that person's actions in the aggregate. One of the leading theories to explain this phenomenon was the "Ecological Systems Theory", first introduced in 1981 by Urie Bronfenbrenner; a Russian-born American psychologist whose earlier work helped with the creation of the *Head Start Program* in 1965. According to *HUD's* analysis of the social conditions impairing the growth trajectory of those born into dire economic circumstances and are forced to live in public housing, Bronfembrenner's theory helped to underscore the power of external forces and familial habitats on its residents. "His theory outlines four nested systems that surround individuals, beginning with the most proximate, the microsystem (for example, the family), and ranging out to the macrosystem, or the larger social and cultural context of our immediate environs," the report noted. "Certain characteristics of microsystems, such as families and neighborhoods characterized by frayed relationships, lack the means to inhibit deviant behavior" ("Neighborhood", p. 34).

For starters, the environmental reasons that sometimes justify youthful misbehavior, underscore the impact of spatial influences on patterns of delinquency. What's more, in order for an individual to have influence, they must first have followers. *Dictionary.com* defines "influence" as *"the capacity to have an effect on the character, development, or behavior of someone or something."* Concomitantly, it also defines "followship" as *"the practice of doing what other people suggest, rather than taking the lead."* Finally, "spatial influence"

is the *"influence of environment on the health, mind, and behavior of human beings"*.
To that end, from a sociological perspective, the relevant research on the
theory of "spatial influence" more than supports the conclusion that
opportunities to participate in criminal offenses are increased in communities
with weak structures and limited social collaboration. Furthermore, as a result
of the external factors that weigh heavily on a youthful offender's decisions,
HUD's report further amplifies the challenges by which individuals like John
Williams, Jr.--a product of his environment--are shaped, impacted and
pipelined into a criminal justice system eagerly awaiting their arrival.
Additionally, other factors driving their thought process may include, but are
not limited, to the following:

1. Delinquent reoffending is spatially dependent rather than spatially diverse.
    This finding is strongest for drug offending, leading us to conclude that
    effective research on juvenile drug offending should incorporate
    neighborhood context ("Neighborhood", p. 48).

2. For some types of offending, especially drug selling, juveniles are likely to
    specialize. This specialization is likely to be influenced by opportunities,
    constraints, and pressures present in the youth's neighborhood
    ("Neighborhood", p. 48).

3. Recidivism offense type is spatially dependent. Residing in a high spatial
    concentration of any particular type of reoffending increases the chance
    that a delinquent youth will recidivate with that type of offense
    ("Neighborhood", p. 48).

4. Geographically defined places provide influences that can increase and
    decrease the likelihood of recidivism, but the nature of these risk and
    protective factors vary widely from neighborhood to neighborhood
    ("Neighborhood", p. 48).

What the *U.S. Department of Housing and Urban Development* conceded, in its
"earth-shattering" admission that crime infested neighborhoods with poor and
desperate people, tend to produce poor and desperate people with a
predilection for criminal activity, also helps to explain some of the choices that
individuals like John Williams, Jr. may make, that steer them onto dangerous
courses.

"As a kid and then a young man, my behavior demonstrated to those who mattered, that I was 'from the streets' but, in fact, a lot of negative consequences came from those experiences," Williams intoned; foreshadowing an inevitable conclusion for a young Black male such as himself. "It led to my being incarcerated several times throughout my life, as a result of my misguided decisions," he lamented. "As far as my incarceration is concerned, I had almost *totally negative* experiences with correctional staff," the former inmate recalled. "I found correctional officers to be very oppressive, very controlling, and very negative in the way that they viewed and treated inmates," he said. "More often than not, there is a generalization amongst the correctional staff at jails and prisons across the country, that all inmates are the same. Obviously, no group of people can all be the same, but there was a very small number of correctional staff, in my experiences, that understood that," John Williams deplored.

"It's a fraternity. A clan. They all stick together! Correctional officers and police make up the biggest gang around," decried the man who has had a front row seat to the world of law enforcement and American jurisprudence. "You want to talk about thugs, like the *Bloods* and the *Crips*? Well the police department is a gang too, and they conduct themselves like a gang! If you do something wrong in prison, they will make sure they beat you down--together--like a gang," he denoted. "Gangs don't come at you one-on-one, they come in groups! In my experience," Williams confessed, "it's pretty much the same thing with the police," he went on. "We see it going on all across America. If you are Black, you are a target. At least that's the way I see it," Williams professed.

"It's unfortunate that there *may* be police who are *not* out here profiling people or having a general disregard for Black life, the repatriated citizen remarked, "but if you are a part of *that* fraternity and do nothing to deter the behavior of your peers, then you are with them, as far as I am concerned. I've got to put them all in the same group," Williams surmised. "They don't arrest other officers they see shooting unarmed civilians. They cover for them. That's what gangs do. They are a group of people with one common cause, and they do whatever they have to do to protect one another. Unfortunately, Black people across America are victimized by these types of officers and their mentality," Williams concluded. What's even more disconcerting, however, is the fact that research and evidence suggests that on both sides of the thin blue line, both police and correctional officers have taken liberties to make life more difficult for many Black males who find themselves in the clutches of the criminal justice system.

In an exposé written by Benjamin Mueller, Robert Gebeloff and Sahil Chinoy for the *New York Times* called, "Surest Way to Face Marijuana Charges in New York: Be Black or Hispanic," young Black males like John Williams, Jr. once was, are not only targeted for criminal enforcement at alarming rates in many parts of the country, but this continued perpetuation of the mass incarceration era remains largely unabated. According to their article, nearly 90% of those arrested for marijuana possession are racial minorities who live in New York City, despite the reality that Blacks and Hispanics make up only 53% of the total population. For John Williams, Jr.'s old neighborhood of Harlem, the enforcement and arrest rates, particularly for low level offenses, dwarfs those of the adjacent, whiter, more affluent neighborhoods it buttresses. "In Manhattan, officers in a precinct covering a stretch of western Harlem, make marijuana arrests at double the rate of their counterparts in a precinct covering the northern part of the Upper West Side. Both received complaints at the same rate, but the precinct covering western Harlem has double the percentage of Black residents as the one that serves the Upper West Side" (Mueller). Highlighting the discrepancy, the *New York Times* story also noted, was the over-policing of minority communities, leading to exorbitant arrest rates and a growing prison industrial complex. "What you have is people smoking weed in the same places in any neighborhood in the city," said Scott Levy, a special counsel to the criminal defense practice at the *Bronx Defenders*, who has studied marijuana arrests. "It's just those neighborhoods are patrolled very, very differently. And the people in those neighborhoods are seen very differently by the police" (Mueller). Moreover, it can be effectively argued that it is because of the way in which some law enforcement officers view Black males that spark many of these interactions to begin with.

Since the expansion of the technological age and the ubiquitous placement of cameras almost everywhere, the world has now become witness to the claims and pleas that Black people in America have made for generations, particularly as it relates to their interactions with the law enforcement community. In some of those complaints, African-American males have decried the alleged planting of evidence and usurpation of their constitutional rights, to include the lack of probable cause itself, when encountering purported corrupt law enforcement officials. In a press release published by the *Vera Institute for*

Justice, an independent nonprofit national research and policy organization in the United States termed, "Research Confirms that Entrenched Racism Manifests in Disparate Treatment of Black Americans in Criminal Justice System", the legacy of bigotry and its far-reaching tentacles into the criminal justice system, have deleteriously impacted young men of color for generations. "The ways in which the criminal justice system operates to disadvantage Black people are systemic and ingrained, and often subtle," the release noted.

"The racial disparities that exist at each and every juncture of the justice system are significant and indisputable. But the reasons behind these disparities are complex and demand deeper understanding", said Nicholas Turner, Executive Director of the *Vera Institute of Justice.* "They are rooted in a history of oppression and discriminatory decision making that has deliberately targeted Black people; in a false and deceptive narrative of criminality; in implicit as well as conscious bias; in the legacy of structural racism and segregation," Turner continued. "We believe that we must reckon with the deep body of evidence of bias that has caused Black communities to become over-incarcerated, overpoliced, impoverished, and burdened with generational suffering" (*Vera Institute*). John Williams, Jr. has sought to reconcile himself with the fact that, in many ways, the shield he came to rely on for every day survival was also one that he would come to be wary of--for every day survival.

"I have had mixed feelings about the police all my life," Williams acknowledged, in discussing the duality of his emotions. "Being the son of a policeman, obviously I was taught to respect law enforcement officers. Furthermore, seeing my dad being such a positive example for both myself and the community, it gave me one view of the police that was very positive. "On the other hand, however, the other experiences that I have had with police officers weren't so positive," he intoned. "Now, I can say that a lot of my interactions with the police were due to my own behavior, but I always felt like the police were excessive in the way that they dealt with the Black community," Williams observed. "It always seemed as if they didn't have respect for me or for my community, so there were always those two competing dynamics," John confirmed. "But after hanging out on the streets for so long, I finally took a stance against law enforcement and what they represented. Ultimately," Williams explained, "my personal experiences with the police overshadowed those things I was taught by my father. Obviously, he attempted to protect me from certain aspects of the police because, in my opinion, he knew that many of his peers weren't good people," Williams speculated. With his perspective being weighed in the totality of his surrounding community, it is still important to note that what belies the impact of his spatial environment--and the implications of his misguided behavior--is a system designed to capitalize upon the intended misfortunes of citizens of color; so much so that it was codified in the *U.S. Constitution* in 1865.

An Unlucky Number?

In the award-winning documentary movie, *13th,* directed by groundbreaking filmmaker Ava DuVernay the history of Black men's entanglement with the American criminal justice system began at the collapse of slavery as an economic institution. As a result, the need to fill a sudden labor gap fueled the beginning of what was known as "convict leasing" and today has morphed into what we now know as the "Era of Mass Incarceration". What is more, as a means of buttressing the Southern economy and codifying a permanent underclass in American society, the *U.S. Congress* passed the *Thirteenth Amendment* to the *U.S. Constitution,* which was submitted to the states by a Joint Resolution of Congress, before finally being ratified when the *Georgia State Legislature* approved the amendment four months before the assassination of President Abraham Lincoln. The amendment, one which continues to impact millions of American today, reads as follows:

❝

Neither slavery nor involuntary servitude, except as a punishment for crime whereof the party shall have been duly convicted, shall exist within the United States, or any place subject to their jurisdiction (U.S. Const. am 13).

In essence, the *Thirteenth Amendment,* while abolishing slavery, also provided a loophole for the re-enslavement of Black people, males in particular, by criminalizing them and then capitalizing, once again, upon their free labor, only this time, as inmates. In her critically acclaimed film, DuVernay comprehensively explored how African-Americans have been dehumanized and degraded as second-class citizens and, as a result, were fair game for economic exploitation. To give credence to their need for continuing a free labor source that would otherwise cost an untold fortune, business and industry leaders needed to demonize the image of Black males and recast the public perception of them from the amiable and pliant men of happiness and mirth, (as it had been shaped in the Antebellum Period with such genial characters as *Uncle Tom* of Harriet Beecher Stowe's 1852 eponymously named book, "Uncle Tom's Cabin"), to dangerous villains that needed to be killed, or convicted and controlled. Then, with the creation of cinematic film, that goal was made all the easier for those who had a vested interest in the continued exploitation of Black bodies; with the proliferation of movie theaters across America offering yet another opportunity to redefine the Black male image as rapacious rapists and insatiable animals. In fact, no other movie was more successful in that effort than the 1915 smash hit, *Birth of a Nation;* a film heralding the creation of the *Ku Klux Klan* as the primary defenders of whiteness in America and the chastity of white women from marauding Black beasts. The popularity of the movie, steeped in the worst of America's racial fears, led to the broad criminalization of Black men, both in public perception and reality, and the birth of slavery by another name: the infamous practice of "convict leasing".

According to the *Equal Justice Initiative's* report, "Convict Leasing", the close of the Civil War ushered in a new form of servitude initially designed to benefit those Southern states who needed cheap labor to meet production demands on their sprawling and vast plantations. To that end, the wholesale criminalization of the formerly enslaved, through the development of these new "Black Codes", as they came to be known, were, in essence a revolving door back to slavery, administered by individual states. "Southern states leased prisoners to private railways, mines, and large plantations. While states profited, prisoners earned no pay and faced inhumane, dangerous, and often deadly work conditions" ("Convict Leasing"). In fact, because the *Thirteenth Amendment* expressly prohibited slavery, new laws sprang up all across the south, most of which only applied to Black people, and subjected them to overly burdensome criminal prosecution for "offenses such as loitering, breaking curfew, vagrancy, having weapons, and not carrying proof of employment. Crafted to ensnare Black people and return them to chains, these laws were effective; for the first time in U.S. history, many state penal systems held more Black prisoners than white – all of whom could be leased for profit" ("Convict Leasing").

According to historical accounts of race and class in America, as chronicled in DuVernay's *13th,* since the demise of slavery as an socioeconomic institution in 1865, and for the next six decades, until the State of Alabama belatedly banned official convict leasing in 1928, the profiteering upon forced servitude was, once again, a means to an end for those willing to use Black bodies as human chattel. Then, in the 1972 re-election campaign of President Richard Nixon, the employment of a racially tinged political game plan known as the "Southern Strategy," a Republican Party electoral initiative to increase political support among Southern white voters by subtly (and sometimes overtly) appealing to racism against African-Americans, helped to usher in what has now become the "Era of Mass Incarceration" that continues unremittingly nearly fifty years later. Positioning himself as the "law and order" candidate, which African-Americans have historically viewed as code-word for "keeping Blacks in their place," Nixon campaigned heavily against what he saw as the primary enemies of American society: Anti-Viet Nam War protesters and Black people. In doing so, he encouraged the widespread arrest of thousands of Black people for low level offenses, fueling a surge in incarceration rates for individuals of color.

In tapes unearthed in the documentary masterpiece, "13th", Presidential Advisor, John Ehrlichman, was recorded bragging about the ultimate goal of "Tricky Dick" Nixon, which was to create a permanent underclass for whites to both objectify and be fearful of, namely Black men in America. "The Nixon campaign in 1968 and the Nixon *White House* after that, had two enemies: the anti-war left and Black people. You understand what I'm saying," Ehrlichman asked. "We knew we couldn't make it illegal to be either against the war or Black... but by getting the public to associate the hippies with marijuana and Blacks with heroin, and then criminalizing both heavily, we could disrupt those communities. We could arrest their leaders, raid their homes, break up their meetings, and vilify them night after night on the evening news. Did we know we were lying about the drugs? Of course, we did" ("13th").

At the beginning of Nixon's second term of office, the U.S. prison population stood at 357,292 people. By the time Nixon's successor, Ronald Reagan, assumed the presidency in 1980, that figure had risen to more than 513,900 people, a large portion of them being African-American men, many of whom were permanently removed from society. As a part of Reagan's ascendancy, he also ushered in a new kind of *"War on Drugs"* which many African-Americans saw as a *"War on Black People"*, one that resulted in the incarceration and separation of an entire generation of men; leaving their children fatherless and their communities more impoverished with every harsh sentence imposed. By 1984, with the crack epidemic holding a tight grip on many urban communities throughout the country, President Reagan commenced a literal war in Black neighborhoods, with police departments and federal law enforcement agencies across the country kicking in the doors of unsuspecting criminals and the innocent alike, arresting thousands of minorities and, in the process, indelibly altering the fate of Black America. Moreover, with the more Draconian sentencing of those convicted of possessing or distributing crack, as opposed to powder cocaine, America's prison industrial complex was strengthened all the more under "The Gipper's" leadership. In fact, in three short years under Reagan's reign the prison population increased nearly 50%, to 759,100 men and women behind bars.

In 1992, the *Democratic Party* led by its nominee, Governor William Jefferson Clinton of Arkansas, determined that the best route to the *White House* was to claim the mantle of being "tough on crime" by "triangulating" the issue of "law and order" in America. Reeling from back-to-back-to-back losses in the 1980, 1984 and 1988 U.S. Presidential Elections, Clinton, along with his running mate, then U.S. Senator Albert Gore, Jr. of Tennessee, decided that his campaign would benefit from "running to the right" of Republican President George H.W. Bush. Four years earlier, then Vice President Bush had won a come-from-behind victory against the Governor of Massachusetts, Michael Dukakis by, once again, demonizing Black men. To achieve his objective, the elder Bush used the doctored image of a scary-looking Willie Horton, a convicted murderer and rapist who, while on a furlough from a Massachusetts state prison, murdered a helpless white woman; stoking latent Caucasian fears of a Black bogeyman and granting Bush four more years at 1600 Pennsylvania Avenue. Midway through George H.W. Bush's tenure, the number of incarcerated Americans had grown to a whopping 1,179,200 individuals.

To outflank Bush on the issue in the next election, Clinton, using his wife, Hillary Rodham Clinton as a surrogate, railed against "super-predators" *(code-*

word for 'Black males who may be repeat offenders'), and successfully campaigned for the idea of flooding America's streets with 100,000 new police officers to help fight the scourge of crime and violence. Once elected, to the presidency, Clinton then tacked further to the right of the political center by championing even tougher criminal justice mandates, including "Three Strikes" laws, which required judges to impose mandatory minimum sentences for those convicted of their third felony, regardless of mitigating circumstances. Additionally, with the passage of Clinton's *Omnibus Crime Bill of 1994*, which also imposed "Truth in Sentencing" guidelines that required convicted criminals to serve a substantial portion of their sentence before being considered for the possibility of parole, the noose around the necks of already desperate Black men was tightened even further, as the Democratically led initiatives would go on to have a devastating effect upon legions of African-American families.

By end of Clinton's presidency in the year 2000, the number of imprisoned people had almost doubled to 2,015,300 people, with African-Americans representing nearly 44% of the total prison population at the time. More than a dozen years later, at the halfway point of Barack Obama's second term as President of the United States, the rate of incarcerated people grew nearly 13%, to 2,306,200 inmates by 2014. Today, with the privatization of many of America's prisons, and the vast expansion of the *Prison-Industrial Complex* which continues to serve as a fount of cheap labor, there are very few signs of anything changing; as companies such as *Corrections Corporation of America* and the *American Legislative Exchange Council* continue to devise ingenious ways to profit off of the backbreaking labor of Black men in chains. Having lived that very experience that so many nameless, faceless men, locked in America's penal institutions endure every day, John Williams, Jr. appreciates the challenges it takes to overcome a life of pain and punishment and has used the footstool of educational enlightenment to shine a path on a brighter future.

"During my incarceration, I encountered a lot of negativity," Williams revealed, "but I always had a thirst for knowledge, and a thirst for learning and I did maintain that. As a result, I met a different group of people while in prison, a group of brothers that took an interest in my education, and nurtured me towards having a greater understanding of the responsibilities of being a Black man. Just as importantly, they helped me to understand that my incarceration, and all of the experiences prior to my incarceration, didn't have to be the last stop for me. I could go back into the community, and not only be a productive member of society, but I could affect some type of change in my neighborhood; to teach young Black men and women that were more positive things that they can do with their efforts. And that's what I had my mind set on doing when I left prison--something positive for the community," Williams declared. "But I am also mindful of the fact that the challenges we face are, of course, by design," he mentioned.

"Today, fifty-plus years after the end of the Civil Rights Movement, Black men in America are still cast in a negative light," the former inmate continued. "And while this movement attempted to address a lot of the issues and concerns that Black people had and still have today, we still have a long way to go," he postulated. "You see, America is built on institutionalized racism. There is a privilege that white people have in our society, where they understand the power they have. In order for the structure of white supremacy to maintain itself, there has to be a class system in place where some people are used and exploited, so that the privileged few can live as comfortable a lifestyle as possible," Williams theorized. "It is a shame that in today's America, we still have modern-day lynching and discrimination against people of color in all areas of human activity, which further demonstrates how deep institutionalized racism is embedded within our culture," he maintained. "In my view, not a lot has changed over the last half-century, it's just disguised in different ways," he went on. "Whites enjoy the same privileges that they have always enjoyed. And Blacks are still catching hell, dealing with the same things we have been dealing with since slavery."

"Today, the *Prison-Industrial Complex* is nothing more than slavery in another form," Williams opined. "If you go back to the *Willie Lynch Letter,* you will see a formula, at the end of chattel slavery, that would keep Black people mentally enslaved for generations to come. Sometimes when we see the behavior of some Black people, we fail to understand that this behavior has been embedded within our DNA and has been passed down to us from one generation to the next," he hypothesized. "For the most part, a majority of our people, in my opinion, don't understand _why_ we behave the way that we do, but it's because that's what those who came before us did to survive. As a Black man, it is frustrating to see my people suffering so much, and the way that the system exploits them in all aspects of American life," Williams noted. "We have not been given the help we need to overcome a lot of the stigma, and a lot of the mental health issues we have, as exemplified by some of our behavior," the redeemed model citizen observed. "In my estimation," Williams said, "we need an entire curriculum that focuses on strategies to counteract the *Post Traumatic Slave Syndrome* we grapple with every day."

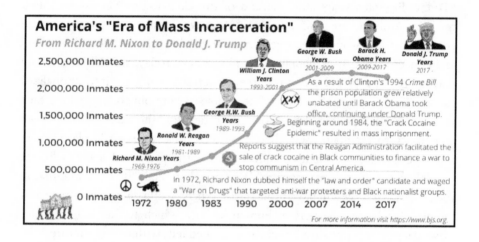

America's "Era of Mass Incarceration"

From Richard M. Nixon to Donald J. Trump

2,500,000 Inmates

2,000,000 Inmates

1,500,000 Inmates

1,000,000 Inmates

500,000 Inmates

0 Inmates

1972   1980   1983   1990   2000   2007   2014   2017

George W. Bush Years 2001-2009
Barack H. Obama Years 2009-2017
Donald J. Trump Years 2017 -
William J. Clinton Years 1993-2001
George H.W. Bush Years 1989-1993
Ronald W. Reagan Years 1981-1989
Richard M. Nixon Years 1969-1976

As a result of Clinton's 1994 *Crime Bill* the prison population grew relatively unabated until Barack Obama took office, continuing under Donald Trump.

Beginning around 1984, the "Crack Cocaine Epidemic" resulted in mass imprisonment.

Reports suggest that the Reagan Administration facilitated the sale of crack cocaine in Black communities to finance a war to stop communism in Central America.

In 1972, Richard Nixon dubbed himself the "law and order" candidate and waged a "War on Drugs" that targeted anti-war protesters and Black nationalist groups.

For more information visit https://www.bjs.org.

Paid in Full?

The United States of America is a nation built upon the fundamental ideals of liberty, justice and freedom. For former felons, however, who fortunately find their way back to society and seek to become contributing and productive members, there are roadblocks at every corner that make it easier, in many ways, to return to prison than it is to return to the community. For example, "Returning Citizens" have difficulties obtaining the basic of human necessities and dignities that make most people feel whole, to include housing and employment, for starters. Moreover, these individuals, a large portion of whom are Black males, are also denied such things as student loans, food stamps and access to the ballot box, all of which can help someone who is struggling to lift themselves up to an ability to fully fend for themselves.

Furthermore, with hiring managers, housing department and rental agents, and social service directors who, in "doing their jobs", oftentimes find themselves actively standing in the way of the lucky break these men need to successfully reintegrate into society, and the results are disheartening.

According to *Oxford Handbooks*, the "Coercive Mobility" thesis assumes that "the cycling of people into and out of prison constitutes an important and distinct form of mobility which can harm the communities that are hardest hit by both crime and, perhaps ironically, crime control policies." As legions of Black men complete their terms of incarceration, and are released back to the counties from which they hailed--with few opportunities for forward progress, scant access to resources, and a stigma that seems to be permanently attached to most formerly incarcerated individuals, the conjoined twins of poverty and desperation are there to greet them at the prison gates. Moreover, the stigma of being a felon, a monster that raises its head every time they apply for a job and have to check "the box" which identifies them as having had prior criminal convictions, conspire together to make the return to society for many of them a nasty, brutish and short affair. With that being said, before properly considering the overwhelming evidence of coercive mobility's impact on communities of color, we must first examine the underlying the dynamics that the effects of the diminished capacity to succeed that most returning citizens pack up and carry with them when they depart the *Department of Corrections*.

In their analysis entitled, "The Effects of Mass Incarceration on Communities of Color," authors Robert Crutchfield and Gregory Weeks of *Issues In Science and Technology*, observed that the challenges repatriating residents have in properly readjusting to life outside of prison is complicated by the emotional challenges they face with waning relationships and few advocates to help them traverse the new terrain. "It is generally accepted that having a good, solid family life lowers the probability of a person becoming involved in crime, and that having employment (especially good employment) does the same. Predictably, those most likely to be sentenced to a term in prison are less likely than others of their age, race, and gender to be involved in a stable relationship or to have been employed in a high-quality job prior to their incarceration," the authors noted. "When men and women return from prison, their family life has an even higher likelihood of having been disrupted, and their competitiveness on the job market is even more diminished than it was before they were incarcerated," Crutchfield and Weeks noted. "Time in prison means that these already marginal people are more marginalized, and they tend to return to living in neighborhoods that are already distressed by the presence of too many disrupted families and high levels of joblessness. They add to the already overcrowded pool of residents likely to not be in good relationships, to not be good prospects as mates, and to be not competitive for the desirable good jobs that will help them stay out of jail or prison and might help their community's dismal economic state" (Crutchfield). As a result of this toxic mix of lack of access and fewer resources to begin with, the chances of keeping them from returning back to prison diminishes as well, as crime tends to increase, in already hard-hit areas.

The *Prison Policy Initiative*, a criminal justice public policy organization that puts the problem of mass incarceration — and the perverse incentives that fuel it — on the national agenda, in their report called, "Out of Prison & Out of Work: Unemployment Among Formerly Incarcerated People," noted that currently, there are more than 600,000 "Returning Citizens" that make the transition from incarceration to liberation each year, most of whom have very few options upon their return to society. According to their investigation of the impact of joblessness amongst repatriated residents, those who have criminal histories are shut out of opportunities for employment, leading to an unsustainable crisis for both the individuals with records as well as the community to which they are returning. "We find that the unemployment rate for formerly incarcerated people is nearly *five times higher* than the unemployment rate for the general United States population," the analysis noted, "and substantially higher than even the worst years of the Great Depression," it continued. "Although we have long known that labor market outcomes for people who have been to prison are poor, these results point to extensive economic exclusion that would certainly be the cause of great public concern if they were mirrored in the general population ("Out of Prison"). Moreover, it goes without saying that employers generally discriminate against those with criminal histories about as much as they do with Black males in general. In fact, according to the *NAACP's* Fair Chance Hiring Fact Sheet, the psychology of racism is so ingrained within the national culture that even white men who have done prison time have just as good a chance and, oftentimes, even better, of getting hired than do Black men with no criminal history and college degrees. But men like John Williiams, Jr., determined never to return to prison again, even though the impact of official policy and social practice demonstrate that the odds are clearly stacked against them, are committed to doing their part to help dismantle what fuels the Prison-Industrial Complex... one inmate at a time.

"While I was incarcerated, I got involved in an initiative called the M.A.N. program. The project, which focused on "Mentoring and Nurturing" (M.A.N.), was designed to help uplift the hopes of incarcerated young men who clearly needed guidance and direction for their lives," Williams explained; detailing the positive effects the program had on his own behavior and those of other prisoners. "M.A.N. was designed to curtail some of the violence that the youths who were in prison were engaging in at the time," he elaborated. "After taking the program to the prison administration and having it approved, we were able to teach many of the young men in the program a variety of life skills that helped them to cope with being in prison. As a part of this initiative," Williams stated, "we taught younger inmates the importance of preventing teenage pregnancies, being better fathers to their children, preventing sexually transmitted diseases, and anything that we felt prisoners could use as a tool to be more successful upon their reintegration into society," the reformed usurper remarked. "We did so, because we realized that many of the youths that were imprisoned had no frame of reference for how to better themselves, while simultaneously dealing with the challenges of prison life. After the first year of the program," Williams observed, "the administration did an assessment and determined that prison violence had actually _decreased_, due in large part to the effectiveness of this unique initiative," Williams beamed. "Yet in still, the prison administration initially approached us about removing the involvement of the inmate population in the facilitation of the program, replacing us with college students as moderators and facilitators. After we voiced our strong objection," he went on, "understanding that a greater impact could be had with these incarcerated youths learning from those who have been down the road that they are heading, they ultimately relented and allowed us to continue."

When it comes to the future of Black males in America, however, particularly those who were once separated from their families due to imprisonment, Williams is hopeful that things will get better over time. "I am very proud of our people for continuing to overcome what we have endured," he stated. "Obviously we have been through a lot, from African colonialism to American slavery and beyond, however I see a lot of positivity associated with being a Black man in America today," the policeman's son declared. "There are Black men out here who are a positive force of nature, brothers with degrees and businesses, for example, who are doing some amazing things," he noted. "With that being said, however, it really doesn't matter—as a Black man—what background you come from, in America, you are still a target," Williams bemoaned. "We get racially profiled not because of our status in society, but simply because of the color of our skin," he theorized. "There have been Black executives, athletes, actors, and more, who have been victims of profiling and discrimination. Even still, I remain optimistic that, as Africans in the diaspora, we are going to band together and address the issues and concerns of our people, our communities, and our neighborhoods, and the larger world. This, however, must be a massive effort if things are ever going to change," Williams postulated. "Black men are fathers, husbands, sons and friends. It's just that the world just doesn't see us that way," he said. To solve the challenges posed by the invisibility that Black males experience every day, Williams believes that education is the most important attainment that Black men can achieve to help position them for greatness in a system not designed for them to succeed.

"If I had the opportunity to give advice to Black males—young and old—I would certainly encourage them to pursue their education at all costs," he declared. "Someone told me a long time ago that we should always seek knowledge--from the cradle to the grave," the self-enlightened survivor intoned. "I am a firm believer that knowledge is power, and most importantly *knowledge is freedom.* Additionally," he elaborated, "I would encourage those brothers to learn to love themselves, first and most importantly, to love God, and to learn to love your brothers and sisters. Regardless of how we may view them, and what they may be going through, we are still a family," Williams emphasized. "Most ethnic groups in America tend to ban together to address the needs of their community. We must do the same. We should begin by pooling our resources, and stop making excuses for why we *should not* deal and do business with one another, as Black people. We must put aside our different religious and sub-cultural beliefs, and embrace the reality that we are all **one** Black family, regardless of where on the globe we come from," the Harlemite extolled. We must not allow anyone to steal away from us **our** legacy," he surmised, "after they have stolen everything else. The time has come for us to reclaim what belongs to us," he went on. "The only way we can do that is through 'Black Unity'", Williams concluded. "At one point in my life, I was a destructive force within the Black community, but that was because I was brainwashed. Today, now that I am enlightened and mentally aware of both my actions and their consequences, I feel a sense of responsibility to address as many of the issues and concerns as I can, because my conscience won't allow me to do anything different. From here on out, my goal is to affect some type of positive change with the time that I have left here on Earth."

(John Williams, Jr.: Reformed Citizen & Justice Advocate)

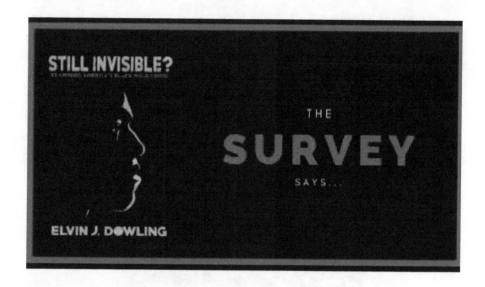

How strongly do you agree or disagree with the following statements?*

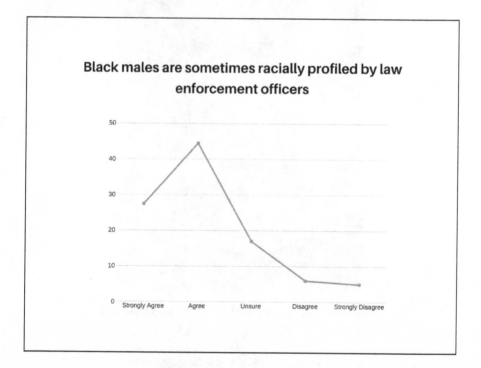

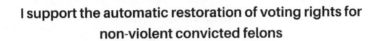

I support the automatic restoration of voting rights for non-violent convicted felons

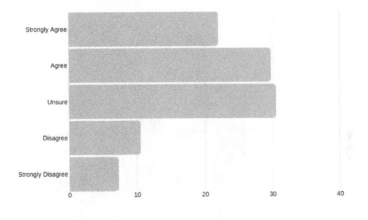

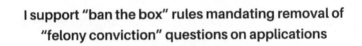

I support "ban the box" rules mandating removal of "felony conviction" questions on applications

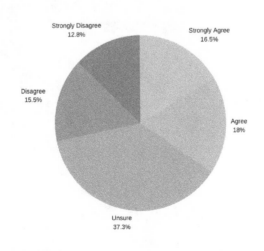

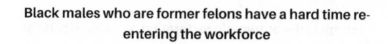

Black males who are former felons have a hard time re-entering the workforce

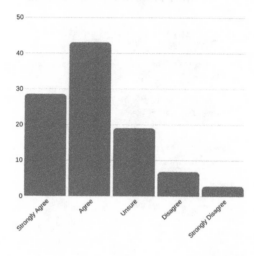

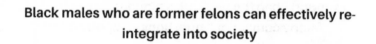

Black males who are former felons can effectively re-integrate into society

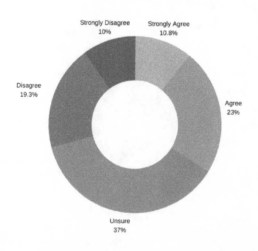

All survey results displayed above are represented by the overall percentage of survey respondents. For more information on our survey methodology, please see the Author's Note, located in the front matter of the book. To review raw survey results, visit: http://bit.ly/stillinvisiblesurvey

BLACK MALES & PRISON: ON THIS WE ALL AGREE...

PROFILED BY POLICE	**RESTORATION OF VOTING RIGHTS**	**BAN THE BOX ON JOB APPLICATIONS**	**TOUGH TIMES AHEAD**
Asian Male Respondents (50.00%) were the only subgroup that "Strongly Disagreed" or "Disagreed" with the idea that Black males are racially profiled by police.	More than half of all respondents (51.75%) Support the "Automatic Restoration of Voting Rights for Former Felons" who have paid their debt to society.	With the exception of White Respondents (32.91%) and Multiracial Respondents (50.00%), most believe that questions concerning past convictions should be banned on job applications.	An overwhelmig number of all respondents (71.50%) "Strongly Agree" or "Agree" with the notion that Black males have a tough time getting hired upon release from incarceration.

Findings by Race

- An overwhelming majority of all White respondents (70.42%) "Strongly Agree" or "Agree" with the statement, *"Black males are sometimes racially profiled by law enforcement officers."*

- 1 out of 3 of all Hispanic respondents (33.33%) were "Unsure" with the statement, *"I support automatic restoration of voting rights for non-violent convicted felons."*

- Nearly 2 out of 10 of all Black respondents (19.23%) "Disagree" or "Strongly Disagree" with the statement, *"I support "ban the box" rules mandating removal of 'felony conviction' questions on applications."*

Findings by Gender

- Almost 4 out of 10 Asian male respondents (37.50%) "Strongly Disagree" or "Disagree" with the statement, *"Black males who are former felons have a hard time re-entering the workforce."*

- More than 8 in 10 Multiracial female respondents "Strongly Disagree" or "Disagree" with the statement, *"Black males who are former felons can effectively re-integrate into society."*

- A strong majority of all Hispanic female respondents (63.16%) "Strongly Agree" or "Agree" with the statement, *"Black males are sometimes racially profiled by law enforcement officers."*

Findings by Age

- More than half of all, ages 18-24 years old (53.19%) "Strongly Agree" or "Agree" with the statement, *"I support automatic restoration of voting rights for non-violent convicted felons."*

- More than one-third of all respondents, ages 55 years and older (34.67%), "Strongly Disagree" or "Disagree" with the statement, *"I support "ban the box" rules mandating removal of "felony conviction" questions on applications."*

- An overwhelming majority of all respondents, ages 25-34 years old (70.08%), "Strongly Agree" or "Agree" with the statement, *"Black males who are former felons have a hard time re-entering the workforce."*

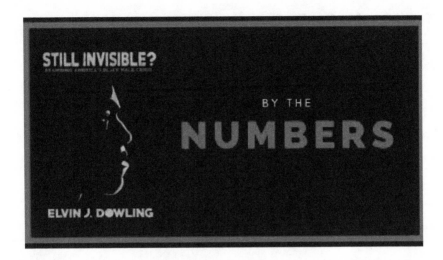

"More Than Their Fair Share!"

- Although Black males make up approximately 6.5% of the U.S. population, they comprise 37% of those incarcerated or otherwise confined in their own homes or in local, state or federal facilities ("Total Correctional Population").

- While white males comprise 31% of the U.S. population, they represent 32% of all prisoners, on par with national demographics. Black males, however, are six times more likely to be locked up ("Total Correctional Population").

"The 'Complexion for the Protection'!"

- Possessing a prior criminal record diminishes the likelihood of getting called back from prospective employers by as much as 50%, making the road to redemption all the more difficult for struggling Returning Citizens ("Fair Chance").

- In the United States of America, white men with previous convictions still have a better shot at receiving a job interview than does a Black man with a degree and no criminal record ("Fair Chance").

"Don't Box Me Out Bro!"

- While many states have passed legislation banning the question about criminal convictions on many job applications, it does not prohibit employers from asking the question during the employment process ("Fair Chance").

- Research has found that "Ban the Box" policies help to increase the chances of those with past criminal records to find meaningful employment, which sets them on the path to successful reintegration into society ("Fair Chances").

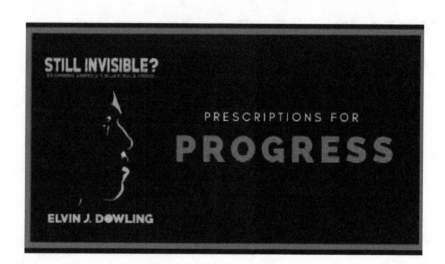

"Good Jobs ... or Desperate Mobs?"

- By providing subsidized jobs aimed at assisting those with past criminal records, with an emphasis on bettering their soft-skills, those deemed "hard to employ" have greater opportunities for long-term success (Doleac, p. 14).

- In developing services that provide support for the formerly-incarcerated as they seek work, that can pay them well; such as construction, chances of recidivism are diminished significantly (Doleac, p. 15).

"A Certificate for Good Behavior?"

- In many jurisdictions across America, former convicts can request that a judge provide them a "Rehabilitation Certificate", which helps them demonstrate their ability to effectively transition back into society (Doleac, p. 19).

- Encourage "Returning Citizens" to seek legal assistance in obtaining "rehabilitation certification" from the courts, where available, to help them reassure potential employers or landlords of their viability (Doleac, p. 19).

"What They Need to Succeed..."

- Create transitional housing options for those released back into society with no place to go, based on evidence-based options, such as group homes, which emphasize self-governance and mutual support ("Housing", p. 7).

- Work with local officials to help former inmates reintegrate, with services that improve family dynamics, increase long-term employment, foster self-improvement, and reduce recidivism ("Housing", p. 8)

Works Cited

1. Harris, Philip W. "The Coaction of Neighborhood and Individual Effects on Juvenile Recidivism." *Cityscape: A Journal of Policy Development and Research - Volume 13, Number 3.* 2011 33. U.S. Department of Housing and Urban Development Office of Policy Development and Research. Accessed 25 November 2019. http://bit.ly/34lEFH9

2. Mueller, Benjamin, Gebeloff, Robert and Chinoy, Sahil. "Surest Way to Face Marijuana Charges in New York: Be Black or Hispanic." *NYTimes.com*, The New York Company. 13 May 2018. ht

3. Vera Institute for Justice. "Research Confirms that Entrenched Racism Manifests in Disparate Treatment of Black Americans in Criminal Justice System." *Vera.org*, Vera Institute for Justice. 3 May 2018. http://bit.ly/33mvBR8

4. "The Constitution of the United States," *Amendment 13*.

5. "Convict Leasing." *EJI.org*, Equal Justice Initiative. Web. 01 November 2013. http://bit.ly/2KU5TwW

6. *"13th."* Directed by Ava DuVernay, with appearances by Melina Abdullah, Bryan Stevenson, Newt Gingrich and Kevin Gannon, director's cut, Kandoo Films and Forward Movement, 2017. *Netflix*, http://www.netflix.com.

7. Frost, Natasha A. and Clear, Todd R. "Coercive Mobility." *The Oxford Handbook of Criminological Theory*, Oxford University Press. December 2012. http://bit.ly/35JkeV7

8. Crutchfield, Robert D. and Weeks, Gregory A. "The Effects of Mass Incarceration on Communities of Color." *Issues.org - Issues in Science and Technology, Arizona State University*. Fall 2015. http://bit.ly/2rvaf73

9. Couloute, Lucius and Kopf, Daniel. "Out of Prison & Out of Work: Unemployment Among Formerly Incarcerated People." *PrisonPolicy.org*, Prison Policy Initiative. July 2018. http://bit.ly/2rBsoA8

10. "Total Correctional Population." *BJS.gov*, Bureau of Justice Statistics - United States Department of Justice. Accessed 30 November 2019. http://bit.ly/33GkxOS

11. "Fair Chance Hiring Fact Sheet." *NAACP.org*, National Association for the Advancement of Colored People (NAACP). Accessed 1 December 2019. http://bit.ly/2rEJ3mh

12. Doleac, Jennifer L. "Strategies to Productively Reincorporate the Formerly-Incarcerated into Communities: A Review of the Literature." *IZA Institute of Labor Economics*, Initiated by Deutsche Post Foundation. June 2018. http://bit.ly/2R6yqmO

Chapter 11: "Hope ... or Nope?"

Exploring the Limitations of Black Political Power

"

You must realize immediately that much of our work is opposed. Our discipline demands therefore that we talk to no one and that we avoid situations in which information might be given away unwittingly."

- Ralph Ellison, "Invisible Man" (Shmoop Editorial Team. 14.120)

The State of Louisiana
Literacy Test (This test is to be given to anyone who cannot prove a fifth grade education.)

Do what you are told to do in each statement, nothing more, nothing less. Be careful as one wrong answer denotes failure of the test. You have 10 minutes to complete the test.

1. Draw a line around the number or letter of this sentence.

2. Draw a line under the last word in this line.

3. Cross out the longest word in this line.

4. Draw a line around the shortest word in this line.

5. Circle the first, first letter of the alphabet in this line.

6. In the space below draw three circles, one inside (engulfed by) the other.

7. Above the letter X make a small cross.

8. Draw a line through the letter below that comes earliest in the alphabet.

   Z V S B D M K I T P H C

9. Draw a line through the two letters below that come last in the alphabet.

   Z V B D M K T P H S Y C

10. In the first circle below write the last letter of the first word beginning with "L".

    ① ② ③ ④ ⑤

11. Cross out the number necessary, when making the number below one million.

    10000000000

12. Draw a line from circle 2 to circle 5 that will pass below circle 2 and above circle 4.

    ① ② ③ ④ ⑤

13. In the line below cross out each number that is more than 20 but less than 30.

    31 16 48 29 53 47 22 37 98 26 20 25

(Actual literacy test used by the State of Louisiana, and given to African-American males seeking the right to vote. The test was designed to be confusingly worded and unanswerable, with the white voter registrar having ultimate discretion on all correct answers).

Not for the Faint of Heart!

"What Happens to a Dream Deferred?"

Famed Italian poet and author of the literary classic "Inferno", Dante Alighieri, once said, *"The darkest places in hell are reserved for those who maintain their neutrality in times of moral crisis."* As America continues to grapple with the challenges of what Black intellectual W.E.B. DuBois once called the *"problem of the color line,"* the need for everyone to pick a side in what could potentially be a fomenting culture clash that could ultimately succeed at weakening our nation from the inside out. Additionally, those who seek to keep the union America has fought so hard to keep together, must begin to rise up to protect the values we often export to others, namely freedom, justice and democracy. Consequently, it is incumbent upon those who are the champions of democracy to incise the cancer of racism in this country, for the sake of the union itself, or we will certainly meet a most perilous fate.

Throughout the course of human existence, the science (and art) of politics has been one of compromise and capitulation, as those who seek a redress of their grievances take their issues to the public square for resolution and progress. As an example of our nation's commitment to the ideals of liberty and justice, those who are brave enough to enter the public arena as elected officials, do so at a very high cost--some much greater than others. Just as much, those political leaders of color who are *truly* committed to making real the promises codified in the *U.S. Constitution*, have historically been forced to work under great risk and danger; as America hasn't taken too kindly to "uppity negroes" insistent upon pushing for systemic change. Furthermore, as the expansion of the franchise became a front and center issue that could ultimately impact the social order of society, Black leaders have, unfortunately, borne the brunt of much of the backlash that has come from those who were desirous of keeping things just the way they are. But times have changed... and so must we.

In today's technologically advanced society, with the proliferation of hostile foreign actors intent on usurping the will of the people through election interference, and those who will stop at nothing to undermine the very foundations of our democratic institutions of government, the time for strong leadership and a unified front against all enemies, foreign and domestic, as never been more important to this country than they are right now. As a matter of fact, history has demonstrated that, when given a chance, African-American men have risen to the challenge, time and again, to fight for the tenets of our faith in this, the land of the free. And if we want to keep it this way, we have got to do something different! You see, by continuing to suppress their innate abilities to help lead us out of the morass of the global dismay that our nation and, indeed our world, finds itself in, America is severely limiting itself when it limits Black leadership. To that end, I propose that we chart a new path that affords free and unfettered access to the ballot and to higher political office for not only Black men, but all people of color. Or, frankly, anyone who calls themselves American and meet the qualifications necessary to have their votes cast and counted. One man. One Woman. One Vote. What's so hard about that?

I Believe in You,

Justitia

Lady Justice

John T. Bullock: "A Man on a Mission"

Vote or Die?

Every morning, on the plains of the African Serengeti, when the sun rises, the slowest gazelle wakes up and knows that it must be faster than the fastest lion or it will be eaten. Likewise, the slowest lion wakes up and knows that it must be faster than the fastest gazelle, or it will starve. And at the end of the night and the dawn of a new day, it really doesn't matter whether you're a lion or a gazelle: "when the sun comes up... you'd better be running." For most of his life, Dr. John Bullock, an up and coming leader in Baltimore City politics, has been running to make a difference in the lives of the least of these through the power of his example. A long-distance sprinter, Bullock is a proud son of "West Philly" as it is known, who continues to pound the pavement in search of solutions for those he serves. A product of one of the scrappiest neighborhoods in the "City of Brotherly Love and Sisterly Affection," Philadelphia, Pennsylvania, Bullock both understands and appreciates the heights to which he has climbed the ladder of leadership, through a long and arduous task that would have made weaker men collapse under the pressure.

"I was raised in a two-parent household, in a close-knot neighborhood in the heart of Philadelphia," declared Dr. John Bullock, an educator and elected official committed to empowering communities and changing lives through the power of his example. "Both of my parents were military veterans, with my mother being a disabled veteran for the latter part of her life," the lanky leader recalled; reminiscing upon a childhood filled with the difficulties and pains of having a parent hobbled by physical limitations. "Over time, even though my family was intact," Bullock noted, "my father had challenges as it relates to consistent, long-term employment over the years. I have also had family members who have struggled with addiction," the professor admitted. "In fact, some of my aunts and uncles are still fighting that battle in many ways today," he elaborated. "In my neighborhood growing up, there were a number of my classmates and neighbors who ended up going to prison and getting killed, as a result of a combination of poor decisions and an environment that predisposed them to violence and tragedy," John noted. "When I was in the sixth grade my first friend, who was only a year older than myself, tragically wound up getting killed. I was only twelve years old. What's more, I also had friends from high school who went to prison--some of whom never came out--but I was fortunate in that my parents always wanted the best for me and helped to steer me in the right direction early on in life," the academician acknowledged.

"In high school," Bullock began, "I had a teacher to ask me _how_ I was able to achieve a number of the successes that I had achieved thus far in my life," he said. "I shared with her the support that I received from both my family and my friends, before she reminded me that _I_ had a role to play in that process as well," the noted scholar recollected. "But more importantly," he elucidated, "I had mentors who invested in me as well. In fact, one of my first professors in undergraduate school told me very pointedly that I **needed** to get a PhD, and that stuck with me until I achieved that goal," Bullock declared. "My high school coach used to encourage me to run, which I still do today. And when I do so, I am reminded of the fact that there are people who are faster than me, but are there to teach me how to reach that next level. As a result, I have learned the importance of putting oneself in a league with those who are striving to achieve the same goals and reach the same heights that you are working on yourself. Then, once that goal is attained, you've got to set another goal for yourself and keep moving forward," he elaborated. "Coming up, my mentors would **force me** to do things that I did not want to do! For example," Bullock explained, "they would tell me things like, _'You're going to go to this debate tournament--whether you like it or not--and you're going to do well_," he laughed. "And I did," the exemplary student intoned. "I say that, as a means of expressing just how I have been very blessed, indeed," the city planner turned city councilman concluded. "My parents prayed for me. Others prayed for me. And I continue to pray for myself," the lifelong Catholic conceded.

"Even though they had not gone to college, my parents expected me to not only **go**, but to **graduate**," Bullock noted, describing a lengthy academic journey that would ultimately lead to his moving to the "head of the class" as an Associate Professor of Political Science; having earned a master's degree in Urban Planning and a doctorate in Government and Politics. "I was fortunate to receive a scholarship to go to college," he went on, "which was great for me. Growing up in West Philadelphia in the 1980's and 1990's, during the height of the crack epidemic, I always wondered why my neighborhood looked the way it did," Bullock queried. "I soon began to realize that the reason my community was the way that it was because people that looked like me were not at the table," the politician pronounced. "In fact, I often say, *"If you are not at the table, then you are on the menu, "* he joked, with a seriousness that hung in the air with the weight of those words. "So, I went to school to study Political Science and that was great for me, and then I soon realized that I wanted to do my part to improve cities. As such, I began working in government in Washington, D.C. for a while," he noted, in explaining his road to the pinnacles of leadership in one of America's most historic cities. "As a neighborhood planner, I learned early on that there are some neighborhoods with fewer resources, which don't have access to the same set of resources as wealthier neighborhoods," he pointed out. "I soon began to realize that this was all about _politics_, and so I went *back to school* to study politics--again--and ended up getting my doctorate degree at the *University of Maryland College Park*," noted the married father of two young boys who will almost certainly blaze impressive paths of their own. But the challenges John's children will face--sooner rather than later--may seem all but insurmountable; particularly if either one of them seek to follow in their father's footsteps and pursue a life of public service.

Throughout the history of the United States, the goal of full participation for African-Americans in the political process has oftentimes been an elusive and moving target. Just as much, it is one that has been fraught with peril, trickery and subterfuge for those Black men desirous of exercising their franchise, both freely and fairly, in what has been trumpeted around the globe as a "democratic society." But the path to both equitable treatment at the ballot box (that is, if they actually made it to the ballot box), and within the halls of government, is one that often finds Black men facing an uphill struggle. In fact, even when they overcome the intentional obstacles placed before them and show up "en masse", to make their opinions heard, Black voices are often muted and stifled by the "powers that be," who sometimes operate from the perspective that "African-American voters should be seen and not heard." Moreover, as Black leaders, community activists, and elected officials continue to work to dismantle the vestiges of racism throughout the country's various levers of government, they do so against the backdrop of smoky, backroom deals that, more often than not, result in policy and praxis that both maintain and strengthen the foundations of white supremacy.

Immediately commencing with the defeat of the South in America's great *Civil War,* and the requirement that formerly enslaved Black males be entitled to the right to vote, with the ratification of the *Fifteenth Amendment,* efforts to curtail Black political empowerment became a cottage industry in many ways; as unscrupulous elections chiefs and violent mobs saw to it that few, if any, Black men could actually get their vote cast and counted without fear of serious retribution. At the same time, white supremacy groups soon sprang up across the country and began to target helpless African-Americans, particularly men, in a reign of terror that resulted in the deaths of countless people of color. Moreover, during the much despised "Period of Reconstruction", which saw for the first time, the election of Black men to the *Congress* of the United States from places like Florida, Georgia, Alabama, Mississippi and South Carolina, gentrified white men with financial interests and calcified conclusions concerning racial superiority---men who were otherwise upstanding individuals and pillars of their communities, chose to cast their lot with vehement racists. In doing so, they joined and, oftentimes, led these treasonous organizations. Furthermore, as a result of their growing racial resentment, the first such group sprang up in 1865, with the founding of the *Ku Klux Klan* by Confederate Colonel Nathan Bedford Forrest of Tennessee; followed two short years later by the establishment of the *Knights of the White Camellia* (11876), the *White League* (1874), and the *Red Shirts* (1875). In fact, each of these groups, while different in both their approach to public relations (as some of them held secret memberships and others were "loud and proud" about who they were and what they believed), were committed in their efforts to eradicate Black political empowerment wherever it was asserted; utilizing mob tactics, arson, kidnapping, murder, torture and physical intimidation to thwart Black men from exercising their franchise. By. Any. Means. Necessary.

According to *The Leadership Conference Education Fund,* founded in 1969 as the education and research arm of *The Leadership Conference on Civil and Human Rights,* the nation's oldest and largest civil and human rights coalition of more than 200 national organizations, in a report called, "Why We Must Confront America's History of Racial Terrorism," more than 4,600 Black men, women and children paid the ultimate price, as they sought to live their lives with dignity and respect and, in doing so, were often publicly executed. "Lynchings were not uncommon, isolated events solely carried out by extremists and vigilantes," the *Fund* observed. "Rather," the report detailed, "terror lynching was widespread, many times committed in front of officials and the entire community in broad daylight," it surmised. Going on to define "racial terrorism" as "a phenomenon used to enforce racial subordination and segregation, and one that was widely supported or tolerated by government officials and the community," the *Fund* also observed that these same upstanding community leaders were oftentimes complicit in serving as judge, jury and executioner--sometimes on the courthouse stairs ("Racial Terrorism"). And that was just phase one of the onslaughts!

_If_ Black Males were able to escape the terror that ran rampant at night, and the not so subtle indignities that were imposed upon them by day (with the operative word being _IF_), and somehow successfully made their way into the local Supervisor of Elections office to register to vote, they were then subjected to a series of institutional roadblocks aimed at thwarting their efforts to have their voices heard in how they would be governed. For example, rampant throughout the South were policies known as "grandfather clauses" which stated that an individual's eligibility to vote depended upon whether or not their grandfather was a previously registered voter who had, in fact, successfully cast a vote. The original grandfather clauses were codified into the new state constitutions during the latter part of the nineteenth century and well into the first decades of the twentieth century. Today, however, long after such onerous requirements as literacy tests in which Black men (before the suffragette movement), and all Black voters thereafter (until the passage of the *Voting Rights Act of 1965*), were required to answer impossible questions-- designed specifically for them to fail--without getting any answers wrong, the subterfuge continued. Moreover, in the dawn of a "New Jim Crow" era in which oppression is not so blatant and "in your face" offensive, elections officials have gotten all the more creative; bolstered by the support of state legislatures across the country ever so worried about Black political expansion.

In a comprehensive survey of "Voter Suppression and Other Election Day Problems", published by the *Center for American Progress*, chronicling the intransigent problem of minority voter suppression in the United States, as evidenced in the 2018 midterm elections, Danielle Root, a director of Voting Rights and Access to Justice for the *Center*, highlighted the fact that--at the end of the day--its always Black voters who suffer most. "Widespread voter suppression—particularly against historically marginalized groups—is a reoccurring problem in the United States," Root wrote; underscoring a history of abuses of Black civil liberties in the purported 'land of the free'. "Each election cycle, untold numbers of eligible Americans are prevented from voting due to barriers in the voter registration process, restrictions on casting ballots, and discriminatory and partisan-rigged district maps," Root continued. "Voter suppression measures can differ by state and even by individual county. And while some voter suppression measures actively seek to discriminate against certain groups, others result from innocent administrative errors and glitches. Regardless of its form or intent, however, voter suppression is relentlessly effective in preventing voting-eligible Americans from contributing to the electoral process" (Root). In parsing the results of the survey's findings, the article went on to observe that, nearly two decades into the twenty-first century, voter suppression continues to remain--particularly for minorities--as American as apple pie.

Below are but some of the findings the *Center for American Progress* uncovered, demonstrating, once again, the lengths to which desperate elections officials will go halt the hands of progress, to include the following tactics:

1. *Voter Registration Problems* - *In Georgia, 53,000 voter registrants—70 percent of whom were Black—were placed in "pending" status by the secretary of state because of minor misspellings or missing hyphens on their registration forms. A federal judge intervened to stop this practice on November 2, 2018—four days before the election—citing the "differential treatment inflicted on a group of individuals who are predominantly minorities" (Root).*

2. *Voter Purges* - *A 2018 report by the Brennan Center for Justice found that between 2014 and 2016, states removed almost 16 million voters from the rolls. Notably, voter purges were particularly prevalent in states with histories of discriminatory voting practices (Root).*

3. *Strict voter ID and ballot requirements* - *Ten states have strict voter ID laws that require eligible voters to present certain forms of government-issued ID before they can vote. A study by the Government Accountability Office found that voter ID laws can reduce participation in elections by between 2 percent and 3 percent (Root).*

4. **Voter confusion** - *On Election Day, voters in several states—including Massachusetts, Wisconsin, and New York—received text messages from various groups and organizations that included incorrect information about designated polling locations, which resulted in people going to the wrong polling places to vote only to be turned away (Root).*

5. **Voter intimidation and harassment** - *President Trump himself engaged in intimidating voters on Election Day, tweeting on the morning of November 5: "Law Enforcement has been strongly notified to watch closely for any ILLEGAL VOTING which may take place in Tuesday's Election (or Early Voting). Anyone caught will be subject to the Maximum Criminal Penalties allowed by law. Thank you" (Root).*

6. **Poll closures and long lines** - *Polling place closures disproportionately affect communities of color, low-income Americans, and young people. For example, since 2012, local officials in Georgia closed 214 polling locations across the state— a move that has disproportionately affected poor and minority voters and made it tougher for them to travel to other voting sites (Root).*

7. **Malfunctioning voting equipment** - *Problems with voting machines—including machines freezing, delayed testing, and malfunction—plagued several jurisdictions in Michigan... with would-be voters leaving polling places without having voted (Root).*

8. **Disenfranchisement of justice-involved individuals** - *Approximately 6 million American citizens are barred from participating in the democratic process as a result of felon disenfranchisement laws. People held in pretrial detention who had not yet been convicted of a crime were also disenfranchised in the November midterms (Root).*

9. **Gerrymandering** - *Politicians in many states have manipulated election districts to choose their voters—rather than having voters choose them. In fact, the Cook Political Report projected that fewer than 1 in 5 congressional districts nationwide were competitive [in 2018] (Root).*

Friends in High Places?

As a result of the challenges that African-American men have historically faced in simply getting to the ballot box, the chances of them electing individuals who will, first and foremost, represent their best interests are oftentimes precarious; as the number of Black Elected Officials is one that, historically, has lagged behind the nation's demographic trends. That is... until recently. According to a write-up by the *Pew Research Center* entitled, "Blacks Have Made Gains in U.S. Political Leadership, But Gaps Remain," the rise in the number of African-Americans elected to public office has increased at a snail's pace over the course of 150 years. In 1870, for example, five years after the passage of the *Thirteenth Amendment* to the *U.S. Constitution*, which simultaneously banned slavery based on race, while legalizing slavery based on criminal status, the *Fifteenth Amendment* provided the opportunity for Black men to exercise their franchise--with strings attached, of course. Moreover, the amendment, which prohibited states from refusing any male citizen the right to vote because of their "race, color or previous condition of servitude," also offered a small sliver of hope for newly freed men and women, by giving them the opportunities, where their numbers so dictated, to elect African-American men to various positions of political power.

The first Black U.S. senator, hailing from the great state of Mississippi, was the Honorable Hiram R. Revels, a Republican who was appointed by the state legislature to fill one year left on the term being vacated by Albert Brown in 1870; as a grand compromise to fall back in favor with the union after the capitulation of the South in the "war of the states." Since then, nine Black Americans have followed in Revels' footsteps; including Edward Brooke of Massachusetts, Barack Obama and Roland Burris of Illinois and Cory Booker of New Jersey. But progress in electing more African-Americans to office has oftentimes been glacial at the federal level as evidenced by the fraction of African-American Senators and United States Representatives to the Congress. "In 1965, there were no Blacks in the U.S. Senate, nor were there any Black governors," the *Pew* report detailed. "And only six members of the House of Representatives were Black. As of 2019, there is greater representation in some areas – 52 House members are Black, putting the share of Black House members (12%) on par with the share of Blacks in the U.S. population overall for the first time in history. But in other areas, there has been little change (there are three Black senators and no Black governors)," the report denoted. Today, the *Congressional Black Caucus*, founded in 1971 as the "conscience of the Congress", is oftentimes a lone but powerful voice, speaking up and speaking out on the issues that matter most to people of color in the country.

From a gubernatorial perspective, African-American political prospects have been even more diminished, as those Black leaders viable enough to be considered for the top spot in state government often fall short on Election Day; resulting in their unceremonious fading into oblivion. For starters, there are no Black governors currently in office today, and there have been only four in U.S. history. Pinckney Pinchback served as a governor of Louisiana for 35 days in the 1870s, following the impeachment of Henry Clay Warmoth for taking part in a fraudulent election of 1872. Additionally, the Commonwealths of Virginia and Massachusetts and the State of New York have each had Black governors, including L. Douglas Wilder, Deval Patrick and David Paterson, respectively. What's of even more consequence for the 1.2 million underrepresented Black people who reside in communities in which they are the majority, yet choose not to run for, or fail to get elected to, public office, is the fact that their authentic voices are not being heard in a way that ensures equitable political representation. As a result, the interests of these same underrepresented minorities are typically left up to the control of individuals who do not share the same cultural experiences, and may not share the same concerns.

In her analysis on the dearth of African-American elected leaders at the local level, Karen Shanton of *Demos*, a liberal think tank organization which champions solutions that will create a democracy and economy rooted in racial equity, called attention to the significant and material gap exists between the numbers of Blacks within a certain geopolitical district and the number of those who actually get elected to office. "Almost a quarter of the municipalities with under representative councils—home to close to half the total underrepresented African-American population—have populations that are majority African America," Shanton reported. "For residents of some of these communities, including the residents of Ferguson [Missouri], the gap between their share of the population and their political representation is especially stark," Shanton continued. "Approximately 77,000 African Americans live in communities in which they make up more than half the population but hold only one or fewer seats on the local council." So, why is it important, if at all, that Black Americans have what demographers have termed "descriptive representation" (i.e. African-American politicians elected to represent the needs, interests and concerns of their constituents which are, more often than not, African-American residents)? Some have theorized that the utility of having someone in office who "looks like you" has the effect of creating civic greater engagement on the part of the populace being in served. "Descriptive representation can be especially valuable in cities like Ferguson," Shanton found, "where there's limited trust between residents and their representatives, but it also seems to promote engagement more broadly. Studies show that African-Americans tend to be more engaged with the political process when they are descriptively represented. They pay closer attention to elections and vote at higher rates when they are represented by an African-American official and are more likely to run for offices that are or have been held by an African-American" (Shanton).

Just as importantly, according to the *Demos* report, studies have indicated that Black officials tend to be more engaged with the Black communities they represent, than do their colleagues who do not happen to be of African-American descent. "Research suggests that African-American legislators are more responsive to African-American constituents than white lawmakers," the report detailed. "They also advocate more forcefully for African-American interests during the legislative process, proposing legislation and making speeches that promote African-American interests at significantly higher rates than non-African American officials. But the challenge of getting past primary elections in which African-Americans don't comprise a sizeable majority (or at least a plurality) of votes to get them across the finish line in first place, remains a consist obstacle to greater Black political representation. There are, however, bright spots within the American political landscape, as savvy and adept politicians in large cities across the country, particularly those that do not have a majority-minority population, have sought to create "gumbo coalitions" of individuals, organizations, political action committees, community groups and skilled campaign operatives; all working together to give deserving and capable Black politicians a chance to lead major municipalities.

As the quintessential example of being able to break past the barriers of entry to the top slot in city government, we need look no further than the Honorable Sylvester Turner, the 62nd Mayor the "Capitol of the Sunbelt" and America's fourth largest city--Houston, Texas. A longtime elected official representing Texas' 139th House District, Turner had previously attempted to ascend to the mayoralty on two previous occasions, in 1991 and 2003, but his efforts fell short both times; losing in a run-off election during his first attempt and placing third the second time he attempted to assume the mantle of leadership for the city. It wasn't, however, until 2015, in a contentious race against businessman Bill King, that Turner was able to win the mayor's race to become only the second Black mayor of Houston; defeating King by 4,082 votes out of 212,696 cast in what would go down--at the time--as the closest race in Houston mayoral history. In doing so, Turner proved that, although difficult, getting elected to key political positions is, indeed, possible, when the candidate is qualified, viable, and willing to never give up on the dream of a better future for themselves and the municipalities they serve.

With an African-American population at the time of approximately 22.5%, Turner would shock the political establishment with his election as mayor, by building upon the strength of his solid reputation for thoughtful leadership and effective advocacy, demonstrating that, for Turner, three times was " the charm" for the able attorney and state legislator turned "Hizzoner". And yet, it is only when individuals like Turner take the keys to city hall that they realize the gargantuan task before them of not only leading the places they live, learn and love, while simultaneously uplifting the communities from which they hail, while walking a calamitous tightrope of "preference to no one and allegiance to all." Be that as it may, Black Elected Officials like the Honorable John T. Bullock, representing one of the most economically distressed districts in the great City of Baltimore, Maryland, understand that the intractable issues which persistently plague Black constituents are ones that will only be solved with a determined focus and collaborative effort on the part of leaders who care.

"I was a first-generation college student, and my mother always had these great dreams for me and would encourage me to use my imagination," Bullock recalled, when discussing his reasons for giving up the creature comforts of home with his wife and young children, for the glare of the political spotlight and the burdens of leadership. "It just so happened that my mom passed away one week before my college graduation, which was devastating and bewildering at that time in my life. What her passing helped me to realize, however, was the fact that I was now a grown man and responsible for my own future," Bullock declared. "In many ways, her passing encouraged me to strike out on my own, while teaching me the importance of never squandering the time that we do have on this earth," the political prognosticator intoned. "So, serving in political office is a way for me to do just that," he opined.

"When I was about six years old, the doctors gave my mother six months to live, and she survived to see me through college. Knowing this reminds me of the fact that we are all on borrowed time and that every day is a blessing," Bullock concluded. "Her eventual passing helped me to reconnect with who I am as a person, first and most importantly," the committed Christian proclaimed. "As a member of the *Catholic* faith, my mother's transition also helped me to reconnect with the church, particularly here in Baltimore, which has a strong *Catholic* presence, while also reminding me of the importance of furthering my education and serving my community," the urban planner turned urban politician reminisced. "As an African-American male," he continued, "I am not unmindful of the fact that even in the City of Baltimore, there is seeming invisibility when it comes to people of color. They are there, but people aren't necessarily thinking about them," Bullock theorized.

"As a community servant and an elected official, I know that it is my job to do just that--to think about the needs of those whom others refuse to see," he went on. "The other part that inspires me about being a Black Elected Official is the fact that I can do something to help stabilize what have become destabilized communities, due to the absence of men," Bullock concluded. "What people don't realize is that many of these neighborhoods are filled with working, trustworthy professionals that include doctors and lawyers and dentists and people just like me who are committed to being a part of the fabric of the community, which helps in the stabilization process. In fact," the promising politico professed, "my neighbors tend to get excited by the very idea that 'Dr. Bullock on City Council' lives in *their* neighborhood and is a part of *their* community. For them (and for me), that means something," he said.

"As a Professor of Political Science, I remember, during my first week of teaching, someone sent a letter to the department chair, who then sent the letter to me, saying: *"Dr. Bullock ought to be teaching African-American history instead of Political Science,"* he said, understanding full well the implications of the letter which were, in essence: *"you've got the wrong person for the position,"* he denoted. "But the course I was teaching was about *American Government*, and I wanted both my students and the administrators to understand that you can't effectively teach *American Government* and urban politics without first understanding _race_, which is an essential component to virtually everything in this country. And I could not teach a class without addressing that fundamental issue. To be honest with you, most of my students had never heard of the various contributions of African-Americans to the establishment of this country," the professor confessed.

"Historically, Black history is relegated to one chapter in a book, in which _'Abraham Lincoln freed the slaves and Martin Luther King Jr. had a dream'_. For me, however, as an educator as well, I make the entire history of the country central to the learning environment of my classroom, and that made for an uncomfortable position for some students. In fact," Bullock admitted, "I have even had some students say to me, _'I don't know if I want to take your class because I don't want to feel guilty,'_" he quoted them as saying. "There are other students who were willing to be open to learning new information, and understanding that they are better for having expanded their horizons. And then, there are still students who are resistant to the idea of learning anything other than something relevant to their own experiences," Bullock confirmed. "Whether we are talking _American Government_, urban politics, or whatever, it is an extremely rare instance when race _doesn't_ play a factor in the equation." So, Bullock continues to insist upon transparency and accountability as the hallmarks of effective leadership and, as such, does not shy away from the responsibility.

"We are at a very interesting juncture in America," the government and politics pedagogue noted, as he took stock of the gains that have come with Black political empowerment and assessed the long road ahead. "We have had, on one hand, the election of Barack Obama as President of the United States, and there was this feeling of "hope and change" and the idea that anything was possible," Bullock stated. "But his election also unleashed an entire barrage of negative repercussions that were already there," he explained. "It's not as if racism just began, but Obama's election, in my opinion, touched a nerve in this country and sparked a desire for some in America to _'take their country back,'_ at least from a political perspective", Dr. Bullock believed. "Lest we forget what happened right here in Baltimore [with the police-involved homicide death of Freddy Gray on April 9, 2015]... And in Ferguson [with the police-involved homicide death of Michael Brown on August 9, 2014] ... And in Milwaukee [with the police-involved homicide death of Philando Castile on July 6, 2016]... And in Baton Rouge [with the police-involved homicide death of Alton Sterling] on July 5, 2016]... And in other parts of the country where unarmed Black men have met an untimely fate after tragic law enforcement encounters. Moreover," Bullock elaborated, "we cannot ignore the fact that the more things change, the more they remain the same."

In fact, in the acclaimed academician's estimation, very little has changed with regard to how Black men in America are treated, particularly by the various institutions of government ostensibly put in place to protect them," the amiable advocate declared. "Clearly nothing is different, except for the fact that we live in the age of smartphones, which enable eyewitnesses to capture video and to share it with others around the world," Dr. Bullock explained. "But the scariest part of the whole thing, is that you can have the demise of defenseless Black men at the hands of the police--on video no less--and, in many cases, it won't even matter." This phenomenon, however, isn't new, as Black leaders throughout history have been targeted--sometimes in broad daylight--and little, if anything, is ever done to prevent it from reoccurring.

BULLSEYE!

A HISTORY OF TARGETED VIOLENCE & MYSTERIOUS DEATHS OF AFRICAN-AMERICAN LEADERS

MEDGAR EVERS: ASSASSINATED JUNE 12, 1963

Evers, the Mississippi Field Secretary for the NAACP, was murdered by gunman Byron De La Beckwith, who shot him in the back with a rifle. Evers passed away in front of his wife, Myrlie Evers, and their two small children.

MALCOLM X: ASSASSINATED FEBRUARY 21, 1965

One week after his home was firebombed, the former Nation of Islam minister, was gunned down by militant Black radicals as he prepared to deliver an address at the Audubon Ballroom in New York City.

MARTIN LUTHER KING, JR.: ASSASSINATED, APRIL 4, 1968

King's home was firebombed, he was physically assaulted, and stabbed before ultimately being gunned down as he stood on the balcony of the Lorraine Motel in Memphis, Tennessee.

FRED HAMPTON: ASSASSINATED DECEMBER 4, 1969

The Deputy Chairman of the national Black Panther Party, Hampton was shot to death by Chicago Police Department Officers as he slept in his bed, in what the police later determined was a "justifiable homicide."

WHITNEY M. YOUNG, JR.: DROWNED MARCH 11, 1971

An avid swimmer, Young was at Lighthouse Beach in Lagos, Nigeria when he "seemed to be in some difficulty," before being swept away. An initial autopsy determined his death was due to a subarachnoid hemorrhage, which is caused by a head injury.

VERNON E. JORDAN, JR.: ATTEMPTED ASSASSINATION & WOUNDING MAY 29, 1980

Jordan, the Executive Director of the Urban League, was shot in the back while on a trip to Fort Wayne, Indiana. Confessed assassin, Joseph Paul Franklin, was later acquitted in 1982.

FOR MORE INFORMATION, VISIT WWW.BIOGRAPHY.COM.

Did We Overcome?

In 1941, at the height of *World War II*, African-Americans were barred from participating in the federal largesse created to support the war effort. As a result, Black men--and women alike--were not allowed to seek government employment and contractor opportunities simply because of the color of their skin. For otherwise qualified individuals who were forced to work menial jobs for low wages, this represented an untenable situation that required either political mediation or direct action to solve a systemic economic problem (for Blacks) created out of racist social policy. In response to the call for change, Asa Philip Randolph, a civil rights and labor leader of the newly unionized *Brotherhood of Sleeping Car Porters,* asked President Franklin Delano Roosevelt to intervene. The president, understanding that, what Randolph was requesting was politically unpalatable, demurred to the idea of upsetting the social order of things; reportedly telling the union leader: *"Phil, if you want me to act on providing civil rights protections in government hiring and contracting for Blacks, then 'go out there and make me do it.'"* Calling his bluff, Randolph threatened to summons 100,000 African-American railroad workers to Washington, D.C. before Roosevelt, feeling the political pressure to come up with a reasonable compromise, issued *Executive Order 8802,* which lifted the ban on Blacks working for the federal government.

In achieving the goal of knocking down yet another barrier to equitable treatment by the government with regard to its citizens of color, Randolph demonstrated both the power and efficacy of one of Black America's most potent political forces—traditional civil rights and social justice organizations. United in a common objective of facilitating social mobility, political progress, and economic access, for Blacks desirous of entering the mainstream of American life, these groups helped to formulate the core of Black political resistance in this country in a way that African-American elected officials could not. In fact, since their inception, civil rights organizations and their leaders have played a pivotal role in forcing American presidents into the pantheon of greatness. Today, organizations such as the *National Association for the Advancement of Colored People* (est. 1909), the *National Urban League* (est. 1910), the *Leadership Conference for Civil and Human Rights* (est. 1950), the *Rainbow/PUSH Coalition* (est. 1971), and the *National Action Network* (est. 1991), among the many other laudatory groups, continue to fight the good fight of faith for some of the most vulnerable American populations.

Known throughout America for its vociferous advocacy of issues that negatively impact the civil rights and liberties of people of color, the *National Association for the Advancement of Colored People*, or *NAACP* as it is commonly known, has proudly assumed the mantle of "outside agitator" in the fight for full equality for more than 110 years. Founded near the close of the first decade of the twentieth century, the *NAACP* sprang up as a result of a deadly race riot that broke out in Springfield, Illinois; inspiring white liberals, led by Mary White Ovington and Oswald Garrison Villard (the progenitors of well-known abolitionists) and Black activists, led by Dr. W. E. B. Du Bois and Ida B. Wells-Barnett, to join forces to effectively address the issue of anti-Black violence in the United States. An organization whose history is so integrally intertwined in the story of America that it is archived by the *U.S. Library of Congress*, in a catalogue called, "NAACP: A Century in the Fight for Freedom," this venerable social justice institution is, perhaps, the most efficacious of all American nonpartisan groups. In fact, having utilized the very same levers of government designed to impede them in their quest for an equitable society, to help them effectively dismantle a suite of Jim Crow era policies that subjugated Blacks to permanent second class citizenship, the *NAACP* has been both lauded and loathed by both Black and White alike, for more than a century of service.

"The *NAACP's* long battle against *de jure* segregation culminated in the Supreme Court's landmark *Brown v. Board of Education* decision, which overturned the "separate but equal" doctrine," the Library of Congress noted in chronicling one hundred years of leadership and service. "In response to the *Brown* decision, Southern states launched a variety of tactics to evade school desegregation, while the *NAACP* countered aggressively in the courts for enforcement. In addition to helping to lead the 1963 March on Washington, the *NAACP*-led *Leadership Conference on Civil Rights*, a coalition of civil rights organizations, spearheaded the drive to win passage of the major civil rights legislation of the era: the *Civil Rights Act of 1957*; the *Civil Rights Act of 1964*; the *Voting Rights Act of 1965*; and the *Fair Housing Act of 1968*," ("A

Century in the Fight"). Today, under the thoughtful stewardship of able men and women, led by its Executive Director, Board of Directors and a membership of 500,000 foot soldiers in the army of justice, the NAACP is poised to parachute into the political landscape at any moment, if and when duty calls.

The *National Urban League*, established just a year after the *NAACP* was birthed, is an economic self-sufficiency and social advocacy organization that has worked to "empower communities and change lives" for African-Americans and other individuals of color since 1910. The *League*, in response to a flood of Black migrants fleeing the South to northern urban centers such as Chicago, Detroit and New York City, was established for the express purpose of addressing the "conditions amongst urban Negroes." Today, with ninety professionally staffed affiliates and 11,000 volunteers, serving 1.7 million people annually in 300 communities across the country, the *Urban League* plays a critical role in drafting policy, promoting best practices and providing direct services for those seeking to uplift themselves and their families through job training, educational equity, political participation and more. In fact, during the tumultuous and oftentimes dangerous civil rights movement, it was the *National Urban League* that provided the infrastructural resources the movement needed to strategize, and plan out the tactics they would use and programs they would implement to move the agenda forward while supporting those putting their lives and safety on the line for the cause of freedom, justice and dignity of the individual. But in doing so, their leaders have frequently been targets of racial violence and even assassination attempts, as they sought to usher in a new era of freedom and justice to be realized by all Americans.

In 1968, a plot was uncovered to murder two of the nation's top civil rights leaders, stoking fear and anxiety throughout the burgeoning movement. According to both news reports and court records, the *Federal Bureau of Investigation's* Counter-Intelligence Program (COINTELPRO) was implicated in the scheme to radicalize two extremists willing to disrupt the movement's forward progress by decapitating its leadership. Moreover, with the goal of halting its continued advancement towards full equality in America, J. Edgar Hoover's *F.B.I.* branded African-American civil rights leaders as "Public Enemy #1" to the law enforcement community. In doing so, the nation's top cop unleashed all manner of government-sanctioned evil against the men tapped by the Black community to lead them to a better life in the land of peace and prosperity; with the goal of distracting, embarrassing and, if necessary, eliminating them from the equation.

According to contemporaneous news report of the ill-fated plot, the civil rights leaders were placed in the crosshairs of political violence, for the crime of standing up for human dignity. "A *Queens County Supreme Court* Justice issued arrest warrants yesterday for two Black militants, Herman B. Ferguson and Arthur Harris, who had been convicted of conspiring to murder Roy Wilkins, executive director of the *National Association for the Advancement of Colored People*, and Whitney Young Jr., executive director of the *Urban League*," the New York Times reported. "Judge Peter T. Farrell noted that the *United States Supreme Court* had refused to hear an appeal in the case and revoked the $10,000 bail for each man. Originally convicted in June, 1968, Ferguson and Harris were freed by a certificate of reasonable doubt by State Supreme Court Justice M. Conroy on Oct. 17 of that year," the Times continued. Just three short years later Young, while swimming with friends during a trip to visit the African-American Institute in Lagos, Nigeria, Young drowned under rather mysterious circumstances on March 11, 1971. Known to be an exceptionally adept swimmer, the conditions under which Young met his untimely demise were as murky as the waters from which they pulled his body.

Immediately following the sudden death of this African-American icon, the *Urban League* moved swiftly to appoint an Executive Director that would continue the forward momentum that Young had established in combatting President Richard Nixon's "tough on crime" strategy that tended to target African-American groups and their leaders who, in the government's opinion, posed a threat to America's social order. In doing so, the organization's Board of Directors settled on Vernon Eulion Jordan, Jr., a nationally known figure who had previously served as the Georgia Director for the *NAACP;* tapping him to be the fifth Executive Director of the venerated institution. As Executive Director, Jordan was ever vigilant against all forms of racism and oppression that made life more difficult for Black people in America, calling on the titans of business and industry to be both fair and equitable in both policy and practice. In criticizing President Ronald Reagan's draconian federal budget cuts that severely impacted the poor and vulnerable, Jordan told the *New York Times*: "I do not challenge the conservatism of this administration. I do challenge its failure to exhibit a compassionate conservatism that adapts itself to the realities of a society ridden by class and race distinction" ("New

York Times"). Furthermore, the outspoken leader would go on to advance the agenda of civil rights in the area of economic access for America's most underserved populations; knocking down barriers of access in boardrooms all across Corporate America. In doing so, however, he racked up his fair share of detractors, one of whom attempted to take his life in the spring of 1980.

While participating in an event at the *Marriott Inn* in Fort Wayne, Indiana, Jordan was marked for death by a roving white supremacist hell-bent on exacting retribution for social gains being made by minorities in America. Joseph Paul Franklin, who would go on to be arrested, tried and eventually exonerated in the May 29th assassination attempt that would lead to the ominous distinction of being the first story to ever be covered by a fledgling new station, *Cable News Network,* better known today as *CNN.* Franklin would later go on to cop to the crime in 1996, while serving six life sentences for a slew of other convictions; successfully avoiding double jeopardy implications. In detailing his depravity for the *Associated Press (AP),* the confessed perpetrator spoke of how he stalked Jordan like an animal, using a ruse to ensnare the unsuspecting activist, before shooting him with an assault rifle. "Franklin said he had come to Fort Wayne from Chicago after failing to stalk and kill Jesse Jackson," *AP* reports connoted, in their shocking headline story, "I Shot Vernon Jordan, Franklin Says."

"In the northeast Indiana city, Franklin said he hoped to target 'race mixers'," the *Associated Press* detailed Joseph Paul Franklin as admitting to, understanding full-well that he could not be re-tried for the crime. "But after hearing a news broadcast that Jordan would be speaking at Fort Wayne's *Marriott Hotel,* Franklin decided to go after Jordan instead. Franklin said he learned Jordan was staying in a corner room at the hotel, waited for dark and parked his car beside a nearby highway. He raised the hood to look like he had car trouble, then waited in the grass with his hunting rifle, about 140 feet from his target" ("Vernon Jordan"). Later on, that night, Jordan, upon returning to his room at the hotel, was shot in the back as he exited a vehicle. "Franklin said he didn't know if it was Jordan, but he fired anyway, sending a 30.06 bullet into Jordan's back near his spine. The wound was so large, a surgeon later said he could put his fist into it ("Vernon Jordan"). The following year, Jordan retired as the leader of one of America's most historic civil rights groups, but the work he engaged in goes on unabated. Today, despite the always eminent threat to its leaders and its attempts at creating a "compassionate community" that is both equitable and just, the *National Urban League* continues to fulfill Jordan's mission of telling the story of African-Americans through the annual release of the "State of Black America Report."

First published under the leadership of Vernon Jordan in 1976, this treatise on Black life in the United States, analyzes the challenges and opportunities faced by African-Americans--from year to year. Measuring both gains and losses of Blacks in the aggregate, the "State of Black America Report" has five key areas of emphasis, including: education, economics, health, civic engagement and social justice. In the 2019 report entitled, "Getting 2 Equal: United Not Divided," the *League* lays out the premise for its continued existence, as it now works to fight the insidious forms of voter suppression that seek to divide minority voters, while sowing discord and confusion, particularly amongst the Black electorate. "It is impossible to untangle voting rights and the ability (or inability) to exercise political power from the history of race in America: a history that has advantaged some while perpetually disadvantaging others," the report highlighted. "Our nation's pursuit of liberty, justice and economic empowerment for *all* hinges largely on the right to determine who will govern us and how," the analysis explained. "Because the right to vote is the price of full admission to participate in our democracy, the *National Urban League* will remain on the frontlines of the battle to protect your fundamental right to vote," the organization forewarned; putting bad actors on notice that the fight for election protection and securing the ballot box will continue; so long as the enemies of the democratic process cease from menacing a determined Black electorate ("Getting 2 Equal").

Supporting the efforts of the civil rights community in advancing the agenda of progress for African-Americans, Black Greek Letter Organizations (BGLO's) also played an integral, if largely unheralded, role in the social and political progress of the country. From their financing of early lawsuits challenging discrimination in various aspects of American culture, such as their funding of litigation in the case of *Sweatt v. Painter* (a *U.S. Supreme Court* decision that successfully overturned the "separate but equal" doctrine of racial segregation established by the 1896 case of *Plessy v. Ferguson)*, to providing bail for jailed civil rights leaders like Martin Luther King, Jr. and many of his devotees, African-American fraternities and sororities have long stood in the gap when called upon to provide "boots on the ground" in the war for equal rights and social justice. Founded on the campus of *Cornell University* in Ithaca, New York in the winter of 1906, *Alpha Phi Alpha Fraternity, Incorporated* was the nation's first BGLO, leading to the eventual formation of eight others, including: *Alpha Kappa Alpha Sorority, Incorporated* (est. 1908); *Kappa Alpha Psi Fraternity, Incorporated* and *Omega Psi Phi Fraternity, Incorporated* (both est. in 1911); *Delta Sigma Theta Sorority, Incorporated* (est. 1913); *Phi Beta Sigma Fraternity, Incorporated* (est. 1914); *Zeta Phi Beta Sorority, Incorporated* (est. in 1920); *Sigma Gamma Rho Sorority, Incorporated* (est. in 1922); and *Iota Phi Theta Fraternity, Incorporated* (est. in 1963).

Together, these organizations which comprise the *National Pan-Hellenic Council,* affectionately known as "The Divine Nine," are politically influential organizations, with combined membership rosters topping more than a million initiates. In close elections, these powerful (and plentiful) groups represent a potent political force that, when called upon, help to turnout the African-American vote time and again in key races across the country. In fact, without their guiding influence, financial support and political prowess, many of the gains of the American civil rights movement may have been delayed, if they happened at all, were it not for the considerable efforts of these dedicated men and women who continue to move on equality in the country. As a member of *Alpha Phi Alpha* and a student of the civil rights movement, Councilman John T. Bullock understands the challenges that Black male leaders continue to face in pressing the agenda forward, as they strive to lead their communities in the face of both existing and emerging challenges.

"When it comes to the gains our country has made with regard to the Civil Rights Movement, I believe that we continue to take a few steps forward... followed by few steps backwards," Bullock bemoaned, detailing his assessment of American progress. "The *March on Washington,* for example, wasn't just a march. It was a march for *jobs and freedom*! So, there was an economic point to the movement," the professor maintained. "In many cases, we have political power that is not undergirded with economic power. It harkens back," Dr. Bullock elaborated, "to the age-old debate between W.E.B. DuBois and Booker T. Washington, and which of their philosophies of *'Education versus Work',* is relevant today," he theorized. "And the truth of the matter is that they **both** are! You have to be able to cast your bucket down and learn how to fish, but you also need to know how to speak *The King's English,"* the political pundit turned professional politician professed.

"When it comes to my young sons, for example, I think about the music that they listen to today, as compared to what I listened to growing up. In my generation, we listened to singers like Marvin Gaye who asked the all-important question, *'What's going on?'*, with the understanding that there was always a *'message in the music'*", Bullock recalled. "I believe, in many respects, that the music was also an extension of the movement itself," he said. "To that end, I think that there needs to be a consciousness about how we are doing what we are doing, when it comes to the battles that lie ahead; especially for the younger people who are now leading the movement," the educator hypothesized. "It's also incumbent upon my generation to create a pipeline of leadership because what has hampered the movement, in many respects, is the fact that the leaders in charge did not necessarily cultivate those who would rise up and take their place," Bullock explained. "I believe that, as elected officials, it is our responsibility to work ourselves out of a job and bring those other generations coming up behind us, to the table." Yet and still, however, being recognized as a part of the conversation is another set of challenges that Black leaders will face, even after they have "arrived".

"I first read the book, *"Invisible Man"* by Ralph Ellison, as a student in high school, and it quickly became one of my favorites. Interestingly enough," Bullock went on, "I didn't read it for class, as my school was in the suburbs and that wasn't happening. But my father, who only had a high school education, owned an extensive book collection that contained this great work. African-American leaders, both then and now, are oftentimes, still invisible," he noted. "Dr. Martin Luther King Jr once said, 'a riot is the language of the unheard.' So, when we talked about the underlying causes of inequities in housing, employment, and education, it doesn't take long for us to figure out that 'invisibility' is really just a symptom of all of these problems," Bullock believes. "But there is also a level of invisibility that I deal with all the time, which is the fact that, in America, we don't expect people who look like me to be a professor or an elected official," he remarked. "In fact, my wife and I have coined the surprise to which people take when they learn of who I am, and what I do as the *"Double O"*, he laughed, before explaining the inside joke. "When I answer their question and respond with the fact that I am a university professor, community organizer and elected official, it is usually followed by Oh?... Oooooooooohhhh! This often happens to me when, after having talked to someone on the phone, I meet them for the first time and introduce myself as Dr. John Bullock, or when I meet my students for the first time and they respond with amazement and curiosity that I am who I say I am," the amiable academician acknowledged.

Today, as the elected representative of the residents of the 9th Council District for the "City that Leads," Bullock is ever mindful of the challenges that he faces in helping to bridge the gap between the community and the various institutions of government that are put in place to serve the public. "Even though the relationship between Black men and the police, for example, continues to be strained, I do believe that there are solutions that can be implemented to help make things better," he declared. "When it comes to the police, it begins by being a part of the fabric of the community," the former urban planner proclaimed. "Black neighborhoods can't be a place where law enforcement officers just police...and go home," he surmised. "It's also important to make sure that our police are properly trained, particularly when it comes to deescalating situations. Everything does not require a gun," Bullock concluded, "and I would say that to young people, as well as police officers. Sometimes it's okay," Bullock said, "to take your lumps and walk away," he reckoned.

"We must also be aware of the cultural context of the communities that are policed, and some of that will only come through the conversations that we have with one another. When people are on an eye-to-eye level with one another, they are more likely to get better information, and build trust," the astute politico noted. "This is what it actually means to do community policing. But it still cuts both ways," he furthered. "When it comes to the African-American community, we have to be mindful of the idea that "when _you_ see something...you say something". Just as importantly, the same rules apply to the police. When _you_ see something you should say something," Bullock implored of all parties involved. "The problem we have is that, sometimes, good police officers cover for bad police officers, when they ought to be turning those people out and rejecting that attitude... but the same thing must be done in Black communities as well. As such, we _all_ have a responsibility to be honest with one another, and that starts with having truthful conversations," Dr. Bullock declared.

As an important part of those conversations, Dr. John T. Bullock also believes that Black males of all ages, perspectives and walks of life, have an opportunity to rise above the circumstances set before them, to achieve their version of the American dream. "If I had the opportunity to give advice to a Black boy, I would encourage them to "embrace your difference," he said. "We all have something that makes us different, but whatever it is that makes _you_ different, understand that it's okay, and wholly embrace who _you_ are. If not, you will spend your entire life running from here to there, trying to figure yourself out. To the young Black adolescent, I would tell him to pursue what you are interested in, and what truly makes you happy. Life ain't a dress rehearsal, so take advantage of the time you have while you are young. Finally, to the Black man, I would remind him to 'tap into your ambition' and to never stop dreaming," Bullock opined. "If you're not moving towards something then you're really not moving anywhere at all."

(John T. Bullock: University Professor & Elected Official)

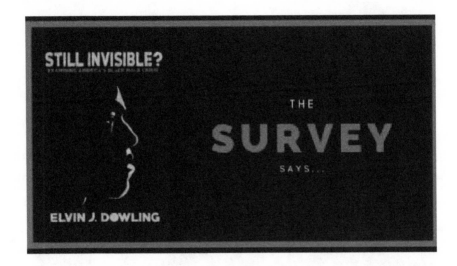

In your opinion, what word(s) would you use to describe Black political leaders are in America? Please include specific names if any come to mind.*

In general, the views of the survey's respondents concerning perceived African-American leaders, whether they were elected or non-elected officials, represented a "mixed bag" of opinions and perspectives--both positive and negative. To that end, the following information provided below consists of highlights of their comments, and a sampling of actual quotes made by some of the survey respondents, including:

- *Most Commonly Mentioned Word(s):* "Effective" (used 126 times) and "Talkers" (used 55 times)

- *Most Commonly Mentioned <u>Positive</u> Attribute Used to Describe Black Leaders:* "Good" (used 33 times)

- *Most Commonly Mentioned <u>Negative</u> Attribute Used to Describe Black Leaders:* "Racist" (used 15 times)

- *Most Commonly Mentioned Name:* Barack Obama (used 54 times)

- *Most Commonly Mentioned Elected/Public Official(s):* Ben Carson (used 12 times), Elijah Cummings (used 9 times), Cory Booker and Kamala Harris (used 8 times each), and Maxine Waters (used 4 times)

- *Most Commonly Mentioned Non-Elected Official(s):* Al Sharpton (used 9 times), Jesse Jackson (used 5 times) and Louis Farrakhan (used 3 times)

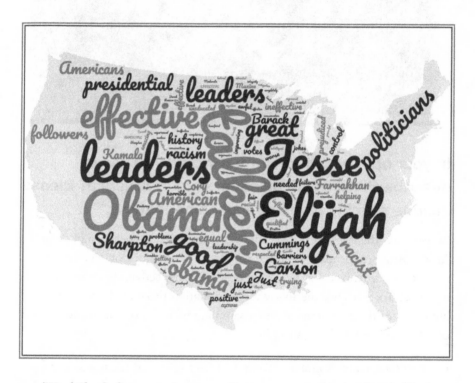

(Word Cloud of names and terms used by survey respondents to describe Black political leaders in America)

Quotes from 18 - 24-Year-Old Respondents

"

Personally, someone's race has absolutely nothing to do with their effectiveness in office. Sadly, I think prejudice exists against Black people, so there are some who would look down upon Black political leaders, but those uneducated, negative opinions shouldn't indicate the political leader's effectiveness. Representation is important, and so there should be Black political leaders in place to challenge those who think otherwise." - White Male

"

Black political leaders are not too effective. They are in those positions for show!" - Black Male

"

We need more in office!" - Hispanic Female

Quotes from 25 - 34-Year-Old Respondents

"

Barack Obama is one of the greatest examples of political leadership in America. Based on his race, he has proven that not all of the Black race are uneducated and related to criminal activity. He also proved that he could be a great leader for our country and he worked to support equality for every race and gender in America." - Asian Female

"

I think they are helping to erase the racial issues we have in this country by showing where you can go, and what you can do, if you push through racial barriers and never give up on your dreams!" - White Female

"

I think Barack Obama was very effective with his policies, but by him being a person of color, I think that hindered him from accomplishing all he wanted to do. I think being a Black politician strengthens the Black communities, but it is hard for them to get things done. For example, we have had only one Black president ever! How are Black politicians supposed to get anything done if they can't get past being a local politician?"   - Other Male

Quotes from 35 - 44-Year-Old Respondents

"

Black political leaders, in my opinion, are not very effective. I think they've succumbed to peer pressure and have often folded when they needed to stand their ground!" - Black Female

"

Unfortunately, I think the Black political leaders who try to do the most for the Black community are ones like Dr. Ben Carson (U.S. Secretary of Housing and Urban Development) and (Former Republican Congressman) Allen West, but they are conservatives, so the media doesn't focus on them. Instead, they focus on people like Al Sharpton, who don't try to help their community at all." - White Male

"

Rev. Al Sharpton is proof that any male, regardless of skin color, can achieve anything they set their mind to!" - Hispanic Male

Quotes from 45 - 54-Year-Old Respondents

"

Barack Obama and Jesse Jackson are horrible!" - Multiracial Male

"

I think Black political leaders in America are just as effective as Whites, if not more effective. I think the only reason that we continue to talk about race is because there is still extreme prejudice against minorities." - Hispanic Female

"

They are as capable and effective as anyone, if they want to be." - White Male

Quotes from 55+ Year Old Respondents

"

White ain't always right!" - Black Female

"

Obama was one of the worst presidents the U.S. has ever had, but not because of his skin color. He was terrible because of his socialistic ideologies. He also made race relations worse by continually baiting society. Obama himself was racist and he hated this country. It shows up in what he said and did. Read his books!" - White Male

"

Black leaders are not very effective because most of them play the race and victim cards. Some of them, like Cory Booker, are actually destructive!" - Hispanic Female

All survey results displayed above are represented by the overall percentage of survey respondents. For more information on our survey methodology, please see the Author's Note, located in the front matter of the book. To review raw survey results, visit: http://bit.ly/stillinvisiblesurvey.

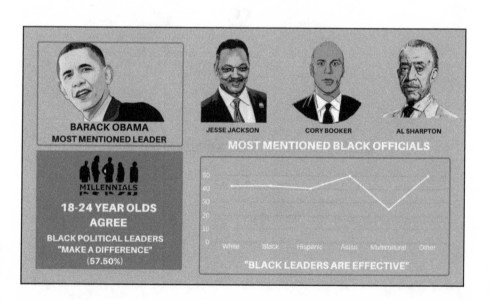

Findings by Race

- More than 1 out of 4 of all White Respondents (26.00%) made comments that can be construed as "negative" as it relates to Black political leaders.

- 1 out of 3 Black respondents (34.57%) rated Black leaders as "Effective" or "Somewhat Effective" and 2 out of 10 respondents (21.14%) saw them as "not very effective."

- Nearly half of all Asian respondents (45.00%) viewed Black leaders as highly effective, with 1 out of 3 of those respondents (15.00%) mentioning President Barack Obama.

Findings by Gender

- 3 out of 10 Hispanic female respondents (31.56%) believe that Black political leaders are "Not Effective" in their roles, with nearly 4 out of 10 (36.82%) rating them as "Effective".

- Asian female respondents were evenly split in their views of Black leaders, with one-third (33.33%) viewing them as either "Effective", "Not Effective" or they were "Unsure".

- More than 4 out of 10 Other male respondents (42.87 %) rated Black leaders as "Effective" as they can be based on the challenges they face in today's political environment.

Findings by Age

- Respondents ages 18-24 years old (57.50%) overwhelmingly believe that Black political leaders are doing an effective job representing the issues of their constituents.

- Half of all Black male respondents (53.83%), ages 25-34 years old, agree that Black leaders are "Effective", while also lamenting that there are still too few of them in office.

- Nearly half of all White female respondents, ages 55 years and older (48.30%) rated Black elected officials and political leaders as both "Effective and "Intelligent".

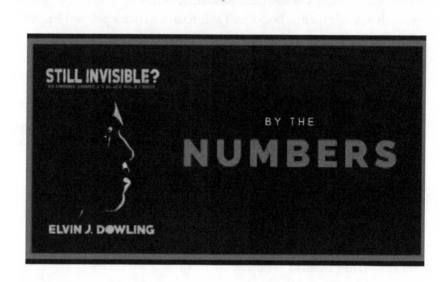

"A Precarious Fate for Black Candidates!"

- Since the passage of the *Voting Rights Act of 1965*, the number of Black Elected Officials of color has grown exponentially, from less than 1,000 nationwide, to more than 10,000 today ("Race in Politics").

- Although African-Americans are 12.5% of the American voting population, they still only make up only 8.5% of state legislatures, 5.7% of city councils, 3% of the U.S. Senate and no Black governors ("Race in Politics").

"To Be Seen and Not Heard!"

- According to academic studies and court rulings, voter suppression tactics helped Donald Trump win the U.S. presidency in 2016 and favored Republican candidates up and down the ballot ("Warping Democracy").

- Nine percent of Black voters in 2018 indicated that they (or someone they lived with) were turned away from the polls for lack of proper I.D or were incorrectly told they weren't on the rolls on Election Day ("Warping Democracy").

"Won't Let Nobody Turn Me 'Round!"

- Civil rights leaders used tactics like canvassing, community organizing, offering "practice sessions" to help voters pass literacy tests and held citizenship education classes to increase Black political participation ("Movement Tactics").

- Often faced with threats of jail time, severe beatings, and death, civil rights leaders ultimately pressured *Congress* to pass landmark legislation, including the *Civil Rights Act of 1964* and the *Fair Housing Act of 1968* ("Black Activists").

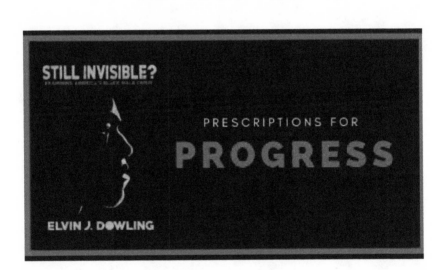

"To Show Up and Show Out."

- The Election Day electorate doesn't always reflect society. Improving the representativeness of candidates and voters, and increasing voter information about policy positions goes a long way towards increased Black turn-out (Born).

- America's political structure has allowed the ascendancy of Black candidates with stellar credentials and moderate politics. Recruiting

candidates who fill that pedigree may assist in electing Blacks to the
highest offices (Bacon).

"Need a Fix? Stop the Tricks!"

- Provide those vulnerable to voter suppression with the facts they need to
  be prepared to vote successfully, including obtaining acceptable forms of
  ID. Anyone with a reliable car can be a part of the overall solution ("How
  to Fight").

- Volunteer as a poll worker on Election Day and encourage voters make
  sure that their vote is properly cast and, whenever possible, to demand
  paper ballots at precincts with malfunctioning equipment ("How to
  Fight").

"Secure the Vote Through Election Protection"

- Encourage *Congress* to update and rewrite the formula that determines
  covered jurisdictions under Section 4 of the *Voting Rights Act*, identifying
  states with problematic histories of racial discrimination ("Section 4").

- Financially support litigation asking courts to require jurisdictions with a
  history of racial discrimination and voter suppression to get federal
  preclearance before changing election laws ("Section 4").

Works Cited

1. Shmoop Editorial Team. "Invisible Man Narrator Quotes   Page
    19." *Shmoop*. Shmoop University, Inc., 11 Nov.   2008. Web. 8 Dec.
    2019.

2. "Why We Must Confront America's History of Racial
    Terrorism." *CivilRights.org*, The Leadership   Conference
    Education Fund - An Education and   Research Arm of The
    Leadership Conference on   Civil Rights. Accessed 4 December

2019.   http://bit.ly/2PcpOJ0

3. Brown, Anna. "Blacks Have Made Gains in U.S. Political Leadership, But Gaps Remain." *PewResearch.org*,   Pew Research Center. 18 January 2019.   https://pewrsr.ch/2Rf3wca

4. Root, Danielle. "Voter Suppression During the 2018 Midterm Elections." *AmericanProgress.org*, Center for   American Progress. 20 November 2018. https://ampr.gs/34PTK4c

5. Shanton, Karen. "The Problem of African American Underrepresentation in City Councils." *Demos.org*,   Demos. 30 October 2014. http://bit.ly/34UcNtX

6. NAACP: A Century in the Fight." *LOC.gov*, U.S. Library of Congress. Accessed 6 December 2019. http://bit.ly/36gJ4fl

7. "Two Convicted in Plot on Wilkins Sought." *NYTimes.com*,   The New York Times Company. 11 July 1970. https://nyti.ms/2PpdjcV

8. *The New York Times*, 23 July 1981, p. 17.

9. "I Shot Vernon Jordan, Franklin Says." *Deseret.com*, Associated Press. 8 April 1996. http://bit.ly/2Yvh1Go

10. Morial, Marc H., ed. "State of Black America Report 2019 - Getting 2 Equal: United Not Divided." *SOBA.iAmEmpowered.com*, National Urban League.   Accessed 6 December 2019. http://bit.ly/340nPg2

11. "On Views of Race and Inequality, Blacks and Whites Are Worlds Apart." *PewSocialTrends.org*, Pew   Research Center. 27 June 2016. https://pewrsr.ch/36j2Mam

12. Brown-Dean, Khalilah. "50 Years of the Voting Rights Act: The State of Race in Politics." *JointCenter.org*, Joint   Center for Political and Economic Studies. Accessed   2 December 2019. http://bit.ly/38lIjmK

13. Newkirk, Vann R., II. "Voter Suppression Is Warping
    Democracy." *TheAtlantic.com*, Emerson Collective.   17 July 2018.
    http://bit.ly/33YZrLJ

14. Crosby, Emilye. "Civil Rights Movement Tactics."
    CivilRightsTeaching.org, A Project of Teaching for   Change.
    http://bit.ly/354x2VU

15. Burmila, Edward. "How to Fight Voter Suppression in
    2018." *DissentMagazine.org*, University of   Pennsylvania
    Press on behalf of the Foundation for   the Study of Independent
    Social Ideas. 11 July 2018.   http://bit.ly/35fbN3K

16. Born, Kelly. "Increasing Voter Turnout: What, If Anything,   Can
    Be Done?" *SSIR.org*, Stanford Social Innovation   Review. 25 April
    2016. http://bit.ly/350uCrC

17. Bacon, Jr., Perry. "The Narrow Path for Black Politicians   Who
    Want to Be President — And How It's   Changing."
    FiveThirtyEight.com, ABC News   Internet Ventures. 23
    August 2019.   https://53eig.ht/38e18bL

18. Desmond-Harris, Jeneé. "Why is Section 4 of the Voting
    Rights Act Such a Big Part of the Fight Over   Voting
    Rights?" *Vox.com*, Vox Media, LLC. 14   February 2016.
    http://bit.ly/2YvPlRA

Chapter 12: What About Obama?

Examining the Notion of a "Post-Racial" America

"

Brother, this is advice from a friend who has been watching you closely. Do not go too fast. Keep working for the people but remember that you are one of us and do not forget if you get too big, they will cut you down ... So, take friendly advice and go easy so that you can keep on helping the colored people. They do not want you to go too fast and will cut you down if you do. Be smart..."

- Ralph Ellison, "Invisible Man" (Shmoop Editorial Team)

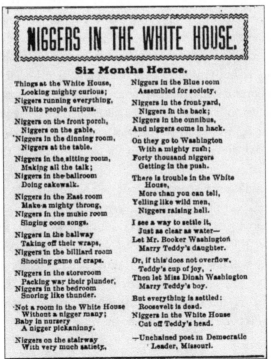

NIGGERS IN THE WHITE HOUSE.

Six Months Hence.

Things at the White House,
Looking mighty curious;
Niggers running everything,
White people furious.

Niggers on the front porch,
Niggers on the gable,
Niggers in the dinning room,
Niggers at the table.

Niggers in the sitting room,
Making all the talk;
Niggers in the ballroom
Doing cakewalk.

Niggers in the East room
Make a mighty throng,
Niggers in the muhic room
Singing coon songs.

Niggers in the hallway
Taking off their wraps,
Niggers in the billiard room
Shooting game of craps.

Niggers in the storeroom
Packing war their plunder,
Niggers in the bedroom
Snoring like thunder.

Not a room in the White House
Without a nigger many;
Baby in nursery
A nigger pickaninny.

Niggers on the stairway
With very much satiety,

Niggers in the Blue room
Assembled for society.

Niggers in the front yard,
Niggers in the back;
Niggers in the omnibus,
And niggers come in hack.

On they go to Washington
With a mighty rush;
Forty thousand niggers
Getting in the push.

There is trouble in the White
House,
More than you can tell,
Yelling like wild men,
Niggers raising hell.

I see a way to settle it,
Just as clear as water—
Let Mr. Booker Washington
Marry Teddy's daughter.

Or, if this does not overflow,
Teddy's cup of joy,
Then let Miss Dinah Washington
Marry Teddy's boy.

But everything is settled:
Roosevelt is dead.
Niggers in the White House
Cut off Teddy's head.

—Unchained poet in Democratic
Leader, Missouri.

(This poem first appeared on October 25, 1901, in Missouri's Sedalia Sentinel newspaper, in response to President Theodore Roosevelt's invitation to Booker T. Washington to dine at the White House.)

Was He the One We Were Waiting On...?

Or Should We Look for Another?

America's 15th President of the United States, James Buchanan, once said: *"If you are as happy in entering the White House as I shall feel on returning to Wheatland, you are a happy man indeed."* For at least one occupant of the most powerful position in the world, truer words have rarely been spoken. Moreover, as Barack Hussein Obama attempts to enjoy a post-presidency that has heretofore been characterized by personal attacks on his professionalism, character and integrity, I'm fairly certain that he would give almost anything for Buchanan's sentiments to apply to him today. In fact, not since the days when John Adams, the nation's second president, officially occupied the mansion that enslaved Africans built, has the idea of Blacks having a significant presence in the *White House* been an issue of social importance that was front and center in the American consciousness. That was until, however, the Obama family took up residence at *1600 Pennsylvania Avenue*. Likewise, the idea of Blacks being a full part of American society at all, has been anathema to those who have sought to maintain the social order of the nation. More importantly, as a country established *by* rich White people, *for* rich White people, ours is a nation that was stolen fair and square--lest we soon forget. Additionally, the idea of having *Black people* at the *White House*, other than in a servant's capacity (of course), was unthinkable just a century ago. Furthermore, as the very notion of a Negro doing anything other than scrubbing toilets, tending the yard, or waiting hand and foot on the president and first family is now considered a throwback to the past, many Americans now subscribe to the notion that our nation has evolved into a "post-racial" society. And that is because times, indeed, have changed... or have they?

In 1901, ignoring the social order of things, President Theodore Roosevelt violated racial protocol by inviting Booker T. Washington, the founder and President of *Tuskegee Institute*, to "the people's house" for dinner. Hoping to build bridges to broader communities, Roosevelt's olive branch was met with derision and scorn, however, igniting a fury the likes of which the nation had never seen before. In this particular instance of racial insensitivity, Midwestern moderates launched a broadside against good old "T.R.", using a small-town paper and a scurrilous poem to let the whole world know just how they felt about Teddy's supper guest. Today, more than a century past the publication of the "shot heard around the world," and years since the afterglow of two terms of the country's first Black president have largely faded from public view, the sentiments expressed back then, were not only applicable during Obama's occupancy of the *Oval Office*, they still ring true today. Furthermore, with the continued dismantling of the hard-fought legacy of a leader who was selfless enough to put himself and his family at risk of grave danger--while subjecting himself to the scorn of an often hostile public--the assault on a decent man's body of work and personal commitment continues...and therein lies the problem.

You see, if you're like me and believe in the idea that allowing those who have done their public duty to "go gently into that good night" (especially if they so choose), then--please--urge your fellow Americans to do the right thing and let Obama do just that. What's more, for all the haters out there who just can't get enough of doing their part to besmirch the 44th president's legacy, I beseech you, dear heart, by the mercies of God—Leave. That Man. Alone.

Please and Thank You,

Justitia

Lady Justice

Myles Barry Caggins III: "An Archetype of Servant Leadership"

Is It All Just Window Dressing?

"I'm Myles Barry Caggins III. I'm 44 years old and I'm an American Negro who was born in Heidelberg, Germany," commenced the commissioned *United States Army Officer (not speaking on the behalf—or as a representative of —the U.S. military)*. The public policy spokesman, in explaining his circuitous route to greatness, has been an experienced warrior in the battles of our time for more than half his life. "I was raised in a military household and relocated to various places throughout my childhood. Most my life was spent growing up in Virginia, but I also spent a considerable amount of time living in Texas and in Germany," Colonel Caggins continued. "In fact, my military career has brought me to many places around the world, including two combat tours in Iraq. It also led me to the *White House*, where I served as a Director for Strategic Communications and Assistant Press Secretary for the Deputy National Security Advisor to the 44th President of the United States, the Honorable Barack Hussein Obama," declared the *Harvard University Kennedy School of Government* alum and stalwart member of the elite *Council on Foreign Relations*, a national nonprofit think tank specializing in U.S. foreign policy and international affairs.

A second generation soldier, Myles is the progeny of a successful military strategist, Colonel Myles B. Caggins, Jr. (*U.S.A. Ret.*) who, himself, commanded troops in battle in Viet Nam and would later go on to graduate from the *National War College*, before embarking upon a successful second career as an operations chief for a Georgia school district before retiring, once again, with honor. The amiable younger colonel's mother, Mrs. Ann Caggins, is an accomplished individual in her own right; having served in key positions at the *American Red Cross* and the *Society for Human Resources Management*, among others. Moreover, the junior Caggins, known as "Barry" to his closest friends, is quick to acknowledge the role that his two most ardent supporters have played in getting him to the pinnacles of American power and prestige: his doting and devoted parents. "I've been blessed with two wonderful parents who've been married for more than fifty years. They were the first and most important influences in life. In fact," Barry explained, "growing up I was always exposed to two-parent households, as both of my parents, who were college educated, spent their time around other couples and families who were married and college educated, so that's all I have ever really known," the angular artisan of *Army* spin acknowledged. "In addition to that, I've had a number of exceptional mentors who are both in and outside of the military, from a variety of different ethnicities, occupations, professions, educational experiences and racial backgrounds, all of whom have contributed in some way to helping me to become the man that I am today," the sagacious soldier surmised.

The circumstances that led Caggins, a formidable competitor who once appeared on an episode of the long running television gameshow, *Jeopardy!*, during one of its "Military Appreciation" weeks (placing second in a come from behind rally that may have been one for the history books had he not run out of time on the show), are as quixotic as his hopscotch childhood. "I'm at the *White House* because I have had people, men and women, Black and White, who have encouraged me and guided me and put me in a place where I was even competitive to interview for the position in which I served," noted one of "the president's men" in the national security sector. "Furthermore, when I came to the *White House,* it happened as a result of me submitting a two-page resume and going through a rigorous vetting process (having applied multiple times before) before I was granted the opportunity to serve. One day," the warrior-stateman recalled, "I received a phone call saying *'Congratulations, we'd like you to come work at the White House',* but it was definitely a long time coming," he remarked. "After working at there for a while, I soon came to realize that my hiring experience was not how it works for everybody," Caggins explained, before detailing a network of exclusive jobs and extraordinary opportunities that are, oftentimes, only available to those on the periphery of power and influence.

"More often than not, people *like me* get jobs *like this* because somebody knows somebody and is in a position to, in essence, pick their own replacement," the colonel conceded. The challenge with such a system, however, is that it does not lend itself to providing equitable access to those same opportunities for individuals who do not have access to the people who can move the levers of government on their behalf. "When that happens," Caggins acknowledged, "and people who look like me are not considered for these extraordinary opportunities to serve their nation and, indeed, the world, it's not necessarily because the people who are driving the decision-making process are racist. Nor is it because they hate Black people," the public relations guru gathered, in assessing reasons why there is a dearth of Black faces working in some of the nation's highest positions--even when the President of the United States is an individual of color. "In my experience", Caggins elaborated, "people pick people for these types of positions whom they know, like and trust. So, at the top of the food chain of government, for the high performers, there are not a lot of Black Americans to begin with, so the ability to put other qualified African-Americans in place to fill these roles is impacted significantly," he maintained. "Sometimes, it's because we don't seek these roles in government, particularly in the national security arena, or because we don't have mentors encouraging us, or we just don't know about the opportunities when they come available," Caggins found. "Whatever the reason, when it comes to Blacks like me in jobs like this, the numbers just aren't there," he observed. Yet, in his considered opinion, Caggins believes that things always improve when "the powers that be" have the political courage to do what some say couldn't (or shouldn't) be done.

With regard to his job at the most powerful office complex on the planet, Colonel Caggins described a decisive chain of command that put him within a stone's throw of the world's most powerful person. "At the top you have the president, who then has a National Security Advisor who, in turn, oversees the *National Security Council (NSC)*. As was the case when I worked at the *White House*, that position was filled by former *United Nations* Ambassador Susan Rice," the foreign policy specialist delineated. "Then there was the Deputy National Security Advisor for Speech Writing and Strategic Communications, Ben Rhodes," Caggins explained, in drawing a visual organizational chart that explained his place on the president's foreign policy totem pole. "Under him," he went on, "we had Ned Price, the *NSC* Primary Spokesman and Special Assistant to the President for Press Operations and then there's me," the military spokesman related. "I served as both an Assistant Press Secretary and Director for Strategic Communications for National Security," the colonel continued.

"I worked daily with--and for--Josh Earnest, the *White House* Press Secretary. With regard to my particular expertise, in layman's terms, I was the *White House* spokesman for a myriad of topics—including Asia defense policy, Guantanamo Bay, multilateral affairs, worldwide human rights, and nuclear weapons and non-proliferation," the longtime foreign policy enthusiast explained. "As a part of this exclusive council staff, there are people of color around me, but in many of the rooms where the final decisions were being made within the national security space, there were not that many minorities and though we might have had Ambassador Susan Rice (a Black woman) at the head of the table, those around the table didn't look much like her--or much like me--sitting over on the side bench," Caggins despaired. To solve, or at least address, what has historically been an exclusive *Executive Branch* in which "whites only" need apply, Myles believes that affirmative steps must be made to ensure inclusivity.

"The *National Football League* has what is known as the "Rooney Rule" which requires them to interview and consider qualified minorities for head coaching positions. I believe the *White House* could do the same," Caggins concluded, imagining a legion of qualified minorities filling the ranks of the executive branch of government. "If an individual is being replaced, the hiring manager or departing employee, should look at all the resumes, see who's being nominated and strongly consider diverse talent, so that we don't always end up with the same type of employee holding positions of significance at this level (i.e. White males from *Yale*)," he joked. "I would say there were probably about 100 other director-level people like myself. But there's just no pipeline to getting more Blacks in position to claim these coveted employment and leadership opportunities," the soldier surmised. "No one says to anyone else, *'Call somebody up and get us some more talented Black people up here,'* the colonel conceded. And therein lies the continuing challenge.

"Now my experiences were not unique. They were often shared by the few minorities with whom I worked with, as I would see them in the hallways and we would share these little talks. One day," Caggins noted, during one of these "watercooler chats" I learned that my soon to be replacement at the *White House* is a guy who was a white male who was fully competent and fully capable for the role that he was going to assume. More importantly, he was doing a great job in the position that he held at the time, but the problem was the fact that I was the last person to know this was the guy who would be replacing me," "Barry" bemoaned. "There's generally some prior knowledge of when you will be rotated out. My replacement," Colonel Caggins explained, "was already selected prior to when I was to be rotated out and, unlike when I interviewed for my position when I sat amongst my peers to be selected, I was not brought into that interview process for the guy that was replacing me. Curiously enough," Caggins confessed, "I found this out from a white male reporter who said to me in passing, 'Hey, I heard this guy is coming up to the National Security office and he's going to be your placement.' My immediate response," Caggins retorted, "was to respond that it was, indeed, interesting that a reporter would know before I would. There's been some discussion," Myles remarked, "about white privilege. Well, for some, it's not white privilege when a group of white males can select another white male for the job, and that white male who receives the job is so confident in his selection, that he can tell a reporter that he will be *nominated* for the role, and its already a done deal, no less. Yet, I was the last person to hear about it, even though I occupied the role at the time," he theorized.

"I never mentioned this to my colleagues, but I'm happy to share this now, so that others can understand how things happened and decisions were made in some of the highest places in government. And, in this case, were happening literally in shouting distance of the first Black president and his Black National Security Advisor," the communications consigliere conceded. "So, in a way, this is a clear demonstration of what it means to be "invisible" in America. But I also believe that if the stories of people like myself never reach the light of day," Myles Caggins maintained, "the broader narrative about the Black male is that he is just somebody who's barely hanging on... scraping by... trying to just walk to the bus stop without getting shot by a cop, or shot by another Black male," the public relations expert explained. "This is the narrative that is often being pushed by some in the media, pushed by some in politics and pushed by some so-called Black leaders, and that's not the totality of who we are," Caggins concluded. The head honcho in charge at "the people's house", however, took as cautious an approach to governing as he did to campaigning, seeking consensus and common ground rather than immediately righting historic wrongs and "reshuffling the deck" by hiring more minorities for positions of power in the bustling *West Wing*.

Change We Can Believe In?

As America's first African-American president, Barack H. Obama faced a barrage of hurdles he had to overcome before winning the nation's top political prize--twice--confounding historians, pundits and prognosticators who believed that his ascension up the ranks of power so quickly was not only improbable but impossible. To that end, the "knives" began to come out--early and often, seeking to take a slice out of Obama's reputation and a pound of flesh (if possible) for the relatively clean-cut community organizer who often described himself as the "skinny guy with the funny name." For starters, before he could even acquire the *Democratic Party* Nomination for President, Obama had to first distance himself from his own pastor and spiritual advisor, the Reverend Jeremiah Wright of the *Trinity United Church of Christ* of Chicago, Illinois. As a faithful follower of the 8,000 member congregation, Obama found himself inspired by the often mesmerizing ministry of the good Reverend Wright, who often preached against despotism, hypocrisy and the history of America from a cultural and religious context that struck a chord not only with the one-day president, but with legions of follower who agreed with this version of "Liberation Theology". The challenge for the young State Senator—turned U.S. Senator from Illinois—turned presidential candidate, was the fact that Wright's bombastic characterization of the deleterious impact of American political policies on the poor and disenfranchised would cause more than just a little political angst. That's because, in the middle of the campaign, Obama had to give an account—not for his own words or deeds—but for the sermonic selections of his pastor; forcing the uber careful president to address the elephant in the room that he had sought to avoid but could do so no longer—Race in America.

On March 18, 2008, before a packed audience at the *Constitution Center* in Philadelphia, Pennsylvania, then candidate Obama, in a speech that ricocheted across the country, confronted a swirling controversy that threatened to consume his campaign--namely the musings of his pastor. In doing so, however, Obama took the opportunity to appeal to the better angels of America's nature. In what would become a historic address entitled, "A More Perfect Union," then Senator Obama described the challenges he faced as a biracial male who considered himself Black, but never denied his white heritage, and how that unique perspective provided him the insight he would need as President of the United States, to help salve festering racial wounds.

Moreover, as a part of his address on race that continues to reverberate through the ages, the erstwhile community organizer who once worked the grounds of the *Altgeld Gardens Chicago Housing Authority* complex, turned man who was one step away from having access to the nation's nuclear launch codes, Obama tapped into his inner sense of purpose to painstakingly deliver a call to America to rise above its history, while embracing it's coming future, with the following remarks:

"

I am the son of a Black man from Kenya and a white woman from Kansas. I was raised with the help of a white grandfather who survived a Depression to serve in Patton's Army during World War II and a white grandmother who worked on a bomber assembly line at Fort Leavenworth while he was overseas. I've gone to some of the best schools in America and lived in one of the world's poorest nations. I am married to a Black American who carries within her the blood of slaves and slaveowners — an inheritance we pass on to our two precious daughters. I have brothers, sisters, nieces, nephews, uncles and cousins of every race and every hue, scattered across three continents, and for as long as I live, I will never forget that in no other country on Earth is my story even possible...

At various stages in the campaign, some commentators have deemed me either "too Black" or "not Black enough." We saw racial tensions bubble to the surface during the week before the South Carolina primary. The press has scoured every single exit poll for the latest evidence of racial polarization, not just in terms of white and Black, but Black and brown as well.

And yet, it has only been in the last couple of weeks that the discussion of race in this campaign has taken a particularly divisive turn.

On one end of the spectrum, we've heard the implication that my candidacy is somehow an exercise in affirmative action; that it's based solely on the desire of wide-eyed liberals to purchase racial reconciliation on the cheap. On the other end, we've heard my former pastor, Jeremiah Wright, use incendiary language to express views that have the potential not only to widen the racial divide, but views that denigrate both the greatness and the goodness of our nation, and that rightly offend white and Black alike...

As imperfect as he may be, he has been like family to me. He strengthened my faith, officiated my wedding, and baptized my children. Not once in my conversations with him have I heard him talk about any ethnic group in derogatory terms, or treat whites with whom he interacted with anything but courtesy and respect. He contains within him the contradictions — the good and the bad — of the community that he has served diligently for so many years.

I can no more disown him than I can disown the Black community. I can no more disown him than I can disown my white grandmother — a woman who helped raise me, a woman who sacrificed again and again for me, a woman who loves me as much as she loves anything in this world, but a woman who once confessed her fear of Black men who passed her by on the street, and who on more than one occasion has uttered racial or ethnic stereotypes that made me cringe.

These people are a part of me. And they are part of America, this country that I love... ("A More Perfect Union")

Throughout the course of his political career, President Obama has had to bury the ghosts of legacies he did not create, the carcasses of mistakes he was not responsible for, and the remains of actions he did not take, forcing him, time and again, into greatness in a way that has visited very few people in public life. And it was in this realm that he tackled the issue of race both in his speech and in his life; with a hopeful optimism that tomorrow can always be better than yesterday. Fortunately, for "Barry" Obama (as the former president is also referred to by his childhood friends), the opportunity to rise or fall to his own level of expectation would go on to mark him as a man with both great abilities and a sincere desire to help heal a hurting nature.

As a reward for his compassion and capacity, Democratic voters elected Obama in primaries and caucuses across the country, allowing him to successfully clinch his party's nomination that summer at the *Mile-High Stadium* in Denver, Colorado, and ultimately win the presidency that fall against U.S. Senator John McCain of Arizona. What's more, this extraordinary achievement in world history would only be celebrated but for a moment, however, as the new president would soon be reminded that he was still persona non grata in the halls of the *U.S. Congress*, particularly when as it related to how he would be treated by the loyal opposition, with obstinate obstructionists who were all too eager to remind him of this political reality. In fact, on the evening of his first inauguration as President of the United States, members of the Republican leadership held a private dinner, called by conservative pollster Frank Luntz, to determine how best to maneuver their party and its positions in the new Obama era, while simultaneously conflating his agenda at every turn. As such, there would be no "honeymoon period" for the first Black president, as the gloves would come off by the time dessert was served at that fateful private repast.

On January 20, 2009, hours after Barack H. Obama became the 44th President of the United States of America, stepping into a national leadership vacuum with an ambitious agenda to make the nation a more equitable and just society, a group of approximately fifteen Republican officials assembled together to not only lick their political wounds, but also to plot a path out of the wilderness and back to political relevance. Having suffered a historic defeat that turned over the *White House* to a Black man for the first time in history, these men were reportedly all too eager to use the personage of the new Commander-in-Chief, to achieve their overall political objective: ensure that the presidency, for Obama, was nasty, brutish and, most importantly, short. In a story covering the dinner by some of the individuals in attendance, the *PBS* show *Frontline*, in a series called, "Divided States of America", the plot to thwart the plans of America's dynamic new leader was hatched in the bowels of a closed door meeting at an innocuous Washington, D.C. restaurant; an event that would theoretically feature Obama's political agenda on a skewer, as an appetizer, and his head on a platter, as the meal's main course.

First reported by cinematographer and journalist, Robert Draper, author of "Do Not Ask What Good We Do: Inside the U.S. House of Representatives," the infamous cabal consisted of a myriad of Republican officials representing both house of congress and the sentiments of millions of Americans, including: Former Speaker of the House Newt Gingrich (R-Ga.), Eric Cantor (R-Va.), Rep. Kevin McCarthy (R-Calif.), Rep. Paul Ryan (R-Wisc.), Rep. Pete Sessions (R-Texas), Rep. Pete Hoekstra (R-Mich.) and Rep. Dan Lungren (R-Calif.). From the Senate were powerbrokers such as Jim DeMint (R-S.C.), Jon Kyle (R-Ariz.), Tom Coburn (R-Okla.), John Ensign (R-Nev.) and Bob Corker (R-Tenn.). According to the *Frontline* account, Luntz, the convener of the event, was initially worried about the event's attendance, wondering if anyone would show up after having been initially dissuaded from hosting the event in the first place, but his prospects soon brightened when the majority of those invited actually arrived, and did so with an eagerness to which Luntz himself did not expect.

"When people gathered, I had no idea who was going to show up. In fact, 15 minutes before — we were 45 minutes into the drinks — 15 minutes before the dinner was to begin, there were only three or four senators or congressmen there, and I thought nobody was showing up," Luntz recalled. "And then they all came, and it was because the parade was late. We actually learned something about Obama on that day: that he was going to be late then, and he's been late ever since," the Republican pollster quipped; hearkening back to a well-worn trope about African-Americans being notoriously late, in what has often been called "colored people time"—a racial stereotype Luntz appeared all too eager to embrace.

"I don't know," Luntz recalled, "eight or nine senators, eight or nine congressmen. The room was filled," he said. Just as important as who was in attendance, was what they would achieve between entrees. "Obama [was] a singularly threatening figure to them, in some ways, because of his offer of bipartisanship. His pledge to end polarization. And they realized that if he were to do that ... These bipartisan bills wouldn't necessarily be viewed as Republican successes, they'd be viewed as Obama's successes and his Democrats' successes," observed Jason Zengerle, senior editor of *The New Republic*. "And they decide[d] that in order to stop Obama from succeeding, they have to deny him the mantel of bipartisanship. Because anything he [did would] accrue to him and...to the Democrats. And they just decide[d] on a strategy of just across the board opposition to deny him anything because they [thought] that even if it is a policy that they ultimately supported or wanted, they won't benefit politically from it" ("Divided States"). Luntz, in characterizing the results of what would be a great political conquest just two short years later, borne out of an idea and a fateful meal that would sustain the hearts and minds of craven politicos for the fierce battles ahead against the "Democratic David" of a new generation of Americans, noted the following: "There was incredible brainpower in that room. Some people were good at language. Some people were good at policy. Some people were good at tactics. Some people understood the media. Others understood the way Washington worked," Luntz said. "And the feeling was that if that group could cooperate, and if that group could lead, that the wilderness might not be a generation away, but it might be more like a few elections away" ("Divided States"). And in that prescient assessment, Luntz was correct.

For his part, Obama and his team were clueless to the brick wall of obstruction that he would encounter when he was merely attempting to fulfill a campaign pledge to reach out to both sides of the political aisle, and independents in the middle; responding with a naïveté that was endemic of a young idealist not grounded in the ways of cutthroat politics. In fact, according to Obama's Assistant to the President and Director of Legislative Affairs, Phil Schiliro, the new president was quickly caught flat-footed with those for whom he had hoped to befriend long enough to get deals done and legislation passed on behalf of the American people. "We didn't know about the [dinner]", Schirillo said. "We didn't know about the Senate caucus meeting where Senator [Mitch] McConnell (R-Ky.), according to Republican senators, said something very similar," he continued. "There were people at the time who were confused by the Republican response because the president started off — not just that first day that he's in Washington meeting with them — but [wanting] to do constant outreach to the Republican side. Those were the instructions to me. And so that's what we did, and he tried to put together policies that he thought would attract Republican support... But we had no idea about that meeting on inauguration night" ("Divided States"). Compounding the obstruction, in an interview to *Fox News* analyst Major Garrett, then Senate Minority Leader, Mitch McConnell of Kentucky, went on record as being opposed to any and every thing that Obama would propose as president of the United States.

According to *Politifact*, Obama's claims of McConnell eagerly playing the role of the brazen saboteur, with an ultimate goal of recapturing 1600 Pennsylvania Avenue were, indeed, true and were also a harbinger of what was to come throughout the entirety of his administration. "The single most important thing we want to achieve is for President Obama to be a one-term president," McConnell said in confirming the intentional intransigence designed to halt the hopeful new president's advances. Meanwhile, at the other end of Constitution Avenue, the *U.S. House of Representatives*, led by then Speaker John Boehner of Ohio, was doing everything it could to stop the progressive new leader's agenda dead in its tracks, especially when it came to his goal of providing universal healthcare for those who were uninsured.

"This is not a time for compromise," Boehner decried. "...We're going to do everything -- and I mean everything -- we can do, to kill it, stop it, slow it down" ("Politifact"). And for the next eight years, despite his ability to get historic legislation passed, including the Affordable Care Act, derisively called "Obamacare" by Republicans, a moniker that was simultaneously embraced as a badge of honor by the president, Obama would be stymied every step of the way. Even more frustrating for the 44th president, was the fact that he would very soon find himself the target of harsh criticism, racist memes, disrespectful treatment and unprecedented obstruction from those with a single, uniting agenda of denying him any achievements or dismantling any successes he was able to eke out via legislation and executive order.

But Racism No Longer Exists... Right?

For Obama, like many of the African-American leaders that proceeded him, none of which made it anywhere near the heights of power that he would achieve, the threat of constant danger was also something that he was forced to live with from the moment he lost his national anonymity when he first addressed the *Democratic National Convention* in 2004 as a candidate for the *United States Senate*. Since then, both as a candidate for President of the United States, through both terms as Commander-in-Chief, Barack Obama was the most threatened leader in the history of America--a nation overflowing with guns and ammunition. In fact, in a sobering post on *DailyKos* called, "President Barack Obama Is the Most Threatened President in History," the number of death threats against the nation's first Black president were both overwhelming and astounding.

"The *Boston Globe* reports that a new internal *Congressional Research Service* report and government sources say there are an unprecedented number of death threats against President Obama -- and that the *Secret Service* is insufficiently funded and staffed to deal with them," the report found. "Obama is the target of more than 30 potential death threats a day and is being protected by an increasingly over-stretched *Secret Service*. He is the most threatened President in history" ("Threatened"). Moreover, from the moment Barack Obama assumed the office of President in January 2009, the rate of threats against the office itself increased 400%. "Some threats to the President have been publicized, including the well-known alleged plot by white supremacists in Tennessee to rob a gun store, shoot 88 Black people, decapitate another 14 and then assassinate the first Black president in American history," the *DailyKos* analysis noted. "Most however, are kept under wraps because the *Secret Service* fears that revealing details of them would only increase the number of copycat attempts" ("Threatened").

What's more, while many made idle threats against the president and his family, all of which required the *U.S. Secret Service* to investigate thoroughly, some attempted to act out their threats, albeit unsuccessfully, providing yet another level of fear and unnecessary angst visited upon Obama and his loved ones. "There have been dozens of people indicted on charges of threatening to harm him since he took office. In 2011, for example, a gunman fired at 1600 Pennsylvania Ave. from Constitution Avenue and at least seven bullets struck the *White House* the president's daughter and mother-in-law were home" ("Threatened"). Several years later, a man armed with a knife was successful at breaching the gates of the most secure compound on earth, and making his way inside the *White House* before being stopped by an off-duty *Secret Service* agent who happened to come across the potential assailant. In addition to the threats against his physical well-being and safety, President Obama also faced a number of jarring and disrespectful moments during his presidency that often reminded him and, indeed all Black males, that America is still a country that has come a long way, but still has a long way to go, when it comes to the issue of white supremacy, racial superiority and the respect of persons of color.

During his first address before a joint session of *Congress* in 2009 on the issue of healthcare, President Obama, while denying that his bill covered undocumented immigrants, was unceremoniously interrupted by Rep. Joe Wilson of South Carolina, who shouted, *"you lie!"* as the president spoke. For his part, the ever-cool Obama simply retorted, *"That's not true,"* before attempting to regain his stride during this first and most important speech of his young administration. Juliet Elperin, a senior writer for the *Washington Post*, in her piece termed, "The Obamas: Refusing to Give In to Hate After Years of Threats," spoke of the vitriol that continues to confront the former leader of the free world and his family; even after he has successfully completed eight "indictment-free" years as President of the United States of America. "Disagree with Obama's politics and policies, sure. That's how it's supposed to work. But there is a viciousness, a racist edge to the hate-speak that echoes the darkest days of American history," Elperin remarked.

From actual threats to verbal disrespect, the former President has often found himself the object of other people's anger and resentment, many of whom are all too eager to let Obama (and the world) know exactly how they feel about him, both personally and professionally. Today, even in the social media sphere, there continues to be little respite for the former president, as he continues to draw the ire of those who remain committed to opposing everything that Obama stands for. "One of the most popular targets is [Former] President Obama, the country's first African American commander-in-chief. It's impossible to utter a single word about... the first family or the president without a blast from the fire hose of hater-ade," Elperin noted. "It can be school lunches, children's books, dresses or kids going off to college. The trolls are there, ripping 'everything Obama' to shreds" (Elperin).

Through it all, however, President Obama stood firm upon his convictions, while doing his part to help America to regain its footing economically, militarily and diplomatically; leaving a legacy of success that cannot be ignored. In fact midway through Obama's second term as president, the U.S. economy had successfully rebounded, unemployment fell below 6% and gas prices had begun to recede considerably from a high of $3.25 at the end of President George W. Bush's terms in office, to $2.50 at the close of his; signaling a renaissance of sorts during the Obama years that saw greater access to prosperity for a growing share of Americans. In a year-end analysis of the state of American life in 2014, *Politico Magazine's* Michael Grunwald, in his report called, "Everything is Awesome," noted that the country had, indeed, moved further away from the precipice of economic calamity during President Obama's hopeful administration. "Crime, abortion, teen pregnancy and oil imports are also way down, while renewable power is way up and the American auto industry is booming again. You don't have to give credit to President Barack Obama for "America's resurgence," as he has started calling it, but there's overwhelming evidence the resurgence is real," Grunwald wrote. "It's a good thing that U.S. wind power has tripled and solar power has increased tenfold in five years. And while it's true that the meteoric rise of the stock market since 2009 has produced windfalls for Wall Street, it has also replenished state pension funds and 401(k) retirement plans and labor union coffers. It definitely beats the alternative" (Grunwald).

Despite the successes of the Obama Administration which were, indeed, "wins" for the American people, a concerted effort to dismantle his political legacy, brick by brick, commenced with lightning speed with the election of his successor to the *White House*; businessman and reality television star Donald John Trump of New York. In fact, from the moment he occupied the *Oval Office*, the 45th president has embarked upon a scorched earth campaign aimed at discrediting, minimizing or all together eliminating, many of the signature achievements made by the nation's first Black Commander-in-Chief.

In covering what could rightly be considered the "Trump Chainsaw Massacre", David Smith of *The Guardian* newspaper reported on the lengths to which Obama's successor has gone to "undo" what Obama hoped he had carved in stone. "When Donald Trump pulled out of the deal to curb Iran's nuclear ambitions, hardline conservatives celebrated, European leaders winced and Barack Obama made a rare, lengthy public statement. Trump's decision was *"misguided"* and *"a serious mistake"*, Obama said, as his signature foreign policy achievement was tossed away," the newspaper reported. What's worse, this withdrawal from a hard-fought foreign policy coup was but the beginning salvo in a one-sided onslaught upon the Obama legacy. "From climate change to criminal justice to international relations, rarely has one occupant of the *Oval Office* appeared so obsessed with taking a chainsaw to the work of another," Smith observed. "During his battle with Hillary Clinton, Trump duly promised to unravel Obama's accomplishments. He described the *Trans-Pacific Partnership (TPP)*, a proposed free trade deal with Asia, as *"a rape of our country"*. He said he is *"not a great believer in manmade climate change"* and vowed to cancel the Paris agreement," The Guardian noted. "He called the Iran nuclear accord a *"disaster"* and *"the worst deal ever negotiated"* and warned that it could lead to a *"nuclear holocaust"* ("*The Guardian*").

For Myles Caggins, III, *"the other Barry,"* understanding the genesis of the sentiments that drive those who hate on others, particularly talented Black men, for very few logical reasons, is essential to understanding the nature of who we are as Americans and the history that fuels that enmity. "Our nation was founded during a time when Black people were three-fifths of a human being", the history buff remarked, "so this is just part of America's DNA. Today, however, in many ways we're still fighting this distinction," Colonel Caggins declared. "As a child, I was told to look both ways before I cross the street. I still do that today. I was told to wash behind my ears," the military strategist recalled, "I still remember to do those things today," he maintained. "I know that sounds silly but I think some of the things that you learn in elementary school should apply to life. Societies can and will evolve... but there are still many people who harbor racial resentment, and long for older days where they yearn for an America that is different from the America that they see today. Even though biology and time have created a 'browning of America', some people want things to stay the way they used to be," Caggins conceded.

"I didn't work too much on the politics side of things, while employed at the *White House*, but I was a keen observer of what was happening politically and I saw, up close, the discussions that happened around the political decisions that were made here in Washington, DC at the time," the army officer acknowledged. "As a neutral and detached observer, it was clear to me that much of the obstruction that happened on Capitol Hill was about stopping President Obama from having a successful agenda, and undermining any accomplishments or any policies that the president believed was going to make the nation better and safer," Caggins concluded. "Many times, we saw President Obama put forth nominees who, for a variety of reasons, were stalled in committee and never got a vote on the floor of the Senate," he surmised. "I'd say the most obvious of these was *Supreme Court* judicial pick, Judge Merrick Garland who, by all metrics, was one of the most qualified persons to have ever been nominated; somebody the Senate unanimously approved for a federal judgeship in years prior. Yet, his nomination was never advanced for a vote and the only expressed or implied reasoning was the fact that President Barack Obama had nominated him," the straight-shooting soldier surmised. "And then there's a number of legislative things that the president just struggled to get through," Caggins ceded. "In my estimation there were people that didn't want him to be successful because he's a Democrat and there are those who didn't want him to be successful because he is a Black man who was president of the United States; but I don't necessarily ascribe racial motivations to folks who were against his political agenda," the colonel concluded.

"Just from my observations of President Obama," Caggins continued, "and the sessions I had with him, I do believe he cares deeply about the conditions of all people around the world. But I also learned that the president is <u>ONE MAN</u>, surrounded by advisors. And *if* you were to go through the background of most of the advisors, and look at their degrees and what they've done professionally, they were a socially elite group of people. As such, their areas of influence didn't necessarily touch the pulse of 'the least of these', namely disenfranchised Americans. In addition to that," Caggins furthered, "people get whipped into a frenzy over the *'Unarmed Black Man Shooting of the Week'*, but that same energy is not applied to the day-to-day needs of real people who are struggling, where the government can make a significant and material difference," Barry believes. "I think if people follow the real teachings of Jesus Christ, not just the *'saved by grace'* and *'everybody makes mistakes Jesus,'* but the Jesus that talks about loving people, treating people right, being disciplined and *then* going out to the nations, I believe our country could solve a lot of problems...particularly as it pertains to poverty," the committed Christian continued. "That is...*if* we cared about poor people," Caggins relented; understanding full well the implications of the old saying which notes, *"if ands and buts were candy and nuts, everyday would be Christmas."* The globetrotting specialist is not convinced, however, that America does, indeed, care about the suffering of her poor huddled masses "yearning to breathe free."

"Why is it in America, we have so many fancy grocery stores, yet so much hunger in this country?," the soldier-statesman asked. "We have *Whole Foods* and *Wegmans* and yet, just a couple miles away from the *White House,* in Southeast Washington, D.C., there's only one grocery store and the food that people are eating from the store lead to a variety of nutritional problems," Caggins observed. "Obviously, kids need to eat healthy foods so that they can learn and grow and are not obese. Whenever there's a crisis," Caggins elucidated, "we quickly manufacture the justification to either *find* or *raise* and then *spend* more money to solve the problem. For example, "the communications strategist went on, "take the Zika virus. Because everyone concluded that this was a public health crisis, our government found $1.4 billion in federal funding to launch a successful fight to combat the spread of the virus. Well, I think $1.4 billion could probably help a lot of young people to have nutritious meals," the international statesman intoned.

"You know," Caggins remarked, "Jesus talks about *'the least of these'.* Why can't kids have access to healthy fruits and vegetables in the United States, where we throw out more food than any other western nation on the planet? Working at the *White House,* I sometimes found it astonishingly disappointing, that we could come up with all of this money for *this* widget or for *that* foreign policy objective, but we couldn't find more money to feed elementary school students--all elementary school students--regardless of what ZIP code they lived in; regardless of where they were born; and regardless of who their parents are," Caggins bemoaned. "Poor people are invisible, still today, and who's their champion?," the colonel queried. "Unfortunately," he concluded, I *still* don't know who *that* is." With that being said, however, Colonel Myles Barry Caggins, III *(U.S.A.),* an accomplished academician and decorated soldier, still believes that there is hope for the future of African-American men, as they strive to fulfill their highest potential.

"For Black boys everywhere, I would remind them to listen closely to your elders; to seek their wisdom and to heed it. For those who are always striving to embody manhood, I would encourage them to find **somebody** that they want to "be like" and find out *how* they got to where they are today. You're going to need mentors and models to make it. Always walk with your head held high and believe that you can," Colonel Caggins admonished. "Furthermore, I would encourage Black males of all ages to ask themselves a simple, but powerful question, and that is—"Why?"

"Why not *you*?" he asked. "*Why* can't *you* be president of the United States? *Why* can't *you* be president of a university? *Why* can't *you* be the best athlete? *Why* can't *you* be valedictorian? *Why* can't *you* open your own medical practice? *Why* can't *you* be the number one realtor in your city? *Why* can't *you* invest in stocks and bonds and be a millionaire by the time you're 30?," he inquired.

"And lastly," the colonel concluded, "I would remind each of them to always remember to be a respecter of all people. First and, most importantly, respect yourself. Always respect women. Respect your family and those who love you most. And just as importantly, treat people with dignity and respect, have good manners and you'll see just how far that will take you!"

(Myles B. Caggins III: Spokesman & Soldier)

How strongly do you agree or disagree with the following statements?

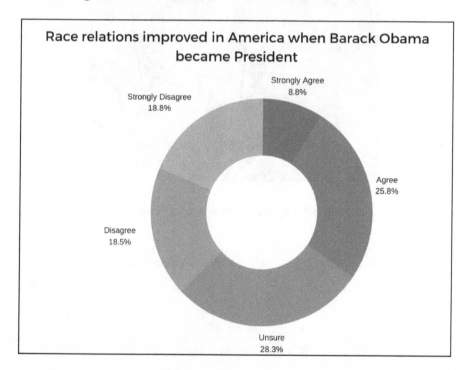

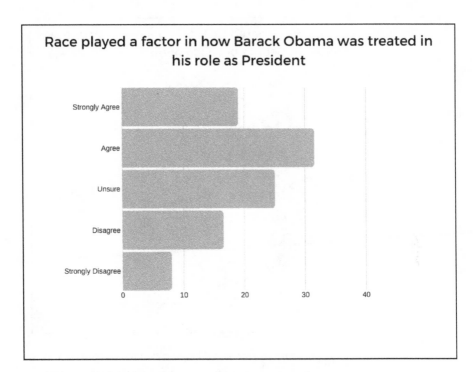

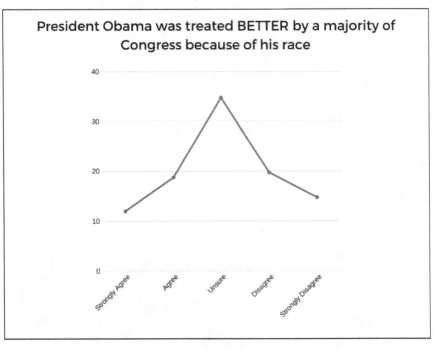

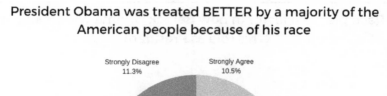

President Obama was treated BETTER by a majority of the American people because of his race

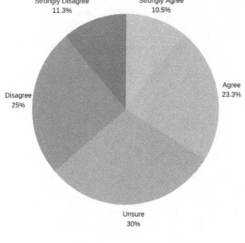

Strongly Disagree
11.3%

Strongly Agree
10.5%

Agree
23.3%

Disagree
25%

Unsure
30%

All survey results displayed above are represented by the overall percentage of survey respondents. For more information on our survey methodology, please see the Author's Note, located in the front matter of the book. To review raw survey results, visit: http://bit.ly/stillinvisiblesurvey.

Nearly 5 in 10 Female Respondents "Agree"

"Race a Factor in How Obama was Treated"

White Males
"Strongly/Disagree"
(47.00%)
"Race Relations Improved
During Obama's Presidency"

AGES 55+ YEARS OLD
"STRONGLY/AGREE"

(41.33%)

"OBAMA WAS TREATED
BETTER BY AMERICANS
BECAUSE HE WAS BLACK"

BLACKS
"STRONGLY/DISAGREE"

(55.76%)

"OBAMA WAS TREATED BETTER BY
CONGRESS BECAUSE OF RACE"

Findings by Race

- More White respondents (39.58%) "Disagree" or "Strongly Disagree" with the statement, *"Race relations improved in America when Barack Obama became President,"* than those who "Agree" or "Strongly Agree" (27.92%).

- An overwhelming majority of Black respondents (67.30%) "Strongly Agree" or "Agree" with the statement, *"Race played a factor in how Barack Obama was treated in his role as President."*

- Nearly 1 out of 3 Hispanic respondents (31.94%) with the statement, *"President Obama was treated BETTER by a majority of Congress because of his race."*

Findings by Gender

- More than one-third of all Female respondents (35.50%) "Strongly Disagree" or "Disagree" with the statement, *"President Obama was treated BETTER by a majority of the American people because of his race."*

- A strong plurality of all Male respondents (44.00%) "Strongly Disagree" or "Disagree" with the statement, *"Race relations improved in America when Barack Obama became President."*

- An equal number of Asian Male respondents (37.50%) either "Strongly Agree / Agree" or were "Unsure" about the statement, *"Race played a factor in how Barack Obama was treated in his role as President."*

Findings by Age

- Nearly 3 out of 10 of all respondents, 18-24 years old (29.78%), "Strongly Disagree" or "Disagree" with the statement, *"President Obama was treated BETTER by a majority of Congress because of his race."*

- Half of all White Male respondents, 55 years and older (50.00%) "Strongly Agree" or "Agree" with the statement, *"President Obama was treated BETTER by a majority of the American people because of his race."*

- More than 4 out of 10 Hispanic Female respondents, ages 35-44 years old (40.47%), "Strongly Agree" or "Agree" with the statement, *"Race relations improved in America when Barack Obama became President."*

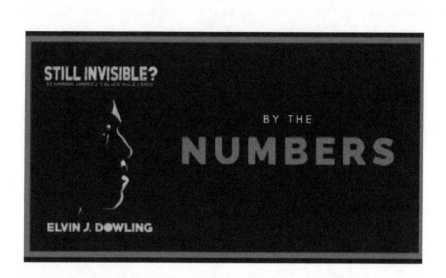

"Making Marks that Can't Be Erased?"

- In February 2009, Obama put forward a $787 billion economic stimulus package that brought America back from the brink or economic ruin, in the wake of the "Great Recession" (Amadeo).

- Championed by Obama as his signature domestic achievement, the *Affordable Care Act* revolutionized healthcare by offering insurance to 20 million people who were uninsured or had pre-existing conditions (Amadeo).

"Despite It All... Obama Stood Tall!"

- Barack Obama was the most castigated, condemned, mocked, insulted and degraded president in U.S. history. Among many scurrilous accusations, he was accused of being a "secret Muslim," and not a U.S. citizen (Stone).

- *Secret Service* protection for Barack Obama and his family began well before earning his party's nomination, based on the number of threats against him, the earliest the service has ever issued a security detail to a candidate (Zeleny).

"The Barack Obama Black-lash Was Real"

- According to *F.B.I.* statistics, there was an increase in hate crimes of 21% in the wake of Obama's election as president, with 9,160 crimes reported and 72.6% of all racially motivated crimes fueled by anti-Black bias (Duquesne).

- Many civil rights groups argue that the *F.B.I,* statistics are flawed, however, as they believe the number of hate crimes are much greater, as the *Bureau* relies on voluntary data provided by local and state officials (Duquesne).

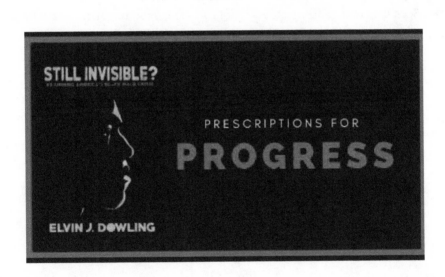

"Rebuild the Dream... Join the Team!"

- Ensure the 44th president's legacy endures by supporting the *Obama Foundation's* mission of building a Presidential Center, providing leadership training and "ensuring young men of color have pathways to opportunity" (Obama).

- Encourage young people, ages 18-25 years old, to connect to the *Obama Community Leadership Corps,* designed to "empower and train young people invested in their communities and eager to make a difference" (Obama).

"Stop the Violence... Increase the Peace!"

- Clearly insist that violence and violent rhetoric are absolutely unacceptable. Language normalizing violence is dangerous and further suggests to others that supporting violence helps them to belong (Kleinfeld).

- Encourage the news media to stop contributing to political polarization by treating every issue as "us vs. them." Rather, insist that they emphasize the complexity of policy outcomes which humanize fellow Americans (Kleinfeld).

"Don't Be Late... When Exposing Hate!"

- Seek help in organizing others to join you in combatting hate, which helps to reduce individual fear. Having allies in the struggle for social progress can be helpful in the fight to eradicate hate ("Fight Hate").

- Hate must always be exposed and rejected. Help news groups achieve balance and depth by providing alternative perspectives. Spread tolerance through social media and other tools, while also exposing animus ("Fight Hate").

Works Cited

1. Obama, Barack. "A More Perfect Union: Barack Obama's Speech on Race." *NPR.org*, 18 March 2008. https://n.pr/2tc7Yi1

2. Farley, Robert. "President Barack Obama Claims Mitch McConnell Says His Main Goal is for GOP to Regain the White House." *Politifact.com*, The Poynter Institute. 30 October 2010. http://bit.ly/36s9mes

3. Breslow, Jason M. "The Opposition Strategy."
   Apps.Frontline.org - *The FRONTLINE Interviews:*   *Divided States*
   of America, Public Broadcasting   Station (PBS). 17 January
   2017.   http://bit.ly/2YIx5oa

4. "President Barack Obama Is the Most Threatened President   in
   History." *DailyKos.com*, BlogPAC. 25 November   2012.
   http://bit.ly/2E8Qp4B

5. Elperin, Juliet. "Refusing to Give in to Hate."
   WashingtonPost.com, Nash Holdings. 31 March   2016.
   https://wapo.st/2rHa09a

6. Grunwald, Michael. "Everything is Awesome." *Politico.com,*
   Politico Magazine. 24 December 2014.
   https://politi.co/35pF9Ni

7. Smith, David. "The Anti-Obama: Trump's Drive to Destroy   His
   Predecessor's Legacy." *TheGuardian.com,*   Guardian News &
   Media Limited. 11 May 2018.   http://bit.ly/2RKn4p4

8. Zeleny, Jeff. "Secret Service Guards Obama, Taking
   Unusually Early Step." *NYTimes.com*, The New   York Times
   Company. 4 May 2007.
   https://nyti.ms/2LSIT1Q

9. Stone, Geoffrey. "Obama Faces Vile Insults Like No Other
   President Has." *ChicagoTribune.com*, Tribune   Publishing.
   11 December 2014.   http://bit.ly/2RUnPMi

10. Potter, Margaret. "Hate Crimes in the U.S., What do the
    Numbers Show?" *Sites.Law.Duq.edu*, Duquesne   Law. 10
    November 2018. http://bit.ly/2PnE

11. "Our Mission." *Obama.org*, Obama Foundation. Accessed 14
    December 2019. http://bit.ly/34kjcxH

12. Kleinfeld, Rachel. "A Short Primer on Preventing Political
    Violence." *CarnegieEndowment.org*, Carnegie   Endowment
    for International Peace. 4 October   2019.
    http://bit.ly/38GAvMz

13. "Ten Ways to Fight Hate: A Community Resource Guide."
    SPLCenter.org, Southern Poverty Law Center. 14   August 2017.
    http://bit.ly/34nai2v

Chapter 13: "Got Any I.D. On You?"

Investigating the Curious Relationship Between Black Men and the Police

❝

You cannot see or hear or smell the truth of what you see... To you he is a mark on the score-card of your achievement, a thing and not a man; a child, or even less – a black amorphous thing."

– Ralph Ellison, "Invisible Man" (Shmoop Editorial Team. 3.314)

(Fugitive slave patrols were groups of armed men in the South who were empowered to stop Blacks at any time and question their citizenship status. African-Americans were then required to show "manumission papers" allowing them permission to be away from their master's plantations—or proving that they were free men and women. Failure to do so could result in violent beatings and, for freed Blacks, enslavement.)

A Thin Line Between Black & Blue

"Can't We All Just... Get Along?"

Dr. Benjamin McLane Spock, an American physician and bestselling author, once said: *"Most middle-class whites have no idea what it feels like to be subjected to police who are routinely suspicious, rude, belligerent, and brutal."* As America continues to confront the obvious fissures dividing the African-American and law enforcement communities, the need to address what ails the peaceful coexistence of these two groups has emerged as a top priority for a nation struggling to become a more perfect union. In his groundbreaking book, "Two Nations: Black, White, Separate, Hostile & Unequal", author Andrew Hacker, an American political scientist and intellectual once accurately described the fraught relationship between minorities and the police when he observed the following: "When whites hear the phrase, *'The police are coming, the police are coming,'* there is an immediate sense of relief. When Blacks hear the phrase, *'The police are coming, the police are coming,'* there is an automatic sense fear", as generations of negative confluences of racism, discrimination and state sponsored violence color their perspective in ways that may never be understood by the mainstream majority of Americans. Just as much, the history of disparate treatment exhibited by American police towards communities of color has been one that is replete with examples of hapless (and helpless) Black people who have been victimized and sometimes killed, in fateful encounters with law enforcement officers. What's more, as America continues to export its values across the globe, the seemingly daily parade of "unarmed Black men shot by police" is truly not helping our image. All of this leads me to the logical conclusion that something must be done, and quickly, to bring us back from one public relations disaster too many.

Before proceeding, it's important for me to note that the majority of police officers in the United States work tirelessly--day in and day out--to ensure that we can all enjoy safe communities that allow us, as Americans, to live, learn and have our being. Moreover, the fact that they willingly place their lives on the line to protect and serve those who need it most, is both laudable and worthy of public commendation. Unfortunately, however, for African-Americans throughout the country, the generational fears they have of the law enforcement community is rooted in the sort of disparate treatment that should make even the most hardened among us wince in shame. Moreover, as Black men in America continue to endure both dehumanization and the indignities associated with being a part of a permanent "criminal class" every time they are asked to "step out of the car" for no apparent probable cause, the relationship between themselves and the police will remain clouded in dissension. Now, that is not to say that there are no Black males who participate in criminal activity. Obviously that's not true. But their rates of criminal activity are no more than any other group in the country (or the world for that matter). Yet, with arrest and incarceration statistics (and a constant media onslaught that rarely tells a different tale), it's hard for any reasonable person—Black or white—to presume otherwise.

So, here's what I propose... Why don't we call a truce? Let's just have everyone go back to their respective corners, Black men and police officers alike, take a "chill pill" and... Just. Calm. Down. Yes, there is anger on one side of the divide and fear on the other and, frankly I can understand why that's so. Hell, all you really have to do is turn on any television set or scroll your social media feed to both fear and loathe either group... but everybody ain't that bad. And not everyone is guilty either... so just cut it out already! For it is only when everyone comes to the table with a level head, and an open mind, willing to consider the idea that both a history of violence against, and an implicit bias towards, Black men in this country does, indeed, exist, nothing will change. And if nothing changes, one day, in the not too distant future, EVERYTHING could change when the tides turn on whites in America and "the rabbit is holding the gun." So, let's get it together people... time is of the essence!

Best wishes for our future,

Justitia

Lady Justice

Officer X: "Sworn to Protect and Serve"

Somebody Called the Police?

"For the sake of anonymity," the decorated police officer began, "I would like to be called *Officer X*, so that I may speak freely about the goings-on inside the law enforcement community," he requested, to which X was respectfully obliged. "I have been a Black police officer for more than twenty-five years. In doing so, I have patrolled every type of neighborhood you can think of, from the harshest inner-city ghettos, to white suburban enclaves and gated communities. As such, I've had a great perspective of what happens out there on the streets," X noted, reminiscing upon many of the beats he walked as a community police officer in the South. "As a child, I came from what I would now consider a poor family, but many at the time probably considered how we lived a lower middle-class existence," the policeman professed. "My mother and father both had a strong work ethic, and both of my parents were present in my life and played an important role in shaping and molding me," he went on.

Not known to mince his words, *Officer X* has spent a career protecting and serving people both in uniform and, when necessary, in civilian gear; fighting "the good fight of faith," with a zealous commitment to ensuring "justice for all" in the land of the free. One of the few law enforcement officers who can credibly claim to have "fought the law and won," X has successfully challenged authorities to change policy and praxis in the treatment of Black law enforcement officers and civilians, drawing the ire of his superiors and elected officials, and the adoration of the community he has served faithfully for more than a quarter-century. With that being said, however, *Officer X's* community crusading has not been without a cost to his own personal safety and peace of mind. To that end, X has often found himself the target of death threats by fellow police officers. In fact, the law abiding lawman has received harassing phone calls at home and other threatening gestures targeted squarely at him, by his fellow "brothers in blue" who, utilizing a proprietary system known as *"Google for cops,"* have sought, unsuccessfully, to silence *X's* vociferous advocacy for the African-American community and a fair application of the rule of law.

"Having other cops run your personal information, unbeknownst to you, simply because you stand up for what's right and insist on equality is alarming, to say the least," the fearless officer declared. "I have been investigated for the most ridiculous of alleged offenses, only to be cleared in the end. I have been unfairly treated as a police officer--by other police officers--and passed over for promotions and additional pay opportunities. To make things even worse, I have even been terminated when I dared to speak up for myself--and vindicated by a court of law in the end," X remarked. "Needless to say, it's not easy being vocal about the issues of racism and discrimination in places and institutions that have a history racism and discrimination," he professed. "But I can't _not_ speak up! When I see a wrong... I am generally inclined to right it. In that way," the decorated military veteran extolled, "I am a lot like my father. He was a man who spoke his mind (which was not easy to do during his era), yet he would tell anybody, with no uncertainty: *"I said... what I said!"*

"My father was born a sharecropper in the early 1900's, in a small town on the border of Florida and Georgia," explained X, a native southerner like his parents and grandparents before him. "He was a hardworking man all of his life, and demonstrated for me the fact that I could do anything I wanted to do if I was willing to work hard to achieve it," the police officer recalled. "Along with his two sisters and his mother, my grandmother, who was born in 1869, just four short years past the abolition of slavery, my father eked out a living harvesting collard greens, beans and vegetables. He did so," X continued, "on a farm owned by a white patrician who thought it was noble of himself to allow them to work for scraps on his plantation," the lawman noted. "With only a mule and a plow, they were able to make just enough money and food to survive, but that was about it. In fact, his grandmother, my great-grandmother, was a slave," the lawman lamented; calling attention to his own proximity to America's most dreaded institution.

"People think it was just a long time ago, but the long arm of slavery continues to touch generations of Americans even today," *Officer X* concluded. "A courageous man all of his life, my father lived to be 95 years old—experiencing America at a time when Black men were preferred to be seen and not heard," *Officer X* declared proudly. "He didn't have the opportunities that I have had to experience the world and also make a difference here at home, as a member of both the military and the police--something he could never dream of doing when he was a child. You see, the police, for him, represented an unyielding authority that was not always a positive force in the community, especially the Black community," *X* observed.

From a historical perspective, the very genesis of American policing (particularly in the South), was borne out of a need to catch and return runaway slaves during the nineteenth century. For *X's* great-grandparents, however, the constant threat of mean-spirited lawmen looking to exact a vicious toll, more often than not for kicks and grins, was a reality they lived with daily. In 1850, the *United States Congress* passed the *Fugitive Slave Act*, as a part of the "Compromise of 1850" between Southern slave-holding states and Northern "Free Soilers" which permitted the recapture and re-enslavement of "persons escaping the service of their masters." In short, if and when an enslaved African--who came to the United States through forced migration--determined that he or she no longer wanted to be whipped, chained and sold at the whims of another human being, decided to run away, they could be hunted down by groups of armed men with shackles and chains and forcibly returned back to permanent subjugation. In fact, even if that formerly enslaved individual found their way to "freedom" in U.S. states north of the Mason-Dixon line, fugitive slave catchers were empowered to abruptly end their quest for asylum in supposedly "free states" at any moment, returning them to a life of misery and servitude.

The origin of modern-day policing is one that has taken two separate and distinct paths in its formative years, depending upon the geographical context in which individual police groups emerged. More specifically, police departments in the North were often organized and structured; with full-time employees and unformed patrols empowered to warn communities about impending danger. In fact, the first official police force began in the "Cradle of Liberty," Boston Massachusetts, in 1838. Following Beantown's formation, police departments sprang up all across northern locales, including: New York City (1845), Chicago (1851), Philadelphia (1855) and Baltimore (1857). Furthermore, according to "The History of Policing in the United States, Part 1", Dr. Gary Potter, a professor at the Eastern Kentucky University's School of Justice Studies, clarified that the concept of organized policing required a series of steps be taken in order to be perceived as credible by community standards.

"These "modern police" organizations", Potter observed, "shared similar characteristics: (1) they were publicly supported and bureaucratic in form; (2) police officers were full-time employees, not community volunteers or case-by-case fee retainers; (3) departments had permanent and fixed rules and procedures, and employment as a police officers was continuous; (4) police departments were accountable to a central governmental authority" (Potter). In the South, however, the path that policing took was much more informal, leading to a brutalizing culture within the "law enforcement" community, filled with "officers" working in a voluntary capacity, or sometimes for hire; many of whom used brute force and sheer violence to keep all Black people in line, whether they were breaking the law or not.

In his article, "Slavery and the Origins of the American Police State", journalist Ben Fountain of Medium, explained how the system of policing in the South took an ugly turn, particularly as it related to its treatment of Blacks. Moreover, the measure of violence meted out was wanton, cruel and fueled by white supremacy and notions of 'taming black savages.' "Slave patrols usually consisted of three to six white men on horseback equipped with guns, rope, and whips," Fountain wrote. "A mounted man presents an awesome figure, and the power and majesty of a group of men on horseback, at night, could terrify slaves into submission," writes Sally Hadden in her fine and useful book Slave Patrols: Law and Violence in Virginia and the Carolinas. Among other duties," Fountain found, "paddyrollers enforced the pass system, which required all slaves absent from their master's property to have a pass, or "ticket," signed by the master indicating permission for travel. Any slave encountered without a pass was subject to detention and beating on the spot, although possession of a valid pass was by no means a guarantee against beating" (Fountain).

According to Fountain's analysis of Hadden's historical work, when individuals were granted certain authorities to do whatever they wanted to do--to other human beings--for the most morally indefensible of reasons, simply because they could, it often led to disastrous results for their intended targets. "[O]ne imagines moreover that gratuitous beatings relieved the tedium and fatigue of nightlong patrols and served to reinforce the notion of who was boss" (Fountain). To create an even heavier presence in an already terrorized Black population, local volunteer officers, often known as "paddyrollers" barged their way into the sleeping quarters of both enslaved and free Blacks, to enforce social norms. "Authority extended to patrolling plantation grounds and entering slave quarters, where the presence of books, writing paper, weapons, liquor, luxury items, or more than the usual store of provisions was cause for beating," the article observed. "Gatherings"—weddings, funerals, church services—were grounds for beating, writes Hadden. Mingling with whites, especially poor whites, or any "loose, disorderly or suspected person": beating. Back talk: beating. Dressing tidily: beating. Singing certain hymns: beating. Even best behavior could earn a lick" (Fountain). After the close of slavery, the loosely formed gangs of roving "law enforcement" mobs were ultimately replaced by groups like the *Ku Klux Klan*, "whose white robes, flaming torches, and queer pseudo-ghost talk were intended for maximum terrorizing effect" (Fountain).

Nothing to See Here?

Today, the perception that policing in the United States has morphed into an amalgamation of the two modalities (i.e. formal and state-sanctioned, and informal and fueled by mob rule), continues to be an issue that remains largely unaddressed to the satisfaction of Blacks in America. In a report published by *The Economist* magazine called, "America's Police on Trial: The United States Needs to Overhaul its Law-Enforcement System," the magazine noted that the gulf of trust in the police which exists between Blacks and whites in America, is as wide as the Mississippi River. "Some 59% of white Americans have confidence in the police, but only 37% of blacks do. This is poisonous," *The Economist* delineated, "if any racial group distrusts the enforcers of the law, it erodes the social contract... But racial division, rooted as it is in America's past, is not easily mitigated" ("Police On Trial"). Moreover, even though police departments are supposed to be employed by officers of the law who are judicious and fair in the administration of their duties, many forces have been infiltrated by white supremacist believers who often use the color of authority to continue terrorizing Blacks in America.

In an ominous warning to both law enforcement communities as well as the general public, the *Federal Bureau of Investigation* raised significant and material concerns about the continued burrowing of racist elements within the heart and soul of police departments all across the country. "In [a] 2006 bulletin, the *F.B.I.* detailed the threat of white nationalists and skinheads infiltrating police in order to disrupt investigations against fellow members and recruit other supremacists," reported Kenya Downs, a digital reporter and senior producer for *PBS NewsHour's* "Race Matters" and education verticals, in her story, "FBI Warned of White Supremacists ion Law Enforcement 10 Years Ago, Has Anything Changed?" "The bulletin was released during a period of scandal for many law enforcement agencies throughout the country, including a neo-Nazi gang formed by members of the *Los Angeles County Sheriff's Department* who harassed Black and Latino communities. Similar investigations revealed officers and entire agencies with hate group ties in Illinois, Ohio and Texas" (Downs). Even still, neither the *F.B.I.* nor local police agencies have taken any meaningful steps to vet law enforcement personnel for links to white supremacy, leaving that task up to social justice organization s and social media advocates to reveal the ties and bring them to the attention of authorities.

Today, the problem with the historic challenges between law enforcement officials and Black men is the fact that, more than 150 years past the institution of slavery, long since the midnight raids of the *Ku Klux Klan*, well past the passage of American civil rights laws that created a theoretically equitable society, and more than a decade since the election of the nation's first Black President, very little has been done to change the dynamics of the "black and blue" relationship. In fact, exasperating the fissures between the two groups are the evidence-based disparities in the application of the law itself, which include: the use of deadly force, violations of due process, racial profiling and other divisive and potentially illegal tactics that are used to ensnare criminals and law abiding citizens alike. For Black Americans, however, the overzealous nature of American policing oftentimes results in a dragnet that scoops up otherwise productive members of society whose primary crime was, apparently, being Black in America. Moreover, in today's era of digital technology, this issue has never been more pronounced; resulting in America seeing with its own eyes what Black men and women have shouted from the rooftops for generations--the fact that Black people in America are unduly treated with violence and cruelty at the hands of those who are sworn to "protect and serve" them. For law and order men like *Officer X*, however, what America is now experiencing with the persistent visual images depicting police violence against Black men is due, in large part, to the proliferation of digital technology; no longer making claims of police brutality it a "cop vs. criminal" version of events.

"Nowadays, because we see images of violence against Black men and women by the police every time we turn around, everybody now believes that police brutality is a new phenomenon," *Officer X* noted. "Clearly it's not a new phenomenon and, if there is anyone who truly believes that, they are--in my opinion--either a racist or are completely illiterate... or maybe both at the same time," he concluded. "Technology has just brought this all to the forefront of the American consciousness," *X* proclaimed. "Having been a cop on the job for most of my professional career, I have rarely seen an instance in which a white suspect is shot, let alone have guns drawn on them, without having first been a clear and present danger to the life of the officer," *Officer X* continued. "So, what you are seeing, in terms of the treatment of Black men by the police, are not anomalies. It is, what it is," he said.

In a thought provoking opinion piece for the *Washington Post* by Ranjana Natarajan, a clinical professor and director of the Civil Rights Clinic at *The University of Texas School of Law*, such arbitrary and capricious treatment of minorities in America by police departments all across the country, have had a devastating impact upon the lives of helpless Black males who often have very little recourse and zero benefit of the doubt when an encounter between the two entities goes awry. "Excessive force by police persists despite the *Constitution's* prohibition on unreasonable searches and seizures," Natarajan reported. "In lawsuits and investigations, the *U.S. Department of Justice* has concluded that a number of major police departments have engaged in a pattern or practice of excessive force. The *Cleveland Police Department* was...

found to be an offender, but it follows a long line of other wayward law enforcement agencies: Seattle, New Orleans, Portland, Newark and Albuquerque among them" (Natarajan).

The *Leadership Conference on Civil Rights,* in a 2011 report on racial profiling called attention to the issue of the disparate treatment of adverse law enforcement actions being visited upon minorities in America at alarming rates, demonstrating that Blacks and Latinos are stopped disproportionately and oftentimes illicitly searched for drugs and other illegal items. "In Illinois, for example, Black and Hispanic drivers were twice as likely to be searched after a traffic stop compared to white drivers, but white drivers were twice as likely to have contraband," Natarajan noted. The *NYPD's* controversial stop-and-frisk program shows similar evidence of racial profiling, with police targeting Blacks and Latinos about 85 percent of the time. In nearly nine out of 10 searches, police find nothing" (Natarajan). Even African-American police officers, many of whom hail from similar circumstances akin to *Officer X,* have been known to aggressively enforce community norms in a way that impacts Black and brown communities harshly.

Nearly fifty years of empirical research has indicated that both Blacks and Whites, in equal proportion, have unconsciously associated "blackness" itself in a negative way, literally coloring the lenses though which they view all Black people in general, and African-American men in particular. Just as significantly, research has also indicated that police officers, who are not immune to the social norms, attitudes and opinions of the general public, are also not immune from implicit racial bias, which sometimes dictates how they may interact with the minority civilian population--even when the police officer happens to be a minority themselves. In an analysis of the book, "The Black Police: Policing Our Own", the *Harvard Law Review* found that Black officers sometimes overstep their bounds when policing majority Black neighborhoods. "Evidence shows that police departments with more Black officers engage in more racial profiling than those with fewer Black officers," the *Harvard Law Review* found. "Data indicates that Black officers are just as likely as their white colleagues to form nonbehavioral suspicions about Black suspects, and that Black officers who stop a Black man are more likely to arrest him than they are to arrest a stopped white suspect. The foregoing might explain why there is only limited evidence that police forces with more minority officers show more equitable patterns of policing," the *Review* concluded. But it is not only the physical violence that is visited upon Black and brown populations by overzealous law enforcement officers, that hurts these communities in profound ways, it's also the economic assaults many minorities experience, via hidden taxes they are forced the pay, through tickets and fines imposed upon them as they simply seek to exist and go about their business. Moreover, from a brass-tacks perspective, oftentimes the priorities of the officers who actively target poor and vulnerable populations, regardless of the race of the officer, are more likely than not driven by higher authorities demanding that officers meet quotas, reduce crime, and fill government coffers... by any means necessary.

In an exposé written by Tess Owen of *Vice News* laying bare the tactics used by a small New Jersey township that created a cottage industry and lucrative revenue stream for the municipality's expanding budget by aggressively targeting African-American and Latino drivers, the issue of police overreach and unconstitutional behavior came to the surface in a way that was clearly undeniable. In fact, according to the report, unsuspecting Black and brown motorists were intentionally targeted for enforcement of even the most minor of civic violations, all of which resulted in an economic boon for the town. In uncovering the unseemly practice, students from *Seton Hall University*, located just seven miles southwest of Bloomfield, New Jersey, the municipality in question, conducted a series of experiments in which they looked at the number of drivers that were stopped and ticketed to see what, if any, anomalies they would uncover. That task would not be easy, however, as New Jersey police officers are not mandated to record the race or ethnicity of an individual on the traffic citation being issued to them, thus requiring the students to attend local court proceedings and gather the data themselves, to which the students willingly obliged; spending more than four weeks of court proceedings to get answers to the questions they were asking.

"Researchers sat in on about 70 hours of hearings and observed 855 ticketed individuals, according to their report. During their observations, they made note of the ethnicity, age, gender, and area of residence for each person who showed up," *Vice News* reported. "The researchers found that Black and Latino drivers were being disproportionately ticketed, accounting for 78 percent of court appearances for traffic violations, despite comprising roughly 43 percent of Bloomfield's population" (Vice News). Moreover, based on the average cost of $137 for each ticket issued by the *Bloomfield Township Police*, minority motorists paid a substantial amount of money in fines issued by the locality. "The *Seton Hall* researchers' calculations suggest that Black and Latino drivers would have paid over $1 million to *Bloomfield Municipal Court* between 2014 and 2015, with Newark and East Orange residents coughing up about $400,000 of the total. The court's budgeted salaries were projected to have more than doubled from $350,600 to more than $760,000 within the same span" (Vice News). In short, by heavily taxing unsuspecting motorists, the small New Jersey enclave was able to expand its municipal staff and operations considerably, often at the expense of poor and vulnerable individuals. For *Officer X*, however, a lawman known within his community as being fair to all and biased towards none, the most effective way to change the nature of policing in America is to change the complexion of the police force itself; through the identification and hiring of more compassionate officers of color. The goal, in *X's* estimation, should be to force "the force" to become more equitable institutions that provide access and opportunity for those men and women of color who have courage and are willing to lay their lives on the line for the protection of others--similar to what he experienced as a soldier in the *United States Army*.

"In 1986," *Officer X* detailed, "I enlisted as a soldier in the *United States Army*. During that time, the U.S. military was, perhaps, the most diverse institution in America, with fifty percent of the noncommissioned officers being men and women of color. For me, this made the Army a place of relative solace from racial animus, particularly with regard to leadership and promotion opportunities," he observed. "In fact, the military was the *least racist* place for a young Black male to be at the time, which was partially why I joined the *Army*. With that being said," *Officer X* remarked, "it should be noted that the majority of the awards and medals, in my experience, seemed to go to the white soldiers that I served with. Even still, I would venture to say that this was one of the few times in my life I was able to operate with a sense of liberty that I have yet to experience as an African-American member of the civilian population," *Officer X* maintained.

"The great thing about the military is the fact that, when a soldier is in the heat of battle, race plays no role in helping one another to stay alive," he observed. Today, as a Black police officer working in what often feels like occupied territories to the residents of communities that are zealously over-policed, the man who once patrolled military outposts in such far-flung places as Iraq and South Korea, is sensitive to the challenges of the young men of color with whom he interacts with every day. Moreover, as he strives to walk a fine line while fulfilling the mission of higher headquarters command, in this instance the state, which has empowered him to enforce law and order on scofflaws and law abiding citizens alike, *Officer X* does so ever mindful of the fact that he is often viewed as persona non grata on both sides of the thin blue line. "I learned very quickly as a police officer that every day when I go to work, I have a position to play. The same thing applies to life. Whenever I encounter a young Black male in performing my duties as a law enforcement officer, my first goal is <u>not </u>to arrest him," *X* stated. "My first goal," the sympathetic public servant said, "is to try to educate him on what may be the error of his ways and talk to him about changing his behavior. The challenge I face, however, as a Black police officer, is that I am *'damned if I do, and damned if I don't'* and my intentions are doubted regardless," *Officer X* acknowledged. "For example," he elaborated, "there was an African-American police officer who was killed in the line of duty in Louisiana. Before he died, however, he posted on social media that he often received hateful looks from people he didn't know, and who didn't know him. And when he was not at work," *X* went on, "and out of uniform, there were those who were very afraid of him... simply because he was Black. I can relate," the longtime lawman conceded, "because I get that all the time."

"When I am patrolling the streets of my city, working hard to help make it a better place to live and raise kids, I get people looking at me with scorn and they don't know anything about me," *Officer X* bemoaned. "When I'm out of uniform, I have people looking at me like I'm going to steal something from them, and they make a point of walking in the other direction--away from me! So, I am invisible everywhere I go, even as a police officer," he said. "Furthermore, in my considered opinion," X observed, "many police officials are inherently racist people and it is exhibited in their hiring practices," *X* lamented. "Even in a city that has a majority Black population, the police force is oftentimes overwhelmingly white. And there's a reason for that," the decorated officer continued. "As a police officer, we have two of the greatest powers vested in an individual in this country: the power to take someone's freedom and, in the right conditions (or the wrong conditions), the power to take someone's life," *Officer X* explained. "So even in majority Black cities, with a Black mayor and a Black city council, it still results in a predominantly white force to police their people. In my view," X opined, "demographics should play a significant part in the hiring and diversity at the police department.

"There are always those folks who say they can't find good Black police officers," *Officer X* theorized, "and will give you every excuse in the world as to why they can't be located for hiring purposes. But if it was a major university football team, there's never a problem finding able Black bodies to do the job," he remarked. "So, to all of those who say *'we can't find them'*, why is it you never have a problem finding Black men to trot off to war?," he queried. These folks never have a problem finding brothers to fill the ranks of the *Coast Guard*, or the *Marines*, or *Navy*, or the *Army*, or the *Air Force*! Yet," *Officer X* elucidated, "when it comes to hiring those same young Black men as police officers within our communities, the system is designed to eliminate them from consideration. They do so," he explained, "by washing these candidates out of the academy for bogus reasons, such as psychological issues, or simply having too many traffic tickets," he noted. "And if you think about it, being a police officer is a damn good job. We get great benefits, healthcare, pension plans... you name it. These are also coveted jobs and limited in number, so the feeding frenzy that occurs oftentimes leaves Black candidates as the "odd men out" over and over again," X conceded. But even when officers like X break through the steel wall and make it to the other side of the "thin blue line," they are met with subtle and sometimes jarring reminders that they are "there by grace" and should be "appreciative of the privilege."

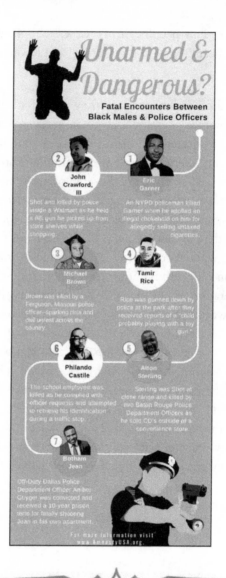

You Think You're One of Us?

In spite of the power that comes with being an agent of the law in the United States of America, the uniform worn by police officers of color does not always make the difference when *they* are the targets of undue police aggression. In one glaring instance in New York City, for example, plainclothes police officers were disciplined for mistreating the city's highest-ranking Black cop, a three-star chief, who was profiled and detained as he minded his own business on a busy city street. According to a news story published by the New York Daily News, in an innocuous headline called, "Plainclothes Officers in Trouble - Didn't Recognize Off-Duty Chief," the issue of police overreach is as real for Black police officers as it is for Black citizens. Based on media posts, Chief Douglas Zeigler of the *New York Police Department* was sitting in his *NYPD*-issued vehicle near a fire hydrant when he was approached by two plainclothes police officers around 7 p.m. that evening. "In his briefing to Police Commissioner Raymond Kelly," the *Daily News* reported, "Zeigler said the two cops, who are white, had no legitimate reason to approach his SUV, ranking sources said. After they ordered him to get out, one officer did not believe the *NYPD* identification Zeigler gave him," continuing to harass and detain the high-ranking law enforcement official ("Off-Duty"). What the decorated Black police chief experienced, however, was mild in comparison to what has happened to other African-American officers who have had the misfortune of being stopped whilst out of uniform or, even worse, accosted while on the job, by fellow law enforcement officers who could care less about the implications of targeting, harassing and even physically assaulting fellow Black police officers.

A notable example of the hatred that can blur the lines between "black and blue," particularly as it relates to how some white officers have mistreated some Black officers (and gotten away with it), occurred during the fall of 2006. In that particular case, Cariol Horne, then a 19-year decorated police officer for the *Buffalo Police Department* in upstate New York, was beaten by a white colleague when she attempted to prevent him from brutalizing an already subdued subject. According to an article in the *Daily Mail*, Horne, a Black woman, responded to a call for assistance from her colleague, Officer Gregory Kwiatkowski, a white male, who was at the scene of a domestic dispute. Upon arrival, Horne witnessed Kwiatkowski violently punching a handcuffed suspect, an African-American male, in the face. What happened next, in Horne's own words, was a violent response to a woman of decency and valor, who would be forced to endure two assaults; one at the hands of her colleague, the other at the hands of her superiors. *"Gregory Kwiatkowski turned [the suspect] around and started choking him. So then I'm like, 'Greg! You're choking him,' because I thought whatever happened in the house he was still upset about so when he didn't stop choking him I just grabbed his arm from around [the suspect's] neck,"* Horne told WKBW ("Daily Mail"). Enraged that she had the temerity to challenge his blatant violation of a Black man's civil and human rights,

Kwiatkowski then proceeded to turn his fury on Horne, punching her squarely in her face. "The punch so was hard that Horne ended up having to have her bridge replaced. She was then injured again as officers dragged her away from trying to defend herself," the *Daily Mail* reported. And then things really took a turn for the worse...

Upon review of the incident by *Buffalo Police Department* brass, the higher-ups determined that it was, in fact, Horne who was wrong for having defended herself, subsequently firing her "for cause" from the department she had served with distinction for nearly two decades. In essence, the "good cop," who was trying to stop abuse by her peer, was fired for "jumping on Officer Kwiatkowski's back striking him with her hands," something that Kwiatkowski himself denied ever happening in a sworn statement (*"Daily Mail"*). As for the "bad cop," an individual who readily admitted to choking a handcuffed suspect and then punching his female co-worker in the face? He was allowed to keep his job after the shameful incident. "It wasn't until he choked another officer at a district station house that he was forced to retire. He was already under investigation for punching another officer while he was off-duty at a local bar" (*"Daily Mail"*).

In another example of questionable force being used against outnumbered Black law enforcement officers by some of their white counterparts, Howard Morgan, a detective for the *Burlington Northern Santa Fe Railroad*, was shot and left for dead by *Chicago Police Department* officers in 2005, after having been pulled over for allegedly driving down the wrong side of the street. "According to police, Morgan opened fire with his service weapon when officers tried to arrest him, which caused them to shoot him 28 times," the *HuffPost* reported. "After being left for dead, he survived and was then charged with attempted murder of the four white officers who brutalized him" (*"HuffPost"*). Eventually, Morgan would be acquitted of three of the four counts against him, but not before paying a heavy price for having the gall to challenge his fellow brothers in blue. "The same jury that cleared him of opening fire on the officers, however, deadlocked on a charge of attempted murder" (*"HuffPost"*). In fact, the 2007 mixed decision sent shock waves through the law enforcement community, causing prosecutors to re-charge Morgan with attempted murder, resulting in his ultimate conviction in 2012. Unsurprisingly, during Morgan's second trial, to which he vociferously protested under double jeopardy rules, a number of procedural roadblocks were conveniently constructed for the defense ultimately leading to the former Black police officer soon becoming a convicted felon in the eyes of State of Illinois. Additionally, according to the *HuffPost* article, many of the "anomalies" that Morgan experienced during his second trial, included the following successful legal machinations:

- *That second jury was never allowed to hear the fact that Morgan had been acquitted of the other charges in a previous trial ("HuffPost").*

- *The van that Howard Morgan was driving at the time of his law enforcement encounter was inexplicably crushed and destroyed without notice or cause before any forensic investigation was performed ("HuffPost").*

- *Morgan was never tested for gunshot residue to confirm whether or not he actually if he even fired a weapon on the morning in question ("HuffPost").*

- *The State never produced the actual bullet proof vest worn by one of the officers who claimed to have allegedly taken a shot directly into the vest on the morning in question. The State only produced a replica ("HuffPost")*

As a result of the second trial, for the same set of criminal charges, Howard Morgan, who was found guilty of attempted murder on fellow police officers, having shot one of the four cops who also shot him, during the fracas. To that end, as punishment for the crimes with which he was charged, Morgan would receive multiple Draconian sentences for daring to fight for his life; including one for 40 years, another for 35 years and two others for 25 years for attempted murder and discharging a firearm at a police officer. Because the sentences were to be served concurrently, Morgan was expected to spend the next 40 years of his life in prison. As a 61- year old soon-to-be retired police officer, the punishment amounted to a death sentence for the sexagenarian, before fate and politics intervened. In 2015 Governor Pat Quinn of Illinois, on his last day in office, commuted Morgan's sentence to "time served" (much to the dismay of the law enforcement community). When considering the fate of similarly situated African-Americans like Howard Morgan, a police officer caught in a life and death struggle in which guns were used to the detriment of all involved, it may be easy for one to assume that law enforcement officials like *Officer X*, are in favor of fewer guns in America--particularly guns placed in the hands of America's most feared population, but that assumption would be incorrect.

"As a Black police officer, I am very aware of the fact that there are too many guns being used against innocent people in our communities, and that needs to stop," *Officer X* bemoaned; explaining the myriad of challenges gun violence continues to have on poor and disadvantaged neighborhoods. "Be that as it may, however, I believe that the best way for African-Americans to protect themselves against the racism and hatred that I see every day on the streets (and on the police force) is for them to be responsible gun owners. Every single household," X implored. "You see, the only reason we have the *First Amendment,* and the rest of our *Bill of Rights*, is because we have a *Second Amendment* that protects them all," said the well-armed former military man. "In my estimation, the only real way for Black people in America to ensure that their freedom is always secured against the tyranny of the majority is if we stay vigilant, stay prepared and, for God's sakes, stay armed!" On that note, however, *Officer X* also believes that the need for African-American men to center themselves and focus their efforts on a community in desperate need of men to fill a critical leadership void.

"As I reflect upon the many words of wisdom that I could impart upon Black males in this country, I have but one critical message I want to leave and hope that they will follow, which is very simple—don't forget *who you are*," X maintained. "And don't forget *where you came from*," he admonished "Be concerned with the issues that are impacting your own community and don't focus all of your energy being worried about everybody else and what they are doing," he went on. "Take care of you and yours. Make sure you help yourself and your own people first, before you worry about anybody else. Finally," X implored, "I would encourage Black males everywhere to never forget about the Black women who helped us to become the men we are today," he declared.

"You know," *Officer X* cautioned, "a lot of people would say that my next statement is racist, but I would encourage Black men to--if possible--marry a black woman," he declared. "*She* is who *you* came from," he continued. "Now, there is nothing wrong with anybody else, but too many Black men, when they make it in America, leave our Black women behind. As soon as we get noticed by society," X theorized, "or get a lot of money, we forget about our sisters. I think we can do a better job of remembering them when we get to where we are going," he concluded. "I truly believe that God loves everybody, but if you can... *if* you can, **love** and **marry** a Black woman!"

("Officer X": Police Official & Public Servant)

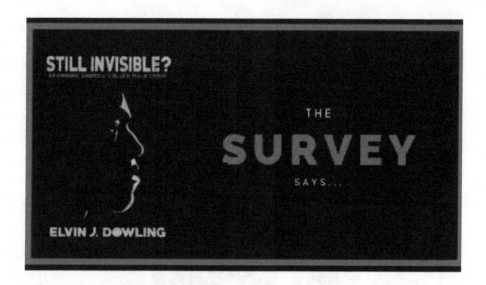

How strongly do you agree or disagree with the following statements?*

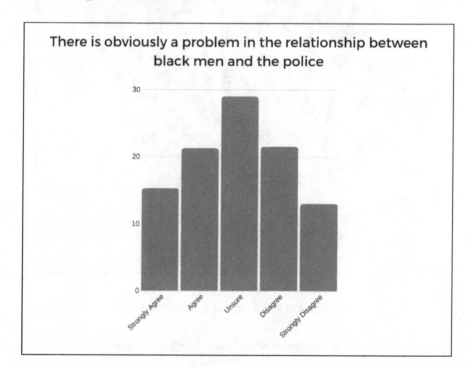

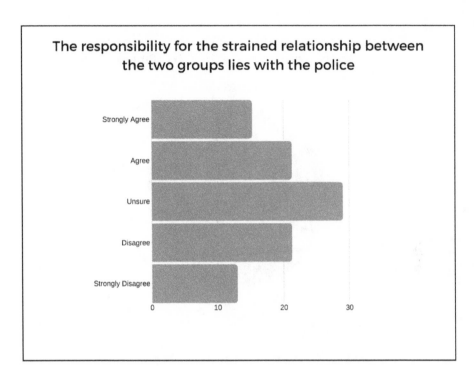

The responsibility for the strained relationship between the two groups lies with the police

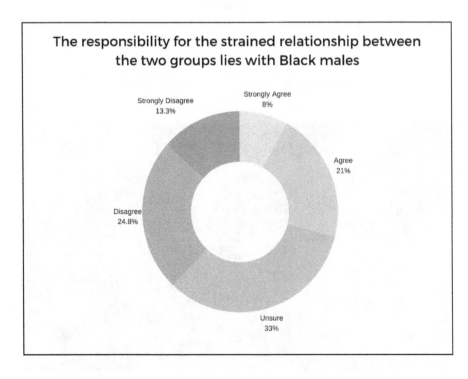

The responsibility for the strained relationship between the two groups lies with Black males

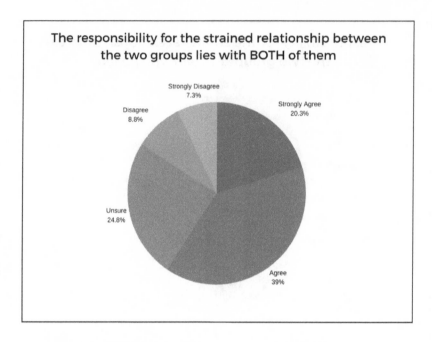

The responsibility for the strained relationship between the two groups lies with BOTH of them

Strongly Disagree 7.3%

Disagree 8.8%

Strongly Agree 20.3%

Unsure 24.8%

Agree 39%

All survey results displayed above are represented by the overall percentage of survey respondents. For more information on our survey methodology, please see the Author's Note, located in the front matter of the book. To review raw survey results, visit: http://bit.ly/stillinvisiblesurvey.

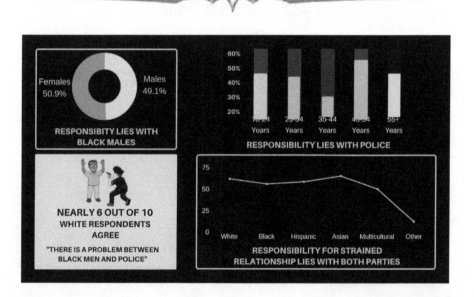

Females 50.9%   Males 49.1%

RESPONSIBITY LIES WITH BLACK MALES

RESPONSIBILITY LIES WITH POLICE

18-24 Years   25-34 Years   35-44 Years   45-54 Years   55+ Years

NEARLY 6 OUT OF 10 WHITE RESPONDENTS AGREE

"THERE IS A PROBLEM BETWEEN BLACK MEN AND POLICE"

White   Black   Hispanic   Asian   Multicultural   Other

RESPONSIBILITY FOR STRAINED RELATIONSHIP LIES WITH BOTH PARTIES

Findings by Race

- More than 3 out of 4 of all Black respondents (76.92%), "Strongly Agree" or "Agree" with the statement, *"There is obviously a problem in the relationship between Black men and the police."*

- Over half of all Asian respondents (55.00%) "Strongly Agree" or "Agree" with the statement, *"The responsibility for the strained relationship between the two groups lies with the police."*

- Nearly 1 out of 3 Hispanic respondents (31.94%) "Strongly Agree" or "Agree" with the statement, *"The responsibility for the strained relationship between the two groups lies with Black males."*

Findings by Gender

- 6 out of 10 White male respondents (60.50%),"Strongly Agree" or "Agree" with the statement, *"The responsibility for the strained relationship between the two groups lies with BOTH of them."*

- 6 out of 10 of all Female respondents (60.00%), "Strongly Agree" or "Agree" with the statement, *"There is obviously a problem in the relationship between Black men and the police."*

- Multiracial male respondents unanimously agree (100.00%) with the statement, *"The responsibility for the strained relationship between the two groups lies with the police."*

Findings by Age

- Nearly half of all male respondents, ages 55 years and older (46.51%) are "Unsure" about the statement, *"The responsibility for the strained relationship between the two groups lies with Black males."*

- Nearly half of all respondents, 18-24 years old (48.94%) "Strongly Agree" or "Agree" with the statement, *"The responsibility for the strained relationship between the two groups lies with BOTH of them."*

- 6 out of 10 Hispanic female respondents (60.00%), "Strongly Agree" or "Agree" with the statement, *"There is obviously a problem in the relationship between Black men and the police."*

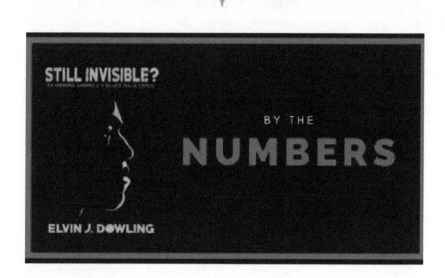

"From Paddy Rollers... to Law Enforcers!"

- Slavery and the control of minorities, including slave patrols and night watches, were two of the foundational pillars of American society shaping early policing and the evolution of modern police departments ("American Policing").

- In 1871, even after Congress passed the *Ku Klux Klan Act*, which prohibited state actors, including police officers, from Klan membership, many cops maintained their allegiance and terrorism persisted ("American Policing").

"Stakes Are Dire? Numbers Are Higher!"

- States that have increased rates of racial segregation, imprisonment, educational credentials, economic disparity, and high unemployment also tend to have higher levels of police violence against Blacks ("Police Shootings").

- African American males are 2.5 times more likely to be killed by police than whites. According to estimates, 1-in-1,000 Black males will be killed by police in their lifetime, and 39 out of 100,000 for whites ("Police Shootings").

"Cutting No Slack Because We're Black!"

- Although the number of minority police officers in U.S. has nearly doubled from 15% to 27% between 1987 and 2013, research indicates that diversity doesn't equate to improved relations between the two groups. ("Racial Makeup").

- Based on statistics, there is no difference in the use of excessive force by Black and white officers. Research also suggests Black officers are more likely to make arrests of Black suspects than are white officers ("Racial Makeup").

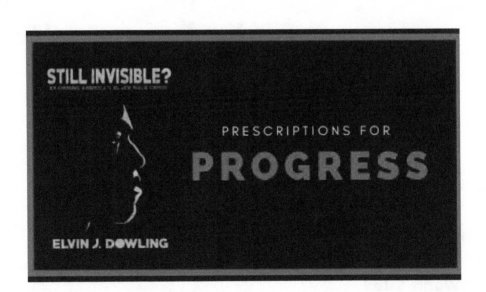

"Insist That Cops Make Bias Stop"

- Demand that strong anti-profiling laws and policies be implemented, to include training officers on the elimination of bias, data collection on traffic stops, and the development of accountability systems (Natarajan).

- Understand that there are *still* police officials and others in leadership and management who don't believe implicit bias is an issue. Insist on awareness training, at all levels, beginning with police leadership ("Implicit Bias").

"Diversify Hiring... But Insist Upon Quality!"

- Insist that cities and municipalities begin to re-evaluate employment criteria, standards, and benchmarks to ensure that they are tailored to attract, select, and retain the most desirable police officer candidates ("Advancing Diversity").

- Encourage those who govern your local police department to reconsider selection criteria that disproportionately screens out underrepresented populations within the community ("Advancing Diversity").

"Open Up... Let the Public In!"

- Demand that local officials insist that police officers employ techniques and other tactics and alternatives to the use of force, including strategies to reduce the likelihood of lethal engagement ("Policing Practices").

- Lobby legislatures to require judges to preside over grand jury proceedings, and to open records to the public of proceedings in police use of force cases ("Policing Practices").

Works Cited

1. Shmoop Editorial Team. "Invisible Man Identity Quotes. 3.314" *Shmoop*. Shmoop University, Inc., 10 July.   2008. Web. 25 Jul. 2019.

2. Potter, Gary. "The History of Policing in the United States, Part 1." *PLSOnline.EKU.edu*, Eastern Kentucky   University - Police Studies Online. 25 June 2013.   http://bit.ly/2PBHE9q

3. Fountain, Ben. "Slavery and the Origins of the American Police State." *Medium.com*, A Medium Corporation. 17 September 2018. http://bit.ly/36JUZlO

4. "America's Police on Trial: The United States Needs to Overhaul its Law-Enforcement System." *Economist.com*, The Economist Group. 11 December 2014. https://econ.st/2Qc6coX

5. Downs, Kenya. "FBI Warned of White Supremacists in Law Enforcement 10 Years ago. Has Anything Changed?" *PBS.org*, PBS News Hour. 21m October 2016. https://to.pbs.org/2Qa5Yyq

6. Natajaran, Ranjana. "Racial Profiling Has Destroyed Public Trust In Police. Cops Are Exploiting Our Weak Laws Against It." *WashingtonPost.com*, Nash Holdings. 15 December 2014. https://wapo.st/2PIqven

7. Owen, Tess. "Driving While Black: Cops Target Minority Drivers in This Mostly White New Jersey Town." *Vice.com*, Vice Media. 11 April 2016. http://bit.ly/2sSPsL2

8. Carbado, Devon and Richardson, L. Song. "The Black Police: Policing Our Own." *HarvardLawReview.org*, The Harvard Law Review Association. 10 May 2018. http://bit.ly/2EC21gJ

9. Gendar, Alison. "Plainclothes Officers in Trouble - Didn't Recognize Off-Duty Chief." *NYDailyNews.com*, Tribune Publishing. 10 May 2008. http://bit.ly/2Q3aU88

10. Spargo, Chris. "Police Officer 'Fired After 19 Years on the Force for Trying to Stop Fellow Cop from Choking and Punching Handcuffed Black Suspect in the Face'" *DailyMail.com.uk*, Daily Mail and General Trust. 23 December 2014. https://dailym.ai/2ZbIOff

11. "Howard Morgan, Black Off-Duty Cop Shot 28 Times By White Chicago Officers, Faces Sentencing." *HuffPost.com*, The Huffington Post. 03 April 2012. http://bit.ly/2SfOIdS\

12. Kappeler, Victor E. "A Brief History of Slavery and the
    Origins of American Policing."
    PLSOnline.EKU.edu, Eastern Kentucky University   - Police
    Studies Online. 7 January 2014.
    http://bit.ly/2PBHE9q

13. Mock, Brentin. "What New Research Says About Race and
    Police Shootings." *CityLab.com*, The Atlantic   Monthly
    Group. 6 August 2019.   http://bit.ly/2ZfpUUJ

14. Bekiempis, Victoria. "The New Racial Makeup of U.S.
    Police Departments." *Newsweek.com*, The   Newsweek
    Daily Beast Company. 14 May 2015.   http://bit.ly/2sbjxFT

15. "Advancing Diversity In Law Enforcement." *EEOC.gov*, U.S.
    Equal Employment Opportunity Commission.   15 October
    2016. http://bit.ly/35P6QPI

16. Lahamon, Catherine, et. al. "Police Use of Force: An
    Examination of Modern Policing Practices."   *USCCR.gov*,
    U.S. Commission on Civil Rights. 15   November 2018.
    http://bit.ly/2MiF1aQ

17. Keesee, Tracie L. "Three Ways to Reduce Implicit Bias."
    GreaterGood.Berkeley.edu, The Greater Good   Science
    Center. 2 July 2015.
    http://bit.ly/2ShE8CZ

Chapter 14: Fixed or Broken?

Probing America's Criminal "Just Us" System

"

Power doesn't have to show off. Power is confident, self-assuring, self-starting and self-stopping, self-warming and self-justifying. When you have it, you know it... This is a power set-up, son, and I'm at the controls. You think about that. When you buck against me, you're bucking against power, rich white folk's power, the nation's power – which means government power!"

- Ralph Ellison, "Invisible Man" (Shmoop Editorial Team. 6.73)

(This 1937 cartoon depiction by Elmer Messner of the Rochester Times Union, was drawn to call attention to the white supremacist ties of President Franklin Delano Roosevelt's appointee as an Associate Justice to the U.S. Supreme Court, U.S. Senator Hugo Black of Alabama.)

"I Once... Was Blind, But Now..."

Will things Ever Change?

At the beginning of his second term of office as President of the United States of America, Franklin Delano Roosevelt, the former Governor of New York who would go on to be the first disabled and longest serving Commander-in-Chief in the nation's history, was given his first of what would be eight nominations to the *United States Supreme Court*. FDR, with his stated aim of "packing the court" with Democrats loyal to his philosophy of governing, nominated then United States Senator Hugo Black of Alabama to the court vacancy, after conservative jurist Willis Van Devanter retired on May 18, 1937. Black, a staunch ally of the president, was known for his championing of a national minimum wage and a maximum workweek. He was also known to be a member of the Robert E. Lee Klan #1 of the "Invisible Empire of the South." A lifetime member of the *KKK*, Black was put forward by a president who, while understanding the implications of such a decision, chose political expediency over personal integrity--regardless of the impact that it would have on generations of minorities who would forever be bound to the decisions made by an avowed white supremacist. It is for reasons like this, and a myriad of others, that African-Americans and other minorities in the country, have an inherent distrust of the judiciary. Moreover, with the ever-present doubt that the American justice system, for people of color, is really "just us", trust in courts is at an all-time low for those who have been continually harmed by the "long arm of the law."

Born more than 330 years ago as a member of French nobility, Charles-Louis de Secondat, baron de la Brède et de Montesquieu, known to the world simply as Montesquieu, was a judge and philosopher who not only helped to develop the concept of "separation of powers", an ideal enshrined in America's most sacred document, but also forewarned of unjust system that perpetrates crimes against its people under the guise of good government and the color of authority. Montesquieu, a jurist by day and savant at night, was a staunch advocate for many of the ideals that make the United States of America the "cradle of liberty" and all that it means to those "yearning to breathe free." Fearful, however, of what both an unchecked executive branch and a rogue judiciary could do to the individual freedoms of the governed, the eighteenth century theorist warned patriots and despots to resist the temptation to circumvent the rights of others when he proclaimed: *There is no greater tyranny than that which is perpetrated under the shield of the law and in the name of justice.* Today, as the primary defender of justice and protector of what makes us all American--the social contract that we hold one another to, enforced through a fair and impartial court system, is in need of desperate reform.

Ever since the days when Rome's famed emperor, *Caesar Augustus*, first introduced me to the public as the embodiment of impartiality, and Tiberius built me a shrine reminiscent of today's courthouses back in 13 B.C., I have devoted my life to the idea that no one is "above the law" and everyone is entitled to "equal treatment under the law." These days, however, I am ashamed and saddened by the reality that due process and a sense of fair play has been perverted by those with wealth and privilege, and, in many instances has become, a "pay to play" environment. Furthermore, I mourn the "doctrine of jurisprudence" that has come to define our justice system: those with privilege and power can step to the front. For those who are poor and powerless the reality is stark in contrast: *"Every man for himself and God for them all!"* I grieve for a nation whose courts are now fueled more by "money, power and relationships", and less by "truth, justice and the American way." And frankly, I don't know what to do about it. How can I go on as the paragon of civility when what I used to represent is no longer reflective of the robe I don every day in courthouses across this land? Be that as it may, however, I am not willing to give up--just yet--on the idea that neutrality can be meted out in temples of justice throughout the land, regardless of race, creed, culture, gender or orientation. *You know ... just like it's supposed to be.*

But herein lies my problem. Every day, in courthouses across America, I stand surreptitiously in the corner, holding aloft a set of scales that are tilted, *ever so slightly*, towards justice. But what I stand for and, more importantly, who stands with me, seems to be misguided, at best, as the goal of filling prisons in response to criminal activity has replaced the idea of compassion and rehabilitation for those deserving of a second chance, and those in need of a fair adjudicator to hear their plaintive pleas. Unfortunately, however, in today's hyper-partisan, zero tolerance society, the idea of being "soft on crime" is about as popular as another hole in your head therefore, as they say in the South, "that dog won't hunt!" To complicate matters, when it comes to her *"tired ... poor ... huddled masses yearning to breathe free..."*, most of whom are minorities, the United States has historically been unyielding when individuals of color become entangled in the criminal justice system. So much so, that American prisons and detention facilities are bursting at the seams with Black males of all ages who may (or may not) be guilty. Moreover, for those helpless souls who must face a Leviathan that chews inmates up and spits them out every day, all day *(and twice on Sundays)*, my very shadow in the corner is a repugnant reminder that justice is, indeed, *not* impartial. In fact, some could rightfully say that it is an entrepreneurial activity. You see, for *them*, justice is a one-edged guillotine, waiting patiently for its next victim. *"First offense? Go to jail... Oh, you forgot your I.D.? Too bad, go to jail! You were just headed back to your mama's house? Not gonna do it anymore... go to jail!"* And it's <u>when</u> they get to jail ... that's when their problems <u>really</u> begin.

In the United States of America, under our system of criminal procedure, when an individual gets charged with a crime, they must first appear before a judge or a magistrate in what's termed an arraignment, where the charging document will be read aloud and the defendant will respond with a plea of guilt or innocence. During this proceeding, the presiding judge will either allow the defendant to walk away without cost, set bail (at a rate that the defendant may or may not be able to afford), or deny bail and remand the defendant into custody, based on the individual's probability of being a "flight risk." Unfortunately for those who don't have "complexion for protection," the flight risks are almost always presumed to be high (at least in the opinion of the court and the prosecutor); thus leading to an overcrowded jail situation because the subject in question can't afford to, or isn't allowed to, get out of jail until a trial is held or their case is otherwise disposed. Moreover, if you're a repeat offender AND a Black male, well darling, you may as well hang it up!

Your chances of walking out of court "on your own recognizance" are relatively infinitesimal and is generally not an option for those who are forced to kneel before my altar of jurisprudence. What torments me most, however, is the fact that these *same* Black males are looking to *me, Lady Justice,* to measure out some semblance of fairness when, more often than not, my hands are tied. Regrettably, however, so long as there are by mandatory-minimum sentencing guidelines, overzealous prosecutors, uber-aggressive law enforcement personnel, dumb defendants and those whose only crime was walking out of the door dressed as themselves, the struggle continues. But what happens when the beast we have created to contain our "national boogeymen" begins to turn its wrath on decent, law abiding white people who haven't done anything that, at a minimum, didn't warrant a fair hearing and a just outcome? What will America do then? As for me, at the rate we are going, I may as well retire. For those citizens of our great land who happen to be people of color, they don't think I am doing anything to make a difference anyway, so what, pray tell, is the point?

But before I put down my *Balance Scales,* which once represented the idea of impartiality and the obligation of the law to weigh the evidence in a caring and thoughtful manner; and I toss aside my *Double-Edged Sword,* symbolizing the ability I once had to enforce the decisions that are made in my midst, in a manner that can cut both ways; and I permanently remove my *Blindfold,* which once obscured my own internal bias, no longer affording me the privilege of rendering probative verdicts, I'm willing to throw myself on the mercy of the court— and give the idea of "justice" one more "college try." Are YOU willing to help me to make America great *for everyone, for once?* If you are, won't you join the team and, together, we can move forward with a meaningful agenda that doesn't tinker around the edges, but dismantles and repairs a system in desperate need of an overhaul? Our republic here at home—and our reputation abroad—deserve no less. Are you with me?

Thank you for all due consideration,

Justitia

Lady Justice

Daryl D. Parks: "An Attorney for the Ages"

"Is That Your Final Answer?"

"I am Daryl D. Parks, Esquire," began the larger than life attorney, humbly introducing himself with an air of aristocracy befitting a modern-day civil rights champion. A "go-to" lawyer, Parks has represented grieving families in times of need and social upheaval in America since graduating from the *Florida State University College of Law* and then passing the Florida Bar Exam in 1995. Since that time, the omnipresent pitchman for equal rights and social justice has been a familiar face on national cable networks, including *Fox News*, *MSNBC* and *CNN*, zealously representing the interests of those who have been wronged and are in pursuit of justice; including the families of the late Trayvon Martin (a South Florida teen who was killed by George Zimmerman, a neighborhood watch volunteer in 2012 as he walked from a convenience store in Sanford, Florida), and the late Michael Brown who was shot and killed by Ferguson, Missouri police officer Darren Wilson in 2014.

"I am the owner of *Parks Law, LLC*, a practice that is primarily focused on civil litigation," the ebullient barrister elucidated. "Our firm has handled such cases as car wrecks and medical malpractice, to nursing home neglect and wrongful death claims. We have also dealt with cases involving ships sinking in the Atlantic Ocean and buildings collapsing, all the way up to the higher profile civil rights cases that you hear about on television and have become a part of the social movement in the country," Attorney Parks acknowledged. In doing so, the loquacious legal eagle poignantly underscored the harrowing heights to which he has ascended, making a mark upon the legal community and American consciousness that can never be erased. Moreover, as a national voice in the fight for a more just and equitable society, Parks, a "country .awyer" from a rural community, has come a long way, indeed; a far cry from

from a rural community, has come a long way, indeed; a far cry from his humble beginnings in Central Florida, having been raised in the shadow of *"The Most Magical Place on Earth."*

"Growing up as a child, I never lived with my natural father," Parks acknowledged, in detailing his early years with a single mother, before she met and married the man who would become the embodiment of fatherhood to him. "When I was about four or five years old, my mother married my stepfather and they would have one child together, my only brother by my mother," Parks recalled. "Even though my stepdad had other children, he and I were as close as any father and son could be, and I credit much of who I am today to the example he set for me. He was a great man," Parks extolled, in a way that only a proud son could do. "My mother didn't go to college, but she was very smart woman who not only valued, but insisted upon, educational excellence. Like a lot of other country Black folks," the counselor concluded, "she lived a very simple life, but it was one that was centered on the need to get a good, quality education and to succeed. In our house," Parks maintained, "you couldn't bring home a "C". The punishment for bringing home anything less than a "B" was a severe whipping," he lamented, with a now mature appreciation for the end result.

"At a very early age, my parents succeeded in putting the fear of God in my heart when it came to excelling in school," the doctor of jurisprudence detailed. "I wasn't coming across my mother's threshold with a bad report card. In fact, the very threat of what would happen "scared me straight", so to speak, keeping me out of trouble and continuing to do well in school." As a result of having the "sword of Damocles" incessantly swinging over his head, Parks became internally motivated to succeed beyond even his own wildest expectations. "I was very driven to have better and have more than what I had access to growing up. I was also a dreamer," the consigliere confessed. "Even to this day, my ultimate destination is _not_ to be a lawyer, as I am planning to do some other things with my life," the always nattily attired attorney admitted.

"America is about business," the barrister bellowed! "As Black people, we need to spend more time teaching _our_ people about how to engage with the business mainstream of the country. Not just barbershops and funeral homes-- all the typical business models one would find in the Black community. I'm talking about developing products and services," Parks implored; with the zeal of courtroom lawyer appealing to a jury's sense of reason and propriety. "Most importantly," he went on, "we need to understand the systems upon which this country was built. My stepfather, for example, had a juke joint that allowed him the opportunity to make money while, at the same time providing a sanctuary for Black people to come and enjoy themselves without the pressures of outside influences that sought to keep us socially confined," Parks proclaimed. "Which is why I also understand the pain of injustice too," the civil rights crusader conceded. "People often ask me, based on the work that I do defending our people against some of the most egregious injustices, whether or not America has progressed as a country. I answer them by saying that I believe, in many ways, that progress has come in the form of a heightened sense of awareness about matters of injustice that are occurring and, just as important, raising the consciousness level of the country and our community about those concerns," the counselor ceded. And it's _those_ injustices that spur legal advocates like Parks and others, into action--fighting for the rights of "the least of these" in the halls of American justice.

In 2011, Daryl Parks was elected by his peers to serve as the President of the _National Bar Association (NBA)_, the oldest and largest association of African-American lawyers and judges in the country. Founded in 1925 as the _Negro Bar Association_, when five Black lawyers were denied membership into the _American Bar Association_, the NBA represents the interests of more than 65,000 attorneys, jurists and law school students in all areas of legal services. During his tenure as leader of the organization, Parks worked with the _American Bar Association_, along with the _National Asian Pacific American Bar Association_ and the _Hispanic National Bar Association_, to fix the gulf between the _ABA's_ ratings of white federal court nominees and its ratings of nominees of color. Additionally, Parks has worked to hold the _ABA's_ feet to the fire on other issues impacting not just African-Americans in the legal profession, but the overall community as well.

"The _National Bar Association_ has impacted my work completely, in that most lawyers of color have needed a place of refuge in this profession," Parks professed. "Not only has the *NBA* been there historically, fighting for the rights of African-Americans and other individuals of color to enjoy the liberties guaranteed to them through American citizenship and enshrined within the *Constitution* of the United States, almost all of the different movements that you have seen throughout our nation's history," Parks surmised, "have been because Black lawyers have taken the lead," he observed. "Whether it was the Civil Rights movement involving Thurgood Marshall or the Black Lives Matter movement, to include what my compatriot in the struggle for human dignity, Attorney Benjamin Crump and I have done in the challenges of today, the nexus that all of these social movements have had are the lawyers who are integrally involved in changing the nature of this country through legal redress," he continued.

"In my earnest opinion, nothing could be clearer than the fact that Black lawyers impact this country significantly, even today," Parks declared. "Most specifically, we tend to be the backbone of our communities in more ways than one. For example," he explained, "many of the Black leaders that assume positions of power and influence in government, are often attorneys. The same can be said in countries like South Africa as well," he theorized. "The training we receive as lawyers, from an intellectual standpoint, provides the foundation that is necessary to not only help our communities, it also positions us to help make meaningful social and political change in this country," the high-powered mouthpiece maintained. Today, however, as the legal system in the United States of America continues to be constrained by an inundation of criminal complaints and charges, the vast majority of which will almost never go to trial, it's clear that it's going to take an armada of attorneys to change the way the criminal justice system churns and burns Black bodies, and penalizes defendants for asserting their rights under law. Moreover, for those who are poor and find themselves in the clutches of the court system, the shock and awe of being remanded to jail or, worse yet, prison (America's very own version of "gladiator school") or "copping a plea" to avoid the carnage, but forfeiting precious liberties in the process, is one that leaves dreams dashed and hope dissipated as the reality of a crushing system is fully realized.

"In Jail Without the Bail?"

For starters, to fundamentally understand how the wheels of justice work in the United States of America, particularly when it comes to low level offenses, one must first understand how the "misdemeanor system" operates. Every day, in courthouses across the country, criminal defendants are encouraged to "pay up" and "plea out" when fighting state charges, or face the wrath of criminal prosecutors who are often put off by those defendants who have the temerity to "challenge the system" by availing themselves of their constitutional rights. What's more, these same criminal defendants, should they not be able to bail themselves out of jail, must then face the inevitable ire of irritable inmates in lockup, and petulant prison guards who, through omission, commission (or both), allow these individuals to be beaten, brutalized and left bewildered--all of whom are innocent until proven guilty by a court of law because they failed to "get with the program." In an opinion piece by the *Washington Post* called, "How the Justice System Criminalizes the Poor — and Funds Itself in the Process," journalist Jonathan Capehart detailed how those trapped in "pauper's prison" pay a steep price for poverty.

"[The misdemeanor system], Capehart noted, "punishes people because they can't pay fines and fees. It punishes people because they can't pay to register their car. It punishes people, often incarcerates them ... not because of the underlying offense, but just because they couldn't come up with the money that was supposed to be the low-level punishment," he observed. "In many ways those fines and fees, that wealth stripping of the poor, is funding the system itself. It's funding court. It's finding probation offices. It's funding public defender offices. It's funding prosecution offices" (Capehart). Furthermore, the same system that incentivizes guilty pleas, also makes life all the more miserable for those who dare to utter the words, *"Not guilty, Your Honor."* And when they do dare to take their chances at trial, many defendants are left to fight against an all-powerful prosecution team, with the keys to the cell dangling in their hands, and often ineffective counsel overburdened by a public defender system that does not afford court-appointed attorneys the time or capacity to vigorously defend their clients.

"We disregard the law in misdemeanor courts all the time," Capehart observed. "The convictions may have been produced without the assistance of counsel. Prosecutors may not have had time to screen those cases and think about them. People are under enormous pressure to plead guilty" (Capehart). In fact, more often than not, if an individual does have a conviction for a previous criminal offense in America, chances are that person's case never went to trial and ended like 97% of all other criminal cases in America--with a plea bargain and the hopes of no further prosecution. "All too often if someone has a conviction, all we conclude is that they were likely to be arrested for all kinds of reasons that may have not had anything to do with the evidence, that they were likely to have been rushed through the process in a speedy way, pressured to plead guilty, and that they were likely to plead guilty, not necessarily because they were guilty, but because they couldn't make bail or they didn't have adequate counsel or because they didn't understand the consequences" (Capehart). But what would happen if there were a significant shift in the criminal justice system, and those being held in abeyance until they received the speedy trial to which they are entitled, actually took their chances at trial? According to legal experts, courthouse chaos would ensue, as the current criminal justice system is simply not equipped or adequately funded to allow everyone the opportunity to "have their day in court." Michelle Alexander, author of "The New Jim Crow: Mass Incarceration in the Era of Colorblindness", in an opinion piece for the *New York Times* themed, "Go to Trial: Crash the Justice System," theorized that the answer to that fateful question is an unequivocal "yes" should otherwise powerless defendants, ban together and dare to reject prosecutorial plea bargains.

"The system of mass incarceration," observed Alexander, "depends almost entirely on the cooperation of those it seeks to control. If everyone charged with crimes suddenly exercised his constitutional rights, there would not be enough judges, lawyers or prison cells to deal with the ensuing tsunami of litigation," Alexander maintained. In doing so, however, the very people the criminal justice system is dependent upon for profits, by shuffling them in and out of court quickly, can potentially upend a criminal "just us" system that heavily impacts communities of color, while simultaneously calling attention to the issues plaguing what many believe to be a broken judicial structure. "Such chaos would force mass incarceration to the top of the agenda for politicians and policy makers," Alexander wrote, "leaving them only two viable options: sharply scale back the number of criminal cases filed (for drug possession, for example) or amend the *Constitution* (or eviscerate it by judicial "emergency" fiat)," she prescribed. "Either action would create a crisis and the system would crash — it could no longer function as it had before. Mass protest would force a public conversation that, to date, we have been content to avoid," she inferred. But the challenge with Alexander's theory, however, is the fact that America's highest court in the land has consistently sustained practices by prosecutors that make it difficult for defendants to resist prosecutorial overtures, threats and demands.

In 1978, the United States Supreme Court ruled that it was, indeed, perfectly permissible for public prosecutors to threaten defendants with life imprisonment for even minor crimes to obtain plea agreements, determining that it was not a violation of Sixth Amendment rights to a fair and speedy trial. Thirteen years later, in 1991, the court also reaffirmed a local prosecutor's ability to threaten life sentences, even for minor crimes, in an effort to induce a defendant to forfeit a jury trial, ruling that it did not violate an individual's Sixth Amendment right to trial. Additionally, the court also ruled that life imprisonment for a first-time drug offense did not violate the Eighth Amendment's protection against cruel and unusual punishment. In a 5-4 ruling, The United States Supreme Court, when considering the facts of the case in Harmelin v. Michigan, determined that the heavy-handed sentencing of a man for drugs was, indeed, justifiable. As chronicled by Oyez, a free law project from Cornell University's Legal Information Institute (LII), Justia, and Chicago-Kent College of Law, the crucial case would be pivotal in opening the door for impertinent inquisitors to use strong-arm tactics to increase conviction rates.

"Following his conviction under Michigan law for possession of over 650 grams of cocaine, Ronald Harmelin was sentenced to life in prison without possibility of parole," Oyez reported. "Harmelin challenged his sentence as cruel and unusual, claiming it was disproportionate to the crime he committed and was statutorily mandated without consideration for the fact that he had no prior felony convictions" ("Harmelin"). In affirming the Michigan Court of Appeals decision, however, the Supreme Court gave a green light to prosecutors to threaten to "throw everything but the kitchen sink" at defendant's fighting criminal charges, thus providing enormous leverage to them when negotiating plea agreements. Consequently, the vast majority of poor defendants, most of whom are Black and Hispanic, by choosing to challenge the system, may immediately commence a hellish nightmare that could be over in days, or weeks, or months, or even years, as they woefully languish in unconscionable misery during what is known as the "pre-trial detainment."

"Feared for Your Life?"

On the other side of the criminal justice equation, of course, are the police officers who not only effect the arrests that clog America's courtrooms, but also have the power to make life or death decisions--at a moment's notice-- with the implied (or expressed) support of prosecutors who will ultimately decide their fates, when instances of brutality against or the deaths of citizens occur during law enforcement encounters. Just as importantly, the enormous power that local prosecutor's wield in forcing plea bargains from criminal defendants is often shelved when it comes to law enforcement officers who find themselves under investigation for excessive or deadly use of force against civilians, many of whom are African-American males. In fact, research indicates that less 1.5% of all police involved homicides ever result in criminal action being taken against the officer. Veritably, more often than not, when a police officer shoots, or even kills a Black suspect, prosecutors will decline to charge the law enforcement officer, especially when they recite the five magic words that serve as a sort of "get out jail free" card for those representing the color of authority: *"I feared for my life."*

In an article by James C. McKinley and Al Baker of the *New York Times*, called, "Grand Jury System, With Exceptions, Favors the Police in Fatalities," the journalists detailed the enormous benefit of the doubt given to law enforcement officers by local prosecutors, when it came to "officer involved shootings", which seem to disproportionately affect men and women of color. "Rarely do deaths [at the hands of police officers] lead to murder or manslaughter charges," observed the *Washington Post* writers. "Research by Philip M. Stinson, a criminologist at *Bowling Green State University,* reports that 41 officers were charged with either murder or manslaughter in shootings while on duty over a seven-year period ending in 2011. Over that same period," McKinley and Baker observed, "police departments reported 2,600 justifiable homicides to the F.B.I." ("Grand Jury System"). To that end, while calling attention to the paltry number of punitive actions being taken against errant police officers prone to shoot first and exercise caution later, is an important community issue, it pales, in comparison to the energy prosecutors expend racking up charges against generally defenseless Black males; using the leverage provided them by the nation's highest court to browbeat them into legal capitulation--even those who are first time offenders in the eyes of the law.

One notable and tragic example of what can happen when these poor, brave souls dare to do what they believe is the right thing in not accepting guilt for crimes in which they earnestly maintain their innocence, can be found in the story of Kalief Browder—a then 16-year old teenager who was arrested and sent to New York City's most notorious jail, *Rikers Island*. Unbeknownst to Browder and his family, he would spend the next three years of his life being dehumanized, tortured, assaulted and degraded by convicts and corrections officers alike in the rodent infested purgatory rife with disease and dismay. In an eye-watering exposé about the tragic circumstances surrounding the arrest and imprisonment of Browder, a once affable teenager from the Bronx, Jennifer Gonnerman of *The New Yorker*, detailed a haunting portrait of stolen youth that has helped to spark a social revolution. As reported in her story, "Before the Law: Three Years on Rikers Without Trial," Gonnerman recalled a tale of woe experienced by the youth and a friend as he walked home in the early morning hours of May 15, 2010, a place he would not see again for years.

"As they passed East 186th Street," Gonnerman wrote, "Browder saw a police car driving toward them. More squad cars arrived, and soon Browder and his friend found themselves squinting in the glare of a police spotlight. An officer said that a man had just reported that they had robbed him," she noted, citing police reports and Browder's own testimony. Before he knew it, both Browder and his friend were handcuffed by police, tossed into the back of a police squad car, and whisked away to the 48th Precinct, with the teens insisting the entire way that they did not rob anyone and were simply on their way home from a party. *"What am I being charged for?"* Browder asked. *"I didn't do anything!"* He remembers an officer telling them, *"We're just going to take you to the precinct"* (Gonnerman). For an impressionable 16-year old kid, Browder believed that to be the truth... but he was wrong. As a consequence of his naïveté, the once gregarious youth would spend the next 1,111 days enduring a torturous journey of solitary confinement, starvation, terror and more, in one of America's most notorious jails. With an ever-present hope, however, that he would be going home soon, Kalief Browder steadfastly maintained his innocence and believed that he would be able to fight the unsubstantiated charges against him in court, come win, lose or draw. Once again, he was wrong.

Having been appointed a public defender by the *Bronx Criminal Court* and unable to post a $900 bond, Kalief was bounced around to nine separate courtrooms, over the process of more than a dozen continuances by prosecutors who continued to offer Browder an opportunity to go home immediately... were he to accept a plea of guilty. Browder refused to do so. As a result, his case was stretched out over years, forcing the teenager who had now come of age locked inside a tiny cell alone, oftentimes without access to showers, while being starved of food by correctional officers who sought to punish Browder for not getting with "the program"—a silent system of exploitation, subjugation and dehumanization forced upon unsuspecting inmates who must forfeit rations, money and sometimes their own bodies to more powerful gang members--or suffer brutal consequences for failure to do so. To make matters worse, "the program" is often run by correctional officers who perform their duties more like storm troopers than public servants, often receiving kickbacks and remuneration from inmates desperate to survive. For Kalief Browder, however, in refusing to "play by the rules", the emotional, social and mental health toll it would take on him, as he languished in one of the nation's worst perditions, was something neither he nor anyone else could truly be prepared for. On the other side of the defendant population, are those who *do* get with "the program" at the beginning of the process, pleading out their cases to reduce jail time, but in doing so, agree to sign away "certain unalienable rights" that they may never, *ever* be returned to them again. By the same token, for those who, unlike Kalief Browder, *did* go to trial and were either unjustly convicted, did not receive a fair trial, or felt as if they had no other choice but to plead guilty to crimes they did not commit and were remanded to the custody of the state or federal government, the stakes are even higher and the penalties much worse.

According to the *National Academy of Sciences*, the most recent statistical data suggests that 4.1% of all inmates currently serving sentences on death row are innocent. *"Evidence of Innocence"*, a television program dedicated to highlighting the travails of those who have suffered the unimaginable injustice of being stripped of their liberty for crimes not of their own doing, has worked to uncover the stories that have long been hidden from public view, but deserve sanitizing daylight, with the hope that systemic change will ensue. "The innocent are sent to jail in alarming numbers. In the past three decades, 2,215 prisoners have been exonerated after going to prison, according to the *National Registry of Exonerations,"* the show reported, "a collaboration between the *University of Michigan* and *Michigan State University* law schools and the *University of California, Irvine*" ("Evidence of Innocence"). And that's just what can be quantified; a number that does *not* include the wrongfully convicted who may have had their sentences commuted to life in prison, for example. Additionally, the fact that even **one** person can be convicted of crimes they were not responsible for and sentenced to death used to be unconscionable in the land of liberty. But now, in many instances, it is the cost of doing business and chalked up as collateral damage in a war of "us vs. them." So how, one may wonder, is this even possible *if* the nation's criminal justice system isn't broken? For poor Black males who happen to catch the eye of unyielding law enforcement officers, aggressive prosecutors and harsh judges, however, the possibility of having one's life upended by a confluence of bogus evidence, coerced confessions and mistaken identity is not only probable, but likely to happen to either themselves or someone they know, over the course of their lifetime.

The *Equal Justice Initiative (EJI)*, a nonprofit organization that "provides legal representation to prisoners who may have been wrongly convicted of crimes, poor prisoners without effective representation, and others who may have been denied a fair trial in their piece", in their piece "Wrongfully Convicted," outlined the challenges facing those who have had the travesty of being locked up on bogus charges befall them. In fact, according to *EJI*, to date, more than 2,500 individuals have been exonerated in the last 30 years alone. Sadly, most of those who were wrongfully convicted and later exonerated spent, on average, 8 years and 10 months incarcerated for crimes they didn't commit. "More than half of wrongful convictions can be traced to witnesses who lied in court or made false accusations," the *Initiative* reports. "In 2018, a record number of exonerations involved misconduct by government officials. Other leading causes of wrongful convictions include mistaken eyewitness identifications, false or misleading forensic science, and jailhouse informants" ("Wrongful Convictions"). To make matters worse, even when authorities discover the unthinkable, the fact that innocent people have been deprived of their liberties, for various and sundry reasons, none of which are justifiable enough to change someone's life inexorably, very little is done to make systemic change.

"Police, prosecutors, and judges are not held accountable for misconduct that leads to wrongful convictions, such as fabricating evidence, presenting false testimony, or refusing to consider proof of innocence", *EJI* noted. "Immunity laws protect them from liability even in cases of gross misconduct. Prosecutors can't be held liable for falsifying evidence, coercing witnesses, presenting false testimony, withholding evidence, or introducing illegally-seized evidence at trial ("Wrongful Convictions"). To that end, many believe the need to elect local prosecutors who are reflective of the communities they serve is of paramount importance in leveling the playing field for majority-minority prosecutorial jurisdictions. That task, however, isn't easy, as there few African-American lawyers who have been successful in being elected as district attorney, but times may be changing.

In 2018, after his failure to charge Ferguson, Missouri police officer, Darren Wilson, in the homicide death of 18-year old Michael Brown in 2014, Robert McCulloch, the 27-year incumbent St. Louis County Prosecutor, went down in resounding electoral defeat when political upstart Wesley Bell, an forty-something African-American attorney and former municipal judge trounced him in the Democratic Primary that summer. Bell, having served on the *Ferguson City Council* prior to being elected, ran a campaign based on progressive ideals that called for the equitable treatment of all St. Louis county residents, regardless of race, when having their cases presented to the prosecutor's office for examination and consideration. In an article published by the *St. Louis American*, a weekly newspaper serving the African-American community of St. Louis County, Missouri since 1928 called, "Wesley Bell Elected St. Louis County's First Black Prosecutor," McCulloch's political luck had finally run out after, once again, failing to call into account actions taken by St. Louis County law enforcement officers that resulted in the needless loss of life. "McCulloch's notoriety went national due to his handling of the Darren Wilson grand jury and Ferguson," the newspaper reported, "giving Bell's primary campaign national attention, as well as furious local organizing. The *American Civil Liberties Union (ACLU)* of Missouri, which does not endorse candidates, made an unprecedented effort to educate the public on McCulloch's record of holding people with misdemeanor offenses who could not post cash bail and the meager results of his diversion program for drug offenders that he initiated after Ferguson" ("Wesley Bell").

Upon assuming office, newly elected St. Louis County Prosecutor Wesley Bell wasted no time in making good in his campaign promises of cleaning up the prosecutor's office, starting with the staff empowered to discharge criminal cases. On his second day in office, he fired the assistant prosecutor who failed to get an indictment against former Ferguson, Missouri police officer Darren Wilson in the 2014 shooting death of 18-year-old Michael Brown. In addition to the personnel changes, Bell enacted structural reforms that were designed to provide equitable justice for all St. Louis County residents, including:

- Declining to prosecute marijuana cases involving fewer than 100 grams. Those with more than 100 grams will only be prosecuted if there is evidence to suggest the marijuana was for sale or distribution.

- Those who are in arrears on child support no longer have to fear prosecution or have their inability to do so be the sole reason probation is revoked.

- Elimination of the request by prosecution for cash bail for all misdemeanor cases.

- Prosecutors may no longer use threats or intimidation tactics to force witnesses to testify in cases being discharged by their office.

Following Bell's example, other African-American attorneys and jurists are taking the plunge, seeking to fill the role of public prosecutor in a means that is just, fair and provides criminal defendants with the trust in knowing that they will be treated with the dignity and respect afforded to them as citizens of a democratic society. Fanon Rucker, for example, an African-American Democrat and former municipal court judge in Hamilton County, Ohio, is seeking to change the tide of history by unseating longtime incumbent Joe Deters, a white Republican, for the position of Hamilton County Prosecutor. In announcing his historic candidacy, Rucker laid out a progressive platform, similar to one enacted by Bell of St. Louis County, and called for reform and integrity in prosecuting criminal cases on behalf of the general public. "I am running to ensure that our system is as responsive as possible to the interests and needs of the victims, the defendants, and most importantly, the community that it serves and are impacted by its policies," Rucker declared in a news conference covered by *WVXU - Cincinnati Public Radio*.

Appointed to the bench in 2007, Rucker has served as a judge, civil rights attorney and prosecutor. The heir of legal royalty, Rucker's father, the Honorable Robert D. Rucker, was the 105th Justice and first African-American appointed to the *Indiana Supreme Court* by then Governor Evan Bayh. Not known for shirking away from a fight, Judge Fanon Rucker believes that his depth and breadth of experience will go a long way towards righting the ship for those who believe that the scales of justice are tilted against them and, as such, has entered the political fray to become one of Ohio's top prosecutors. "We will enact policies that will focus on the aggressive prosecution of violent crimes," Rucker declared, "provide continued support of victims after the court process, staff an office with those focused on the foundation principles of justice and reduce overcrowding in our jails and prisons," he continued ("WVXU"). Furthermore, with a platform that includes creating a *Conviction Integrity Unit (CIU)* to ensure that prosecutions were carried out fairly, and a policy of recommending "Own Recognizance Bonds" for nonviolent offenders, Rucker's goal of reforming the criminal justice system in his buckeye community is one that is laudable and worthy of replication, irrespective of his political fate. Accordingly, with the fates of millions of erstwhile productive members of society hanging in the balance, it is plain to see that who the prosecutor is matters--particularly for those hoping to avoid criminal convictions--and the ever-present scarlet letter that comes with every conviction.

In the United States of America, for example, once an individual becomes a convicted felon, there are a number of rights that they will no longer be able to exercise as citizens of the country. For starters, those who have a felony record face a number of difficulties when attempting to reintegrate themselves into society, which includes their inability to exercise their franchise or receive public assistance, as a result of their criminal history. In fact, according to the article, "What Rights Do Convicted Felons Lose?," published by *Legal Beagle* , an online community of people with Juris Doctor (J.D.), Master of Laws (LL.M.) and Doctor of the Science of Law (J.S.D.) degrees who aim to simplify and make it easier to navigate through legal information, "convicted felons face a number of difficulties when attempting to reintegrate themselves into society," to include, but are not limited, to the following ("Felons"):

WHAT RIGHTS DO YOU LOSE AS A CONVICTED FELON?

WHY "COPPING A PLEA" IS A ONE-WAY TICKET TO SECOND CLASS CITIZENSHIP

THE RIGHT TO VOTE

Most states bar those convicted of a felony from voting. Even after completing their sentence, former felons are still prohibited from voting for a set period of time, if not forever, depending upon where they reside.

THE RIGHT TO HOLD PUBLIC OFFICE

Many states bar convicted felons from seeking or holding public office. Also, if someone is a current office holder and is convicted of crimes, they may be removed from office.

THE RIGHT TO BEAR ARMS

Having any type of criminal record generally bars convicted felons from purchasing, owning or possessing a firearm. What's more, licensed firearms dealers are required to run mandatory background checks for criminal history and not sell to those with a record.

THE RIGHT TO TRAVEL ABROAD

While convicted felons in the U.S. are not prohibited from obtaining a passport, they still face severe restrictions with international travel, and foreign countries retain the option of refusing entry to the formerly incarcerated.

PUBLIC SOCIAL BENEFITS

There are a number of restrictions imposed upon those who are convicted felons, to include residing in public housing, applying for financial aid, accepting food stamps, and benefitting from Supplemental Security Income.

MOVING TO ANOTHER STATE

The U.S. Constitution's "Full Faith and Credit" clause requires states to respect the rulings and judgments of other states, thereby frustrating efforts of convicted felons to leave the past behind.

 6 FACTS YOU SHOULD KNOW BEFORE SIGNING A PLEA AGREEMENT...

FOR MORE INFORMATION VISIT
WWW.LEGALBEAGLE.COM

For the young Kalief Browder, however, a teenager who had never been in any serious trouble with the law, losing all of the aforementioned rights and "privileges appertaining thereto" was a nonnegotiable proposition that he was willing to fight for... all the way to the end. For that, he would pay a heavy cost. After continued delay, legal obstruction, and procedural maneuvering, the prosecutor in Browder's flimsily constructed case, having failed to produce any witnesses, corroboration, or physical or digital evidence tying Browder to any crimes related to the stolen backpack, ultimately relented and dropped all charges against Kalief on May 29, 2013. His case never even went to trial. Unfortunately for Browder, however, the damage had already been done.

In writing a requiem to a teenager failed by a system designed to treat him as invisible, entitled "Kalief Browder, 1993-2015", Gonnerman of *The New Yorker*, tapped into the depths of Kalief's hopelessness, in telling the story of a young man who had simply given up on life, hanging himself in an upper bedroom of his childhood home as his mother sat, unaware, downstairs. "During that time [of his unjust imprisonment], he endured about two years in solitary confinement, where he attempted to end his life several times. Once, in February, 2012," Gonnerman wrote, "he ripped his bedsheet into strips, tied them together to create a noose, and tried to hang himself from the light fixture in his cell." On June 6, 2015, after multiple unsuccessful attempts to end his internal suffering, fostered by a paranoia that had been induced through years of solitary confinement, Kalief Browder became a figure for the ages when he finally succeeded in ending his own life. "That afternoon, at about 12:15 P.M., he went into another bedroom, pulled out the air conditioner, and pushed himself out through the hole in the wall, feet first, with a cord wrapped around his neck," Gonnerman reported.

"His mother was the only other person home at the time. After she heard a loud thumping noise, she went upstairs to investigate, but couldn't figure out what had happened. It wasn't until she went outside to the backyard and looked up that she realized that her youngest child had hanged himself" ("1993-2015"). Kalief Browder was 22 years old. As tragic as Browder's story may be, unfortunately it is not an unusual experience for the countless number of Black males, whose names we will never know, who endure similar fates at the hands of the criminal justice system. The only difference between themselves and Browder, is the fact that no one knows their names. But for the son of one of Attorney Parks' clients, the late Trayvon Martin, his name, like Browder's will ring through the ages as a symbol of perverted justice and a reflection point on the very humanity of Black men in America.

Born February 5, 1995 to Sybrina Fulton and Tracy Martin in South Florida, Trayvon Martin was a precocious child who exhibited an early interest in aviation, with dreams of becoming a pilot as an adult. A young teenager struggling to find his way, Martin sometimes found himself in trouble in school for behavioral issues. Having been suspended several times from school before being shipped off to his father's home in the Central Florida town of Sanford, Florida, some 233 miles away from the familiar environs of his hometown of Miami Gardens, Trayvon was a boy in search of himself when he died. In fact, it was during this fateful time—as Martin was seeking to reprioritize his life—that he would meet a tragic fate when he was stalked and shot by a neighborhood watch volunteer by the name of George Zimmerman.

In a *Biography* story about his brief but impactful life called, "Trayvon Martin: 1995-2012," the young man with no previous criminal history, who would go on to spark a movement felt around the world, soon found himself the subject of a stranger's undue attention as he walked back to his father's home from the local 7-11 store. Having just purchased a bag of candy and an iced tea, Trayvon attempted to make his way back home when, unbeknownst to him, Zimmerman began trailing him on foot, while phoning Martin's "suspicious activity" in to the local police department. Even after being told by police emergency operators to discontinue stalking Martin, the 28-year old Zimmerman continued his pursuit remarking, *"these assholes... they always get away."* This time, Zimmerman was determined to make sure that didn't happen, shooting the child as he fought, in vain, for his life--exactly three weeks after his 17th birthday. What's more, after the tragic death of the unarmed youth, law enforcement officials were reticent to charge Zimmerman with a crime, as he cited Florida's notorious "Stand Your Ground Law," which allows citizens to use deadly force if they believe their life or the lives of others are being imminently threatened. After Zimmerman's multiple protestations of his own innocence according to the law, and an intensive investigation, he was eventually charged—forty-four days later—with second degree murder.

"The trial began on June 24, 2013, after the selection of an all-female jury. The following month, on July 13, 2013, the six-member jury acquitted Zimmerman of murder, triggering mostly peaceful protests in several American cities" ("Biography"). For the parents of the teen who will remain forever young, however, the American court system had failed them in their pursuit of justice for their son. For others, however, there is a strong belief that the system did not fail the Martin family but rather, it worked as intended. In a thought-provoking piece for The Atlantic called, "Trayvon Martin and the Irony of American Justice," award winning author, Ta-Nehisi Coates theorized that the criminal justice system is, in fact, NOT broken... it's been fixed the entire time.

"The injustice inherent in the killing of Trayvon Martin by George Zimmerman was not authored by a jury given a weak case," Coates opined. "The jury's performance may be the least disturbing aspect of this entire affair. The injustice," he explained, "was authored by a country which has taken as its policy, for the lion's share of its history, to erect a pariah class. Moreover, the internationally acclaimed author believes that the failure to convict George Zimmerman is, in essence, endemic of a history of dehumanization aimed squarely at people in America of African descent. "It is painful to say this: Trayvon Martin is not a miscarriage of American justice," Coates bemoaned, "but American justice itself. This is not our system malfunctioning. It is our system working as intended" ("American Justice"). Consequently, the death of Martin, and ultimate exoneration of Zimmerman, marked a watershed moment in American history, reminding many of the August 28, 1955 lynching of Emmett Till; exactly eight years to the day that Martin Luther King, Jr. would deliver his "I Have a Dream" speech, and fifty-three years to the day that Senator Barack Obama would accept the Democratic Party nomination for President of the United States. Moreover, this incident of international concern, was so potent to the issue of race relations in America that it prompted President Barack Obama to deliver an address to the nation, in the White House Rose Garden, where he made the following remarks that, for many White Americans, was a step too far for what they had hoped would be a "racially neutral" president:

"

You know, when Trayvon Martin was first shot, I said that this could have been my son. Another way of saying that, is Trayvon Martin could have been me 35 years ago. And when you think about why, in the African American community at least, there's a lot of pain around what happened here, I think it's important to recognize that the African American community is looking at this issue through a set of experiences and a history that doesn't go away.

There are very few African American men in this country who haven't had the experience of being followed when they were shopping in a department store. That includes me. There are very few African American men who haven't had the experience of walking across the street and hearing the locks click on the doors of cars. That happens to me -- at least before I was a senator. There are very few African Americans who haven't had the experience of getting on an elevator and a woman clutching her purse nervously and holding her breath until she had a chance to get off. That happens often.

And I don't want to exaggerate this, but those sets of experiences inform how the African American community interprets what happened one night in Florida. And it's inescapable for people to bring those experiences to bear. The African American community is also knowledgeable that there is a history of racial disparities in the application of our criminal laws -- everything from the death penalty to enforcement of our drug laws. And that ends up having an impact in terms of how people interpret the case...

And let me just leave you with a final thought that, as difficult and challenging as this whole episode has been for a lot of people, I don't want us to lose sight that things are getting better. Each successive generation seems to be making progress in changing attitudes when it comes to race. **It doesn't mean we're in a post-racial society.** *It doesn't mean that racism is eliminated. But when I talk to Malia and Sasha, and I listen to their friends and I seem them interact, they're better than we are -- they're better than we were -- on these issues. And that's true in every community that I've visited all across the country... ("Remarks by President").*

For Obama, and for many other Americans, consoling a family and a community after such a tragic loss, both of Martin's life and his case for justice in the criminal courts, might seem as if it were the right thing to do, but for others it was the declaration of racial identity. In a story by Monica Potts of *Vogue Magazine* termed, "Barack Obama, Trayvon Martin and the Presidency," the mere suggestion that anything other than justice had been served was heresy. "As Nikole Hannah-Jones showed in an interview with a white Iowan who had voted for Obama but switched to Republican Donald Trump this year, this was a turning point for many white Americans," Potts reported. "Obama really turned her off when after a vigilante killed a Black teenager named Trayvon Martin, he said the boy could have been his son," Hannah-Jones wrote about the voter, Gretchen Douglas. "She felt as if Obama was choosing a side in the racial divide, stirring up tensions." As the attorney of record for the family of the late Trayvon Martin, Daryl D. Parks understands all too well the physical dangers that Black males face every day, simply trying to exist in an often hostile and judgmental society, and the antipathy people like himself faces when they dare to speak out against it.

"I understand the concept of being invisible, in that this country seems to not see us... Definitely not as equals," Attorney Parks declared. "This country has never, really, seen African-Americans as *humans*, *let alone equals*, and therein lies our problem," he maintained. "One of the reasons that George Zimmerman probably got off is that they [the jury] just couldn't see Trayvon as "their son." In fact, part of the defense strategy was to portray Trayvon as "*something,*" not *someone*, who could have, in theory, been a child of any of the members of the all-white, all female jury," he theorized. "With that being said, however, this concept of African-American men being invisible in today's society, in my opinion, has both justification and, to some extent, is a figment of the imagination," especially for those who tend to make excuses for bad behavior and a willingness to try and help themselves. "In that regard," the barrister elucidated, "it's incumbent upon Black males to take the time to do the things that need to be done, to gain the attributes that white people deem credible in twenty-first century America," Parks opined. In his opinion, this begins with Black males striving to get a good education, a good job, and conforming to civil society in ways that are acceptable to most Americans. "Anything else," Parks admonished, "gets you x'ed out in their eyes, and that makes you invisible to them," he continued.

"Here's a concept I've often heard white people use when assessing the humanity of Blacks: *"Are they a good person?"* What does that really even mean," he queried, before answering his own question. "What it means is that there are some in our society who <u>still</u> believe that if they think you are a 'good person', that somehow gives us some sort of limited access to their world. If they don't believe you to be a *'good person'*," he continued, "then they put you in that 'other world', where they see you as invisible and unworthy of consideration," he concluded. "At that point, you are not even a *'good person'* or a person at all, you are an *"it"* or a *"thing"* to them," the barrister bemoaned. "Unfortunately for a lot of Black men, we are put in that *"it"* or *"thing"* category really quick," he lamented.

"The other part of the equation, in my estimation, is this..." Parks began, in explaining his theories on race and culture in America. "There are some white people who always want to lord over somebody else, which could probably be said of other races of people as well, he acknowledged. "But there are <u>**some**</u> who have this insatiable desire to be superior to somebody else, even other white people" Parks elucidated. "In one of my many travels around the world, for example, I was on a very nice *Norwegian Cruise Line* ship, in the middle of the Caribbean Sea," the accomplished attorney remembered. "A middle-aged white man from the Buckhead area of Atlanta, Georgia walked up to me and asked, *"Do you know me?"*, Parks described. Befuddled and a bit bemused, he responded, *"No...I don't think I do."* Suddenly," Parks recalled, "he says, *"This is* **my** *boat!* Without skipping a beat, I responded, *"No shit -- **YOU** are Mr. Norwegian!?,"* the incredulous counselor retorted. "I would have never thought that YOU *actually* made the trip," he quipped. "You see," Parks explained, "this rich white guy thought it was nothing to walk up to the first Black guy he saw at sea, to say something so ridiculous. It's a mentality," Parks proclaimed, "and that's a prevailing sentiment in the country right now. This is why," he believes, "it is incumbent upon those of us who are lawyers, to assume the role of protectors of our people and defenders of democracy," he concluded.

"When it comes to the danger facing Black men in America today, I believe that we are more of a danger to ourselves then white people are to us," the counselor conceded. "As a community, Black people have to go back to the concept of a civil society, as the foundations of our democracy really rest on the principle of civility. We have to understand where we live and by whose rules we are required to operate," he said. "In my estimation, a lot of brothers need to take the time to be a little bit more civil to one another. To that end," Parks went on, "I do think that our people have to be a lot more responsible for ourselves... and we are not," he mourned! "So many times, in so many instances, we just don't hold each other accountable. Just as important, we don't make people grow up to be responsible for themselves, for their communities and for the world around them," Parks observed. "So that's an issue," he maintained, "and it's something we need to address right away."

"As a general rule of thumb," the prolific spokesman proclaimed, "I believe that Black people spend way too much time and energy on the issue of police brutality," he concluded. "There are plenty of other issues that are taking Black people's lives, that cry out for someone's energy. The lack of affordable healthcare options and educational disparities, for example, are causing far more damage, as a whole, to our race, than the unacceptable number of Black males who are needlessly killed by the police. Mind you," Parks explained, "this is not to minimize a critically important issue to our community and our nation. But it is certainly not our biggest problem," he concluded. "Finally, I think it is important for all Black males to look for examples they can follow, as they strive to make something of themselves in a society where the odds are stacked against them. Today, *if you believe the mainstream media*, our Black heroes just aren't out there, and that... I do <u>**NOT**</u> believe," he exclaimed. "We just have to highlight those individuals, and tell their stories. Until then," Attorney Parks declared, "I will continue to advocate for the least of these," he concluded. "And fight for their rights until hell freezes over ... and then I will fight on the ice!"

(Daryl Parks: Civil Rights Attorney & Law Firm Owner)

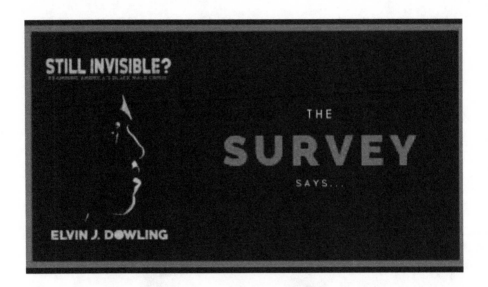

Do you believe that bias against Black males exists within the American criminal justice system?*

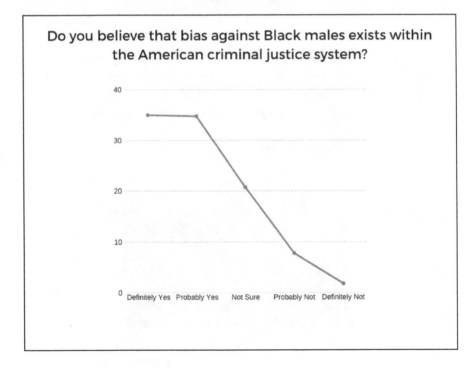

How strongly do you agree or disagree with the following statements?*

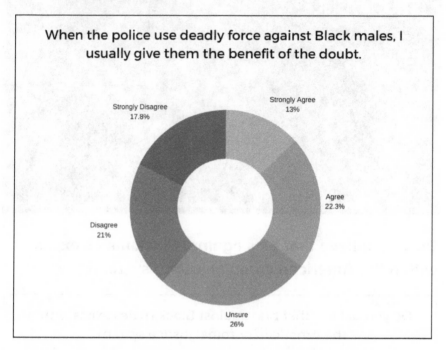

When the police use deadly force against Black males, I usually give them the benefit of the doubt.

Strongly Disagree 17.8%
Strongly Agree 13%
Agree 22.3%
Disagree 21%
Unsure 26%

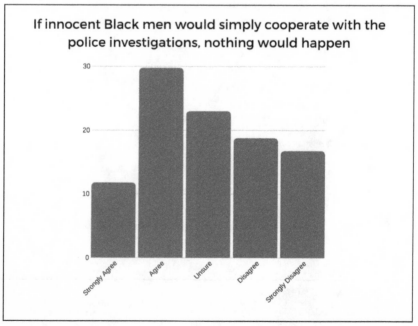

If innocent Black men would simply cooperate with the police investigations, nothing would happen

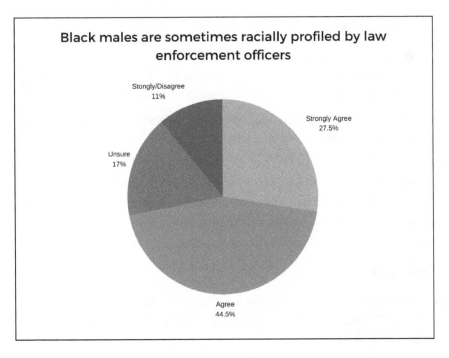

Black males are sometimes racially profiled by law enforcement officers

- Stongly/Disagree 11%
- Strongly Agree 27.5%
- Unsure 17%
- Agree 44.5%

All survey results displayed above are represented by the overall percentage of survey respondents. For more information on our survey methodology, please see the Author's Note, located in the front matter of the book. To review raw survey results, visit: http://bit.ly/stillinvisiblesurvey.

In God We Trust?

Justice Delayed...Is Justice Denied

1 Strong Majority Believes Bias Exists
Nearly 7 out of 10 respondents (69.75%) are in agreement that racial bias exists against Black males in the criminal justice system.

2 Nearly Even Split On Police "Use of Force"
Just over a third of all respondents (35.25%) are willing to give the police the benefit of the doubt when force is used; with 38.75% "less likely to do" so, and 26% "unsure".

3 Plurality Say Black Men Should Comply
More than 4 out of 10 respondents (41.50%) believe that innocent Black males should comply with police investigations and nothing will happen to them.

4 Most Agree That Racial Profiling Is A Problem
Only 11% of all respondents disagree with the idea that Black males are racially profiled by police

Findings by Race

- Nearly 9 out of 10 of all Black respondents (88.46%) say "Definitely Yes" or "Probably Yes" when asked the statement, *"Do you believe that bias against Black males exists within the American criminal justice system?"*

- One third of all White respondents (33.33%) "Strongly Agree" or "Agree" with the statement, *"When the police use deadly force against Black males, I usually give them the benefit of the doubt."*

- More than half of all Asian respondents (55.00%) "Strongly Agree" or "Agree" with the statement, *"If innocent Black men would simply cooperate with the police investigations, nothing would happen."*

Findings by Gender

- 7 out of 10 of all Female respondents (70.50%) "Strongly Agree" or "Agree" with the statement, *"Black males are sometimes racially profiled by law enforcement officers."*

- More than 7 out of 10 of all Male respondents (71.00%) say "Definitely Yes" or "Probably Yes" when asked the statement, *"Do you believe that bias against Black males exists within the American criminal justice system?"*

- More than 4 out 10 Hispanic female respondents (43.40%) "Strongly Agree" or "Agree" with the statement, *"When the police use deadly force against Black males, I usually give them the benefit of the doubt."*

Findings by Age

- Nearly half of all respondents, ages 18-24 years old (48.94%), "Strongly Disagree" or "Disagree" with the statement, *"If innocent Black men would simply cooperate with the police investigations, nothing would happen."*

- Nearly 7 out of 10 of all White respondents, ages 55 years and older (69.49%) "Strongly Agree" or "Agree" with the statement, *"Black males are sometimes racially profiled by law enforcement officers."*

- 7 out of 10 of all respondents, ages 25-34 years old (70.08%), say "Definitely Yes" or "Probably Yes" when asked the statement, *"Do you believe that bias against Black males exists within the American criminal justice system?"*

"Convicted on Lies...Sentenced to Die!"

- According to the most conservative estimates by the *National Academy of Sciences*, at least 4.1% of all defendants sentenced to death in the United States are innocent of the crimes to which they were convicted ("Innocent").

- Even though death sentences make up less than one-tenth of 1% of all prison sentences in the United States, they account for 12% of all exonerations, representing 1 innocent person for every 130 death row inmates ("Innocent").

"Membership *Really Does* Have Its Privileges!"

- Each year, nearly 1,000 people die as a result of police involved shootings. In 98.5% of all cases, local prosecutors decline to bring charges against officers, even in the most egregious circumstances (Ross).

- Since 2005, 98 local police officers have been arrested for killing citizens while on duty; 35 were convicted (3 for murder), 22 were acquitted by a jury, 9 acquitted by a judge, 10 cases were dismissed, and 21 cases are pending (Ross).

"No Voice. No Vote. No Joke!"

- 1 out of every 3 Black men in America have a felony conviction, rising from 13% in 1980 to 33% in 2010. During that same time period, the number of Black men remanded to prison more than doubled ("Felony Convictions").

- More than 6.1 million Americans are barred from voting in elections due to felony conviction laws, with African- Americans comprising 38% of this group of legally disenfranchised citizens ("Felony Convictions").

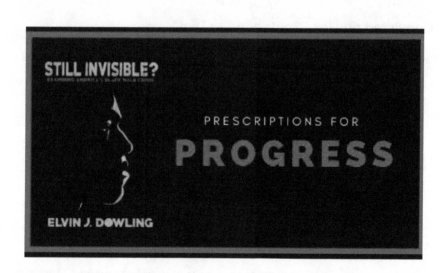

"Help Those Who Can't Help Themselves."

- In many American states, those who have been wrongfully convicted or incarcerated receive $0 by means of a just recompense. Encourage elected officials to pass laws mandating compensation for the exonerated ("Justice").

- Support organizations assisting the wrongfully accused to secure affordable housing, provide psychological counseling, legal services to obtain public benefits, expunge records, and regain custody of children ("Justice").

"Demand Change... Starting with the D.A."

- Since 2000, the policy of "building more prisons" has had zero impact on crime. Rather than focusing on their own convictions rates, insist that prosecutors focus on reducing recidivism and harm to the community ("Gatekeepers").

- Despite large numbers of minorities in the criminal justice system, there are few non-white prosecutors. Encourage diverse, reform-minded attorneys to become prosecutors and run for district attorney ("Gatekeepers").

"A Voteless People ... A Hopeless People!"

- Work with community groups and religious institutions that provide support to help returning citizens turn their lives around, with programs that include mentoring, housing placement and job training ("Re-entry").

- Millions of Americans, especially Black males, have lost their right to vote through felony disenfranchisement. Lobby your state legislature to restore voting rights for the formerly incarcerated ("Re-entry").

Works Cited

1. Capehart, Jonathan. "How the Justice System Criminalizes the Poor — and Funds Itself in the Process." *WashingtonPost.com*, Nash Holdings. 29 January 2019. https://wapo.st/2ZsAl7p

2. Alexander, Michelle. "Go to Trial: Crash the Justice
   System." *NYTimes.com*, The New York Times   Company. 10
   March 2012.   https://nyti.ms/34RAanbn

3. "Harmelin v. Michigan." *Oyez.org*, Cornell University -
   Legal Information Institute. Accessed 25   December
   2019. http://bit.ly/2EP8jK1

4. McKinley, James C. and Baker, Al. "Grand Jury System,
   With Exceptions, Favors the Police in Fatalities."   *NYTimes.com*,
   The New York Times Company. 7   December 2014.
   https://nyti.ms/2Su7azC

5. Fletcher, Michael A. "Evidence of Innocence" on TV One
   Tells the Stories of the Wrongfully Convicted."
   TheUndefeated.com, ESPN. 4 June 2018.
   http://bit.ly/2ZxkUe5

6. "Wrongful Convictions." *EJI.org*, Equal Justice Initiative.
   Accessed 27 December 2019.
   http://bit.ly/2Qtap7t

7. Jordan, Sandra. "Wesley Bell Elected STL County's First
   Black Prosecutor." *STLAmerican.com*, The St.   Louis
   American. 6 November 2018.
   http://bit.ly/2Quin0b

8. Weingartner, Tana. "Judge Fanon Rucker Enters Hamilton
   County Prosecutor's Race." *WVXU.org*,   Cincinnati
   Public Radio. 14 October 2019.   http://bit.ly/2Q6LCqS

9. Gonnerman, Jennifer. "Before the Law: Three Years on
   Rikers   Without Trial." *NewYorker.com*, ⊠Condé   Nast. 6
   October 2014. http://bit.ly/2MrX3r2

10. Blank, Chris and McDowell, Rebecca. "What Rights Do
    Convicted Felons Lose?" *LegalBeagle.com*, Leaf   Group Ltd. /
    Leaf Group Media.   http://bit.ly/2sduZ41

11. Gonnerman, Jennifer. "Kalief Browder: 1993-2015."
    NewYorker.com, ⊠Condé Nast. 6 October 2014. 7   June 2015.
    http://bit.ly/39bkxdH

12. Coats, Ta-Nehisi, "Trayvon Martin and the Irony of

American Justice." *TheAtlantic.com*, Atlantic   Media. 15 July
2013. http://bit.ly/35YNsj5

13. Potts, Monica. "Barack Obama, Trayvon Martin, and the
Presidency." *Vogue.com*, ⊠Condé Nast. 22   December
2016. http://bit.ly/2QkeYRH

14. "Remarks by the President on Trayvon Martin."
ObamaWhiteHouse.Archives.gov, The White House   - Office of
the Press Secretary. 19 July 2013.   http://bit.ly/2EWGzDe

15. "National Academy of Sciences Reports Four Percent of
Death Row Inmates are Innocent."
InnocenceProject.org, Innocence Project. 28 April   2014.
http://bit.ly/2EVmux2

16. Ross, Janell. "Police Officers Convicted for Fatal Shootings   Are
the Exception, Not the Rule."   *NBCNews.com*,
NBCUniversal.   https://nbcnews.to/2QtJkkC

17. "Race & Justice News: One Third of Black Men Have
Felony Convictions." *SentencingProject.org*, The   Sentencing
Project. 10 October 2017.   http://bit.ly/2MC0BqW

18. "Justice After Exoneration." *WitnessToInnocence*.org,
Witness to Innocence. Accessed 27 December   2019.
http://bit.ly/2spqqU0

19. Rooks, Robert. "The Successful Reentry Project: Working
Towards Justice, Dignity and Redemption."   *NAACP.org*,
The National Association for the   Advancement of Colored
People. November   2010. http://bit.ly/2Sxytck

Chapter 15: Do Black Lives Really Matter?

Examining Political Protests in the iPhone Era

"

I didn't understand in those pre-invisible days that their hate, and mine too, was charged with fear."

- Ralph Ellison, "Invisible Man" (Shmoop Editorial Team. 2.98)

(The photo above is a depiction of the Deslondes Slave Rebellion. Charles Deslondes, an enslaved Haitian, led America's largest slave revolt in 1811, having compiled a group of 200-500 slaves and Maroons and then marched from the sugar plantations on the German Coast [Mississippi River] to the City of New Orleans—terrorizing white Southerners in the process.)

"Time to Get Back to Basics"

Can't We Start All Over Again?

In his book, "All I Really Need to Know, I Learned in Kindergarten," author Robert Fulghum spoke of the fundamental lessons learned by the young—and the young at heart—as they open their eyes to the realities of the world and those around them. *"All I really need to know about how to live and what to do and how to be, I learned in kindergarten,"* Fulghum found. *"Wisdom was not at the top of the graduate school mountain, but there in the sand pile at Sunday School."* Today, however, as America works feverishly to forestall a looming racial inferno that has the potential to consume and destroy our "shining city on a hill," something must be done, and quickly, to address the natives who have clearly gotten restless and are no longer content with taking the *"tranquilizing drug of gradualism."* To that end, dear heart, in my last missive to you for a while, I hope to proffer some final words of wisdom that, if heeded, can go a long way towards bridging our nation's clear racial divide. If ignored, however, I fear a divisive and uncertain fate for the "land of the free", "home of the brave", and country we call home.

Since the height of the worldwide slave trade, Africans forced into bondage in America have sought to overthrow their captors as early, and as often, as possible; staging revolts, rebellions and running away—anything they could do to help them *"live free or die."* In fact, many of those who determined that they would rather be six feet under, than to be held captive and in chains, were unwilling to let anything separate them from their very own "pursuit of happiness". In doing so, they had no qualms if that necessitated their destroying property and taking lives when they deemed it necessary; stoking fears of racial revenge in the hearts and minds of many in the majority. In responding to the cyclical unrest that periodically tears at the fabric of our society, the Reverend Dr. Martin Luther King, Jr. apocalyptically affirmed what many already knew America, after centuries of winking her eye, nodding her head and saying "not a mumbling word" continues to remain tone deaf and mute on matters of moral courage. *"A riot is the language of the unheard,"* Dr. King warned us. *"And what is it America has failed to hear? ... It has failed to hear that the promises of freedom and justice have not been met. And it has failed to hear that large segments of white society are more concerned about tranquility and the status quo than about justice and humanity."*

As natural born and/or naturalized citizens of the greatest nation on earth, we are taught, in no uncertain terms, that the United States of America is a refuge of *"liberty and justice for all."* More importantly, the foundational tenets we ascribe to as a nation, such as treating our neighbors with love and respect, showing kindness to the immigrant and stranger, and exhibiting grace and mercy, not only for those who *"do* get things they *don't* deserve, but also for those who *"don't* get things that they *do* deserve." Further, if we are to continue to keep the republic that was bequeathed to us by our nation's founding fathers in the summer of 1776, imbibing these canons by "practicing what we preach" is as important to our cultural development as country, as "reading is fundamental". To that end, for those of us who are in the majority, yet have compassion for those within the minority, it's important for you to remember—and never forget—that there are those who understand, much more than you will ever comprehend, what it's like to be constantly given "the short end of the stick." So, mind your manners (please and thank you) and hearken to *their* voices for a change. You may even be pleasantly surprised at just how much you'll learn —if you listen twice as much as you speak.

As Americans, one of the leading core values we share is the idea that, at the end of the day—when it's all said and done—we are stronger when we stand as one. In short, *"we may not have all come over on the same boat, but we're in this ship together!"* Today, however, as we enter the age of slacktivism and W.I.F.M. (i.e. *"What's in It for Me?"),* we have replaced the idea of *"What's mine is yours and what's yours is mine,"* with *"Every man for himself and God for us all."* **And that has got to change.** You see, as the universe's sole superpower, there are nation's desirous of knocking us off of our exalted pedestal and taking our place in the world. Moreover, they believe that America's best days are behind us, writing us off as a "has-been" country rife with hypocrisy and fueled by racism and greed. Additionally, it is no accident that hostile forces around the globe are actively seeking to subvert our government's integrity and upend our way of life. But _we_ know we are better than that—or at least we believe that we can be—and that's what makes our nation great!

Another one of those key principles that separate us from the rest of the flock, as a nation to be admired, is the idea that, in America, it is important for us to always do the right thing— even if it's unpopular. But that pertains to all of us. You see, if America is ever going to truly be "America" to all who call her home, our nation can no longer sustain a cultural model built on a foundation of lies. Moreover, we must expose the lies that continue to promote the fallacious notion that _"white is always right."_ To achieve this goal, it will require us to deconstruct the unjust institutions that provide sanctuary for the majority—at the expense of the minority—which is easier said than done. But it's possible.

The late professor Leo Buscaglia, known to many during his lifetime as "Dr. Love," best summed up what I believe to be America's limitless potential when he said:

❝

"To laugh is to risk appearing a fool.
To weep is to risk appearing sentimental.
To reach out to another is to risk involvement.
To expose feelings is to risk exposing your true self.
To place your ideas and dreams before a crowd is to risk their loss.
To love is to risk not being loved in return.
To hope is to risk pain.
To try is to risk failure.
But risks must be taken, because the greatest hazard in life is to risk nothing."

Today, as we prepare to turn over the reins of our nation to a new generation of leadership, the time has come for all of us to get back to the basics of what it truly means to be an American. That includes "doing the right thing," treating others the way we would want to be treated and "sticking together"—always with a willingness to take the risks that need to be taken to

"Make America Great ... My Friend!" Finally, beloved, you must never forget that there will be times when it seems as if the whole world is against us—and it is—but we've got to remain united. There will be days when it seems as if *every time* we take one step forward, we're knocked two steps back ... but keep the faith. Don't lose hope. Change is <u>still</u> possible... if only we just believe!

Farewell for now,

Justitia

Lady Justice

Roy M. Tatem, Jr.: "Taking it to the Streets"

Can You Hear Me Now?

"My name is Roy M. Tatem, Jr. and I am originally from Virginia Beach Virginia, but I currently reside in Phoenix, Arizona," opened the skilled political activist and recognizable community leader. "I grew up in a pretty middle-class environment as a kid, and I don't really have the sort of "rags to riches" upbringing that usually accompanies what it means to be Black and later become successful in America," the trusted political operative intoned. "In fact," he said, "I grew up in a loving two-parent household with hardworking, blue collar parents who taught me the value of leadership and commitment early on as a child. My mother," Tatem continued, "was a teacher, and my father worked for the *United States Department of Defense*, repairing aircraft carriers for the military," he recalled. "Even though I was raised in a relatively middle-class community, but even still, I was not immune to the societal situations impacting people of color in this country, while attempting to successfully navigate my community as a young Black man," he declared.

"When I was twelve years old, my parents separated, but for the first dozen years of my life, I am proud to say that I grew up in a two-parent household. By the time that I reached my teenage years, however, although I was shuttling back and forth between my mother and father's homes, I was kept relatively busy so that the change in my home situation did not negatively impact me during those most formative years. In fact, as a teenager, I had a burgeoning sports career, participating in every sporting activity that I could enroll in, from football to track. I bring this up," Tatem explained, "to reflect on the fact that those years flew by, from the time my parents split up, until the day of my high school graduation," he noted. "As a result, I was always busy in some type of activity or sporting event, and too tired to run the streets and get in trouble," Tatem observed, grateful that his parents continued to place his well-being at the forefront of their responsibilities, regardless of the deterioration of their own relationship.

"My family is the core of my value system," Tatem proclaimed, noting the esteem to which he held his parents who invested their time, energy and attention into him becoming a man of excellence. "As a kid growing up, I will say that my mother definitely served as that spiritual anchor for me, always admonishing me to trust in God, lean not to my own understanding and pray without ceasing," the devout husband and father declared. "On the other hand, my father was my first hero. He was also my first idol and first teacher. Together, both of them helped me to appreciate who I was, and always gave me a sense of self-affirmation even when the world did not reflect what I knew to be my truth," the community leader conceded. "So, I have always had my own sense of identity, courage, and confidence, so to speak, and I owe it all to my parents," Tatem professed.

"One of the important aspects of my early upbringing that I want to speak to," he continued, "was the fact that there were not many places where I _had_ to go, outside of my own home, to get something that I needed," he recalled. "I'm talking about basic human needs, like food, shelter, water and love," the activist admitted. "There was never a time where I had to worry about something going wrong, or being evicted or kicked out of the house, or the water not being on," he explained. "That was not my upbringing, as my parents worked hard to ensure that I had a strong sense of security," he explained. "When you talk about Maslow's hierarchy of needs, the parenting that I received put me in the middle of that pyramid, where safety and love and all of the basic needs of the human being were absolutely taken care of. Therefore," Tatem intoned, "even at a very young age, I always believed that I could pursue my own level of self-actualization, and that has served me well," he concluded.

"In 1994, I matriculated to *Virginia State University*, in Petersburg, Virginia, where I began to pursue an interest in politics as a college student," Tatem declared; detailing a long history of political activism that has taken him from "sea to shining sea" in support of political candidates seeking the highest office in the land. "Upon graduation from college in 1998, I was able to get a job on *Capitol Hill* in the *United States Senate*. Since then, I have not only worked on three U.S. presidential campaigns, I am now the owner and operator of my own company, *Vanguard Strategies and Consulting, LLC*, where I provide consultative services in the areas of politics, business and personal development for individuals and companies," he continued. As a sought-after political operative with a solid reputation for "getting things done," Roy also served as the National Deputy Director for African-American Outreach *(personally responsible for Black political engagement for half the country)* for the 2016 insurgency campaign for the Democratic Party nomination for President of the United Sates by the former Mayor of Burlington, the Honorable Bernie Sanders—a United Senator from Vermont. "From a civic engagement perspective, I also serve as President of the *East Valley NAACP*, where we work to turn personal passion into an organized strategy aimed at implementing best practices that address an array of community concerns," Tatem detailed.

"During my time on *Capitol Hill*, I worked for then Senator Charles "Chuck" Robb of Virginia," who was also the son-in-law of the late United States President Lyndon Baines Johnson, having wed the president's daughter, the former Lynda Bird Johnson, in 1967. "January 2, 1999—my first day on the job— was also the first day of the impeachment trial against President William Jefferson Clinton in the *United States Senate*," the history buff recalled. "By the time I came on board as a staff member to Senator Robb, one of the jurors in the case against the president, the issue was already a political 'hot potato' that ultimately landed in my lap as the 'low man on the *Tatem-* pole," he joked. Nonetheless, Tatem was grateful for the opportunity to be an eyewitness to history on behalf of the people of the Commonwealth of Virginia. Since that time, Roy has not only worked on the issues impacting "real people" in a "real way" with those at the highest levels of government, he has also challenged those same authorities when necessary; fighting for the rights of the "least of these" on behalf of the nation's oldest civil rights organization.

In the Fall of 2011, the *NAACP* launched a process to develop a strategic plan to address the major areas of inequality facing Blacks and other individuals of color in twenty-first century America. Branded by the organization as "Game Changers for the Twenty-First Century," the direct action approach of today's *NAACP* is deliberate and intentional; based on six key areas of interest and concern to the marginalized and oppressed peoples of the country, including: Economic Sustainability, Education, Health, Public Safety and Criminal Justice, Voting Rights and Political Representation, and Expanding Youth and Young Adult Engagement. Moreover, as a new generation of leadership takes the stage and attempts to move the agenda of minority empowerment and equal opportunity to the forefront of the American consciousness once more, millennials, a group to which Roy Tatem, Jr. is not too far removed, have now become "the new foot soldiers" on the frontlines of the battle for social justice. In a story under the same byline by Sarah Ruiz-Grossman, a reporter for the *Huffington Post,* those born between 1980-2000 are now beginning to take up the torch of leadership and courage, in cutting edge ways no less, definitively proving that this is <u>NOT</u> their father's revolution.

"Since the November [2016] presidential election, waves of people have taken to the streets in protest — and young people are leading the charge," Ruiz-Grossman found. "Among people who have taken any form of political action in their lifetime, 24 percent of 18- to 30-year-olds say they've gone to a rally or demonstration since the election, compared to only around 10 percent of people ages 30 to 44; 45 to 64; or 65 and older," the *HuffPost* reported. "Young people also rank protest as one of the two most effective political actions one can take, alongside calling or writing their representatives," to bring about meaningful change in America (Ruiz-Grossman). In fact, in one of the most comprehensive studies on millennials and their involvement with causes to date, Rai Masuda, President of the *Achieve Agency,* an advertising firm whose expertise lies in the four pillars of storytelling, web design, digital marketing and social media, observed just how differently young Americans view activism from those in older generations. Furthermore, the research demonstrates that millennials, despite popular conception, are willing to lay their lives on the line for issues of importance to them—so long as that goal can be achieved before brunch or yoga class.

"The report reveals that while millennials remain passionately interested in improving their world, they base their political decisions on what causes each candidate supports and no longer primarily look to traditional institutions to effect societal change," Masuda detailed. Furthermore, in analyzing the "2016 Millennial Impact Report," Masuda noted how *"Generation Y"* is as equally determined—as was their parents —in changing the way the United States treats its most vulnerable populations, but only on their own terms, and in ways that are unique to their contemporary worldview. "Millennials are quickly normalizing the change-making lifestyle—one in which cause engagement is embedded in their everyday lives and identity—while at the same time losing faith in government and other established groups to make a meaningful impact" (Masuda). As such, the following causes and concerns, according to the report, are of paramount importance to the millennial generation, to include (but not be limited to) the following:

- **Voting** - Most reported supporting positions from both sides of the political divide concurrently; splitting their votes almost evenly between the Democratic and Republican candidates for President of the United States in 2016 (Masuda).

- **Activism** - Most Gen. Y'ers believe that "making a difference" is important and as such, more than half (52.50%) identify themselves as "advocates". (Masuda)

- **Issues:** The leading issues of concern among high school/no degree participants include criminal justice reform, employment and wages (Masuda).

- **Trust in Government:** Unsurprisingly, millennials do not tend to trust in government to right the wrongs in American society. Consequently, they are often actively engaged in signing petitions, volunteering for causes, advocating for issues on social media platforms as ways to enact change (Masuda).

Just as important as their willingness to get involved in the defining social issues of our time, many in the millennial generation also understand that the impetus for lasting social change in America is up to those whites who are willing to lay aside their own personal bias, in search of a higher truth. In her article, "It's Now Up to Whites to Dismantle Racism," Stephanye Watts, creator of the web series "Year of the Real Black Girl," in writing for *TIME*, discussed how those within America's majority must do the heavy lifting of enacting systemic change, *if* America is truly to become a more just and equitable society. "Hear me out, white people," Watts exclaimed, "the ball is completely in your court. You created the mess, so it's up to you to clean it up. Black people," Watts wrote, "as much as we've tried, can't dismantle racism. White people created the social construct of race to subjugate people of color, so you are the only ones who can change it," she continued. "Black people do everything you ask us to do. We get college degrees, work in corporate America, and speak the Queen's English. Yet," she continued, "to many of you, we're still just 3/5 human. White people (and our President) love to reference Dr. Martin Luther King Jr. as a role model for how to behave in a time of unrest. What they always forget is that despite the fact that he was a well-dressed, well-behaved Christian pastor, he was still murdered," Watts bewailed.

What's more, the columnist, decried, for those whites who *"get it,"* while also understanding the incredible odds stacked against the average man or woman of color in America, it is important that they stand up and have their voices counted in the chorus of change in America. Moreover, the need for them to stand in the gap for those members of the minority community who have no one to stand for them, is just as important now as it was during the civil rights movement of the 1950's and 1960's. "Black people have done everything we can do," Watts said with an air of resignation that the difficult work of racial reconciliation and healing must begin with those in the majority. "Fixing this is up to white people now... We appreciate you for standing in solidarity, but it's only half your battle," she opined. "The second and most important step is to share what you know with the more prejudiced white people around you... Trust me, they'll believe you over us."

With that being said, however, in order for the nation to truly engage in a meaningful discussion, Watts, like many other Black Americans, believe that inflammatory distractions and racist red herrings must be dispensed with if Blacks and whites in America truly want to change the historic nature of their love-hate relationship. "White people of America," she implored, "I beg of you, stop bringing up Black-on-Black crime. It's irrelevant to the question of why a Black man who kills another will be put under the jail, while a white police officer doesn't even get charges sent his way. That is where our anger lies," Watts intoned. "This is why we're flooding the streets and disrupting life as usual. Murder is murder, and all of our lives are equally precious, so why is there a discrepancy in penalties?," she asked (Watts). So, what can be done to turn the tide of race relations in America? In the opinion of many Blacks, those whites willing to become "trusted allies" in the fight for human dignity for all Americans, must emerge from the shadows and take their rightful place at the table of progress and brotherhood.

Will You Practice What You Preach?

In her engaging commentary on the need for whites in America to step up and speak out on issues of race and culture in the country, Melanie Morrison of *Yale Divinity School* called on those who mean well to do the right thing by joining the fight to undo discrimination. "To understand what it means to be white in America and break the silences that surround it requires arduous, persistent, and soul-stretching work," remarked Morrison, an educated white woman from the Ivy League admitted. "Sadly, too many of us stop short of that deep work. We assume that our good intentions and eagerness to help are enough," she hypothesized. "We come into multiracial gatherings or organizations expecting to be liked and trusted. But trust isn't something we are granted simply because we finally showed up. Trust has to be earned, again and again," Morrison maintained. "Or better said, we need to become trustworthy white allies, people passionately committed to eliminating systems of oppression that unjustly benefit us."

For Morrison, and similarly situated members of the majority culture, being white in America has its own set of benefits that are hard to deny. "One meaning of being white is that we are granted unearned privileges and structural power simply by reason of our race, without regard for our personal attitudes, values, and commitments," Morrison confessed. As such, the thoughtful theologian theorized that some whites actually do more harm than good when rushing into minority communities proffering themselves as the solution to everything that ails Black people. "How do we do this?," Morrison asked. "By presuming we can speak for others, imposing our mission and outreach projects on others, discounting as "ungrounded" the fears and criticisms voiced by people of color, dismissing their pain as overreacting, accusing them of "playing the race card" when they call us on our oppressive behavior, and then shifting the focus to our hurt feelings. Our work as allies," Morrison asserted, "must always and everywhere be grounded in humility, collaboration, and accountability. This means becoming engaged in organizations led by people of color, respecting the priorities they identify as strategies for change, and sustaining our engagement over time" (Morrison). As a confederate with people from across the racial divide, Roy Tatem, Jr. agrees with the notion that everyone must be involved, particularly those with power, in building a "beloved community."

"As president of the *East Valley NAACP,* I represent the interests of people of color east of Phoenix, Arizona—which is the fifth largest city in America," the modern-day civil rights champion explained. "The East Valley comprises nine relatively affluent communities, including Tempe, Mesa, and Scottsdale, Arizona. Although there are a number of communities that many Black people here call home, there is no solid "Black block" of neighborhoods here in the East Valley. With that thought in mind," Tatem related, "the minority community in my area is generally comprised of educated people of color who have access to a significant level of means. Furthermore, their children attend schools that are fairly integrated and reside in communities that are fairly integrated," he remarked. "When law enforcement officers are interacting with the constituency groups I represent," he declared, "especially Black men, my role is to ensure that they are being treated fairly and not being profiled," the protector of personal freedoms proclaimed.

"As you may know, the East Valley falls into Maricopa County, and prior to 2016, Maricopa County had a notorious Sheriff by the name of Joe Arpaio, known to the world as "Sheriff Joe," Tatem denoted, describing a man both celebrated by many on the right side of the political spectrum for his "tough on immigration" tactics, and scorned on the left for the way he treated people of color while in power as the county's top cop. "Sheriff Joe, as he was called by most people, was known to be very hard on people of color in general and the Latino community in particular. In fact," Tatem elucidated, "the county eventually lost a federal lawsuit for racial profiling, _right here_, so there is a culture of aggressive policing of Black and brown people in this community," he stated. "To that end, I have intentionally worked to develop relationships with the majority of the police leadership, and other individuals that can be potential allies in the continuing quest for dignity and justice in America."

"When there is a police shooting, or report of police misconduct, I get a phone call and through my work with the _NAACP_, I investigate and seek to resolve those issues and seek to get some semblance of justice for those who have been potentially victimized," Roy remarked. "The police leadership, in my opinion, understands the need to have fair and equitable policing practices, however, that same level of understanding needs to be conveyed all the way down to the rank-and-file police officers," he maintained. "Many African-American males in communities like mine, often have the police called on them by a citizen, pedestrian, resident, or local business owner, because they feel 'unsafe', for whatever reason. Once Black males around here encounter the police, however, many of them are looked at by law enforcement _'as guilty until proven innocent,'_" Tatem noted, describing some of the circumstances that lead to many of the complaints he receives from those who believe they have been aggrieved. "The challenge with that, however, is that there is often no _'probable cause'_ to believe that someone has committed a crime," Tatem declared. "In those instances, they should just be left alone. Unfortunately," he conceded, "some police officers overstep their roles as peace officers, in an effort to intimidate citizens or extract potentially damaging information that can then be used against them, when they deal with citizens of color. And that," the advocate and activist admitted, "is why we have to protest!"

"Let's be honest," Tatem confessed, "some police officers are involved in white supremacist activity, and should not be involved in police work at all," he exclaimed. "When an individual is entrusted to protect and serve the community and are paid with taxpayer dollars, they should not operate with a sense of bias when dealing with the community," he went on. "Furthermore, when it comes to the rank-and-file police officer, I believe we need to have a more educated police force patrolling our streets. These are people with the power of life and death in their hands," he noted, "therefore, there should be continued education and sensitivity training for them to become better officers as they strive to serve the community," he concluded. When it comes to the plethora of negative police interactions that are pervasive in public perception, however, Tatem is convinced that there is nothing new under the sun.

"I believe that what we are seeing today, is nothing different than what has been happening to Black men for centuries," Tatem theorized; hearkening back to the martyrs of a bygone era who were sacrificed on the altar of hate and ignorance so that ensuing generations could live. "With the proliferation of technology, the power of social media and the fact that everyone has a camera in their pockets, the world is now seeing what Black people experience every day in this country," he furthered. "There are killings, and other civil rights violations against Black men that are going on in real time, and I will say that there is no difference in what was happening in the past, and what is occurring right now. "Most recently," Tatem noted, "we commemorated the brutal lynching of Emmett Till on August 28th, 1955, who was killed in Mississippi for allegedly whistling at a white woman. Were it not for the insistence of his mother, Mamie till, who decided to have an open casket funeral, allowing the media to publish the photos of a disfigured 14-year old child, whose only crime was being Black in the South, the world may never have known the true brutality of white supremacy," Roy remarked. "For many of us, growing up in the South, we all learned the story of Emmett Till in a way that made us aware of some very real dangers that were out there in society waiting to befall us the moment we made a wrong move," the powerful politico professed.

"In my opinion, the government is not doing enough to address the negative issues that impact African-American men in this country," the activist ceded. "In fact," Tatem said, "we really have yet begun to address the historic justices in our democratic system. For the first time ever," he went on, "we have heard the subject of reparations discussed in a presidential debate—in 2019. In modern day political parlance, that has never happened! To that end, I think it is important for us to address the issue of restorative justice, economically, for the descendants of slaves. Not to mention," Tatem asserted, "there are a number of issues we have to tackle as a nation, if we are to ever be a 'free society' for all Americans," he noted.

"There is an old expression in the African-American community which says,

'When white America catches a cold, Black America gets pneumonia'. As Black people in this country," Roy concluded, "we unfortunately get the worst end of every ill that America faces. Additionally, the government has still not fully addressed the needs of the Black community in general, and Black men in particular, because they look to us as a source of labor," Tatem speculated. "They look to us as entertainment. They look to us as sports players," he went on, "but they don't look to us as equals. In fact," he theorized, "we need look no further than the *National Football League (NFL)*, which has sent a clear and direct message to able-bodied, strong Black men, which is simple and succinct: "If you want to pursue a career in football, you had better leave that social justice stuff behind, because it is not welcome here in the *NFL*," he hypothesized. "In short, what they are saying to African-American men is, 'we want your body, we want your speed, and we want your muscle,' Tatem intoned. "But what we don't want is your brain. Nor do we want your opinions when it comes to the American justice system," he concluded. With regard to his assessment of both the *NFL* and its stance on the social justice protests that have marked "America's game," Tatem is not alone, as there are others (many of whom are not African-American) who agree that the *League* has capitulated to the desires of a complacent majority who prefer their athletes simply "shut up and play"—without ever speaking up for marginalized and oppressed in the ongoing struggle for human dignity and self-respect.

"Do We *Have* to Pick Sides?"

In his opinion article for the *Chicago Tribune* entitled, "Why Do Whites Oppose NFL Protests?," Steve Chapman, a member of the newspaper's editorial board, offered a simple yet powerful explanation for the antipathy that America's majority has for those who dare to disrupt a game with their plaintive cries for equality. "The *Black Lives Matter* movement is... unpopular among whites....The negative opinions could be attributed to the noisy, disruptive marches the group has held or to the occasional outbreaks of violence that have resulted," Chapman admitted. "But if you don't like how *Black Lives Matter* pursues its agenda, you should welcome the *NFL* players' approach. It's silent; it's not disruptive; and it's entirely nonviolent," Chapman posited. "It doesn't block traffic, occupy police or frighten bystanders," he wrote. Even still, the majority of whites not only oppose protesting sports stars, preferring to burn the jerseys and paraphernalia of protesting Black athletes or even better (in the opinion of many) having their careers placed on indefinite hold, as is the case with former *San Francisco 49'ers* quarterback Colin Kaepernick; an erstwhile talented athlete in the prime of his career who has been effectively sidelined since he decided to silently take a knee during the playing of the country's national anthem.

"Critics say it's disrespectful to the flag," Chapman pronounced, "but no flags are harmed — and it could be taken as a form of respect for the flag to mutely signal your belief that the ideals it represents are not being realized," he observed. "Every time unrest erupts in Black communities in response to some perceived injustice, finger-wagging whites wonder why Blacks can't express their dissent in an orderly, law-abiding way. But every time African-Americans protest peacefully, the same whites object to the message, the tactics, the purpose or the slogans" (Chapman). In concluding his assessment of the reasoning behind the animus displayed against those who dare to speak out against injustice, Chapman ceded that there are some whites, despite the method in which Blacks express their displeasure at being woefully mistreated by entities that are supposed to protect them, who may never be satisfied. "Are there better ways for them to make their point? Maybe so," Chapman acknowledged. "But it wouldn't make much difference. To many whites, the only good Black protest is no Black protest," he said. When it comes to social protests, however, whether on (or off) the playing field, or in the streets for that matter, some have postulated that a coming race conflagration is on the horizon, should America fail to change the way it treats its most vulnerable citizens.

In 1968, the year in which he was assassinated in the kitchen of the *Ambassador Hotel* in Los Angeles, California, U.S. Senator Robert F. Kennedy of New York spoke to the challenges expressed by those who protest and take to the streets in America when they believe their concerns are not being addressed in a reasonable and timely manner, when he said:

``

Some who accuse others of inciting riots have by their own conduct invited them ... This much is clear; violence breeds violence, repression brings retaliation, and only a cleaning of our whole society can remove this sickness from our soul. For there is another kind of violence, slower but just as deadly, destructive as the shot or the bomb in the night. This is the violence of institutions; indifference and inaction and slow decay. This is the violence that afflicts the poor, that poisons relations between men because their skin has different colors. This is a slow destruction of a child by hunger, and schools without books and homes without heat in the winter. This is the breaking of a man's spirit by denying him the chance to stand as a father and as a man among other men. And this too afflicts us all.

A TIMELINE OF BLACK PROTEST

FROM SLAVE SHIP REBELLIONS TO "BLACK LIVES MATTER"

1811

Deslondes Slave Rebellion
Began January 8
Charles Deslondes, a Haitian slave, led an uprising of hundreds of slaves who marched on white plantations, from Mississippi to New Orleans, Louisiana.

1831 REBELLION

Nat Turner Slave Rebellion
August 21 - 23
In a horrifying slave uprising led by Nat Turner in Southampton County, Virginia, rebel slaves killed from 55 to 65 people, with at least 51 victims being white.

Amistad Slave Revolt
July 2
After freeing themselves, captive Africans, led by Sengbe Pieh, revolted against and overthrew the crew of "La Amistad", a slave ship, before making a landing off the coast of Long Island, New York.

1839 REVOLT

1967 RIOT

Detroit Riots
July 23 - 28
Also known as the "Detroit Rebellion," the urban uprising occured when police raided an unlicensed, after-hours bar, resulting in 43 deaths, 1,189 injuries, 7,200 arrests and 2,000 buildings destroyed.

Los Angeles Riots
April 29 - May 4
Unrest began in South Central Los Angeles after a jury acquitted Los Angeles Police Department officers in the brutal beating of motorist Rodney King, which had been videotaped, widely viewed, and considered by many to be an excessive use of force.

1992 RIOT

2015 PROTESTS

Baltimore Protests & Riots
April 18 - May 3
Protests broke out when Baltimore Police Department officers arrested 25 year old Freddie Gray, who sustained injuries and later died while in police custody.

For more information visit
www.history.com.

Today, as the United States of America continues to experience periodic "seasons of discontent," the issues sparking civil disobedience and, in some cases rebellion, throughout its history, continue to plague her today. In an eye-opening exposition for *TIME* called, "The Coming Race War Won't Be About Race," basketball great Kareem Abdul-Jabbar pointed to the ominous storm clouds looming just off of the horizon, with a potential to have natural disaster implications, should America choose to ignore forecasts warning of a racial tsunami headed its way. In fact, according to Abdul-Jabbar, the only factor holding America back from enacting true, systemic change in the way we police, protect and serve communities of color, is the ability of the nation's aristocracy to keep its proletariat class continually at odds with one another. "The *U.S. Census Report* finds that 50 million Americans are poor. Fifty million voters are a powerful block if they ever organized in an effort to pursue their common economic goals," the sports legend proclaimed. "So, it's crucial that those in the wealthiest *One Percent* keep the poor fractured, by distracting them with emotional issues like immigration, abortion and gun control so they never stop to wonder how they got so screwed over for so long," he postulated.

"Rather than uniting to face the real foe—do-nothing politicians, legislators, and others in power—we fall into the trap of turning against each other, expending our energy battling our allies instead of our enemies," Abdul-Jabbar deduced. Moreover, if things are to ever change for the better in America, the six-time "*Most Valuable Player*" (MVP) for the *National Basketball Association*, believes that the poor and vulnerable members of society must come together to oppose hypocrisy and marginalization whenever it raises its ugly head. "The middle class has to join the poor," Abdul-Jabbar explained, if the nation is to ever become a 'more perfect union'. "Whites have to join African-Americans in mass demonstrations, in ousting corrupt politicians, in boycotting exploitative businesses, in passing legislation that promotes economic equality and opportunity, and in punishing those who gamble with our financial future," he warned, or the consequences could be dire.

For many white Americans, however, the very thought of joining African-

Americans in the fight for racial justice and social equality, is one that leaves them frightened and concerned that their ability to continually set the agenda as America's super-majority is being threatened and is coming to a close. Hua Hsu, a professor of English at *Vassar College*, in an article for *The Atlantic* called, "The End of White America?," postulated that the changing demographics of the nation are driving some Caucasians, who are feeling an enormous sense of pressure, to reject the cries of equality from minorities. In doing so, however, they often cling to the mistaken belief that a "win" for Black Americans is a "loss" for whites. "Whether you describe it as the dawning of a post-racial age or just the end of white America. We're approaching a profound demographic tipping point," Hsu wrote. In point of fact, in a 2008 *U.S. Census Bureau* report detailing the shifting demography those groups currently categorized as racial minorities, to include Blacks and Hispanics, and Asians, who will assume the mantle of "majority" in America by the year 2042.

In analyzing the tension that some feel as the "browning" of the nation continues, Hsu, in quoting white men she interviewed, observed that there is genuine angst amongst this powerful group of Americans who used to represent an overwhelming majority of the population. *"'I think white people feel like they're under siege right now—like it's not okay to be white right now, especially if you're a white male,'"* one respondent noted. *"'There's a lot of fear and a lot of resentment,'"* another said. Yet another respondent declared, *'We used to be in control! We're losing control!'* In seeking to tamp down the concern, Hsu noted the importance of reassuring those who may be concerned about this coming demographic shift, that there is always room at the table for those who are willing to advance our nation's most enduring motto, *'E Pluribus Unum—'Out of many, One.'* According to Hsu, "I always tell the white men in the room, *'We need you...We cannot talk about diversity and inclusion and engagement without you at the table. It's okay to be white...* But people are stressed out about it," And that stress sometimes leads to a theoretical "circling of the wagons," for some white Americans who are beginning to feel outnumbered and, in a proverbial sense, outgunned.

As a follow-up to his initial piece in *TIME*, Kareem Abdul-Jabbar, a man who has served as a global ambassador for peace and camaraderie throughout the entirety of his lifetime, in a second piece entitled, "White People Feel Targeted by the Ferguson Protests—Welcome to Our World," encouraged those who are currently in the majority to consider the feelings of the minority and *why* they protest for change. "Many white people think that these cries of outrage over racism by African-Americans are directed at them," Abdul-Jabbar inscribed, "which makes them frightened, defensive and equally outraged. They feel like they are being blamed for a problem that's been going on for many decades, even centuries, " he maintained. "They feel they are being singled out because of the color of their skin rather than any actions they've taken. They are angry at the injustice. And rightfully so. Why should they be attacked and blamed for something they didn't do?," Abdul-Jabbar queried. "Which is exactly how Black people feel. Every. Single. Day." As a man who keeps his ear close to the ground and his "hands to the plow", Roy Tatem, Jr. believes that part of the challenge America faces, even today, is its unwillingness to deal with the love-hate relationship it has with Black people.

"As Black men in America, the concept of being 'invisible' takes on a number of connotations and meanings for me, as our bodies are always seen, however, our voices are not always heard—and our perspectives are not always appreciated," Tatem denoted. "Just as importantly," he postulated, "our intellect is not always respected. As such, I totally appreciate the work of Ralph Ellison in *"Invisible Man"*, but nowadays, I believe it takes on a very complex concept because America loves Black bodies, for different reasons. They love us for our work ethic (despite the narrative that we are lazy), for entertainment, for sport and for play. Yet and still, our opinions have yet to be respected, our bodies have yet to be cherished, and our intellect—as we have seen with the election of Barack Obama, who had an Ivy League degree, was president of the United States and was still assumed to be *lacking* or somehow *deficient*," he repined. As a means of remedying this problem, particularly as a community, Tatem believes that African-Americans, and other individuals of color, should turn their focus inward and begin to love themselves (again), regardless of the opinions of others.

"When we talk about Black men harming other Black men," Tatem explained, "the only way that you can harm someone that lives where you live, who looks like you, and is probably someone you know, love, or have some affection for, is because there is a deep sense of self-loathing and _that_ is a mental disease which impacts a number of people in our community. In my opinion," the civil rights defender declared, "this self-loathing, if you will, is _not_ something a person was born with, but rather is something that is manufactured by society and then adopted by the individual," he said. "To that end," Tatem explicated, "this lack of self-love is not by accident, and so we have to work to reverse the self-hatred that has been taught to us for generations," he surmised. "We have to *learn* to love ourselves. Likewise, we have to *un-learn* the hatred we have of ourselves. More importantly, we have to *re-learn* how to reaffirm ourselves—and one another," Tatem posited.

When it comes to his views of the future of Black men in America, Tatem, the former government guru, believes that the opportunities are endless. "From my perspective, the current state of the Black male is amazing," he exclaimed. "We have more Black men in college. We have more Black men with money. We have more positive representations in our community, and that can be empowering in and of itself," Tatem declared. "The narrative is that we are *always* struggling, or we are at the bottom of every list, or that we lack in many areas of American life. To a certain extent, that is true, but we have a lot of examples of Black men excelling in all areas of endeavor, and being successful in the process. In my belief," Tatem uttered, "what we focus on grows," he said. "For the first time in our sojourn in America, we can point to someone that has been successful, who looks like *us*, and we can model them," he concluded.

"To that end, if I could offer one piece of advice to Black males, I would keep it quite simple—READ—as early and as often as you can!," Tatem emphasized. "I know that it seems overly simplistic," he continued, "but when I think about the potential that *we* have through the power of reading, it cannot be ignored," he noted. "When you look at people like Malcolm X, who used to be 'Detroit Red' in an earlier phase of his life, running the streets and participating in every illicit activity you can think of, however, when he went to jail and began reading, a transformation took place and everything changed for him," Tatem said. "He went from being a local criminal involved in illegal activity, to a world leader, but it all began with an earnest willingness to *learn* and *read*—even when he was in prison. "For Malcolm X, the lights and the microphones came later," Tatem said. "But his true metamorphosis came in a 4'x6' cell. Consequently," he elaborated, "what I would say to any young Black male is this: don't wait until you're in the darkest time of your life to change the world," he admonished. "You can start that right now! Malcolm X read everything he could get his hands on. He read history," Tatem explained, "he read Shakespeare, he read political books. He even copied out the entire dictionary, therefore making sure that his language and use of words were powerful. And for you, as a Black man in America, it takes that same type of commitment to get to the next dimension of your abilities to succeed."

"Someone may be reading this book in prison, one day, wondering what they can do to make *the next chapter* of their life, *the best chapter* of their life, and *that* journey begins with reading," Tatem expounded. "Even if you are a college student or a professional athlete, take the next step by picking up books that feed your mind," he advised. "As African-American men, we have much more power than we give ourselves credit for. A lot of times," Tatem deduced, "we may look at our situation and think that everything is just *so* bad. But we have to make gradual changes, and shifts in our thinking, in order to improve our own lots in life. It may not happen overnight," he furthered, "but if we chart a clear path, stay the course, and practice discipline, then we can enhance our own trajectory."

"As Black people," Tatem continued, "we have *so many* positive examples to look to, to turn our situation around," Tatem acknowledged. "It doesn't have to be as extreme as going to prison to force you to turn things around. In my opinion," Tatem went on, "*'nothing is as powerful as a changed mind'*. You don't have to wait for the government to change," he continued, "or the president to change, or your congressman to change, or your local elected official to change, or your boss to change—to do something different TODAY. *YOU* have the power to change *YOU* right NOW!"

(Roy M. Tatem, Jr.: Political Activist & Community Leader)

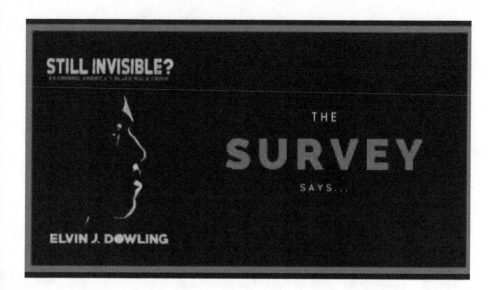

How strongly do you agree or disagree with the following statements?*

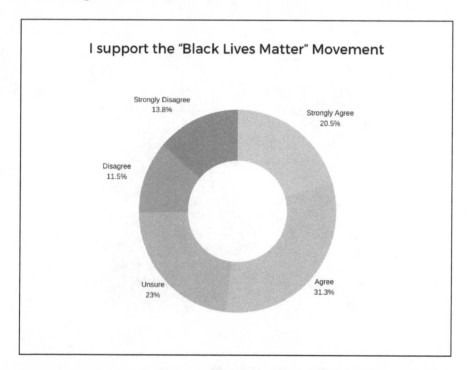

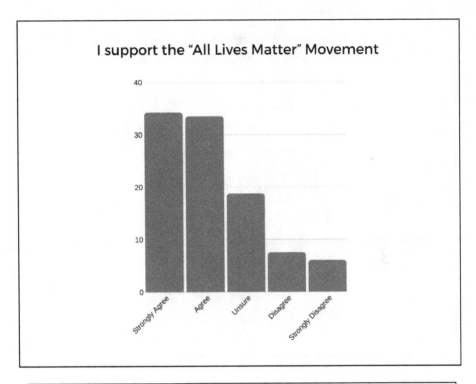

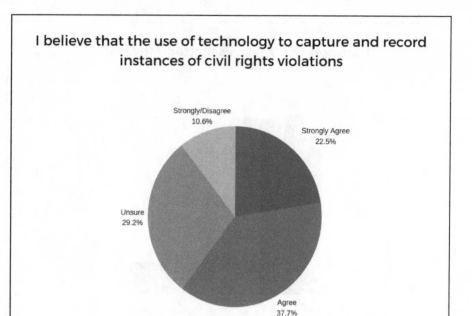

I believe that the use of technology to capture and record instances of civil rights violations

Strongly/Disagree
10.6%

Strongly Agree
22.5%

Unsure
29.2%

Agree
37.7%

All survey results displayed above are represented by the overall percentage of survey respondents. For more information on our survey methodology, please see the Author's Note, located in the front matter of the book. To review raw survey results, visit: http://bit.ly/stillinvisiblesurvey.

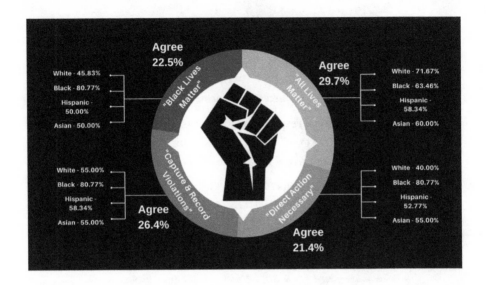

Findings by Race

- Nearly half of all White respondents (45.83%) "Strongly Agree" or "Agree" with the statement, *"I support the 'Black Lives Matter' Movement."*

- More than 6 out of 10 Black male respondents (63.46%) "Strongly Agree" or "Agree" with the statement, *"I support the 'All Lives Matter' Movement."*

- More than half of all Hispanic respondents (52.77%) "Strongly Agree" or "Agree" with the statement, *"I believe that direct action, including protests, are necessary to achieve change in America."*

Findings by Gender

- 8 out of 10 Multicultural female respondents (83.34%) "Strongly Agree" or "Agree" with the statement, *"I believe that the use of technology to capture and record instances of civil rights violations."*

- 3 out of 4 Asian male respondents (75.00%) "Strongly Disagree" with the statement, *"I support the 'Black Lives Matter' Movement."*

- 1 out of 4 Hispanic male respondents (24.53%) are "Unsure" when asked how they feel about the statement, *"I support the 'All Lives Matter' Movement."*

Findings by Age

- 1 out of 3 Black Male respondents, ages 55 years and older (33.33%), "Strongly Disagree" or "Disagree" with the statement, *"I believe that direct action, including protests, are necessary to achieve change in America."*

- Half of all White female respondents, ages 18-24 years old (50.00%) "Strongly Agree" or "Agree" with the statement, *"I believe that the use of technology to capture and record instances of civil rights violations."*

- Half of all Other respondents (50.00%) "Strongly Agree" or "Agree" with the statement, *"I support the 'Black Lives Matter' Movement,"* with the other half (50.00%) "Unsure".

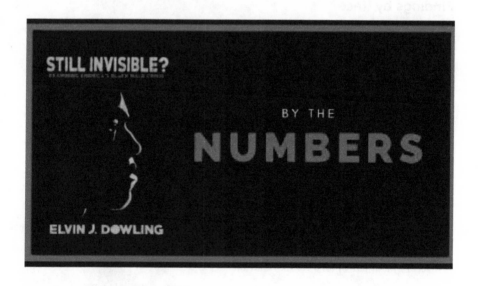

"Partisanship *'Won't Fly'* with Generation Y!"

- Without fanfare, millennials are redefining what it means to be "liberal" or "conservative". Reticent to be perceived as adversarial, they prefer "advocate" to "activist" when describing their cause engagement ("Impact").

- Desirous of government becoming less partisan, millennials believe that elected officials should be more accommodating and open minded on issues of social justice, and often support candidates who agree ("Impact").

"Seeking White Allies. Please Apply Within."

- As advocates of social justice and equality, one must first understand that "allyship" is a process that involves a lot of listening and understanding that "ally" is not an identity, but a lifelong process that requires hard work ("Allyship 101").

- A white ally does not remain silent when confronted with racism, but challenges and seeks to deconstruct it by challenging systemic oppression, even at their own personal risk ("Allyship 101").

"There's No Doubt ... People Turn Out!"

- According to data gathered from the *Crowd Counting Consortium*, in 2017, there were 425 total marches involving 4,124,543 people throughout the United States of America ("Protest Patterns").

- The most commonly protested issue in America by region, include: Immigration (Southern Border and the Northeast), Civil Rights (Central states) and racial injustice (Southern states) ("Protest Patterns").

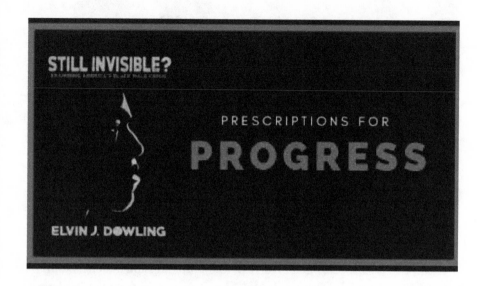

"From the Screens... to the Streets!"

- Tap into the power of "triggering events" such as murder, abuse of power or outright hostility, to organize the community, understanding that "triggering events" tend to break the status quo ("Engage", p. 11).

- Take online activism offline by engaging in informational activities (i.e. interviews), symbolic activities (i.e. boycotts), organizing activities (i.e. networking), and civil disobedience activities such as sit-ins ("Engage", p. 15).

"Become a 'Friend to the End'"

- Those who consider themselves "White Allies" must always be mindful of not asking people of color to carry the burden of convincing fellow whites of their own humanity ("Against Hate").

- When seeking to be an effective white ally, be sure to listen to the concerns of those with whom you stand in solidarity. Voices of allies are critical, but it's important to remember that it's someone else's life on the line ("Against Hate").

"Either Go BIG ... or Go Home!"

- To spur lasting change, protests must be *un*-ignorable. As such, protest organizers must first determine how long the protest will last, know who will be involved, and seek to avoid death and destruction ("Making Protest Work").

- Coalesce overlapping protest groups under a united banner. Take advantage of large numbers of people who want to advocate for the same spate of values and channel that collective energy into action ("Making Protest Work").

Works Cited

1. Shmoop Editorial Team. "Invisible Man Narrator Quotes   Page 4." *Shmoop*. Shmoop University, Inc., 11 Nov.   2008. Web. 30 December 2019.

2. Ruiz-Grossman, Sarah. "Millennials Are the Foot Soldiers   of The Resistance." *HuffPost.com*, The Huffington   Post. 23 February 2017. http://bit.ly/2QrACn4

3. Masuda, Rai, "Research Shows Millennials See Activism in Different Way Than Previous Generations."   *AchieveAgency.com*, Achieve Agency, LLC. 15 Match   2017. http://bit.ly/357da3J

4. Watts, Stephanye. "It's Now Up to Whites to Dismantle Racism." *Time.com*, TIME USA, LLC. 8 December   2014. http://bit.ly/2F7S2Qc

5. Morrison, Melanie S. "Becoming Trustworthy White Allies. Reflections. *Yale.edu*, Yale University Divinity   School. Accessed 29 December 2019. http://bit.ly/2ZAhAyZ

6. Chapman, Steve. "Why Do Whites Oppose the NFL

Protests?" *ChicagoTribune.com*, Tribune Publishing.   26 September
2017. http://bit.ly/2SDKE7e

7. Abdul-Jabbar, Kareem. "The Coming Race War Won't Be
    About Race." *Time.com*, TIME USA, LLC. 17   August 2014.
    http://bit.ly/2ZBfdfo

8. Hsu, Hua. "The End of White America?" *TheAtlantic.com*,
    Atlantic Media. January 2009. http://bit.ly/368Jl4h

9. Abdul-Jabbar, Kareem. "White People Feel Targeted by the
    Ferguson Protests—Welcome to Our World."   *Time.com*,
    TIME USA, LLC. 26 November 2014.   http://bit.ly/2ZBfdfo

10. "The 2016 Millennial Impact Report: Cause Engagement   During
    a Presidential Election Year."
    TheMillennialImpact.com, Achieve Agency. Accessed   31
    December 2019. http://bit.ly/35eAIE3

11. "White Allyship 101: Resources to Get to Work."
    DismantleCollective.org, Dismantle Collective (a   fiscally
    sponsored project of Community   Ventures). Accessed
    31 December 2019.   http://bit.ly/2ZGNeuP

12. Caruso, Catherine. "Count Love Project Reveals Protest
    Patterns." *BU.edu*, The Brink - Pioneering Research   from Boston
    University. 15 November 2017.   http://bit.ly/35fbHIE

13. Dookoo, Sasha R. "How Millennials Engage in Social Media
    Activism.: A Uses and Gratifications Approach."   *Etd.FCLA.edu*,
    University of Central Florida.   Accessed 31 December
    2019.   http://bit.ly/2u8eeHX

14. Eller, Ryan. "6 Ways for White Allies to Stand Against
    Hate." *Time.com*, TIME USA, LLC. 18 August   2017.
    http://bit.ly/37qydjg

15. Resnick, Brian. "4 Rules for Making a Protest Work,
    According to Experts." *Vox.com*, Vox Media, LLC.   23 April 2017.
    http://bit.ly/2F8BB6z

Afterword

"Where Do We Go from Here?"

❝

Something, perhaps, like a man passing on to his son his own father's watch, which he accepted not because he wanted the old-fashioned timepiece for itself, but because of the overtones of unstated seriousness and solemnity of the paternal gesture which at once joined him with his ancestors, marked a high point of his present, and promised a concreteness to his nebulous and chaotic future."

- Ralph Ellison, "Invisible Man" (Shmoop Editorial Team, 18.70)

(Black males in America continue to experience more significant and material challenges than do their white counterparts. Even still, many continue to remain focused on achieving success, leading a religious life and are, generally, more optimistic than most that things will—eventually—get better).

Message to Millennials: *Chaos or Community?*

"*OUR* Time Has Come!"

The socio-political and economic forces that exacerbate the undercurrent of racial discrimination towards Black men is no secret. This book has taken careful, deliberate steps to remind some and teach others of this man-made phenomenon that continues to distort itself into the new millennium. And yet, the question does remain: **What next?** Often, books like these might overshoot their objective; Elvin Dowling's methodical uncovering of the truth could leave many feeling like that very truth is too insurmountable to overcome. As a millennial and young Black man, I feel no such fear in standing up to the proponents of institutional and social racism because the data and thoughts within this book empower me. It is with this power that I hope to deliver a message of strength to my generation of peers, specifically young Black men, but truly all young individuals of various religions, ethnicities, genders and so forth.

Before I begin, it's important to have a firm grasp of our purpose as a generation. To do so, we must look to the past, much like watching an Olympic relay race – a race where one sprinter passes a baton to another. Every generation of Black Americans, from the Civil War to today, has been tasked with accomplishing both a tactical and spiritual mission in furtherance of full equality. The tactical mission refers to an objective that is political or technical in nature; the spiritual mission refers to a psychological or otherwise non-technical purpose that said generation must achieve. If a generation achieves both of their missions, they not only make it easier for the next generation, but they also push all of us that much closer to the promised land of equality. If the baton is fumbled however, it makes it that much more difficult for the next sprinter to run their part of the race.

Take a look below at my attempt to simplify this concept:

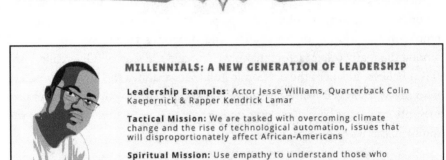

MILLENNIALS: A NEW GENERATION OF LEADERSHIP

Leadership Examples: Actor Jesse Williams, Quarterback Colin Kaepernick & Rapper Kendrick Lamar

Tactical Mission: We are tasked with overcoming climate change and the rise of technological automation, issues that will disproportionately affect African-Americans

Spiritual Mission: Use empathy to understand those who disagree with us or with who we may disagree

GENERATIONAL TIMELINE	LEADERSHIP EXAMPLES	TACTICAL MISSION	SPIRITUAL MISSION
POST-RECONSTRUCTION GENERATION	FREDERICK DOUGLASS & HIRAM REVELS	PURSUE HIGHER EDUCATION	OVERCOME PSYCHOLOGICAL EFFECTS OF SLAVERY
JIM CROW/HARLEM RENAISSANCE GENERATION	BOOKER T. WASHINGTON, W.E.B. DUBOIS & LANGSTON HUGHES	DEFER TO WHITES AND OBEY STRICT SEGREGATION LAWS	PRACTICE HUMILITY AND PATIENCE TO SURVIVE
CIVIL RIGHTS GENERATION	MARTIN LUTHER KING, JR., & MALCOLM X	USE BOYCOTS AND CIVIL DISOBEDIENCE TO GAIN ACCESS	HARNESS THE POWER OF SOLIDARITY
POST-CIVIL RIGHTS GENERATION	JESSE JACKSON & BARACK OBAMA	ASSIMILATE WITH LARGER AMERICA AND FIGHT FOR ECONOMIC INCLUSION FOR ALL BLACK PEOPLE	& POLITICAL INFLUENCE

Every generation, from the *Civil War* to Civil Rights, completed their mission fully. It wasn't perfect or ideal, but they accomplished their objective. But then came the Post-Civil Rights Generation, our parents, aunts and uncles. And that, in my opinion, is when things truly began to change You see, it was this generation of Blacks that were the first to *truly* assimilate with White America. In the process of acculturation, however, our parents got just a bit *too* comfortable. They didn't have to fight as hard for economic inclusion as our grandparents did for Civil Rights. And why should they have done so? Things were better... right? In fact, it was because they believed that "things were better" that they ultimately adopted the American individualist mentality and put aside some of the community ideals that brought our people strength. Many Black folks moved into White suburbs and became homeowners. Many went off to top colleges. Meanwhile, the less fortunate amongst us fell further behind, due to persistent poverty, lack of meaningful employment, housing discrimination and America's failed "War on Drugs", among the many other factors that have stood in the way of full equality. And this, I believe, is where the economic gulf that separates the few Black people who have achieved some measure of success, from the overwhelming majority who are barely making ends meet. _This_ is where the baton was fumbled. But it's not over until we win...

My reasoning for walking you through this mini-history lesson is to clarify, first and most importantly, why we millennials feel the way we feel--and why the time for change is NOW! You see, our parents told us to go to the top colleges so that we can get a good job when we graduate; now we are saddled with hundreds of thousands of dollars in debt and no way to pay it off without having to move back in with them. Our aunts and uncles encouraged us to become homeowners; now it makes little sense to be tied down to a single location when the careers of today and the jobs of tomorrow are so much more mobile and transient. Our school system forced us into classrooms but didn't give us the tools to succeed and, in doing so, created a school-to-prison pipeline that is working as it was intended. Our teachers shepherded us away from hard sciences like coding and software engineering; now Black folks make up less than 3% of employees at any given tech company, a field that's becoming more in-demand every day.

On January 20, 2009, Barack Obama became the most powerful man in the entire world. The very next day, however, he still owed money on his student loans to Harvard University School of Law. Think about that! The most important position on the planet, assumed by a Black man no less, and even _he_ was still paying his student loans. Having been born in an age of the digital revolution, it is clear to me, and most of my contemporaries, that what our parents _didn't do_ (or perhaps know _how_ to do) was to fight for our economic inclusion. Being smart about our money. Owning, instead of financing depreciating assets. Investing money, instead of squandering resources. For you see, when they assimilated into larger America, they became susceptible to the scheme that is run by larger America. In doing so, they discovered that the ice wasn't necessarily *colder* and the grass wasn't always *greener* on the other side. So, where does that leave us today? How do we pick up the baton and fight for both economic inclusion AND the issues our generation has to contend with, such as climate change and automation? Well... the answer can be found in the actions of a rather interesting messenger: musical artist *Young Thug*.

Who is *Young Thug*, you ask? He's the *"Uber of Hip-Hop"*. A walking Silicon Valley of experimentation in music and ideas. One of the first trap artists to openly wear dresses while professing ambivalent sexuality within his music. *Young Thug* is the epitome of the millennial generation and has a bevy of notable outspoken fans, from Barack Obama to Elton John. For the unenlightened, what makes *Young Thug* different is that he's risen through hip-hop HIS way. He helped rap/trap music evolve by adding his own flavor to the mix. In *Young Thug*, I see an opportunity for many of us to reflect these attributes in our generation's own fight for equality. In short, it's time for us to do this *our* way. For our generation to succeed, we have to realize that WE possess the tools to solve the problems I enumerated above. Following the traditional model set by our parents' generation will NOT work for us. In fact, following the traditional model set by larger America is a failing choice as well. It's a trap. As the future leaders of this nation, we need to be smarter about our end goals and work to make them a reality. Moreover, simply adhering to a process because it's what we are "supposed" to do needs to be retired as a concept and philosophy as well. Instead, we need to think outside the box.

Evidence of "out-thinking" the establishment already exists. Inmates are finding creative ways to get educated. Parents are rejecting school systems that discriminate against young Black children and creating new types of schools. Young Black entrepreneurs are bypassing MBA programs and starting their own businesses; taking real risks and gaining practical experience in the process. High school dropouts are using *YouTube* to learn how to code and gain industry skills. We are resourceful and *that* skill needs to become our *new* norm.

To that end, here's a working formula for achieving success, not only for those in my generation, but for those to whom we will one day pass the baton:

[DigitalTechnology+Ownership]xIngenuity = EconomicInclusionandMobility

- **Digital Technology** within the formula refers to leveraging, learning, and adopting anything that involves the use of digital technology. In today's twenty-first century economy, that can mean coding and software engineering as viable options for a sustainable future. It can also mean coming up with new and better ideas that leverage any use of technology to help build a better future.

- **Ownership** within the formula refers to economic ownership. For example, musicians are now being encouraged to own their masters. Putting your money into a high yield savings account that appreciates in value and/or owning assets like stocks are also important. Most importantly, be certain that YOU owning your ideas.

- **Ingenuity** within the formula refers to the unique mindset that only our generation possesses, due to our intrinsic use of and interaction with technology. Take this story for example.

❝

I once saw a video of a three-year-old who was given a book. He took that book and swiped on it like an iPad. Not once did the boy attempt to turn a page of the book. That boy was given a concept that has been handed down for hundreds of years and saw it in a new light.

Essentially, we can take traditional ideas and concepts and look at them in a completely new way. Likewise, if we can find ways to harness the power of the digital and information age, and own the investments and ideas we have, I believe we can achieve economic mobility and financial stability in twenty-first century America. Moreover, we must always remember that the true power of economic mobility lies in the fact that it gives us many more options. Options to fight climate change. Options to uplift our communities. Options that allow us to make **_our_** mark on the world that can never, **_ever_** be erased!

#StayWoke,

Kendall Finlay

Author's Note: *Kendall Finlay is a 2017 graduate of the University of Pennsylvania, where he studied Political Science and Government. An aspiring attorney, Kendall has served as a Legal Analyst for Facebook, one of the world's most powerful social networks.*

(Kendall Finlay: Millennial Leader & Rising Star)

Works Cited

1. Shmoop Editorial Team. "Invisible Man Memory and the   Past
   Quotes Page 2." *Shmoop*. Shmoop University,   Inc., 11 Nov. 2008.
   Web. 6 Nov. 2019.

Postface

Lest We Soon Forget!

" "

They were all such a part of that other life that's dead that I can't remember them all. (Time was as I was, but neither that time, nor that "I", are any more.)"

- Ralph Ellison, "Invisible Man" (Shmoop Editorial Team, 2.7)

(Emmett Till was a 14-year-old Black boy who was lynched in Mississippi on August 28, 1955, after being accused of offending a white woman. The savage nature of his death was shown in newspapers across the country, while the accused perpetrators of Till's death were acquitted of murder.)

"The Revolution Will _NOT_ Be Televised!"

So, What Are _YOU_ Waiting On?

Each year, just as sure as the sun rises in the east, sets in the west, our compatriots in the struggle for human dignity and social equality, our Jewish brothers and sisters from around the world, take the time to recollect and call attention to the horrors of Hitler's hate-filled holocaust. _"Evil flourishes when good men do nothing,"_ it's been said, which is why they always remember. Our friends are justified in their reflections and united in their aims—_"The world must never forget!"_

We must never forget that America is a nation established on Judeo-Christian principles by white slave owners who "wanted to be free." Tens of millions of Africans were bartered into bondage, by their own brothers and sisters no less, then tossed overboard slave ships during the dreaded _Middle Passage_; to be drowned in chains or eaten by sharks, never reaching that distant shore. _"Before they'd be enslaved, they'd be buried in their graves.'_ As lovers of freedom, we cannot forget!"

We must never forget the face of Emmett Till, after his body was retrieved from the murky depths of the Tallahatchie Rives. A young man gone too soon, Till never realized the winter of his discontent, having his life snuffed out one fateful summer that would unfortunately be his last. _Too many lives... too many lies._ _"How quickly we forget!"_

We must never forget the day that the Rev. Dr. Martin Luther King, Jr. was shot and killed on the balcony of the Lorraine Motel, taken in a rage of hate and despair by "the hate that hate produced". The "drum major for peace" shot down like a dog—in the _"greatest country in the world."_ _Too much information... too little time._ _"We mustn't let anyone forget!"_

We must never forget the terror of the Orlando Nightclub massacre, the fear invoked by the Charleston Church shooting and the mayhem of the Marjorie Stoneman Douglas High School shooting, and other tragic incidents that remind us every day of the depths of depravity to which our society has sunken. Yet, many parents continue to neglect their children and then they wonder why "Cain killed Abel". _"Too much time for everything else? We had better not forget!"_

We must never forget my brother, Kalief Browder, who was sacrificed on the altar of "American Justice"—a system that robbed him of his youth, abridged him of his basic human rights, and denied him due process—before washing his blood from their hands and clearing their conscience of his fate. *"His life mattered ... 'Black Lives Matter'!* ***Please don't forget!"***

In 2008, Barack Obama called on each of us, as Americans, to answer the call of "service above self," by doing <u>our</u> part to perfect <u>our</u> union. In the same manner, he also admonished each and every one of us to "be the change" we seek to see in the world. Today, as America continues to grapple with two pervasive and insidious enemies that are difficult—but not impossible—to defeat, the twin evils of apathy and selfishness, we must never forget that the former creeps into our minds to convince us that *"somebody else is going to do it"*, and the latter hides behind hollow prayers, like *"God bless me and my three...us four—and no more!"* "Change will not come if we wait for some other person or some other time. We are the ones we've been waiting for," Obama reminded us. *"Truer words have never been spoken... **Commit them to memory —and never forget!"***

In his compelling composition, "The Power of One," poet Ashish Ram prophetically proclaimed:

"

One song can spark a moment,
One whisper can wake the dream.
One tree can start a forest,
One bird can herald spring...

One vote can change a nation, One
sunbeam lights a room
One candle wipes out darkness,
One laugh will conquer gloom...

One voice can speak with wisdom,
One heart can know what's true,
One life can make a difference,
You see, it's up to you!

For those who gave their lives in the quest for freedom—*we owe it to them not to forget!*

For those descendants of kings who were once enslaved—*we must never, ever forget!*

And for those generations of Americans yet to come. who are depending on us to leave them a nation better than the one we inherited, *we must tell the stories of those who can no longer speak for themselves — so that no one **ever forgets!***

So long as the bank accounts of justice in this country are still marked "insufficient funds," and the verbal promissory note of American democracy isn't worth the paper it's printed on—***we shall not forget!***

*"Early to bed, early to rise ... work like hell and organize—**Lest we soon forget!***

One Love,

Akeem Browder

Akeem Browder

Editor's Note: *Akeem Browder is the Founder & Executive Director of the Kalief Browder Foundation. A 2016 Green Party candidate for Mayor of New York City, Akeem placed fourth in a race that attracted nearly seventy qualifying competitors. An active leader in the justice reform movement, Browder successfully lobbied the New York State Assembly to pass "Kalief's Law" in 2016, to ensure that persons arrested receive a speedy trial, and pressured New York City officials to permanently shutter the notorious Rikers Island jail, currently scheduled for closure in 2027.*

(Akeem Browder: Movement Leader & Justice Reformer)

Works Cited

1. Shmoop Editorial Team. "Invisible Man Memory and the Past Quotes Page 2." *Shmoop*. Shmoop University, Inc., 11 Nov. 2008. Web. 31 December 2019.

"OUT OF THE DARKNESS & INTO THE LIGHT"

Still Invisible? Illuminates Joys & Pains of African-Americ
Males; Offers Meaningful "Prescriptions for Progress"

FINALLY A BOOK TO REMIND US "NOT ALL HEROES WEAR CAPES"

"Unlike Any Other Book You've Read!"

It has often been said, "The journey of a thousand miles begins with the first step." For more than 400 years, the United States of America has sought to ignore what Black intellectual, Dr. William Edward Burghardt DuBois, once called the persistent "issue of the color line"—especially as it relates to African-American males. Even still, despite having initially been dragged to the shores of the country in the hulls of slave ships as forced labor with no inalienable rights and "questionable humanity" Black men have excelled in every area of human endeavor, while working to make a strange land their home.   For some, however—even today—the indomitable spirit that Black men possess is threatening to a belief system predicated upon an inherently racist belief that Blacks are inherently inferior to whites.

n this gripping tome highlighting the highs and ows of Black life in America, as experienced by t's men and boys, **Still Invisible?** pays homage o one of America's most enduring literary works, Invisible Man" by Ralph Ellison, while helping to eshape the Black male narrative—from rederick Douglass to Freddie Gray.

TAKE A PEEK AT WHAT'S INSIDE:

Each chapter highlights stories of history, hope and healing.
Book features some of America's "unsung heroes."

www.StillInvisible.com

STILL INVISIBLE?
"EXAMINING AMERICA'S BLACK MALE

POLL: BLACK MEN ARE BOTH LOVED & LOATHED IN U.S.

The Results Are In...

In an effort to better understand the attitudes, opinions and beliefs of people from across the country, this project commissioned a proprietary survey that "looked like America"(demographically speaking that is). Our goal was to obtain the best and broadest base of opinions about Black males in the United States. With a margin of error of +/- 5%, the survey received the unfiltered views of 400 Americans, from all walks of life, residing in 44 states. Additionally, 50% of the respondents were women and 50% were men (and all were 18 years of age and older).

The survey's findings, in many ways, offered a window into the thinking of our fellow citizens and what they truly feel about African-American men. Some interesting tidbits include:

- The group that tended to express distrust and/or antipathy the most towards Black Males were Asian respondents of all ages and genders.
- A significant number of White women were willing to give Black males the benefit of the doubt on issues of social justice.
- A persistent number of Black males (13%) were quite critical of other Black males on almost every issue.

Each chapter of *Still Invisible?* features three useful tools to help the reader to *learn and do more,* including: "The Survey Says", "By the Numbers" and "Prescriptions for Progress" (see examples on right).

www.StillInvisible.com

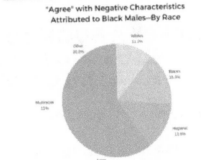

"Agree" with Negative Characteristics Attributed to Black Males—By Race

Pt. I: Building A Framework

Elvin J. Dowling
Author & Activist

Introduction: Are Black Men In America "Still Invisible"?
Theme: Why _This_ Book Is Different

African-American males continue to lag behind most racial subgroups in the country. Through a combination of in-depth interviews, surveys, research, and anecdotal evidence, this book seeks to determine what ails, and just as importantly, how to effectively address, the challenges facing Black men in America.

What We Learned

To as great an extent as possible, this book endeavored to present the ideas and issues contained herein, in a fashion that does not draw any conclusions or make assumptions but rather, presents historical data and observational analysis in a way that allows you—the reader—to consider the questions asked in each chapter, before drawing your own conclusions.

Alcee L. Hastings
Congressman & Statesman

Foreword: "Forward Ever ... Backwards Never!"
Theme: Never Give Up the Fight!

As the longest serving member of the Florida delegation to the U.S. House of Representatives, "Judge Hastings" as he is often referred, has experienced the ups and downs of life in America as an outspoken Black male leader. Having been impeached as a federal judge for crimes in which he has steadfastly maintained his innocence (after having been acquitted by a jury of his peers), and run for office—and lost 8 times—before a successive string of victories that has placed him in the pantheon of the longest serving Black Elected Officials, Alcee Hastings is an African-American leader not defined by other people's opinions.

What We Learned

Having been diagnosed with stage 4 pancreatic cancer, Congresman Hasting—In the battle of his life—encouraged Black males to "keep fighting the good fight of faith"—despite the odds against them.

Ralph W. Ellison
Author & Genius

Dedication: Remembering the "Invisible Man"
Theme: Paying Homage to an American Classic

Nearly seventy years have passed since Ralph Ellison released his seminal novel, "Invisible Man," to critical acclaim in 1952. In doing so, he not only demonstrated a Black man's ability to author an enduring work, he also highlighted the intractible issues faced by Black men in a society that renders them "invisible".

What We Learned

Each chapter of this book opens up with a relevant quotation from Ellison's momentous work, a subtle but constant reminder of the fact that, for Black males in America, when it comes to racial progress in the United States, "the more things change, the more they remain the same."

Pt. II: "From Boys to Men"

Gregory Diggs
Educator & Advocate

Chapter 1: Born With a Birthmark?
Theme: Black Boys & Secondary Education

From the moment they take their first breath, to their first day of kindergarten, to high school graduation, Black boys are often stereotyped, suspended or expelled from school, and are often referred to law enforcemen officers for disciplinary infractions t are often considered minor offenses for other racial groups.

What We Learned

- Black boys have a 50/50 chance of remaining in poverty for the rest of their lives, even if they are born into wealth.
- From preschool to high school, Black boys are suspended three times as much as white boys in America.
- Black boys with disabilities are often forced iinto mechanica restraints by school officials more than any other race of children in America.

Joseph C. Phillips
Actor & Commentator

Chapter 2: Don't They All Look Alike?
Theme: Debunking Broad Generalizations

For centuries, Black men have been negatively stereotyped as somehow "less than", prone to criminality, or otherwise undesirable. Understanding the genesis for many of the pervasi prejudices facing Black males is helpful when attempting to stri at the core of internal bias. By analyzing many of the tropes and myths about Black men, we are able to delve deeper into the complex issues governing racial attitudes in America.

What We Learned

- Media platforms often portray Black males in a negative fash on news programs and in subservient roles on screen.
- Some whites believe Blacks possess superhuman powers ar as such, don't experience pain to the same degree they do.
- Studies show that Black males, when encountering police, a perceived to be larger in size and therefore more dangerous

Will Moreland
Author & Coach

Chapter 3: What Do You Call A Black Man with a Ph.D.?
Theme: Higher Education & Social Mobility

For nearly 200 years, Blacks have sought upward mobility and social acceptance in America by obtaining college degrees an joining the military. Even still, many Black males face systemic obstacles in their efforts to survive and thrive in academia and armed forces.

What We Learned

- Due to the biased nature of many standardized tests, many the result of creating a lifetime of inequality.
- Black males have the lowest college completion rates of ar racial subroup in America.
- Black soldiers are disciplined three times as much as white

Pt. III: Media & Money

Andre Showell
Journalist & Influencer

Chapter 4: Mo' Tea, Suh?
Theme: How the Media Shapes the Black Narrative

Through the use of various communications platforms, the media (to include news organizations and advertisers) contributes to the shaping of opinions and perspectives on Black males in America. Moreover, with a constant need to maintain and gain viewership, negative imagery of African-American males has become a staple of entities reliant upon "black villains" to keep spectators engaged

What We Learned
- Black males, featured in 7 out of 10 negative news stories, are overwhelmingly represented in an unfavorable light by the press.
- In America, Black males are often mistakenly defined by the "Five D's": Dumb, Deprived, Dangerous, Deviant and Disturbed.
- For 25 years, despite the fact that crime has dropped, Black males are still being incarcerated at alarming rates in America.

Kelvin Boston
Economist & Advisor

Chapter 5: What's the Difference Between 3/5 and 87%?
Theme: Black Economics/Devaluing Black Male Labor

Since the landing of the first slave ship off of the coast of Virginia in 1619, Black makes have been coveted for their ability to provide a consistent and reliable labor source for profiteers—at little to no remuneration for themselves. Today, however, Black males are still the lowest paid wage earners of all similar racial subgroups in America.

What We Learned
- More than one-third of all Black children live in single-parent households led by women with little economic security.
- The Gross Domestic Product (GDP) of Black America is less than half that of White America.
- The average African-American household has less than 1/10 of the wealth held by white households.

Jose Thompson
H.R. Expert &
Entrepreneur

Chapter 6: Can You Help A Brother Out?
Theme: Black Male Unemployment

Black males continue to face an uphill struggle when seeking employment opportunities. What's more, even when they lack a criminal record and earn college degrees, Black males still have fewer chances of getting a job than do their white counterparts who may have criminal convictions and no formal education.

What We Learned
- The unemploiyment for Blacks remains twice as high as the rate for whites, regardless of nation's economic conditions.
- The only group in America more unemployed than Black males are teenagers.
- Black males with past criminal convictions are persistently unemployed and are deemed by many to be "unemployable"

Pt. IV: Body, Mind & Soul

Patrick C. Hines
Physician & Inventor

Chapter 7: We Sick, Boss?
Theme: Black Men & Physical Health
African-American men tend to live sicker and die quicker than any other racial subgroup in the country. Moreover, Black males succumb in ways that are often tragic and, in many instances, avoidable—with young Black males leading the way in deaths due to homicide and law enforcement interactions.

What We Learned
- Black males are nearly three times as likely to be killed by police than are white males.
- On average, Black males tend to live 7 years fewer than all other racial subgroups in America.
- Black men suffer from preventable diseases more than anyone else, and suicide is the 3rd leading cause of death for Black teens.

Justin S. Hopkins
Therapist & Practitioner

Chapter 8: Will They Ever See Us?
Theme: Black Men & Mental Health
The issue of mental health disease is one that is often viewed as sign of weakness in the eyes of many African-Americans. To that end, Black males often avoid seeking treatment for a myriad of mental health maladies, thereby exasperating pre-existing conditions like depression and Post Traumatic Stress Disorder.

What We Learned
- Black males who are unemployed and have no source of income suffer higher rates of stress, anxiety and suicide.
- In 75% of all Black male suicides, firearms are often used to effectuate their death.
- Less than 2 out of every 10 Black males seek professional psychotherapy services when dealing with mental health issues.

Timothy Tee Boddie
Pastor & Professor

Chapter 9: Must Jesus Bear the Cross Alone?
Theme: How the Mainstream Church Ignores Black Believers
As the most devout group on Christian believers in America, Black churchgoers continue to face history of repression, marginalization and lack of empathy from America increasingly hostile mainstream denominations which often fail to speak to issues impacting Black people daily.

What We Learned
- Nearly half of all Black believers attend regular worship services, the highest rate of all other racial groups.
- Almost half of all Americans no longer support organized religion, regardless of the denomination.
- Many Americans no longer hold members of the clergy in esteem, with pastors ranking below police officers in general public perception.

Pt. V: Love, Faith & Hope

John Williams Jr.
Reformed Citizen

Chapter 10: Where Is the Love?
Black Men & the Prison Industrial Complex
Beginning with the passage of the 13th Amendment to the Consitution, effectively criminalizing blackness at the end of slavery, and expanding precipitously during America's "War o Drugs", Black men have been incarcerated at disproportinate rates for more than 150 years. Today, with millions of African-American males imprisoned across the country, the U.S. leads the world in the number of people it locks up annually.

What We Learned
- African-American men are six times more likely to be incarcerated in the United States during their lifetime.
- Formerly incarcerated Black men seeking employment upon release from lockup are 50% more likely to NOT get a callback for a job ninterview.
- Without "ban the box" policies, Returning Citizens face an uphill climb in reintegrating back into society.

John T. Bullock
Professor & Politician

Chapter 11: Hope ... Or Nope?
Theme: Examining the Limitations of Black Political Power
In the United States of America, the concept of "one person, one vote" is, perhaps, the single most unifying power citizens possess. Black voters, however, are often targeted for election suppression and African-American leaders, whether elected or appointed, have often been targeted with harassment, violence and death for daring to challenge governmental policy.

What We Learned
- Although the number of Black politicians in the U.S. has increased significantly over the last 50 years, their ranks still lag behind other racial subgroups, based on demographics.
- During the 2018 election cycle in the U.S., 1 out of every 10 Black votes were suppressed using a variety of tactics.
- Despite threats and reprisals, Black leaders have been successful at passing meaningful social justice legislation.

Myles B. Caggins III
Spokesman & Soldier

Chapter 12: What About Obama?
Theme: Analyzing the Concept of a "Post-Racial" Society
The election of Barack Obama as President of the United States represented "Hope" and the idea that, in America, anything was possible. Today, however, both Obama's policies and America's racial progress gains are actively being dismantled.

What We Learned
- Under Obama's leadership, Congress passed the Affordable Care Act (ACA), insuring an additional 20 million Americans.
- During his two terms in office, Barack Obama was the most threatened President in the history of America.
- According to FBI statistics, racially motivated hate crimes against Blacks increased during Obama's presidency.

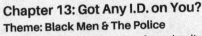

"Officer X"
Lawman & Servant

Chapter 13: Got Any I.D. on You?
Theme: Black Men & The Police

Since the mid 1800's, when formal police departments sprang up in the Northeast, and informal marauding mobs roamed the South searching for runaway slaves, Black males have had a contentious relationship with the law enforcement community. Today, with the senseless deaths of unarmed Black men at the hands of the police becoming a frighteningly regular occurrence, the gulf between the two groups continues to widen with each tragic encounter.

What We Learned

- Despite efforts by Congress in 1871 to curtail police participation in groups like the KKK, many still maintain ties.
- Poor, racially segregated states with high unemployment, tend to have increased rates of police violence against Blacks.
- Black police officers tend to arrest Black potential suspects more than their white conterparts and there is no difference in the use of force on Black males by African-American officers.

Daryl D. Parks
Attorney &
Entrepreneur

Chapter 14: Fixed or Broken?
Theme: Black Males & Criminal Justice

The American justice system is overrun with Black males, as the prison industrial complex is both unforgiving and inflexible when it comes to scofflaws of color. Sanctioned by courts that depend on plea agreements, cash bail, and over-burdensome fees, African-American males continue to represent a ready source of revenue for state governments and private corporations who profit from their pain.

What We Learned

- Black males convicted of capital crimes are exonerated at twelve times the rate of the death row population.
- In nearly 99% of all cases involving police involved shootings, local prosecutors decline to seek charges.
- 1 out of every 3 Black males in America are saddled with a criminal conviction, barring them from voting in elections.

Chapter 15: Do Black Loves Really Matter?
Theme: Political Protest in the iPhone Era

Blacks in America have used civil disobedience as a means of bringing about social justice reform. Through slave rebellions, ric and protests, African-Americans have risked life and limb to achieve equitable treatment in American society. In today's fractured America, however, the voices of trusted white allies is a critical component to the the success of social justice movemen —now more than ever!

Roy M. Tatem, Jr.
Activist & Leader

What We Learned

- Millennial protesters are willing to join the cause for social justice reform, but are only interested in doing it "their way".
- White allies must be willing to confront racism when it occur